D0630029

8/75

HARVARD HISTORICAL STUDIES

PUBLISHED UNDER THE DIRECTION OF
THE DEPARTMENT OF HISTORY

FROM THE INCOME OF

THE HENRY WARREN TORREY FUND

VOLUME XXXIV

HARVARD HISTORICAL STUDIES

HARVARD UNIVERSITY PRESS
CAMBRIDGE, MASS., U. S. A.

THE INFLUENCE OF THE COMMONS ON EARLY LEGISLATION

A Study of the Fourteenth and Fifteenth Centuries

BY

HOWARD L. GRAY

Marjorie Walter Goodhart Professor of History
Bryn Mawr College

CAMBRIDGE

HARVARD UNIVERSITY PRESS

LONDON: HUMPHREY MILFORD

OXFORD UNIVERSITY PRESS

1932

To

PROFESSOR CHARLES HOMER HASKINS
with appreciation of
his inspiring scholarship
and his unfailing kindness.

PREFACE

For several patent defects of this volume the author asks the indulgence of any who may read it. Some of these defects arise from its introductory character; for it is far from being a comprehensive treatment of even a single century of parliamentary history. It may seem to be the description of a formal rather than of a fundamental aspect of its subject, inasmuch as it relates largely to the final stages of the legislative process rather than to earlier ones in which formative influences have play. Its progress is from later and fuller evidence to that which is earlier and fragmentary; and this method not only sometimes leads those who adopt it to attribute to an early time features which are really later but it likewise departs from the logical development of a theme. The chapters, again, are often laden with dull summaries of legislation, occasionally not free from repetition; and blunders have probably been made in attempting to summarize in a sentence or phrase bills which are often verbose or obscure.

In excuse for these defects I can only plead the desirability of making an initial examination of a subject little studied of late; the necessity of utilizing first the more obvious documents at hand; the convenience of a method which supplements somewhat the reticences of the documents; and, finally, the scientific demand that all evidence of one sort be adduced, voluminous and obscure though it be.

Three gentlemen have been good enough to read the manuscript — Professor W. E. Lunt, Professor Conyers Read and Dr. G. O. Sayles. They have made valuable suggestions for its improvement without in any way associating themselves with such shortcomings as remain. I am grateful for their help.

To Dr. Sayles I am further indebted for information which I have incorporated in the text, as the notes will show. The officials of the Public Record Office have, as always, been most helpful.

H. L. Gray.

Bryn Mawr, September, 1932.

CONTENTS

ABBREVIATIONS[1]

Documents in the Public Record Office (P. R. O.).

A. P. .... Ancient Petitions.
C., C. & C. P. .... Chancery, Parliament and Council Proceedings.
E 175 .... Exchequer, Parliament and Council Proceedings.
C 65 .... Chancery, Parliament Rolls.

Printed Sources.

Stats. .... *Statutes of the Realm.*
R. P. .... *Rotuli Parliamentorum.*
Proceedings .... *Proceedings of the Privy Council.*
C. P. R. .... *Calendar of Patent Rolls.*
C. C. R. .... *Calendar of Close Rolls.*

[1] The sources and literature are described in Chapter III and in the introduction. I have taken the liberty of further abbreviating *Rot. Parl.,* since the reference occurs so often.

INTRODUCTION

THE indifference of scholars to parliamentary history which with two noteworthy exceptions prevailed for some time after Stubbs, Gneist and Riess completed their monumental works came to an end twenty years ago. It was dissipated by Professor McIlwain's original study, which maintained that in its beginnings parliament was primarily a judicial body. This view was adopted and other aspects of the evolution of parliament were discussed in Professor Pollard's stimulating survey.[1] To-day special and extended research is being devoted to the early history of parliament by several scholars. Messrs. Richardson and Sayles are examining, classifying and interpreting all parliamentary records to 1377.[2] Professor Pollard is engaged on an exhaustive study of the reformation parliament of 1529. Professor Neale is re-editing the journals of Elizabeth's reign and will naturally rewrite the

---

[1] W. Stubbs, *The Constitutional History of England*, 3 vols. (Oxford, 1874-78; 4th-6th eds., 1903-1906). R. Gneist, *Englische Verfassungsgeschichte* (Berlin, 1882); English trans., P. A. Ashworth, 2 vols. (London, 1886). L. Riess, *Geschichte des Wahlrechts zum englischen Parlament im Mittelalter* (Leipzig, 1885). F. W. Maitland, *Memoranda de Parliamento*, Rolls Series (London, 1893). L. O. Pike, *A Constitutional History of the House of Lords* (London, 1894). C. H. McIlwain, *The High Court of Parliament and its Supremacy* (New Haven, 1910). A. F. Pollard, *The Evolution of Parliament* (London, 1920). D. Pasquet, *An Essay on the Origin of the House of Commons* (Cambridge, 1925). This is a revised translation of the French study which first appeared in 1914. Professor Lapsley's brief preface is a clear statement of divergent views about the essential character of early parliaments.

[2] H. G. Richardson and G. Sayles, " The Early Records of the English Parliaments," " The Parliaments of Edward III " in *Bulletin of the Institute of Historical Research* (London, 1923, etc.), vols v, vi, viii, ix; " The King's Ministers in Parliament " in *English Historical Review*, vols. xlvi, xlvii (1931-32). New light is thrown upon procedure in the parliament of 1376 in the text of and the introduction to *An Anominalle Chronicle, 1333-1381*, ed. V. H. Galbraith (Manchester, 1927).

parliamentary history of that period. Professor Notestein has long devoted himself to similar and searching labours on the parliamentary records of the early seventeenth century. Only the period from 1377 to 1509 seems at present to be neglected. Without aspiring to exhaustive treatment of the parliaments of these years, this volume endeavours to follow at least one thread of development. It inquires into the influence which the commons as a body exerted upon the legislation of the period; and, to make the subject precise, statutory legislation is primarily considered.[3]

Whatever novelty the inquiry may have lies perhaps less in the conclusions which may be reached than in the method employed to reach them. The influence of the commons upon the legislation of the fourteenth and fifteenth centuries has not been a neglected subject. Among modern historians Stubbs gave it most careful attention. As a result he reached the conclusion that the revolution of 1399, if not indeed movements of the preceding century, introduced into the central government of the realm democratic features which found expression in the activities of the youthful house of commons. For him the reigns of the Lancastrian kings extending over the first half of the fifteenth century were a period of popular control. Nor was he inclined to admit any noteworthy decline in the powers of the lower house as the century advanced. Indeed he formulated an oft-quoted generalization that toward the middle of the century the authority of the commons was consolidated and expanded by an innovation in procedure. In place of procedure by petition there was substituted procedure by bill, a change which rescued the commons from the attitude of petition in which they had spent their early years and insured that measures which they formulated would

---

[3] Upon non-parliamentary legislation (see McIlwain, *op. cit.*, pp. 134-136, 315-321) the commons could naturally have no influence. Considerable parliamentary legislation was non-statutory and much of this did not originate with the commons. In due course, however, the commons assent to it was sought.

henceforth undergo little change when and insofar as these were approved by king and lords.[4]

At first sight there might seem to be ample evidence from the records of fourteenth- and fifteenth-century parliaments that the commons exerted an extensive influence on statutory legislation. A superficial comparison of statutes with what were called commons petitions[5] discloses that many of the former arose from the latter. The same comparison, however, reveals that the relationship appears to have been as characteristic of the second half of the fifteenth century as it was of the first half. During the time of Edward IV, when not much legislation of importance was enacted by parliament, it may have mattered little whether statutes were prompted by the commons or by the king, council and lords. During the reign of Henry VII, however, when there came to be considerable legislation of first rate significance, it did matter considerably who took the initiative. Present-day historians of the sixteenth and seventeenth centuries are inclined to look upon the period of the Tudors as one characterized in general by absolutist tendencies, derogatory to popular control of administration and legislation. And they see the dominance of such tendencies as early as the reign of Henry VII. Professor Notestein is convinced that the commons did not emerge as an effective force in national life until the seventeenth century. Views of this sort naturally conflict somewhat with the attribution of parliamentary legislation throughout the fifteenth century to the initiative of the commons. A reconciliation of Stubbs thesis with that of later writers can, of course, be attained by explaining that the commons enjoyed a somewhat brief tenure of power, which they afterward lost. Perhaps this has become the accepted view. But it relies upon no precise examination of the evidence, especially of that sup-

---

[4] *Op. cit.,* ii. 608-609. See below, pp. 46, 177-83.

[5] In the following chapters the phrases commons bills, lords bills and commons petitions are treated as generic terms and are written without apostrophe.

plied by the fifteenth century. Wherefore the rise of Tudor absolutism rests upon a slightly uncertain foundation.

That uncertainty surrounds our knowledge of the parliamentary activity of the fifteenth century is partly due to the fact that scholars have hitherto relied for information about it upon an enrolled record. Stubbs and others who have described it have been dependent upon the so-called rolls of parliament. At the end of a mediaeval English parliament after the time of Edward II the clerk drew up a summary account of the business which had been transacted and this became for practical purposes the final record to which reference was henceforth made. Individual documents with which the members of parliament had been immediately concerned, largely bills of one sort or another, were filed in chancery. Apparently no one henceforth troubled much about them. Many if not most of them have been lost; and historians, like officials, have attended only to what were enrolled. Under the name *Rotuli Parliamentorum* the enrolled records of parliament from the reign of Edward I to that of Henry VII inclusive were printed in the eighteenth century. Nothing can detract from the value of these volumes, perhaps the most important source for our general knowledge of English history during two centuries. But the rolls of parliament have the defects of all enrolled records in the omissions which they properly allowed themselves and in the less excusable tendency to become stereotyped. For the second reason, the later rolls are perhaps less trustworthy than the earlier ones; and there is the greater need to interpret them in the light of the documents from which the clerk of parliament compiled them. Such interpretation of the rolls and, in consequence, of the activities of parliament historians have not undertaken. To attempt it is the innovation of the present volume.

So restricted an objective involves, of course, serious limitations of treatment. In any complete history of parliament attention would be given to such topics as the qualifications, election and social status of members of the commons, the

evolution of parliamentary privilege, the minutiae of procedure, the significance of the legislation enacted, the control
of extraordinary taxation and the administration of justice.
Without aspiring to comprehensiveness of this sort, a comparison of the rolls with the surviving documents from which
they were compiled may nonetheless elucidate one matter. It
may explain to what extent approved bills, however they may
have been enrolled, were of commons' origin. Since nearly
all statutes after the time of Edward II arose from such approved bills, the outcome will be an account of the influence of
the commons upon statutory legislation during almost two
centuries.

Inasmuch as this approach to parliamentary records is
through the individual bill, it involves some description of
parliamentary procedure. The rolls are not very informing
about this. Nor, indeed, is the original material upon which
we propose to rely in interpreting them. Owing to these
reticences it may be permissible to adopt the plan of proceeding from the better known to the less known. What seems to
be the first satisfactory and fairly full account of the treatment of bills in the house of commons dates from the early
seventeenth century. As we pass to the sixteenth century,
procedure regarding bills is revealed to some extent in the
journals of the two houses. Since the earliest of these is the
lords' journal of 1509, it seems a convenient stepping-stone
in a progress to the less explicit records of an earlier time.
Hence the first two chapters of the following study are a
summary sketch of a seventeenth-century description of procedure in the commons and of a sixteenth-century lords' journal. The second gives further assistance in admitting of comparison with the parliament roll of the same year and in thus
introducing us to the type of enrolled record upon which we
shall henceforth have to rely. For interpreting this record in
the fifteenth century the simplest method is to compare the
bills of certain selected parliaments with the form which they
assumed when the clerk enrolled them. Thus we take the

step necessary to discern the structure of the parliament roll. When once this structure has been ascertained, we possess, so to speak, a key for the interpretation of all the parliament rolls of the two centuries in relation to the bills which they record. In pursuance of the policy of proceeding from the better known to the less known, it seems best to inquire first into the activity and initiative of the commons in the second half of the fifteenth century, i.e., the last half-century of the printed rolls. With the ground thus cleared we may turn sharply to the beginning of the commons' influence on legislation in the first half of the fourteenth century and follow its history thence to 1450. Contrasted with commons bills throughout the entire period are the far more numerous private bills. Something must be said about how they too came eventually within the scope of the commons' influence. Lastly, since much parliamentary legislation in due course assumed the form of statute, ordinance or act and was as such enrolled on the statute roll, some note must be taken of these final embodiments of new law. Thus even a restricted study of certain early parliamentary records, especially of those which are available only in manuscript, is bound to have considerable scope. But if it elucidates in some measure the commons' influence on legislation during two centuries, it will perhaps have dispelled some of the obscurity in which the subject is now enshrouded.

THE INFLUENCE OF THE
COMMONS ON EARLY
LEGISLATION

CHAPTER I

PARLIAMENTARY PROCEDURE IN THE EARLY
SEVENTEENTH CENTURY

ALTHOUGH descriptions of procedure in parliament survive from the reign of Elizabeth, notably that of William Lambard, the fullest early account of the passing of bills is one written by Thomas Richardson, who became speaker of the commons in 1620.[1] We have it only in an eighteenth-century transcript, which the copyist has left incomplete. The transcriber apparently was not interested in the comparison between seventeenth-century practice and earlier practice, which Richardson himself had elaborated; for he breaks off soon after copying the sentences, "And thus much concerning the passage of Bills according to the modern practice. In antient times the Course was very differing (as elsewhere shall be declared). But that ancient order, as it was nothing so curious as this, so was it not so safe for the Subject, as by comparing both together will easily appear."[2] Although we are thus left without Richardson's possibly valuable comment on earlier practice, his description of the procedure which he himself administered is precise and adequate. Briefly summarized its principal features are as follows.

The treatment of bills was practically the same in both houses. "Bills originally preferred to the upper House have such proceedings in that House in all points as Bills preferred to the Lower House have there; only, when any Question is made in the upper House, the Tryal thereof is by holding up

---

[1] Lambard's Treatise is Add. MS. 5123 and is entitled "Some certaine notes of the Order, Proceedings, punisshments and priviledges of the lower house of Parliment." Richardson's Treatise is Add. MS. 36856. I am indebted to Professors J. E. Neale and W. E. Notstein for reference to these works.

[2] Add. MS. 36856, f. 45 b.

of hands and, if they be doubtful there, by telling of the polls without dividing of the House."[3]   While, therefore, Richardson's description professedly relates to bills in the commons, it may be taken as descriptive also of bills in the lords.

Each house treated the bills of the other with even greater respect than it showed to its own measures.   Evidence of this appeared in connection with the amending of bills sent from one house to the other.   If a committee of the commons saw "Cause to make some amendments in them [the bills coming from the lords], they ought not to Interline or rase or make any other alteration in the Bill itself as they do in their own Bills, but in paper thereunto annexed they ought to express in what line and in what words they desire the amendments to be made.   If upon the Report thereof the House shall approve the doing of the Committee, then ought the Bill with the paper affixed to be sent to the upper House to be accordingly amended by the Lords if they shall so think good.   So likewise ought the Lords to do when they desire alterations in any Bill passed from the lower House unto them."[4]   Each house would, therefore, go no further than suggest to the other that it amend a bill which it had formulated.   The same sensitiveness to independent action appeared in connection with a complaint of the lords in 23 Elizabeth. They then maintained that, when they had sent down a bill to the commons, the latter body should not proceed with a similar bill, presumably its own, without conference.   But, says Richardson, this "was spoken by the Lords at a Conference and answered by the Committees of the lower House

[3] Ibid., f. 44 *b*.

[4] Ibid., f. 40.   Richardson goes on to say that in 29 Elizabeth, when the lords desired to amend a commons bill touching labourers, they sent down their "amendments in Parchment and the parchment formally indorsed, Soit baille aux Comons.   To which, Exception being taken, there was much Contestation about it between the Houses and Precedants sought up and at last Resolved it ought to be in paper without any Indorsement at all" (f. 40 *b*).

they might lawfully do so."[5] Since the incident belongs to the time of Elizabeth, it may suggest that the commons' insistence on concurrent powers was more meticulous in the half-century before Richardson wrote than it had been at an earlier time.

Bills offered in the two houses were of four sorts: private bills, public bills, bills of subsidy, and bills of general pardon. Bills of general pardon, says Richardson, "are sent engrossed by the King to the Lords where they are read once and Passed and then sent down to the Commons where they are also read but once." Such bills might not be amended, since "the Subject must take [them] without any alteration."[6] The acceptance of them was couched in a formal phrase of gratitude: "Les Prelates, Seigneurs et Comunes en ceste presente Parlement assembles an nom de touts vous autre Subjects Remercient treshumblement votre Majestie et prient Dieu vous doner en sante bone vie et longe."[7]

"The Bill for Subsidy is usually drawn by some of the Kings Counsell after the Substance thereof for the Number of Subsidies and fifteens to be Granted, and the Times of Payment are first agreed upon in the House. The Preamble thereof containing the Causes of the Grant is usually drawn by some Principal members of the House, Selected Committees for that purpose."[8] Lambard at an earlier date was equally explicit. "After mencion made for a subsidy the devise and dealing therein is committed to divers who agree uppon articles which they doe bringe in to be ordered by the house that Mr. Attorney generall shall Drawe it into forme of an Act; which done, it hath three readings and soe passeth as other bills doe, but yet commonly the consideracons in the Preamble is penned by some Committees whereof some be alwaies of the privy councell." Already Lambard had ex-

[5] Ibid., f. 39.
[6] Ibid., f. 30 note; f. 32.
[7] Ibid., f. 45 b.
[8] Ibid., f. 30.

plained: " The bill of subsidy is offered by the commons only for the Lords, [who] besides the Comon usage for other bills doe send it to the house againe after that they have thrice read it; and there it Remayneth to be carryed by the Speaker when he shall present it, 18 May, 23 Elizabeth." This seems to imply that money bills originating with the commons were thrice read in the lords, then returned to the commons, and finally presented by the Speaker to the king. Lambard further explains: " The manner is, when a subsidye is graunted, to carry it alone and the pardon to the King, leavange the rest of the bills in the chamber; and this is done to prepare the Royall assent to the rest and to present the Subsidye and give thanks for the Pardon." [9]   The royal assent to the subsidy bill was embodied in the response: " Le Roy remercy Ses loyeulx Subjects, accept leur beneVoleur, et auxi le vult; " or in Lambard's briefer formula, " Le Roi rende grand mercies." [10]   Subsidy bills voted by the clergy were, like the general pardon, read only once in each house; for like it they could only be accepted.

While bills of general pardon and bills of subsidy were thus differentiated as originating respectively with king or commons and, for the rest, requiring only formal assent, it was otherwise with private bills and public bills. Private bills, which were also called " particular " bills, were in every way held in less regard than public bills. It was almost an impertinence to introduce them. " It hath at some times been Ordered that everyone that preferreth a private Bill should pay 5 li. to the poor, which was done 43° Eliz. toward the end of the Parliament when they were troubled with much Business; but it holdeth not in other Parliaments." " There hath been often orders in the House that after nine of the clock, when usually the House groweth to be full, they should not be troubled with the Reading of any private Bill." " Public Bills are in due Course to be preferred in Reading and Passing

[9] Add. MS. 5123, f. 21.
[10] Richardson, f. 45 b; Lambard, f. 22.

before private." [11]   When public and private bills were sent together from the commons to the lords the latter were presented last.[12]   Private bills were drawn differently from public bills, "usually by Councillors of Law not being of the House and Sometimes by those of the House and that for their Fees. . . ." [13]   Once passed, a particular bill "shall be filed upon Flaws and that shall Suffice unless the Party whom it particularly concernes will Sue to have it Enrolled, then it may be enrolled to be sure." [14]

In contrast with this impatient and slightly disdainful treatment of private bills, both houses gave prolonged and serious consideration to public bills. These were "usually drawn by Such of the House with the Advice of Lawyers as of themselves are earnestly inclined to the effecting of Some publick Good . . . ; which being finer written in paper with wide Lines they are either by some Member of the House publicly presented to the Speaker in the House with some short speech setting forth the Usefulness of a Law in that behalf or are delivered in private to the Speaker or the Clerk of the Parliament to be presented to the House at some time convenient; and it is the Choice of the Party to prefer his Bill first into the Upper House or into the (House of Commons, which he list and as he shall think it may most advantage his Cause. Many times upon the motion of Some one of the House wishing a Law were made . . . a Committee is purposely appointed by the House to drawe a Bill to that Effect; which being done, one of them presenteth it to the Speaker. This is usual in Cases of great Moment and Difficultie. . . . Bills for the Revival, Repeal or Continuance of Statutes are usually drawn by Law-

---

[11] Richardson, f. 31.

[12] See below, p. 13.

[13] Richardson, f. 30 b. He added that the latter method "cannot be but very inconvenient Seeing afterwards they are to be Judges in the same Cause." Cf. the ordinance of 1372, which declared that practicing lawyers might not be knights of the shire since they often presented the private bills of their clients in the name of the commons (R. P., II, 310).

[14] Ibid., f. 17 b.

yers being members of the House, so appointed thereunto by the House upon Some nominacion to that purpose made, which is usual at the Beginning of every Parliament."[15]

A private or public bill thus drawn and presented to the Speaker or the Clerk was ready for its successive readings. Of these there were three in either house, and each house gave to the bills of the other three readings.[16] Three readings of a bill are apparent in the first journal of the lords in 1509 and in the first journal of the commons in 1547. But it was left for Richardson in the seventeenth century to tell us fully about them. On the first reading, the clerk, being told by the Speaker which bill to read, read the title and afterward the bill. The Speaker, taking the bill, repeated its title and "open[ed] to the House [its] Substance," either trusting to his memory or using the "Help" or the "Breviate" which was filed to the bill. "At the first Reading of the Bill it is not the use for any man to speak to it but rather to consider thereof and to take time 'till the Second Reading." Occasionally, but seldom, there was debate when a bill was clearly hurtful to the commonwealth "and so not fitting to trouble the House any longer." Even then the Speaker would not put the question unless much pressed, unwilling to subject the bill "to such a Hazard." If put to a vote and rejected, the bill was to be noted by the Clerk in his journal as not further read.[17]

Although a bill might come to its second reading on the day after the first reading, two or three days were usually allowed to elapse that members might have more time to think upon it. Then the Clerk again read the bill and again the Speaker repeated its title and read his Breviate, declaring this to be the second reading. If thereafter no one objected to its "matter of form," the Speaker could, if it was a commons bill, put the question whether it should be engrossed; for formal trans-

[15] Ibid., f. 30.
[16] Ibid., f. 40.
[17] Ibid., ff. 31 b-32 b.

ference to parchment was the mark of passage on second reading. Usually, however, before this was done the House called for the committing of the bill, and anyone wishing to speak against its matter or form was heard. If the vote was for commitment, the Speaker "put the House in mind touching the naming of Committees." Thereupon any member might name any other "to be a Committee" and the Clerk should note in his Journal any name which "in that confusion he can distinctly hear." When "a convenient number of Committees" was named, the Speaker should "put the House in mind to name the time and place" for their meeting. These the Clerk should enter in his journal and announce along with the "committees'" names, as soon as "the House is in Silence." If it was a bill coming from the lords which was up for a second reading, the question should be, not for its engrossing, since such bills were already engrossed, but for its commitment. If no commitment was desired, the lords bill passed to its third reading.[18]

When the members of the committee, all of whom might speak freely, had "fully resolved touching the Bill and the Amendment thereof, one of them . . . ought to make Report thereof to the House, opening the Substance of the things amended and the Reasons thereof." He should stand beside the Clerk while the latter read the amendments twice, assisting him through difficulties of interlining and bad writing. The Speaker, now taking the amended bill, put the question for engrossing. Again, as before commitment, there might be debate. If the vote was against engrossing, the Clerk should enter in his journal that the bill was dashed and should make the same record on the back of the bill along with the

[18] Richardson, ff. 33 *b*-34 *b*. Lambard agrees as to the commitment of bills. "And if the more voices will have yt committed, then must the Speaker entreate them to appoint the Committees. And that donne theire names and the tyme and place of meeting and the day of theire Reporte shall be indorsed uppon yt" (Lambard, f. 8). Ordinarily a bill was not re-committed; but in matters of importance it might be, usually to the same committee.

date. If the vote was to have it engrossed, it was the office of the Clerk to do this. And on the back of the bill, not within, he should write its title. Similarly, bills coming from the lords should have their titles already engrossed on the back, in defect of which they might be returned.

Some two or three days after a bill was engrossed it was offered by the Speaker to be read the third time, and this for its passage. Usually it was not now presented alone but along with other bills also engrossed, as many as five or six. Notice of the presentment was given and special attendance asked. First private bills were read "untill the House be grown to some fullness," then public bills. On the third reading "the matter is debated afresh and for the most part it is more Spoken unto this time than upon any of the former Readings; when the argument is Ended, the Speaker, still holding the Bill in his hand, maketh a Question for the passage in this Sort: As many as are of the mind that this Bill should pass say, Yea." And the Clerk recorded in his journal the favorable or unfavorable vote.

"Upon the Bill thus passed (if it be a Bill originally Exhibited in the lower House) the clerk ought to write within the Bill on the top toward the Right hand these Words

Soit baille aux Seigneurs.

If a Bill passed be a Bill originally begun in the upper House, then ought the Clerk to write underneath the Superscription of the Lords, which always is at the foot of the Bill, these words

A ceste Bille Les Comons sont assentus." [19]

Elsewhere, however, Richardson tells us that, if a bill was first delivered to the lords and passed them, "they use not to make any Indorsement but to send the Bill to the Comons," who on approval endorsed it as described.[20] Lambard noted that, "if the Lords agree to any bill sent unto them from the

[19] Ibid., ff. 35-37.
[20] Ibid., f. 18.

lower house, it must be indorsed, Les Signeurs ont assentes." [21]
We shall see that the lords' endorsement of a bill, whether
their own or a commons bill, whether with approval or disapproval, is of relatively late origin.

Having explained the manner in which a bill was thrice
read, Richardson discussed at some length the process of
amendment. A simple and brief amendment was made in one
way but a longer one differently. If the lower house wished
to amend one of its bills upon third reading and "the amendment thereof will not much deface the Bill nor spend much
time, the use is to cause the Serjeant to call in the Clerk that
did Ingross it (being usually a Servant to the Clerk of the
House) and to Cause him standing at the Table by his master
in the presence of the whole House to amend the same according to their Direction. Sometimes if the Amendments be but
of a few Words it is done by the Clerk himself writing a fair
Hand." [22]

If, however, the amendment was longer, it took the form
of a "provisoe" or of an "addition." Neither is defined further than is implied in the respective words. If anyone wished
to offer a proviso to a bill originating in the lower house, it
should, before the bill was engrossed, be offered on paper. After the engrossing of the bill it should be offered on parchment.
The reason for offering it on paper was that it might receive
any amendment in committee. When the proviso along
with the bill was returned by the committee, the Speaker
should put a special question whether it should be engrossed.
If this was denied, he proceeded to third reading without the
proviso; if accepted, he should have the proviso engrossed and
present it along with the bill on third reading. Many times on
second reading the proviso was debated and "sometimes Committed or Amended at the Board." If the bill with the proviso annexed passed on third reading, the Clerk wrote upon it
to the right, "Soit baille aux Seigneurs avesque un provision

[21] Lambard, f. 12 *b.*
[22] Richardson, f. 37 *b.*

annex"; and on the proviso itself he wrote, "Soit baille aux Seigneurs." The rules governing provisos applied to additions with a difference. The Clerk's inscription instead of mentioning a proviso ran "avesque une Schedule annex; for that which containeth an Addition is called a Schedule." [23]

When either house wished that a bill coming from the other house be amended, we have seen that such amendment was suggested on a paper affixed to the bill when it was returned in the hope that the other house might see fit to amend its own bill. In such cases a lords bill approved by the commons with suggested amendments was returned "with these words underneath the Signing of the Lords at the foot of the Bill

A ceste Bille avesq les Amendments les Comons ont assentus."

If the commons wished to alter some proviso or schedule sent from the lords, they naturally tendered such an amendment also on paper. Finally, if the lower House passed " a Bill sent from the Lords with some Additions by way of Schedule (whichever containeth some new Clause or intire branch added to the Bill) or with some Proviso to be added thereunto, the same ought to be signed as a new Bill, "Soit baille aux Seigneurs." [24] These details of procedure show not only independence of spirit on the part of either house but furnish inscriptions which, in so far as they appear at an earlier time, may be of assistance to us.

When the commons had passed some five or six bills, they appointed at the suggestion of the Speaker one of their principal members to carry them to the lords. Sometimes, " to grace some one Bill," they sent it alone. Then this bearer was "usually attended by 30 or 40 of the house as they please and are affected by the Business." Once the lords returned a bill because it was attended by only four or five. When the messenger with his company came to the bar of the lords he presented the bill or bills with three " Congees " to

[23] Ibid., ff. 39-40.
[24] Ibid., ff. 40, 40 *b*.

the "Lord Chancellor who of purpose cometh to the Bar to receive them." The order of presentation was (1) bills coming originally from the lords; (2) commons bills sent back by the lords to be amended; (3) new public bills "marshalled according to their Degrees in Consequence"; (4) private bills "in such order as the Speaker pleaseth." Lords bills sent to the commons, if "ordinary Bills," were dispatched by two doctors of civil law who were "Masters of the Chancery" and attendants in the upper house, sometimes accompanied by the clerk of the crown also attendant there. Bills of greater moment were "usually sent down by some of the Judges, assistants in the Upper House, accompanied with some of the Masters of the Chancery." Approaching the table where the Clerk sat they made "Congies" and, informing the Speaker that the lords had sent to the commons certain bills, they read the titles, delivered to him the bills and departed with three further "Congies." [25]

The last stage in the passage of bills was the securing of the royal approval. This was "usually deferred till the last day of the Session," although it might be given at any time during the parliament. Despite much discussion "whether the Royal Assent given to any one Bill doth not *ipso facto* conclude that present session," the House decided in the time of Philip and Mary and again in James I's last parliament that it did not. The comparatively recent ruling implies that such conclusion of a session was exceptional in the sixteenth century and probably almost unknown in the fifteenth. If the inference is correct, the earlier usage must have been that the king's assent to all bills, except perhaps subsidy bills, was given on the last day of the session.

It was not necessary that the king himself be present in parliament to give approval since by a decision of 33 Henry VIII letters patent under the great seal signed by his hand sufficed. The clerk of the crown read the titles of the bills

---

[25] Ibid., 43 *b*-44 *b*.

in the order of their consequence; and as the title of each was read, the clerk of parliament pronounced the royal response according to instructions from the king. "If it be a publick Bill to which the King assenteth, the Answer is

Le Roy le voet.

If a private Bill allowed by the King, the answer is

Soit fait come il desire.

If a publick Bill which the King forbeareth to allow,

Le Roi se avisera." [26]

The responses to subsidy bills and to general pardons have already been given.[27] Lambard says that the French phrases were pronounced by the clerk of the crown.[28] Certainly it would seem to have been more appropriate for the clerk of parliament to have read the titles and for the clerk of the crown to have pronounced the king's responses.

[26] Ibid., ff. 45, 45 *b.*
[27] See above, pp. 5, 6.
[28] Lambard, f. 22.

CHAPTER II

THE LORDS' JOURNAL AND THE PARLIAMENT
ROLL OF 1509

PERHAPS the next point at which we can best stop in a retro-
gressive approach to parliamentary procedure in the fourteenth and fifteenth centuries is the first year of Henry VIII;
for from 1509 comes the first journal of either house of parliament, the first narrative of what was done day by day. It is,
of course, the journal of the lords, since we have no commons'
journal earlier than 1547.[1] If in the early seventeenth century, and probably in Lambard's day as well, the expedition of
bills in both houses was the same, it may perhaps be assumed
that in 1509 the commons were conducting their affairs much
as the lords were. Whether this assumption is justifiable or
not, the lords' journal of 1509 furnishes valuable evidence
about parliamentary procedure in at least one house. It has a
further value in assisting us to make a transition to that type
of parliamentary record which alone survives for the fifteenth
century. Before 1509 our knowledge of parliamentary activity has to be got from the rolls of parliament, which are
summary accounts of the transactions of the lords with incidental references to the commons, drawn up at the close of
each parliament by the clerk. For further study, therefore,
it will be of service, not only to examine the lords' journal of
1509 but also to compare it with the parliament roll of that
year.[2]

The lords' journal of 1509 is not altogether a precise record. Bits of information about the progress of certain bills
are omitted, especially about the passage of some which we

---

[1] *Journals of the House of Lords, 1509-1714,* 19 vols. (s. l., s. a.) I, 1-9.
[2] *Journals,* I., 1-9; P. R. O., C. 65/131. It would be better to draw conclusions from an examination of several journals, but the scope of this
chapter scarcely permits it.

know were approved.[3]   A few other points remain obscure.[4]
But if we assume that all approved bills were treated like
those which are most fully described or if we make a composite picture derived from the progress of several bills, we
shall not be badly informed.

The lords sat from 21 January to 23 February inclusive, a
period of five weeks during which they transacted business
on twenty-three days.   On four other days, when the chancellor and other lords were absent in convocation, the treasurer
adjourned the session.[5]   During the five weeks there were
introduced for their lordships' consideration fifty-two bills.
Of these twenty-nine failed of passage while apparently
twenty-three received the approval of both houses.   Of the
latter all except three were enrolled on the parliament roll and
became statutes or acts.   Two of those not enrolled merely
provided for the repeal of earlier statutes — possibly the reason for their non-enrollment.[6]   In the Journal, all bills are

---

[3] The second reading is sometimes not noted.

[4] The bills connected with Empson and Dudley are perplexing. On the
second day before the conclusion of the parliament a *Billa concernens Dudley at Empson et eorum la Atteynt et Convictionem in Parliamento* was
read twice and the next day a third time. On the last day it was *recepta . . .
noviter formata,* was approved and was sent to the commons with at least
one *additio* and one *proviso* (see below, p. 23, n. 35). No act for the attainder
of Dudley and Empson appears on the parliament roll or on the statute
roll. On both, however, there is an act, not referred to in the journal,
exempting from their attainder lands which the attainted men held in trust
for others. It is possible that this was the *additio* or the *proviso* referred
to in the journal. The entries for the last two days are somewhat con-
fused, indicating a rush of business.

[5] 26, 31 Jan., 5, 15 Feb. On three of these days bills were received or were
dispatched to the commons, but none was considered.

[6] Of the three not enrolled, one, a *Billa de Forestis et de Feris extra suas
clausuras . . . interficiendis,* is fully described as read three times in the lords
then sent to the commons, approved by them, and on being returned to the
lords, " expedita " (29 Jan., 4, 6, 7, 16 Feb.) ; another, a *Billa de Adnullacione
Statuti contra Pannarios editi tempore Richardi III,* was received from
the commons on 21 Feb., and promptly approved by the lords (" quam
Domini approbarunt; lecta est coram dominis tertio ") ; the third, a *billa pro
annullacione cuiusdam Statuti editi anno undecimo Henrici Septimi,* was
received from the commons and read on 16 Feb., was read a second time

referred to by Latin titles; but it will be more convenient to use the English titles by which approved bills were designated on the parliament roll.   For convenience, too, they may well be referred to in the order in which they are there recorded, although such was not the order in which bills were considered and passed.[7]   The twenty enrolled as acts are printed with the same titles in the *Statutes of the Realm;* but earlier editions

on 18 Feb., and on 19 Feb. was passed (*expedita*), presumably on third reading.

[7] On the parliament roll the acts of the session are enrolled as follows:

1. An Acte for the expences of the King's Howsehold.
2. An Acte for the assignement of money for the King's greate Warderobe.
3. An Acte for confirmacion of Lettres Patents made to Quene Katheryn for her Dower.
4. An Acte for the restitucion of Roberte Ratclyffe, Knight, Lord Fitzwater.
5. An Acte for a Subsidy to be granted to the Kynge.
6. An Acte for the repealinge of a Statut for Fyshinge in Island.
7. An Acte concerning the making of Wollen Clothes.
8. An Acte concerning Receyvors [certain revenues to be paid to John Heyron, the king's " general Receyvour "].
9. An Acte that Informacions uppon Penall Statuts shalbe made within three Yeres.
10. An Acte for the trewe Payment of the King's Customes.
11. An Acte for repealing of a Statut concerning Justic[es] of Peace.
12. An Acte concerning Coroners.
13. An Acte agaynst Escheators and Comyssioners for makinge false retornes of Offices and Commyssions.
14. An Act for the taking of toll at Staynes Bridg for repayring therof.
15. An Act that noe Lease shalbe made of Lands seised into the Kyng's Hands but in certayne cases.
16. An Act agaynst Perjury.
17. An Acte for Admyttance of a travers agaynst an untrew Inquisicion.
18. An Act agaynst carrying out of this Realme any Coyne, plate or Jewells.
19. An Act agaynst wearing of costly Apparrell.
20. An Acte concernyng lands made in trust to Empson and Dudley.
[21. (Not enrolled). An Act concerning forests and wild beasts].
[22. (Not enrolled). An Act for the repeal of the statute of Richard III concerning cloth-workers].
[23. (Not enrolled). An Act for the repeal of a certain statute of 11 Henry VII].

Henceforth these numbers will often be used to designate briefly the bills from which the acts arose.

of the statutes printed only the last fifteen of them and did so with entire justification.[8]

If we note what the Journal tells us about the passage of approved bills, the record is somewhat as follows. All bills received at least three readings; and the first formal appearance of a bill was on its first reading. How a bill came to the lords before first reading is seldom explained. The Journal usually notes only that it had been " received " or that it had been received to be read — "*recepta legenda.*" Four or five bills besides the subsidy bill came from the commons.[9] Another bill was in the hands of the " Porter " before it came to first reading.[10] Four bills before or after first reading were given to the king's attorney and the king's solicitor for

[8] *Stats.*, III. 1-9. The *Statutes* place last the five which are enrolled first on the parliament roll and the editors noted that they had not been hitherto printed. The fifteen others are acts of wider import and for this reason seemed to earlier editors the only ones worthy to be designated statutes. In so thinking earlier editors were correct. Never in the fourteenth or the fifteenth century were subsidy indentures or acts for the maintenance of the king's household or great wardrobe regarded as statutes and enrolled on the statute roll. It was only after the statute rolls failed the editors of the *Statutes of the Realm* that these editors began to print as statutes material which was not traditionally such. From the days of Richard III they drew for their subject matter upon the parliament roll and were generous in printing much of what they found there. But all of the " acts " which they print thereafter should not be looked upon as " statutes " in the earlier significance of the term. (See below, pp. 138, n. 23, 150, n. 37 and ch. xi).

[9] See below, p. 30, n. 54. About the origin of another bill, that ratifying Queen Katherine's dower (no. 3), there is some doubt. It was first read in the lords on 30 Jan., was sent to the commons on 5 Feb. after its third reading on 4 Feb., and was returned from the commons on 16 Feb., to be again read and approved on 18 Feb. The roll of parliament, however, suggests that this bill originated with the commons, noting that it *exhibita est Regi . . . per communitatem Anglie.* In the fifteenth-century rolls of parliament this phrase implies commons' origin; but it may have been employed loosely by 1509. Wherever first introduced, the bill was official in character and had already on introduction been phrased in the form of an act — *in forma Actus compilata*, as the roll puts it.

[10] The bill for the making of woolen cloths: 11 Feb., *recepta; Habet Porter;* 14 Feb., *lecta prima vice.* " Porter " may have been a personal name. But it is never accompanied by a title and the functions of the bearer were humble.

revision.[11]   Such action suggests that it was possible for criticism and hence for debate to arise on first reading.   One of
the bills coming from the commons is described on first reading as a bill which the lords *discussed* and thought should be
revised.   In the next session, on second reading, it was sent
back to the lower house for such revision.[12]   Another bill,
this one unsuccessful, seems also to have been discussed on
first reading.[13]   If there was debate on first reading, it cannot
in general have been prolonged.   Two bills are said to have
had their first and second readings on the same day [14]; and
four others for which no second reading is recorded must have
been expedited in like manner, since the third reading came
on the day after the first.[15]   Often the second reading fell on
the day after the first or on the day of the next session.[16]   We
are told of only two bills for which the interval was longer.[16a]

It is more likely that debate arose in connection with second reading.   We have just seen that it was after second
reading that a commons bill was returned to the lower house
for revision; and a second commons bill was treated in the

[11] The bill touching escheators' false returns was on 24 Jan. *tradita Attornato et Sollicitatori Regis reformanda,* on 25 Jan. *lecta iam bis* and on 28
Jan. *tunc tertio lecta.* A bill *Pro Libertatibus Ecclesie Anglicane* was treated
similarly but was on 24 Jan. *bis lecta.* The bill against wearing costly apparel was on 24 Jan. *tradita Attornato reformanda* and on 25 Jan. *lecta iam
prima et tradita est Attornato et Solliciatori.* The bill for exporting gold
was on 30 Jan. *lecta iam prima,* on 1 Feb. *tradita est Regis Attornato ac
Solliciatori emendanda* and on 7 Feb. *lecta secunda vice.*

[13] The bill for informations made upon penal statute was first read in the
lords on 1 Feb., *quam Billam Domini disputando censerunt esse reformandam;* on 4 Feb. it was *lecta secunda vice [et] missa ex mandato Dominorum in Domum Inferiorem reformanda.*

[13] A bill concerning letters of privy seal, which failed of final passage, was
read on 1 Feb. and given to the " Porter," *quam Billam Domini in certis
verbis decreverunt esse amplicandam.* In the next session on second reading the Journal notes, *super quam Domini deliberandum fore duxerunt,* and
we hear no more of it.

[14] Above, n. 11.

[15] Bills 6, 12, 16, 4; 29 and 30 Jan., 19 and 20 Feb.

[16] Bills 3, 10, 18, 9, 11, 14; 30 Jan.-1 Feb., 1 Feb.-4 Feb., 14 Feb.-16 Feb.

[16a] Bill 21; 29 Jan.-4 Feb., with two sessions intervening; bill 18, 1 Feb.-
7 Feb., with four sessions intervening during which the bill was revised.

same manner.[17]   Except in one instance, and this a government bill making provision for the king's wardrobe, the third reading seems never to have fallen on the same day as the second.[18]   Usually it occurred in the session following the second reading[19] or even, as we have seen, in the session after the first.   For no successful bill is there clear evidence of a session intervening between second and third reading, although there is such testimony touching a bill which failed of passage.[20]

If these intervals suggest that little time was usually allowed for debate on second reading, they also suggest, in conjunction with the intervals between the first and the third reading of those bills for which no second reading is recorded that usually no time was allowed for committment to a committee.   Of the twenty-three bills passed by the lords only three, over and above those sent back to the commons, were clearly given an interval of more than one session between first and third readings; and in the case of one of them the delay was due to turning the bill over to the attorney for revision.[21]   Since in general such expedition prevailed, committees would have had little time for deliberation.   If a commons bill was sent back to the commons for amendment this was done after second reading in the lords.   A third reading apparently occurred only after the bill had been received from the commons a second time and in amended form.

Although there is no indication that the lords in 1509 submitted bills to a committee on second reading, there are two or three bits of evidence that a bill might be engrossed after second reading.   The bill for repairing the bridge at Staines was on first reading given to Master Eliot to be revised.[21a]   In

[17] The bill for repealing a statute concerning justices of the peace was first read on 1 Feb. and, when read a second time on 4 Feb., was sent back to the commons for amendment.

[18] 22 Feb.

[19] Bills 13, 21, 3, 10, 14, and probably others.

[20] See below, p. 21, n. 26.

[21] Bills 18, 7, 21.   In the case of bill 7 two sessions intervened between first and third reading, and in the case of bill 21 three.

[21a] Eliot was the king's sergeant-at-law.

the next session the revised bill was read and passed and was given to the "Porter" *ad scribendam*.[22] This may, of course, merely signify that Master Eliot's changes were to be incorporated; but the Porter's action sounds very like the later engrossing. The Journal is clearer in the case of two bills which passed the lords but not the commons. One related to the treatment of boats in creeks. On 30 January it was first read and in the next session on second reading the lords voted that it should be written *on parchment*, then be read a third time and thereafter be sent to the Commons.[23] A second unsuccessful bill was directed against privilege of clergy. First read on 14 February it was turned over to Master Eliot, presumably to be revised. In the next session it was again read, was passed, and was given to the Porter *ad scribendam in munda*. In the following session it was read, approved, and sent to the commons.[24] In the case of both these bills engrossing after second reading is pretty clearly indicated.[25]

On third reading debate seems to have been unusual but possible. What usually followed third reading was acceptance on the same day and dispatch on this day or the next to the other house. Three bills, to be sure, came up for third reading, yet were not sent to the commons.[26] They must have

---

[22] On 14 Feb. the bill was first read and *tradita Magistro Eliot reformanda;* on 16 Feb. it was *lecta et expedita et habet Porter ad scribendam.*

[23] . . . *decreverunt Domini hanc Billam in pergamenam scribendam et in die Lune* [this was Friday] *tertio legendam et in Domum Inferiorem mittendam.* . . .

[24] The Journal says that the reading on 16 Feb. was the third, but this seems to be a mistake.

[25] In the parliament of 1511 the bills first received by the lords were *in papiro (Journals,* i, 11).

[26] The bill *Pro Patentibus Fortiliciorum concessis ad vitam* was first read on 25 Jan. and was then given to the attorney to revise. It was read a second time in the next session. The third reading was delayed until 6 Feb. The bill *de Promotoribus et Commissariis . . . amovendis* was first read on 6 Feb., when the lords ordered that the names of the men censored be added, was again read on 11 Feb., when it was given to the Porter *ad reformandam,* and was finally read a third time on 14 Feb. with the names annexed but with no indication that it was sent to the commons. Of the bill

been rejected at this stage and the rejection may imply debate. The custom of bringing up several bills together for third reading, described by Richardson, seems not yet to have arisen. Although occasionally two or three third readings occurred on the same day, it would scarcely be justifiable to see in this any intentional grouping of bills. The bearers of lords bills to the commons were usually two, the persons most often designated being the clerk of parliament and the king's attorney, with occasional mention of the king's solicitor. A lords bill accepted by the commons and returned to the upper house is in two instances said to have been read a fourth time before it was finally passed.[27] Often the only phrase applied to a bill so returned is *expedita*[28]; and sometimes not even this occurs, although it is clear that the bill became an act.[29]

We have just seen that three bills came up before the lords for third reading but were not thereafter sent to the commons. Two other bills, approved on third reading were sent to the lower house but there is no record of their passage there.[30] Only when bills received the approval of both houses did they become acts of parliament. Often the two houses co-operated readily and agreed upon the adoption of bills without further ado or amendment. Of the twenty-three bills passed in this parliament, eleven seem to have been so adopted.[31] Another was returned to the commons that they might note on it their approval.[32] In another instance the lords amended one of their

pro resumptione Officiorum Regine only the third reading is recorded (22 Feb.).

[27] The bill regarding fishing in Iceland was returned from the commons on 1 Feb. and *lecta una vice;* the bill touching the Queen's dower was returned from the commons on 16 Feb. and on 18 Feb. was *lecta et approbata [et] expedita*.

[28] Bills 9, 10, 19, 21.

[29] Bills 2, 7, 8, 12, 14, 16, 18.

[30] The bill for the treatment of boats in creeks (30 Jan., 1, 4 Feb.) and the bill relating to benefit of clergy (14, 16, 18 Feb.).

[31] Bills 2, 3, 6, 7, 8, 13, 15, 16, 21, 22, 23.

[32] The bill for Staines bridge, after its three readings in the lords, its dispatch to the commons and its return thence was *remittenda ut annotetur quod a Domo Inferiori confirmetur* (20 Feb.).

own bills after it had been returned by the commons, but apparently on their own initiative. When it was sent down in amended form the commons duly approved the change.[33]   In another instance the lords, after sending a bill to the commons, seems to have dispatched a second one on the same subject four days later.[34]   In like manner the commons may have dispatched to the lords an addition to one of their bills already sent up; for, touching the attainder of Empsom and Dudley, after the lords had thrice read a bill presumably of commons origin, they received on the day after third reading the bill *noviter formata*. Promptly they ratified what they called an addition with a proviso and sent it to the commons.[35]

If in the case of fifteen of the bills passed by the parliament of 1509 there was ready concurrence between the two houses, there was less prompt agreement touching the remaining eight. In four instances the commons amended lords bills; in four the lords amended commons bills.[36]   One of the commons amendments consisted of two words.[37]   Elsewhere the commons added provisos where the lords had already done the same. To the proviso which the lords had attached to their bill for the restitution of lord Fitzwater the commons added

[33] The bill against costly apparel after its three readings, its dispatch to the commons and its return was, on 20 Feb., *lecta et emendanda*. On 22 Feb. it was again *adduct[a] a Domo Inferiori et per utramque Domum expedita.*

[34] The bill against the exportation of gold and jewels, after being twice referred to the attorney for revision and being thrice read, was sent to the commons on 19 Feb. On 23 Feb. the *Billa concernens Asportacionem Monete cum alia Billa de eadem materia a Domo Superiori prius in Inferiorem missa et utraque remissa est in Domum Communem.*

[35] On 23 Feb., the day after third reading, *recepta est Billa de Attinctu . . . noviter formata*. On the same day *quedam Additio cum Provisione annexa super attinctum Empson et Dudley lecte sunt et approbate et misse in Domum Communem*. The addition and proviso may, of course, have been the lords' own (cf. above p. 16, n. 4).

[36] Bills 12, 4, 1, 10 and 5, 17, 9, 11.

[37] On 20 Feb. the bill about coroners was *adducta a Communibus emendanda in duobus verbis.*

three more [38]; and to the single proviso which the lords had added to the bill for the household, the commons added four.[39] One bill was three times read in the lords, was sent to the commons and was returned; whereupon the lords voted that it should again be sent to the lower house to be "reformed." Apparently the commons had suggested or made unsatisfactory changes.[40]

More numerous and apparently more significant than the commons' amendments to lords bills were the lords' amendments to commons bills. When the subsidy bill, presumably already accepted by the commons, was introduced in the lords, two provisos were added—one in favour of the Hansards, the other in favour of the staplers. The two were introduced separately, were apparently each read three times, were sent separately to the commons, who approved them, and were finally passed along with the bill itself. Thereupon the act with two provisos annexed was given to Sir Thomas Lovel, speaker of the commons, and to his associates at the bar of the lords.[41] The bill for the admittance of travers against an untrue inquisition was returned to the commons two days after the first reading (probably on second reading) to be revised (*reformanda*). On the same day it came back and presumably was passed at once.[42]

Two other commons bills gave rise to more prolonged negotiations. The one requiring that information upon penal stat-

---

[38] On 20 Feb. after third reading the bill was sent to the commons *cum uno proviso*. On 22 Feb. the bill was returned from the commons *cum quatuor provisionibus eidem annexis . . . et lecta cum suis provisionibus.*

[39] On 18 Feb. this bill was *missa in Domum Inferiorem cum uno proviso;* on 22 Feb. it was *adducta a Domo Communi cum provisionibus quinque eidem annexis.*

[40] This bill, providing for true payment of customs, had its third reading on 4 Feb. and next day was sent to the commons. On 8 Feb., when it was *adducta a Domo Communi, Domini decreverunt iterum in Domum Inferiorem mittendam et reformandam.*

[41] 16, 18, 21, 22, 23 Feb. *Actus subsidii cum duobus Provisionibus annexis liberatur Thome Lovel, mil., et sociis suis ad Barram hic.*

[42] 20 and 22 Feb.

utes should be made within three years was the one which, on
first reading, the lords *disputando* thought should be revised,
noting that the king should have three or four years instead
of one in which to follow up actions of this sort.   On second
reading the bill was sent back to the commons for revision.
The change just noted was indicated but also others *prout in
Billa continebatur.*   Four days later the bill was returned, presumably with the desired changes, and the lords gave assent.
But two weeks later and on the day before the end of parliament they sent what was now called the act to the commons
with the limitation that it endure only until the next parliament.   On the same day the commons accepted the limitation
and the act was thus *expedita.*[43]

The bill repealing a statute concerning justices of the peace
was also returned to the commons after second reading, this
time with the comment that it ought to apply not merely
to persons dwelling in certain places but also to those who had
been born there.   When four days later it was a second time
brought from the commons and read before the lords, the
latter pronounced that it ought again to go to the lower house
to be amended.   It was sent for this purpose next day.   When
it came back some days later it was still unsatisfactory in
lacking the date at which it should become operative and in
other respects.   Hence Bryknell and Gremesby were com-
missioned to go from lords to commons *ad tractandum tam
pro reformatione eiusdem Bille et quum inciperet habere
vigorem.*   This is almost a committee of conference between
the houses.[44]

The amending of these four commons bills by the lords
seems to follow the general lines of procedure indicated by
Richardson.   The repeated use of " reformanda " as descriptive of what was expected when a bill was returned by the
lords to the commons implies that, if the lords suggested the
amendment, they none the less expected the commons to for-

[43] I, 4, 8, 22 Feb.
[44] I, 4, 8, 9, 16 Feb.

mulate it and either incorporate it in the bill or add it to the bill as a proviso. This is reminiscent of Richardson's account of how either house suggested to the other its amendment on paper rather than on parchment in order to avoid any appearance of dictation. It was in the seventeenth century one house's tribute to the independence of the other. That the lords were meticulous in 1509 in thus referring desirable amendments to the commons is a matter of some importance; for it is not improbable that there had been a time when the lords' revision of a commons bill was merely incorporated in the king's response to it and was not returned to the lower house for assent. To discover whether this was once the custom and, if so, when the change to a more respectful procedure occurred will be one of the problems of the fifteenth century.[45]

Our reconstruction of parliamentary procedure in 1509 has been based on the methods employed in passing the twenty-three bills which received the assent of both houses. Only occasional reference has been made to the twenty-nine which failed of approval, and this in connection with debate on first or third reading or in connection with engrossing. Of the twenty-nine, six came to a first reading, two to a second, and six to a third. After third reading three of the six were sent to the commons. The remaining fifteen bills were merely presented and are described as *recepta* or *recepta legenda* or *recepta et respectuatur*.[46] Why so many bills got no further than presentation or than first or second reading need not concern us. The brevity of the session may have had much to do with it. The three bills which were thrice read but not sent to the commons have an interest in suggesting rejection on third reading and possible debate.[47] Of the three which were sent to the commons, two must have been rejected there, since nothing more is heard of them.[48] But the third had a

[45] See below, pp. 261-2, 278-86, 320-24.
[46] E.g., bills introduced on 11 Feb. and 20 Feb.
[47] Cf. above, p. 21.
[48] Cf. above, p. 22.

more unusual fate. After its passage by the lords on three readings in three successive sessions, its dispatch to the commons and its return thence eleven days later it was again read before the lords on 8 February. The pronouncement now was *non placuit et tradita Collyngborn*.[49] Whether the lords were dissatisfied with their earlier action or whether the commons had made unacceptable changes is not clear. Although there would still have been time to amend the bill during the session, nothing apparently was done.

The Journal concludes with information about the final stages of the bills passed by both houses. On the last day of parliament at 5.00 P.M. in the *Camera Crucis* with the king on the throne and all the lords and commons present the speaker of the commons in a laudatory address presented to the king certain indented letters recording the grant of a subsidy of many thousand pounds.[50] The chancellor, consulting the king, made answer. Then at the bidding of the king he ordered that all acts made in this parliament be read and made public. The clerk of the crown and the clerk of parliament proceeded to read them and also the declaration of royal will written on the back of each.[51] The last assumed the phraseology of Richardson's day, "Le Roy le vult," "Le Roy se advisera," "Soit fait come il est desire," while the bill of subsidy was endorsed, "Le Roy remercie ses Communes . . . lez Graunts ac accepte et . . . approve [with the provisions annexed]."

The Lords' Journal of 1509 thus shows how largely the procedure described by Richardson was existent a century before

---

[49] This bill *Pro Libertatibus Ecclesie Anglicane* was twice read on 24 and 25 Jan., and a third time in the session of the 28th.

[50] " . . . quasdam literas indentatas subsidium quoddam multarum millium librarum summas in se continentes Regie optulit Majestati." 23 Feb.

[51] " . . . Cancellarius Acta omnia in presenti Parliamento . . . edita et facta ex Mandato Domini Regis recitari et publicari jussit, quibus ex ordine (ut moris erat) per Clericum Corone per initia recitatis et lectis et singulis per Clericum Parliamenti responsione secundum annotationes Regie voluntatis Declarationem a dorso scripta facta per hec verba. . . ."

he wrote. Although we do not learn who prepared bills, the revision of the lords bills was the task of the king's attorney or of the attorney and the solicitor. In the lords, bills were subjected to three readings. They might be debated, possibly on the first reading, pretty clearly on the second, not improbably on the third. They were sometimes engrossed on second reading, and may have been on third. The lords sometimes added provisos to their own bills or even sent to the commons a second bill to supplement one already dispatched. The commons similarly in one case sent to the lords a bill *noviter formata*. Not only did each house amend or revise its own bills but each amended the bills of the other. Amendments of this sort were referred to the house in which the bill originated, were usually accepted by it and were returned as provisos. Thereupon the bill was passed (*expedita*) by both houses and was ready for the royal assent or dissent. This was given on the last day of parliament and was inscribed on the back of the bill. What we miss from Richardson's account is little more than the submission of bills to committees on second reading and certain details about the treatment of provisos and exceptions. Finally, although the Journal's narrative applies primarily to the lords, it is not unlikely that procedure in the commons was similar if not indeed the same.

As has been pointed out, not only may the procedure of 1509 serve as a *terminus a quo* for investigations into fifteenth century procedure, but a comparison of the Journal with the parliament roll of 1509 may elucidate the structure of earlier parliament rolls upon which we shall henceforth have to rely so largely. The parliament roll of 1509 was drawn up by the clerk and is signed " John Tayler, manu propria, clerico parliamentorum." [52] It adds little to our knowledge of the proceedings of this parliament and it omits nearly all that the Journal tells us about the passage of bills. It has no record of three bills which seem to have been passed or of the at-

[52] The roll is in MS. only, C. 65/131.

tainder of Empson and Dudley.[52a] It describes, as does the
Journal, the opening of parliament. In enumerating the so-
called triours of petitions it adds the names of four men, designating each as "chevalier," thereby indicating that they were
members of the commons. The Journal may have neglected
them because they were not members of the lords. The roll
proceeds to record the acts passed, designating them in the
margin with the titles which we have already adopted. Following the fifth act appears the statement: "Item diverse
communes petitiones . . . exhibite erunt . . . Regi . . .
quarum tenores cum responsionibus . . . per Regem ex assensu dominorum . . . ac comunitatis . . . factis et in dorsis
insertis [are as follows]." Fifteen acts follow with the king's
response attached to each. It is always the same, "Le Roy
le vuelt."

The fifteen acts themselves assume the form in which they
appear in the *Statutes of the Realm*. Each begins with one or
more explanatory "whereas" clauses [53] and then passes to the
enacting clause. The latter runs, "Be it therefore enacted by
the king with the assent of the lords and commons in this present parliament assembled" or more briefly "by authority of
this present parliament." Provisos are often incorporated,
some of them embodying the amendments which the Journal
describes. In an act in its final form it is difficult and at
times impossible to distinguish between provisos which inhered
in the original form of the bill, provisos which were added later
by the house which sponsored the bill and provisos which
were added by the other house. This is the more unfortunate
since the last sort of proviso is significant, telling, as it does,
something about the relations existing between the two houses.
The difficulty will become sharply apparent in the fifteenth
century when there are no journals to instruct us and when
we see the provisos only as they appear in the final form of
the act. The obscuring of this information is perhaps our

[52a] See above p. 16, notes 4, 6.
[53] Sometimes "wherefor," "where," "forasmuch."

most serious loss in passing from the journals to the rolls; but happily fifteenth-century rolls are somewhat more informing about provisos than is the roll of 1509.

A marked divergence between the lords' journal and the parliament roll in 1509 is the apparent failure of the latter to distinguish between acts which originated with the lords and those which originated with the commons — between lords bills and commons bills. Indeed, the roll seems intentionally misleading; for it sometimes enters what the Journal shows to have been lords bills under the caption "communes petitiones." To be sure, the Journal itself is occasionally ambiguous regarding the origin of bills. Of the fifteen acts which arose from the "communes petitiones" of the parliament roll it designates clearly only four as in origin commons bills.[54] Certain of the fifteen must, however, have originated with the lords. Two bills which gave rise to two of them were already before the lords on 24 January, the day after the commons had presented the speaker, and hence before bills could have been passed in the lower house.[55] Since four others were read on the 29th and still two others on the 30th, the days on which the fourth and fifth sessions of the lords took place, we should have to assume that the six were given somewhat rapid consideration in the lower house if we were to maintain that all of them originated there.[56] Bills which were clearly of commons' origin did not reach the lords until 1 February, the day of the sixth session. Hence it is very likely that as many as a third of the bills designated as "communes petitions," and probably a larger number, originated with the lords rather than with the commons.

The explanation of this anomaly is partly teleological, partly historical. The fifteen bills in question, whether originating with lords or commons, were public bills and were to become

[54] Bills 9, 11, 15, 17. The last two are described as *misse a domo Communi, remisse sunt in eandum Domum reformande* (22 Feb.).

[55] Bills 13 and 19.

[56] Bills 6, 12, 16, 21 and 10, 18.

public acts. For enrollment it mattered little what had been their origin; all were to become statutes. And if the caption "public bills" would have been more appropriate than "commons petitions" the latter had in its favour long usage. In 1509 it was a survival from a time when most bills so designated on the parliament roll were actually of commons' origin. A once precise and more or less pertinent designation of them had, however, in course of time become blurred; and the clerk, intent on the future rather than on the past of public bills, retained the old caption when enrolling them, indifferent as to whether this was longer applicable to all the bills which it introduced.[57]

Although the parliament roll of 1509 grouped its last fifteen acts together as arising from commons petitions, careless of whether they were commons bills or lords bills, it did not so designate the first five which it records. Simple explanations for this are at hand. One of the acts was that for a subsidy, one was a private act, three were official in character, touching the court.

According to the Journal, the subsidy bill, originating of course in the commons, did not reach the lords until 16 February. We have seen how the lords then added two provisos, which the commons in turn accepted, how they later delivered the act with the two provisos to the representatives of the commons at the bar of the upper house, and how on the last day of the session, the speaker of the commons presented the subsidy to the king in the form of an indenture (*littere indentate*) receiving therefor the king's thanks. Touching all this the roll merely says that the commons with the assent of the lords granted to the king a subsidy, which it describes, and that the king thanked the commons for it, approving it with the two provisos annexed. Fifteenth-century accounts of subsidy bills in the rolls will be a little more informing than this, enough so to disclose some of the features described in the Journal.

[57] See below, pp. 286, 94, 102, 115-16.

The one distinctly private bill passed in 1509 was for the restitution of lord Fitzwater. We have seen how it was first introduced in the lords (but as late as 19 February), was sent to the commons with two provisos, was amended there by two more, and, with a final proviso added by the lords, was passed. The parliament roll merely enrolled the bill and the five provisos without distinguishing the origin of any of the latter. It did, however, describe the bill clearly as a private petition presented to king, lords and commons by Robert Ratcliffe, kt., lord Fitzwater.[58] Thereby it revealed that its usage was to enroll private bills apart from public bills. Fifteenth-century rolls of parliament will not only conform to this usage but will furnish a clue for discovering whether private bills originated in the lords or in the commons.

The three other bills of the roll of 1509 which are recorded before commons petitions are alike in being of an official nature and in providing for the needs of the court. One related to the expenses of the king's household, another to the assignment of money for his wardrobe, and the third was the ratification of letters patent assigning to Queen Katherine her dower. The first two apparently were introduced in the lords before they were in the commons, although as late in the session as 16 and 21 February. The third was probably also first read in the lords and as early as 30 January.[59] All were pretty clearly read three times before they were sent to the commons.[60] Thus the three bills, as they appear in the Journal, were like other lords bills. Actually there was a difference. None of them had the general import which the last fifteen bills of the parliament roll had. Although they were

---

[58] " Item . . . petitio exhibita est . . . Regi . . . per Robertum Ratclyf, militem. . . ." It is addressed " To the Kyng . . . and to the lordes . . . and the commons," and asks that the king grant the petitioner's request with the assent of the lords and commons.

[59] See above, p. 18, n. 9.

[60] This is carefully noted of two of them. Only a first reading is recorded of the household act; but, since this occurred on 16 Feb. and the bill was not sent to the commons until 18 Feb., a third reading probably intervened.

to become acts of parliament like the latter, they had a lesser statutory significance. It was logical to separate them on the parliament roll from public bills. For this we shall find that there was abundant precedent, as there was in the case of subsidy bills and private bills. All of these usages lead us, as does the character of the " commons petitions," to a study of the development of the parliament roll in the fourteenth and fifteenth centuries.

The parliament roll of 1509 leaves us with disappointments, but also with clues and with questions. It fails to reveal clearly whether provisos to a bill were added by the house in which a bill originated or by the house to which it was sent; but it does not forbid the hope that earlier rolls may be more explicit or that the bills in their original form may clear up obscurities. It fails in the second place to distinguish, as the Journal also often does, between bills originating with the lords and bills originating with the commons. It even adds an element of confusion by grouping both under the caption " commons petitions." But again it admits of the possibility that earlier rolls may throw light on this grouping and that some earlier phraseology may enable us to make the desired distinction. It finally sets apart from the body of commons petitions, which, when granted, became public acts, certain other bills and resultant acts. These comprise a subsidy bill, a private bill and official bills. In Richardson's seventeenth-century phraseology subsidy bills and private bills formed categories co-ordinate with public bills.[61] We now learn that the parliament roll recognized the same categories and added perhaps a fourth. In this it is more discriminating than the Journal and reconciles us somewhat to becoming dependent upon earlier rolls of a similar character. To these rolls and to other parliamentary records of the fifteenth century we must now turn.

---

[61] Of his fourth type of bill, the general pardon, there was no example in 1509.

CHAPTER III

PARLIAMENTARY RECORDS OF THE FOURTEENTH AND
FIFTEENTH CENTURIES

The surviving records of the proceedings of parliament in the fourteenth and fifteenth centuries are of the same type as the records of the sixteenth century, with the regrettable absence of the journals. The three stages of elaboration in which they appear are (1) the original bills, (2) the parliament rolls and (3) the statute rolls. The original bills are those which were sent from one house to the other in engrossed form. They often came to bear on their face or back certain inscriptions and they were finally conveyed to chancery for preservation. They were before the clerk of parliament when at the end of the session he drew up in enrolled form his record of parliamentary activities. They were also before whoever redrafted them, so far as redrafting was necessary, to make them into acts or statutes, a work finally embodied in the statute roll. In sixteenth century studies of parliament they may be more or less neglected since they tell us little that cannot be found in either the journals or the rolls; but in earlier centuries, when the journals fail us, greater reliance must be placed upon them. In short, the following examination of fourteenth- and fifteenth-century parliamentary procedure may be described as an attempt to make original bills compensate for the absence of journals in elucidating the rolls. They will by no means compensate fully or even satisfactorily. But in conjunction with an explicitness in fifteenth century rolls somewhat greater than that of the roll of 1509, they will tell us considerable about the nature and expedition of parliamentary business.

The history of parliament in the fifteenth century has hitherto been written almost entirely from the record of the parliament rolls and the statute rolls (*rotuli parliamentorum, rotuli de statutis*).   The former constitute a series somewhat broken at first, but well preserved from the middle of the fourteenth century.[1]   The latter are in contrast.   The most imposing statute roll is the first, containing the statutes of the three Edwards; in the fifteenth century the statute rolls deteriorated and did not survive the reign of Henry VII.[2]

Both parliament rolls and statute rolls are enrolled records and have the virtues and defects of enrolled records generally. Enrollment, whether in chancery or in the exchequer, looked to the preservation in compact and final form of information which was of permanent interest to the departments concerned. Much that was of seeming unimportance was disregarded, the form of what was preserved was often changed, summarized or perfected, and the method by which the final record was evolved is often obscured.   The enrolled customs accounts, for example, are a uniform and an extremely summary digest of the varied and detailed information contained in the so-called particulars of accounts submitted by the collectors at the various ports.   Similarly the enrolled household accounts summarize briefly the detailed expenditures recorded in the "particuli" of the keeper of the household for any year.

Because the parliament rolls and the statute rolls embodied in compact and final form the record of the activities of successive parliaments, the desirability of printing them has long since been recognized.   Editions of the statutes appeared from the fifteenth century until the more satisfactory *Statutes of the Realm* were published by the Record Commission early in the nineteenth century.[3]   Six volumes of the *Rotuli Parliamentorum* made public the enrollments of the clerk of parliament up to the reign of Henry VIII.[4]   But the first stage in which

[1] Maitland, *Memoranda*, pp. ix, xv, xxiv, lxv; Richardson and Sayles, *Early Records*.

[2] See below p. 390.

[3] *Statutes of the Realm* (1235-1713), Record Com., 11 vols. (London, 1810-28).   See I, pp. xxi-xxv.

[4] *Rotuli Parliamentorum*, 6 vols., [c. 1783].   Index, 1832.   There are justi-

parliamentary bills survive has been very imperfectly revealed in print. Practically none of those which were enrolled, and only certain of those which were not enrolled, have been printed. The editors of the *Rotuli Parliamentorum* made it a practice to print after the rolls of certain parliaments a few unenrolled bills " ex originalibus in turri Londoniensi." Such were bills which were left unanswered, or failed of passage, or, as private bills, while granted, were not enrolled. Although the value of these is considerable, it is unfortunately diminished by the carelessness of the transcribers who sometimes printed but sometimes did not, any inscriptions which may have been written upon them.[5] What has been available, therefore, for the study of original bills in the parliaments of the fourteenth and fifteenth centuries is a series of casual illustrations sometimes imperfectly printed and consisting only of bills not enrolled. Yet it is not improbable that original bills may tell us much; for the clerk of parliament in his enrollment may have omitted or abbreviated what perhaps all contemporaries knew and took for granted, but what we to-day can only conjecture about. Hence the method adopted in the following study is to rely primarily upon the unprinted records of fourteenth and fifteenth century parliaments, interpreting in the light of them the enrolled record of the clerk. When in this way we have learned something about the technique of procedure and the clerk's method of recording parliamentary proceedings, we may be in a position to discover more or less fully what was the influence of the commons upon the legislation of the fourteenth and fifteenth centuries.

The unprinted records of fourteenth and fifteenth century parliaments which were before the clerk when he drew up his

fiable abbreviations after the reign of Edward IV. Most of the rolls of Volume I were not written by the clerk (cf. Richardson and Sayles, *Early Records*). In Volume I of the *Journals of the House of Lords* are printed the parliament rolls of 4-27 Henry VIII but not those of the first two parliaments of the reign (pp. i-ccxlii).

[5] E.g., see below, p. 365, n. 69. For further careless transcription, see below, p. 347, notes 34, 35.

roll, are, so far as these survive in the Public Record Office, grouped for the most part in three series. The first is called Ancient Petitions and numbers upwards of 20,000 documents. These include, however, petitions addressed to the king or his council when no parliament was sitting and others addressed to the chancellor. No one has ascertained how many of them are parliamentary petitions properly so called, but perhaps nearly half of them are such. They have been subjected to several regroupings which have sacrificed the bundles in which they were originally filed and have left them in no temporal sequence.[6] The new unprinted catalogue of Mr. R. L. Atkinson goes a long way toward dating such as furnish internal evidence therefor. But it still often happens that an important petition can be dated only approximately. The series for the most part comprises what Richardson would have called private bills, few public bills being included. From various bundles now distributed throughout this series the editors of the *Rotuli Parliamentorum* drew their "originales ex turri Londoniensi." When they made their selection the bundles had not yet been so disorganized as they later became, and the printed originals have therefore the virtue of being usually correctly dated. Since, moreover, the earlier ones seldom bear inscriptions such as the transcribers of later ones sometimes missed, the printed copies of the former are satisfactory. Of the possibly eight or nine thousand parliamentary petitions, three-fourths or more are from the reigns of the three Edwards and of Richard II. Inasmuch as those of the three Edwards belong to a period when the commons as a body had little to do with private petitions, those later than 1377 are the ones which reveal any influence which the commons may have acquired relative to the passage of private bills. But among these are the ones which are unsatisfactorily printed.

The second and third series of parliamentary records of the fourteenth and fifteenth centuries which furnished material for the clerk's enrollment are described in the modern classifica-

[6] *Lists and Indices, No. 1,* Rolls Ser. (London, 1892).

tion of the Record Office as " Chancery, Parliament and Council Proceedings," and "Exchequer, Parliament and Council Proceedings." They are now conveniently arranged in thin volumes or files each containing from ten to thirty documents. The chancery series comprises for the two centuries some forty files, the exchequer series five, together with some fifty rolls. In both series documents of the fourteenth century are so greatly outnumbered by those of the fifteenth that they may be described as belonging to the latter century. In this they differ markedly from the Ancient Petitions. And they differ from them also in character; for the two series contain relatively few private petitions but do contain a considerable number of what Richardson called public bills and bills of subsidy. Since such bills early came to be of greater importance than private bills, the two series in question comprise our most valuable material for the study of parliamentary procedure. They comprise, too, the documents which seem to be antecedent to the statute rolls. These documents were formulated at about the time that the clerk drew up the parliament roll; and they mark a stage intermediate between the passing of bills in parliament and the enrolling of such of them as were to form statutes.[7]

It is thus from sources grouped in five ways that most of the subject matter discussed in the following chapters is drawn. All of these sources are preserved in the Public Record Office and two of the five groups are printed. Because the latter are enrolled records, they stand in need of some interpretation; and the other three groups, which are separated from one another by no very logical grouping, supply in a measure the means for interpreting them. Such explanations as we can discover apply primarily to the parliament roll, this being the immediate record of parliamentary activities. To a study of the characteristics of the various sorts of bills and of the way in which they appear on the roll we may, therefore, at once apply ourselves.

[7] See below, pp. 392-93, 395, 397-98.

CHAPTER IV

TYPES OF BILLS ENROLLED ON THE PARLIAMENT ROLL

INASMUCH as our method turns largely upon seeing how bills of all sorts were recorded on the parliament roll, a precise comparison of the original form of certain selected bills with the form which they assumed when enrolled will be pertinent. It happens that for the last thirty years of the fifteenth century original bills have largely disappeared but that for the parliaments of the years 1453-1465 they are fairly numerous. Records of parliaments of the middle of a century should normally be typical of the century as a whole if its parliamentary procedure underwent no great change. To be sure, the parliaments of these years happen to be the first ones which were under Yorkist control and for that reason may in some respects have differed from Lancastrian parliaments. But they furnish satisfactory illustrations of the different types of bills characteristic of both the fourteenth and the fifteenth centuries and of the manner in which each type was enrolled on the parliament roll. An understanding of these technical matters is essential to any study of the parliamentary records of the two centuries.

In comparing bills in their original form with their enrolled form we may retain the types to which Richardson introduced us. Most infrequent and least important was the bill of general pardon. Only one such was granted during the last half of the fifteenth century, and this belongs to the June-July session of the parliament of 1455.[1] The original bill has disappeared leaving us merely its enrolled form. The roll relates how the chancellor declared that the king on his own initiative granted his pardon to all his lieges who might wish to avail

[1] *R. P.,* V, 283.

themselves of it according to the tenor of a "cedule" now
deposited in chancery.   The schedule follows, assuming the
form of letters close addressed to all "ballivi et fideles."   No
response from either house or any further action is recorded.
Since the chancellor's declaration was enrolled as if it had been
made at the time of the prorogation of parliament, it is not
unlikely that the pardon was read before lords and commons
together and, of course, read but once.   Whether their acceptance took the form of an expression of gratitude as it did
later must remain obscure.   The designation of the bill as a
"cedule" is noteworthy.

Subsidy bills were often passed in fifteenth century parliaments.   Sometimes they were little more than authorizations
for the continuance of the existent customs duties, either the
wool subsidy or tunnage and poundage.   Sometimes they were
grants of fifteenths and tenths.   Both sorts assumed the same
form, which may be illustrated from two subsidy bills of 1453
and two of 1463-1465.   One bill of 1453 granted tunnage and
poundage, a subsidy on wool and a subsidy on resident aliens;
another of that year granted a half-fifteenth and a half-tenth;
one of 1463 conceded a fifteenth and tenth; and one of 1465
tunnage and poundage and the subsidy on wool.[2]

What is common to the four and indeed to all subsidy bills
of the century is that they took the form of indentures.   The
upper margin is serrate as it was in all feet of fines.   The
granting of a subsidy was a transaction between king and commons in which apparently each party retained one-half of the

---

[2] C., P. & C. P. 29/1, 29/2, 35/3, 35/9; *R. P.*, V, 228, 236, 497, 508. The
fifteenth and tenth of 1463 was first granted as an "Aide nomine auxili." Of
this "Ayde of the somme of xxxvii m. li," £31,000 were to be assessed
upon localities as this amount had been in preceding grants of a fifteenth
and tenth when £6,000 had been remitted. The £6,000 was now to be
paid but only by those who had lands and tenements to the yearly value
of 20 s. or goods to the value of 10 marks — property qualifications twice
as high as those set for contributors to the £31,000. Later the commons
got the £6,000 remitted and the name " ayde " changed to the customary
" fifteenth and tenth " (*ibid.*, p. 498).

twice written contract.[3]   In its own phraseology it was a grant
made to the king with the assent of the lords.   Each of the
four indentures begins in words which were usual throughout
the century: " To the worschip of God, we your pouer Communes . . . commen to this youre present Parliament . . . ,
by th' assent of all the Lordes spirituelle and temporelle . . .
graunt by this present Indenture to you oure Soveraigne
Lord. . . ."   On neither the face nor the back of the indentures is anything written to show how they were originally
drawn up or how or where they were read.[4]   Seldom do indentures of this period or of an earlier time bear an inscription
of any sort.   On one of the four under consideration is written
the king's response, but this, as we shall see, was in the nature
of an innovation.

Seldom, too, was there attached to indentures of these or of
earlier years any amendment apart from the provisos included
in the grant.   Three provisos were included in the grant of the
subsidy on aliens in 1453; but they were inserted in the indenture as an integral part of it.   Genuine amendments, however,
were attached to two of the four indentures.   The grant of the
half-fifteenth and half-tenth in 1453 was amended in a manner
almost unique by an erasure and substituted words.   The bill
as amended provided that the first half of the subsidy be payable at the feast of the Purification, which must have been that
next following and hence in 1454, and that the second half be
payable at the feast of the Nativity of St. John the Baptist in
1454.   The name of the last feast (not the year) has been inserted after an erasure.   Since the writer had to cramp his
words to insert them in the space, it is likely that the original
date was some feast bearing a shorter name.   It is likely, too,
that it fell later than the Nativity of St. John the Baptist, since

[3] Since the commons must have kept their part of the indenture, incipient records of that body are suggested.

[4] On the dorse of the tunnage and poundage indenture of 1453 is written
" Concessiones subsidiorum fac[torum] . . . Regi anno xxxi," evidence that
it was outermost of a bundle or file; and on the dorse of the grant of a
half-fifteenth in the same year appears, " Concessio medietatis xv et x."

the two halves of a subsidy were not usually made payable within six months. Inasmuch as earlier payment would have been to the advantage of the government, the change was probably made after the bill had left the commons. It was probably inspired by the government and may have been made in the lords. There is no clue as to how the assent of the commons to the change was got, if, indeed, it was got.

The action of the government in amending a subsidy bill is more clearly seen in the indenture of 1465, which granted tunnage and poundage and the wool subsidy. The indenture in itself is noteworthy in making various stipulations as to how the money was to be spent. At the bottom is written the king's response noting his acceptance, his thanks and his approval of the stipulations " ovesque cestes II provisions a cest endenture annexes." Attached are two short membranes containing the two provisions. At the end of one of them, which exempts from the subsidies the free chapel of Saint Martin the Great in London, is written " per manus proprias xviii die marcie in Camera parl[iamenti] "; and a little to the right is the further note, " Be this provision added to the bille of subsidie and to the bill of [cord]waners." The other annexed proviso secured to the Hansards their privileges. On the back of it is written " per manus Henr[ici] Sotyll de mandatu Regis super actu subsidii xvi die Marcii in camera parl[iamenti]." Henry Sotehill had been attorney general since 20 April, 1461.[5] Thus it becomes clear that in 1465 provisos could be and were annexed to a subsidy bill in the parliament chamber. The king himself annexed such; more often probably the attorney general did so at his command. And it was perhaps in the latter way that the date for the payment of the subsidy of 1453 was changed.

Richardson, it will be remembered, explained that the royal assent to a subsidy bill was written upon it in the words " Le Roy remercy ses loyaulx Subjects, accept leur beneVoleur et

[5] C. P. R., 1461-1467, p. 6.

auxi le vult." Lambard's formula was briefer, "Le Roi rende grand mercies." On the subsidy bill of 1465 the royal response, written in French, although the indenture was in English, ran as follows: "le Roy, considerant les bones coers de ses Co[mmun]es enfaisauntz a luy lez grauntes avauntditz, mesme les grauntes accepta et leur molt entierment remerciea, leur ottroiant qe toutz autres articles et peticions en cest endenture contenuz soient faitz sicome ils sount desires ovesque cestes II provisions a cest endenture annexes." Upon no other surviving indenture of the fifteenth century is there written at such length the royal response. The reason for it in this case is apparent. The commons had inserted in the indenture certain petitions which required an answer and the king wished to attach to his answer two provisos. For contemporaries the more important part of the response was the latter part. For us, however, the first part, which must have seemed a matter-of-course preface, is more interesting. It shows that as early as 1465 the royal response to a grant of subsidy was of the same tenor as it was in the sixteenth and seventeenth centuries and was somewhat more verbose in phrase. It might further be written on the indenture. But this was probably not yet the accepted rule as another of our four subsidy bills shows.

The indenture granting the half-fifteenth of 1453 bears no inscription on either face or dorse. Yet the parliament roll tells us that after the speaker of the commons had in their name read the grant, presumably before the lords, the chancellor tenderly thanked them and the king with his own lips added, "Nos vobis intime regratiamur et ne dubietis quin vobis erimus graciosus et benevolus Dominus." Twelve years before 1465, therefore, the royal gratitude was expressed verbally but not recorded on the indenture. The custom of so inscribing it was a development of the second half of the fifteenth century.

This reference to the parliament roll brings us to the enrollment of subsidy bills. The method can be described briefly. The indenture was in all cases transcribed verbatim, always with an introduction, seldom with any further comment. The introduction was always some variant of the following sentence, which prefaced the grant of the half-fifteenth of 1453: " Memorandum quod prefati Communes in presenti Parliamento coram Domino Rege Secundo die Julii Anno predicto comparentes per Thomam Thorp, Perlocutorem suum, declarabant qualiter ipsi de assensu Dominorum Spiritualium et Temporalium . . . concesserunt prefato Domino Regi medietatem unius Quintedecime et Decime . . . sub certa forma in quadam Indentura inde confecta et Domino Regi die illo in eodem Parliamento exhibita contenta deducend[a] de Laico populo Regni Anglie levand[a]. Tenor cuius Indenture sequitur in hec verba." [6]

From this, no more than from the original indenture, can much be learned about the preparation and passage of the subsidy bill. That the assent of the lords was secured — a phase of which there is no trace in the indenture — is disclosed; but whether this was attended by three readings and by a return to the commons is obscure. The presentation to the king was pretty clearly the last stage in the passage of the bill and the most formal one. Since the final stage in the passage of bills in the seventeenth century was the reading of their titles and of the king's responses usually on the last day of the session, it might be thought that the presentation of fifteenth century subsidy bills to the king occurred at that time.[7] Sometimes it did. The indenture for the half-fifteenth of 1453 was presented on 2 July, on which day parliament was prorogued until 12 November.[8] Earlier in the session, however, and indeed twenty-two days after its beginning on 6 March, the speaker of the commons had presented to the king two other subsidy indentures. One of them was the grant

---

[6] R. P., V, 236.

[7] Lambard, to be sure, explained that in his day the subsidy bill was usually carried to the king before other bills were. See above, p. 6.

[8] R. P., V, 236.

of tunnage and poundage, of the subsidy on wool and of the
subsidy on aliens, the original copy of which survives; the
other was the grant of an entire fifteenth and tenth, of which
the original has disappeared. The sequence of events in this
parliament is fairly typical of the fifteenth century. The government, if it could, secured its subsidies early in the session;
if it could not, it accepted a grant on the last day. Hence the
presentation of subsidy-indentures might occur either early or
late. The parliament roll, in dating the presentation of the
indenture, as it usually does, adds considerable to our knowledge of the success of financial negotiations in parliament; it
adds a little to our knowledge of procedure by showing that
subsidy bills might pass through all stages early in the session or might, like other bills, reach their final stage only as
the session closed.

A final observation about bills of subsidy is that they were
almost never known to the fifteenth century as bills. They
were "indentures" or at most "indentured schedules." There
were approaches to the later terminology in two bills of the
parliaments of 1453 and 1463 respectively. In 1453, when the
commons granted to the king the levy of 13000 archers, the
grant took the form of a "billa indentata." It was phrased
like a subsidy bill and, although the original does not survive,
it was undoubtedly an indenture.[9] Again in 1463, when the
commons granted the king £37000, calling the sum an aid
(auxilium), instead of the usual fifteenth and tenth, the document was called an indenture. But, when in a later session of
the same parliament they asked that £6000 be remitted, as had
become usual in collecting a fifteenth, and that the grant itself
be a fifteenth, they referred to the first transaction as an
"act." [10] Such departures as these from the accepted nomen-
clature were unusual.

Nor were bills of general pardon referred to as bills. They
were "pardons" or "cedules." The term bill was reserved for

[9] *Ibid.,* p. 231.
[10] *Ibid.,* pp. 497, 498. See above, p. 40, n. 2.

Richardson's other types of bills, private bills and public bills. For both sorts, too, another designation was even more often employed. They were petitions, and at an early date we meet the words petition and bill used as equivalent terms.[11] Obviously neither the grant of a subsidy nor the bestowal of a general pardon could be called a petition. Public and private bills, however, we shall find, originated as petitions to the king. The term was, therefore, in early days quite as appropriate for them as the term bill.

The interchangeability of bill and petition in parliamentary parlance of the fifteenth century is challenged by an important passage in Stubbs' *Constitutional History;* for in describing the difficulties which the commons experienced in securing observance of promises made them, difficulties which, he thought, arose from their "attitude of petition," Stubbs contrasted petition and bill. "The remedy," he wrote, "was the adoption of a new form of initiation; the form of bill was substituted for that of petition; the statute was brought forward in the shape which it was intended ultimately to take, and every modification of the original draft passed under the eyes of the promoters. This change took place about the end of the reign of Henry VI." And he quotes from Ruffhead's *Statutes* the phrase "quaedam petitio exhibita fuit in hoc parliamento formam actus in se continens."[12]

Variants of this phrase, as we shall see, occur from 1461 onward and have a certain significance. We shall see, too, that toward the middle of the fifteenth century a change probably took place in parliamentary procedure, which affected the

---

[11] In 1383 one request in a commons petition was "q'en ce present Parlement et chescun qe serra soient toutes les Billes respondez et endossez des toutes les liges qe ne poent avoir autre remedie qe par Petition . . ." (*R. P.,* III, 162, par 50). In 1433 a bill of the town of Poole was introduced as "une autre Petition," but the response to it began, "The Communes ben assented to this Bill . . ." (*ibid.,* IV, 444-5). In 1450 the reply to one of the "petitiones communes" began, "As to the first article of this Bille . . ." (*ibid.,* V, 183, 201).

[12] Stubbs, *Constitutional History,* II, 608-609.

form assumed by private and public bills at the time of their passage. But it is misleading to characterize this change as a new form of initiation in which a bill was substituted for a petition, or to prove that it occurred by citing such a phrase as Stubbs quoted. A measure introduced for parliamentary consideration was throughout the century called indifferently a petition or a bill. Innovations which took place related to the answer made or the amendment offered, not primarily to the nature of the measure as introduced.[13]

Indeed from the early years of the reign of Edward III petitions were called bills. Relative to private petitions we then find such phrases as, " il avoit bote bille en soun [the king's] dereyn Parlement," "Veigne la Bille devant le Conseil " and " il ad sui per Bille en votre Parlement."[14] In 1351 the commons petitioned that no statute be changed "par nule Bille especiale de singuler persone."[14a] Throughout the fifteenth century the commons assent to a petition ran, "A cest bille les Communes sont assentuz."[15] A bill was, of course, not an oral petition, but was something written. An accusation in the parliament of 1390 was made "si bien par bille come par bouche."[16] Indeed, any brief written composition might be called a bill. A correspondent of John Paston, describing the death of Suffolk in 1450, declared that he had "wesshe this litel bille with sorwfulle terys."[17] A technical meaning, nevertheless, arose in the wardrobe as well as in parliament. There a written promise to pay a wardrobe debt was called a bill.[18]

If the term bill was normally used to designate petitions presented in fourteenth- and fifteenth-century parliaments, these bills were in turn classified by contemporaries as private

---

[13] See below, pp. 178-83.
[14] *R. P.,* II, 13, 14, 32.
[14a] *Ibid.,* p. 230, par. 39.
[15] See below, pp. 370, 373; see above, p. 10.
[16] *R. P.,* III, 288.
[17] *The Paston Letters,* ed. J. Gairdner, 6 vols. (London, 1904), I, no. 93.
[18] *R. P.,* II, 36. The usage probably dates from the days of Edward I or from an even earlier time.

petitions and commons petitions — the private and public bills
of Richardson's day.   Their Latin designations were "speciales" or "particulares," and "communes."   In the parliament of 1437 it was provided that certain lords of the king's
council with the aid of the justices should reply authoritatively
to petitions left unanswered at the rising of parliament, "tam
communes quam speciales Petitiones"[19]; and the original petitions of the parliament of 1449-50 were tied up in bundles on
the back of one of which is written in a contemporary hand
"Communes petitiones Anno XXVII," and on the back of an-
ther "Particulares petitiones in parliamento anno XXVII.[20]
In 1348 the commons were told "qe touz les singulers persones qe vourroient liverer Petitions en ce Parlement les ferroient liverer au Chancellor Et qe les Petitions touchantes les
Communes ferroient liverer au Clerc du Parlement.[21]   In 1363
parliament continued in session considering "les Petitions
baillez par les Communes et autres singulers persons . . ."[22];
and in 1371 the commons asked "qe toutes leurs Billes . . .
et toutes autres . . . si bien celles qe sont pur severalles Persones, Villes ou Contees come celle qe sont pur les Communes
suisdites de lour Grevances" be given to certain lords to consider and answer.[23]   In each of these instances the distinction
between private petitions and commons petitions is clear.   It
will be convenient to call the petitions of the commons commons petitions rather than common petitions, the term used by
Stubbs and Pollard; for, since petitions may with propriety be
called bills, the logical "common bill" might seem odd.   Later
usage has accustomed us to commons bills.   And we have already adopted a further modern usage in omitting the apostrophe which might be used.

[19] *Ibid.*, IV, 507.   In 1422, when unanswered petitions were similarly entrusted to the council, they were described as "si bien de ceux qe baillez
sont per les Communes . . . come d'autres . . ." (*ibid.*, p. 174).

[20] C., P. & C. P. 27/11; A. P. 1348.

[21] *R. P.*, II, 201.

[22] *Ibid.*, p. 280.

[23] *Ibid.*, p. 304.

Actually, the categories private bills and commons bills were not all-comprehending in the fifteenth century, even apart from subsidy indentures and general pardons. Bills appear which were neither of private nor of commons' origin, but clearly originated with the lords or with the government. They were a second sort of public bill. In examining, therefore, the form assumed by fifteenth-century bills before and after enrollment, we shall have at least three groups of them: private bills, commons bills and lords or government bills. Private bills will in turn assume two forms, determined by whether they were to be first presented in the lords or in the commons. We may expect, therefore, four types of phraseology arising from the character of bills as private or public and from their initiation in lords or commons. As it happens the parliament roll is not always very clear in making these distinctions. Hence it is important to see precisely what form each type of bill assumed in its original as well as in its enrolled form. Our illustrations are, as before, drawn from the years 1453-1465.

Private bills first introduced in the lords were not addressed to that body but to the king. The petition of Henry Wentworth in 1465, asking that the attainder of his father be not to the disparagement of himself and his heirs, illustrates the formulae of address and appeal, while the inscriptions written on it reveal how approval was given. The notes added in the enrollment on the parliament roll explain how the bill was expedited. The appeal ran: "To the King our Liege Lord. Mekely besecheth . . . youre humble Subgett . . . Henry Wentworth [reciting in detail the circumstances of the attainder] . . . Wherefore please it your Highness . . . to ordeigne, establissh and enact by th' advis and assent of the Lordes Spirituell and Temporell and the Comons in this youre present Parlement assembled and by th' auctorite of the same Parlement [that Henry inherit as if there had been no attainder]." Above the text of the original bill is written the sign manual of the king in his own hand, "R. E."; below the

text the phrase, " A cest bille les Co[mmun]es sount assentuz ";
and on the back of the bill in a formal hand, not the king's,
" R[esponsi]o: Soit fait come il est desire." [24]   The appearance of the royal sign manual on a bill is in the nature of an
innovation, since it is seldom found before the time of Edward
IV and not always in the early years of his reign.   The inscription on the dorse of the bill recording in a chancery hand the
royal assent was, before 1463, sufficient.   The words of this, it
will be noted, were precisely those which were used in Richardson's day.   The assent of the commons, too, was given in
the sentence which, Richardson says, was employed in his time
by the lower house in approving a lords bill.   Since the bill was
engrossed on parchment, its appearance after passage was like
that of any private bill of the seventeenth century originating
in the lords, except that it bore no inscription noting the approval of that body.

When Wentworth's bill was enrolled it was introduced by
the phrase, " Memorand[um] quod quedam Petitio exhibita
fuit Domino Regi in presenti Parliamento per Henricum Wentworth . . . in hec verba." The text of the bill follows and then
we are told about its passage.   " Que quidem Petitio Communibus . . . transportata fuit.   Cui iidem communes assensum suum prebuerunt sub hiis verbis, A cest Bille les Communes sount assentux.   Quibus quidem Petitione et assensu in
dicto Parliamento lectis, auditis et plenius intellectis, de avisamento et assensu Dominorum Spiritualium et Temporalium
. . . eidem Petitioni respondebatur in forma sequenti, Soit
fait come il est desire." [25]

This recital of the fortunes of the bill adds somewhat to our
knowledge, although not so much as we might wish.   It tells
us little about readings in either house and nothing at all about
committees.   It does explain, however, that the bill was " carried over " from lords to commons.   It records the words of
the commons' assent and the return of the bill to the lords,

[24] A. P. 1418; *R. P.*, V, 548.
[25] *Ibid.*

where bill and assent were both read. The reading of a bill in the lords on its return from the commons, even though no amendment had been made, was not unusual, it will be remembered, in 1509. If we may trust the enrolled account of 1465 to give correctly the sequence of procedure, such a final reading was customary in the fifteenth century. Only after it had taken place and the assent of the lords had been given was the bill ready for the final approval of the king. In the case of Wentworth's bill the words of this approval as written on the dorse of the bill were reproduced in the enrollment.

Brief as is the description of the treatment of Wentworth's bill in the parliament roll, it is considerably more detailed than similar descriptions of earlier date. A private bill of 1461, though in its original form like Wentworth's and similarly inscribed, was enrolled summarily. An introduction stated that a petition was shown to the king in parliament by Thomas Lumley; and, following the record of the text, a single sentence relates that after the bill had been read and understood in parliament it was with the advice of lords and commons answered in the words, " Soit fait come il est desire." [26] There is nothing more.

Since private bills were often enrolled with this brevity, how are we to know in cases where no original survives that they were first introduced in the lords? When the explanations of the roll are so grudging and so ambiguous, may the bill not have been introduced in the commons? Only an examination of such bills as Lumley's in their original and in their enrolled form justifies an answer. In point of fact all comparisons of fifteenth-century private bills with the statements accompanying their enrollment establish one conclusion. If the enrolled private bill begins with an appeal to the king and proceeds to ask that he ordain with the assent of lords and commons

---

[26] C., P. C. P. 52/8/3; *R. P.,* V, 486. The original has no royal sign manual and the inscribed commons assent runs, " A ceo les comyns sount assentuz."

what the petitioner wishes, the original bill, if granted, was inscribed with the words, " A ceste bille les Commons sount assentuz." Since this inscription never appears on bills origi- nating in the commons, the inference that the bill came from the lords is justified. This deduction is of marked assistance in reading the parliament roll; for, no matter how brief is the statement attending the enrollment, it is always possible to identify private bills originating in the lords by their phrase- ology.

The value of this clue will become clearer from an exam- ination of private bills of a second and different type, those which were first introduced in the commons. Typical of such is a petition of James Strangeways presented in 1461. Its opening words were, " To the discreet Commyns of this present Parlement: Sheweth to your grete wisdomes . . . James Strangways " and others how certain lands once theirs have come into the king's hands but could rightly be restored. The petitioners then proceeded to their appeal: " Wherefore please it youre wisdomes tenderly to consider the premisses and to besche the King our Soverayn Lord that he will ordeyn and establisch by the advis and assent of his Lordes Spirituelx and Temporelx and of his Commyns in this present Parlement as- sembled and by auctorite of the same " that James recover the lands, transmitting them on his death to his fellow peti- tioners.

In the original form of this bill, which is carefully engrossed, the introductory words, " To the . . . Commyns of this . . . Parlement," are written above the text itself. Also above and to the right is written in a different hand the sentence, " Soit baille as s[eigneur]s." On the back of the bill is the same inscription as appeared on Wentworth's bill, " R[esponsi]o: Soit fait come il est desire." [27]

Like all other private bills this one was enrolled with an introductory and with a concluding sentence. The former runs, " Item quedam Petitio exhibita fuit . . . Regi in pre-

[27] C., P. & C. P. 52/8/5; *R. P.,* V, 485.

senti Parliamento per Communes Regni Anglie . . . ex parte Jacobi Strangways, Militis, et aliorum . . . sub eo qui sequitur tenore verborum." After the text the clerk noted the fortunes of the bill. "Qua quidem Petitione in Parliamento predicto lecta, audita et plenius intellecta de avisamento et assensu Dominorum Spiritualium et Temporalium . . . et ad requisitionem Communitatis predicte respondebatur eidem in forma sequenti, Soit fait come il est desire."

In one respect this petition is like the two already quoted. The royal response is inscribed on the back in the same words and the enrolled record of it is the same, "Soit fait come il est desire." In two other respects, however, Strangeways' petition differs from Wentworth's and Lumley's. It is addressed to the commons and begs that body to entreat the king to grant it with the assent of the lords. It further bears the inscription "Soit baille as seigneurs," whereas the other petitions were inscribed "A ceste bille les Communes sount assentuz." These two features, the phraseology of the bill and the inscription on its face, demonstrate its introduction in the commons and its despatch to the lords. Of the assent of the latter body there is no trace other than the king's assent.

The two distinguishing features of Strangeways' bill are apparent in its enrolled form. The text supplies the address to the commons and the request that they intercede with the king and lords; and, although the sentence which dispatches the bill to the lords is not reproduced, there is substituted for it the introductory information that the bill was presented to the king in parliament by the commons, while the final comment of the parliament roll is that the approval of the king and lords was in response to the commons' request. Often this last item is omitted. A bill of James, earl of Wiltshire, presented in 1454, is precisely like that of Strangeways' both in its original and in its enrolled form except that the description accompanying the latter omits "ad requisitionem Communitatis."[28] This matters little. And even if the introduc-

---

[28] A. P. 1358; *R. P.,* V, 257.

tion to either bill had neglected to say that it was presented by the commons, the phraseology of the bill itself would have made the matter clear.

Thus private bills first introduced in the commons, like private bills first introduced in the lords, bear marks of identification in the words which they employ. Whenever the original bills have disappeared and when the inscriptions which indicate, on the one hand, commons assent or, on the other, dispatch to the lords are omitted in the enrollment, as they always are, still no doubt need arise as to the character of the bill. It is sufficient that the parliament roll record it. To be sure, the clerk in his introduction usually distinguished between bills presented to the king by the petitioner and bills presented to the king for the petitioner by the commons. But even if he failed to do so, the words of the bill suffice. Private bills first introduced in the lords addressed the king and asked him to grant a request with the assent of lords and commons; private bills first introduced in the commons addressed that body and asked that it beseech the king to grant a request with the advice and assent of the lords.

Before leaving private bills we note that they were not always the bills of one person or even of one person and his relatives or associates. Bills which were presented by groups or men, sometimes corporate, sometimes not, were in the fourteenth and fifteenth centuries considered private bills. Such groups were the men of a town or county, a body of merchants or artisans, a group of officials or monks, a university or a collegiate chapter. A petition from such a group employed in its original form the same phrases of introduction and appeal as did a private petition; in its enrolled form it was introduced and its acceptance described in the formulae which have been recited above. We shall have occasion later to distinguish bills of this sort from the wider category of private bills to which they belong and it will be convenient to designate them as group bills or petitions. Meanwhile it is sufficient to cite two illustrations to show how such group petitions were identical in form with private bills.

In 1454 the mayor, constables and society of the merchants of the staple addressed the king, asking that with the assent of lords and commons they be secured in the repayment of 10,000 marks loaned for the payment of soldiers' wages at Calais. The phrases employed were those of Wentworth's bill, and below the text was written "A ceste bille les Commyns sount assentuz." In the upper left-hand corner the abbreviation "irro" (*irrotulatur* or *irroluletur*) either recorded or ordered enrollment. The enrollment was in the briefer language of Lumley's bill. The only divergence from the form or from the enrollment of a private bill first introduced in the lords lay in the royal response. Instead of the customary "Soit fait come il est desire," both bill and parliament roll recorded the sentence, "Le Roy le voet." Richardson, it will be recalled, declared that this was the seventeenth-century response to a public bill, and we shall see shortly that such was also the usage of the fifteenth century. This single divergence from the forms characteristic of private bills introduced in the lords may prove significant in our later discussion of group bills. Meanwhile we may formulate the generalization that, with the possible exception of the response, group bills were phrased like private bills and were often enrolled like them.[29]

Even touching the response there need be no exception in the case of many group bills. This is true of one which illustrates primarily introduction in the commons rather than in the lords. In 1461 the "pore Tenauntes and Commyns of the grounde of Northwales" begged the commons to pray the king that with the assent of the lords he declare certain Welsh misdoers who held Hardleigh castle to be traitors unless they should surrender promptly. The bill is like Strangeways' in every respect — in the words of address and appeal, in the inscribed "Soit baille as seigneurs" and in the royal "Soit fait

[29] A. P. 4968 and *R. P.*, V, 248.

come il est desire." It was enrolled, too, with the same introductory and concluding sentences.[30] Apparently, therefore,
the divergent response of the staplers' bill was not altogether
characteristic of group bills. Actually the response to them
might be like the response to private bills or it might be like
the response to public bills. And this brings us to the consideration of public bills.

Public bills introduced in the lords differed in phraseology,
in the inscriptions written on them, and in their enrolled form
from public bills first introduced in the commons. The contrast was like that arising between private bills which were
introduced in the upper house and those which were introduced in the lower. A bill to provide money for the king's
household, presented to the lords in 1454, and another attainting certain lords, presented in 1461, illustrate the type. The
first was addressed " To the Kyng owr Soveraigne Lord." An
explanatory clause began with " Forasmoche " and explained
how purveyors had not paid for goods and chattels taken.
This was followed by an appeal "that it may please your
Highnesse . . . to ordeyn and establyssh by th' advys and assent of the Lordes Spirituell and Temporell and the Communes
in this your high Court of Parliament assembled and by the
authority of the same " that certain specified sources of income
may be set apart for the household's expenses. Below the bill
was written, "A cest Bille les Commyns sount assentuz," and
on the back of it, "Le Roy le voet." [31]

The enrolled form of the bill reproduced the text and added
explanatory matter. Its preface ran, "Item quedam Cedula
exhibita fuit . . . Regi in presenti Parliamento in hec verba."
Its concluding description explained, "Cui quidem Cedule
prefati Communes assensum suum prebuerunt sub hiis verbis,
A cest Bille les Commyns sount assentuz. Quibus quidam
Cedula et assensu in Parliamento predicto lectis et plenius intellectis eisdem de avisamento et assensu Dominorum Spiri-

---

[30] C., P. & C. P. 52/8/4 and R. P., V, 486.
[31] A. P. 1187 B.

tualium et Temporalium . . . responsum fuit . . . Le Roy le voet." To the king's assent were attached three provisos, which were appended.[32]

The bill of 1461 for the attainder of certain lords, while resembling the household act in type, differed from it in minor features. It had no address to the king but began with " forasmuch " clauses, which ran on to great length. Then, instead of the impersonal appeal of the household act, it proceeded to an affirmation, viz., " It be declared and adjudged by th' assent and advis of the Lordes Spirituelx and Temporelx and Commyns that [Henry VI and many of his partisans be attainted]." The commons' assent and the king's approval were inscribed in the words used relative to the household bill, save that the assent employed the word " act " and the approval stipulated " ovesque cest provision a cest bille annexe."

The enrolled form of the bill, too, employed the sentences used for the household bill but with two additions. The introductory sentence explained, " Item, quedam Cedula, formam Actus in se continens, exhibita fuit . . . Regi"; and the sentence following the text stated, " Qua quidem Cedula Communibus Regni Anglie . . . transportata fuit." [33] We shall have occasion later to examine the statement about a cedule assuming the form of an act. This aspect of it did not affect the bill from the point of view now under consideration. But it is satisfactory to be told that the bill was carried over to the commons and it is important to know that the effective part of it following the " forasmuch " clause might assume the form of an affirmation. Indeed, in the second half of the fifteenth century public bills introduced in the lords usually did assume this form, although they did not in the first half of the century.

The features apparent in these two bills and therefore characteristic of public bills originating in the lords were: (1) the absence of an appeal made to the king by any person or group, the appeal, if it appears, being impersonal; (2) the occasional

---

[32] *R. P.,* V. 246.
[33] C., P. & C. P. 52/8/11; *R. P.,* V, 476-483.

substitution for the appeal of a statement that the king declares, ordains or enacts; (3) the prefacing of the impersonal appeal or the royal action by a "forasmuch" clause or clauses; (4) the record of the commons' assent, which might refer to the measure as bill, cedule or act; and (5) the expression of the king's approval by "Le Roy le voet." Occasionally there were derivations from these characteristics, the first and second of which were already alternative. The "forasmuch" clause might disappear. A household bill of 1455 began baldly, "Memorandum, it pleaseth the king . . . ," but continued in the accustomed manner.[34] More perplexing is an occasional variation in the king's response and this leads to a comparison between public and private bills submitted to the lords.

In some aspects these two types were alike. Whether the bill was public or private, the commons expressed their approval in the sentence already so often quoted. If the public bill was expressly addressed to the king and appealed to him, in this it resembled a private bill save that the appeal was impersonal. If the public bill happened to be without the "forasmuch" clause, one feature which differentiated it from the private bill disappeared. There remained the words of the king's approval. In the years 1453-1465, as in Richardson's day, the approval of private bills ran, "Soit fait come il est desire"; of public bills, "Le Roy le veut." Although there is no difference in the content of these two expressions, they apparently already had a different past. It would not be surprising, however, if in bills which were private in content but public in form, the king on his own initiative doing a favour to some individual, there should be some fluctuation in usage. This, indeed, is what we find.

In 1465 the king confirmed to Anne, duchess of Exeter, grants of land previously made her, and in 1461 he bestowed upon his mother Cecilie, duchess of York, an annuity of £400. The former bill began, "The Kyng . . . of grete zele and

[34] C., P. & C. P. 30/2; *R. P.,* V. 320.

tendre affection which . . . he hath unto . . . Anne . . .";
the second, "The Kyng remembring that he hath granted by
his Letters Patentes. . . ." Both declared that he now
"graunteth . . . by th' advice and assent of the Lordes . . .
and Commens . . ." the respective favours. Both were inscribed with the commons' assent, the first using the phrase
"A cest act . . .", the second, "A cest bille les Commyns
sount assentuz." Similar as the two were, however, the royal
response to the first was, "Le Roy le voet"; to the second,
"Soit fait come il est desire." [35] The explanation is that both
bills were essentially private in so far as they conferred favours
upon individuals and both were technically public in declaring
the king's will without petition addressed to him. When it
came to the point of inscribing the response, the official who
phrased the king's will had in mind in one instance the private
content of the bill, in the other its public form. In the latter
he was technically correct. But the illustrations show that the
response to public bills which related to individuals sometimes
deviated from the normal response to public bills. This occurrence is so unusual, however, that our five characteristic
features of public bills originating in the lords need be modified only by inserting relative to the king's response that it
was *usually* in the words, "Le Roy le voet."

No difficulty ever arises in recognizing a public bill originating in the lords if its original form survives. Identification,
however, is not always so obvious if it survives only as it is
enrolled. For the enrolled form often omitted the words of
the commons' assent and of the king's approval and might at
worst add no explanatory sentence whatever, merely transcrib-
ing the bill. A household act of 1455, in sharp contrast with
that of 1454 described above, was enrolled with neither introductory nor concluding sentence. Only the text of the bill was
reproduced, although the original shows that it received the
usual inscriptions of approval.[36] Precisely the same is true of

---

[35] C., P. & C. P. 35/12, 52/8/8; *R. P.,* V, 548, 483.
[36] C., P. & C. P. 30/2; *R. P.,* V, 320.

the bills for the duchess of York and the duchess of Exeter. Often, however, there was an introductory sentence and a more important concluding one, the latter telling of the commons' assent but not reproducing it. In 1454 a bill for the repeal of the household act of 1450 took the form of an impersonal appeal to the king: " Please it the Kyng by th' assent of the Lordes . . . and the Communes . . . to ordeyne and stablisshe [that the act be void]." Assent of commons and king were in the usual phrases, the latter with a proviso annexed. The clerk of parliament in enrolling this bill prefaced it with the statement, " Item, quedam Petitio exhibita fuit . . . Regi in presenti Parliamento sub hac serie verborum." At the end he said nothing about its being carried to the commons nor did he give the words of their assent. Such assent was merely noted in the sentence with which he concluded: " Qua quidam Petitione in Parliamento predicto lecta, audita et plenius intellecta, de avisamento et assensu Dominorum Spiritualium et Temporalium ac Communitatis Regni Anglie . . . respondebatur eidem in forma sequenti, Le Roy le voet [with one proviso]." [37]

Inasmuch as most of the originals of public bills originating in the lords have disappeared, the reader of the rolls of parliament has to identify bills of this sort from their enrolled form. When this is accompanied by explanatory matter, all or nearly all of the five characteristics outlined above can be easily discovered. When, however, the explanatory matter shrinks and disappears, the characteristics which are inherent in the bill have to suffice. One of these is the introductory " forasmuch " clause, a feature not characteristic of any other sort of bill. Nearly always such a clause occurs and it is of great value for purposes of identification. If the bill contains none such, there remain only the appeal and the enacting clause. The appeal, in turn, occurs only in certain of these bills, in the earlier rather than in the later ones. If there is

---

[37] *Ibid.*, pp. 272, 247. This is almost the only instance in which the editors of the rolls have printed both the original and the enrolled form of a bill.

an appeal, it should normally be an impersonal one, "Please it the Kyng," as in the bill of repeal just quoted. This feature, like the "forasmuch" clause, is valuable for identification. Finally, if for the appeal is substituted an affirmation of the king's will, this should normally assume some such form as "Be it declared and adjudged by the assent of lords and commons" or "The King with the assent of lords and commons ordains and enacts." Since this affirmation was not characteristic of private bills, it supplies a clue alternative to that of the appeal and valuable when there is no appeal. What we learn, therefore, is that public bills originating in the lords often have to be identified in their enrolled form by two features only, (1) the employment of a forasmuch clause and (2) the impersonality of the appeal, or, barring this, the affirmation of the king's will approved by lords and commons.

Before leaving public bills originating in the lords, it is desirable to give them a name which shall be less cumbersome and less ambiguous. May they not be called lords bills? We shall soon have no hesitancy in calling bills originating in the commons commons bills. The analogy would seem to be close. But there will be no doubt that bills originating in the commons nearly always took form there and expressed the desire of the commons. It is not so clear that fifteenth-century bills which first appeared in the lords were drafted by that body and expressed its desires. Nearly all bills which seem to have originated with the lords were of an administrative or official character. Such were those which have been cited — the two household acts, the bill for the repeal of a household act, the bill for the attainder of Henry VI and his adherents, the bills for the duchess of York and for the duchess of Exeter. Such, too, was a bill of 1454 designating five noblemen to safeguard the sea.[38] Seldom, indeed, does the parliament roll record a bill the purport of which indicates that it was drafted by the

---

[38] C., P. & C. P. 29/4; *R. P.,* V, 244. It was enrolled without comment, but the original is inscribed with the assent of the commons and of the king.

lords. A bill originating with the government, on the other hand, and presumably embodying the wishes of the council, would be naturally introduced in the lords. At the end of the thirteenth century Fleta associated the council closely with the lords in referring to the king as being present in his council in his parliaments.[39] The councillors then and in the following century were largely lords and in any event would normally have been present when the lords were in session. In 1509 a household act and a wardrobe act, presumably of government origin, were first introduced in the lords. Without, therefore, denying that some bills originating in the lords were genuine lords bills, we shall not be greatly misinterpreting the fourteenth and fifteenth centuries by calling such bills official or government bills. This implies no more than that they were as a rule drafted in the council rather than in that enlarged council which constituted the house of lords.

In contrast with official bills originating in the lords were public bills originating in the commons. Contemporaries called them in Latin " communes petitiones " and in French "communes petitions." We may call them commons petitions or commons bills. They were the most important bills presented in parliament for more than a century and their significance appears particularly by contrasting them with official bills. Official bills, as we have seen, often and somewhat inconsistently addressed the king and appealed to him. The appeal, however, was always impersonal. Commons bills also addressed the king, but did this less impersonally. They always began with a set phrase which was never used in official bills. This was " Prayen the Commons " or " Beseechen the Commons " or something very similar. Whereas, further, official bills asked the king to grant a request with the assent of lords *and commons*, commons bills naturally asked him to grant the favour mentioning only the assent of the lords.

---

[39] " Habet enim Rex curiam suam in consilio suo in parliamentis suis." *Fleta, seu Commentarius iuris anglicani* . . . lib. ii, ch. 2. (London, 2nd ed., 1685), p. 66. Cf. Pollard, *op. cit.*, pp. 24-34.

Petitioners would not ask that anything be granted with their own assent. As a corollary we shall not expect to find on a commons bill the familiar inscription, " A cest bille les communes sount assentuz." Instead of it there should be some inscription dispatching the bill to king and lords for consideration.

A commons bill of 1461 illustrates these features and admits of examination both in its original and in its enrolled form. It runs: " Prayen the Commyns in this present Parlement assembled that, for so much as John Waleys [and others have offended against King Edward], It please our seid Soverayn and Liege Lord by th' avis and assent of the Lordes Spirituelx and Temporelx being in this present Parlement and by auctorite of the same to graunte, ordeyn and stablissh [that they appear before the bench or stand attainted of high treason]." Above the text is written in a different hand, " Soit baille as s[eigneur]s "; and on the back of the bill, " R[esponsi]o: Le Roy le voet."

This bill is enrolled with fuller explanation than attends most commons bills. An introductory sentence tells us, " Item quedam Petitio exhibita fuit . . . Regi . . . per prefatos Communes sub eo qui sequitur tenore verborum." After the transcription of the text the roll continues, " Qua quidam Petitione in Parliamento prodicto lecta, audita et plenius intellecta, de avisamento et assensu Dominorum . . . et ad requisitionem Communitatis predicte taliter fuit responsum eidem, Le Roy le voet." [40]

The characteristics of a public bill originating in the commons, or for brevity a commons bill, thus appear somewhat more clearly in the original bill than in its enrolled form. Foremost is the inscription, " Soit baille as seigneurs," which disappears in the enrollment. For it is substituted the explanation that the bill was presented in parliament by the commons and, after being read, received the assent of the lords. This, to be sure, would be adequate information if the roll

---

[40] C., P. & C. P. 52/8/9; *R. P.*, V, 483.

always supplied it. Unfortunately it seldom does. A second characteristic of the bill against John Walys is that the king's assent was inserted on the back as "Le Roy le voet." These were the words of the royal assent to an official bill, the other type of public bill, but different from the "Soit fait come il est desire" of private bills. They were always carefully enrolled. A third characteristic of the bill is the appeal, introduced by "Prayen the Commyns" and asking that the king take action with the assent of the lords. Since this inhered in the text, it is as readily apparent in the enrolled as in the original form of the bill. In so far then as commons bills were enrolled like this one against John Walys, the enrolled form presented two of their three characteristic features. But one of the two, the phrasing of the king's response, they shared with official bills. Hence only a single characteristic remained which was peculiar to an enrolled commons bill — its introductory "Prayen the Commons" and the appeal that the king act with the assent of the lords. In the case of enrolled bills, we shall always have to infer that this characteristic, when it appears, implies that we are reading a commons bill which in its original form also bore the inscription, "Soit baille as seigneurs."

This somewhat detailed examination of private and public bills as they were drawn up and enrolled in the middle of the fifteenth century has revealed four types of them. The characteristic features of these types are most apparent in the original bills. Enrollment usually disregarded two or three features but occasionally added an item, such as the carrying of a bill from the lords to the commons. The types and the characteristics which determine them may now be summarized.

Private bills originating in the lords were addressed to the king and asked him to grant with the assent of lords and commons some favour to an individual or group. On them were written sentences which indicated the assent of commons and king respectively, viz, "A cest bille les Communes sount assentuz" and "Soit fait come il est desire." When the bills were enrolled, the first of these sentences was likely to disappear and even the second might do so. There remained as indicative of the nature of the bill only the phraseology of the address and appeal with, at best, the royal response. Private bills originating in the commons were addressed to that body and asked its intercession with the king for the granting of some favour to an individual or a group. On them were written two sentences, the first dispatching them to the lords with "Soit baille as seigneurs," the second, recording the king's assent in the words quoted above. On enrollment the sentence of dispatch disappeared and even a statement that the bill came from the commons might be omitted. So, too, might be the king's response. But the distinctive phraseology of the bill itself always insures identification.

Public bills originating in the lords, and in view of their subject matter perhaps not inappropriately to be referred to as official bills, sometimes addressed the king and sometimes did not. If they did, the appeal was impersonal; if they did not, there was substituted for the appeal an affirmation of the king's will. In either case an explanatory "forasmuch" clause nearly always introduced the bill. On the original bill were written the commons' assent in the usual phrase and the king's assent in the words, "Le Roy le voet." On enrollment both expressions of assent might disappear and only the "forasmuch" clause and the impersonal appeal or the affirmation of the royal will remain to serve for identification. But these are distinctive enough to suffice. Public bills originating in the commons may properly be called, as at the time of their origin they were called, commons bills or petitions. They addressed the king in the set phrase "Prayen the commons" and asked that he grant with the assent of the lords some favour to the commonalty. On them were written two sentences, the one dispatching the bill to the lords in the words employed for private bills and the other recording the king's assent in the words employed for public bills. The sentence of dispatch disappeared when the bill was enrolled, but the royal response was usually recorded. As with other bills the best clue to the identification of a commons bill lies in the phraseology of its address and appeal. For them this was as distinctive as it was for private bills originating in the commons and rather more distinctive than the phraseology of official bills or of private bills originating in the lords.

To distinguish these four types of bills is never difficult if the original bill survives. Nor is it usually difficult if we have merely the enrolled record. From the latter alone, however, some doubt may occasionally arise whether the bill was an official one or a private one addressed to the king. We have seen how the response to an official bill in favour of the duchess of York took, perhaps carelessly, the form appropriate to a private bill. The doubt most often arises in connection with group bills the content of which is to some degree official. The private bill of the staplers quoted above asking for repayment of a loan advanced to pay soldiers' wages at Calais might have been an official bill if the initiative in paying the debt had come from the government.[41] Another Calais bill, one of 1453, although technically private, was still farther on the road towards being an official bill. It ran: " For the suerte and saufgarde of the Towene and Castell of Cales' . . . and for redy payement to be had for wages and vitaillement of the Soudeours and Officers [there] . . . Please it the Kyng . . . to ordeigne and establisshe by auctorite of this same Parlement [payment as specified]." Although this bill does not survive in its original form, an *inspeximus* of it does, which records the commons' and the king's assent. Both are phrased in the sentences appropriate to private bills. And, indeed, the enrolled record tells us that the petition was presented by the treasurer and victualler of Calais, received the assent of lords and commons and was answered " Soit fait come il est desire."[42] If, however, there had been no inspeximus and if the enrollment had been without explanatory sentences, we might well have thought the bill an official one. It is official

---

[41] Cf. above, p. 55.
[42] C. 76/137, m. 17; *R. P.,* V, 235.

in content, has a substitute for a "forasmuch" clause, and is impersonal in its appeal.

To show how slight is the transition to an official bill, we may note still another Calais bill of 1453 enrolled immediately before the one just quoted. It runs: "Forasmuche as it is nedefull and expedient hasty provision to be made for reparations and workes to be done at Caleis . . . , the Kyng, therefor, by th' advys and assent of his Lordes . . . and Communes [sets apart certain income]."[43] No original of this bill is discoverable and no explanatory sentences are added in the enrollment. The bill is badly transcribed. But it is clear from the phraseology as well as the content that it was an official bill. Why this bill should have been official while its companion, providing for the payment of the soldiers, was put in the mouths of the treasurer and victualler, is not clear. To pay the soldiers at Calais was as much the government's business as to repair the works. Perhaps, however, the treasurer and victualler took the initiative through a realization of the difficulties. The three Calais bills at least teach us that we must be prepared sometimes to face ambiguity regarding bills which were more or less official in content, which were enrolled (as the bill for the soldiers was not) without explanatory sentences, and which do not disclose very clearly whether their appeal was personal or impersonal. Uncertainty on the last point, fortunately, seldom occurs; for in nearly all cases which might otherwise puzzle us, the personal or impersonal character of the appeal is readily discernible. And this is sufficient for the identification of the bill as private or official.

Another ambiguity regarding official bills has also occasionally to be reckoned with in the second half of the fifteenth century. Occasionally, though rarely, the government, in order to put its measures in the mouth of the commons, had bills which were properly official bills presented as commons bills. A noteworthy illustration is the affirmation or "declaration" of the title of Edward IV. This began with a "forsomoch"

[43] *Ibid.*, p. 234.

clause expanded at length and introductory to a statement that
"the Commyns . . . besech . . . their . . . Soverayn Lord
Kyng Edward the fourth that by th' avis and assent of the
Lordes Spirituellex and Temporelx . . . his right and title to
the seid Coroune . . . be declared [with elaborate specifica-
tions]." [44]   The purport and the tone of this bill stamp it as
official, while the forasmuch clauses take a first step in making
it such. Yet it was made to assume the form of a commons bill.
The vital clause in it is an appeal of the commons, not a statement of the king's will; the original bill is inscribed "Soit baille
as s[eigneur]s," and the explanatory sentences of the enrollment say that the bill was presented by the commons and was
answered at their request.   The political situation, of course,
explains the anomaly.   It would have been awkward for a
king who had just overthrown his predecessor to declare his
own title.   It was better that the declaration come from his
subjects and come in the form of a petition.   So a compromise
bill was drafted.   It did not begin with "Prayen the commons"
as commons bills usually did. Instead, it was introduced by the
"forasmuch" clause, characteristic of official bills.   But after
the first intrusion of the official hand, the bill was modeled on
the forms of a commons bill.   A curious hybrid resulted, but
one justified by the circumstances.

Less explicable and less justifiable was a bill of 1454, official in essence but assuming the form of a commons petition.
It asked that the king's step-brothers, the earls of Richmond
and Pembroke, be assured of all rights of Englishmen and
confirmed in all privileges and possessions granted by the king.
Its appeal ran, "Excellentissimo . . . Principi Domino nostro
Regi Supplicamus . . . nos, Communitas huius Regni . . . ,
quatinus . . . dignemini . . . de avisamento et assensu . . .
Dominorum Spiritualium et Temporalium . . . statuere . . .
quod prefati Edmundus et Jasper declarentur vestri Fratres
uterini. . . ."   Two schedules were appended.   On the bill was
inscribed the commons' dispatch, "Soient baille as S[eig-

---

[44] C., P. & C. P. 52/7; *R. P.*, V, 463-467.

neur]s," and the king's assent, " Soit fait come il est desire
ovesque certeins provisions a y cest bille annexez." The enrolled record explains that the petition was presented by the
commons and was answered at their request.[45]   This petition
might have assumed the form of a private bill, or of an official
bill or of a commons bill.   It was in essence like the official
bills for the duchess of York and the duchess of Exeter respectively, which have already been quoted.   It might equally
well have been presented to the king by his brothers as a
private petition.   That it assumed the form of a commons
petition was probably for the purpose of securing popularity
for the two earls.   Neither this petition nor the one touching
the title of Edward IV was enrolled along with other commons petitions of the respective parliaments in which they
were presented.   They were grouped rather with official bills
and private bills.   This circumstance alone stamps them as
unusual and assures us that their divergence from the normal
types of bills was exceptional.

[45] C., P. & C. P. 29/6; *R. P.*, V, 250.

CHAPTER V

THE STRUCTURE OF THE PARLIAMENT ROLL

THE differentiation of the types of mid-fifteenth century bills and the examination of the manner in which each type was recorded on the parliament roll have been undertaken not as ends in themselves. So far as the differentiation has been successful, it should reveal how the clerk in drawing up the roll entered upon it bills of various types. If in successive parliaments some system is perceptible in his entries, it becomes possible to speak of the structure of the parliament roll. The structure of the roll of 1509 has already been examined, primarily to see how bills which the journal of the year describes more fully were then enrolled. We may now inquire whether fifteenth-century rolls were like the later one and whether by any good fortune they are more informing. It is to be hoped that they are, since little besides them survives, apart from original bills and the statute roll, to inform us about the proceedings of parliament.[1]

Just as illustrations of different types of bills have been drawn from the rolls of the parliaments of 1453-1465, so the structure of the parliament roll may be studied from the rolls of the same years. The parliaments in question were six in number. Owing to adjournments, each of the first two was continued into a second year, while the sessions of the last were separated by an interval of nearly two years. We shall henceforth designate the six as the parliaments of 1453-4, 1455-6, 1459, 1460, 1461 and 1463-5. Because the second

---

[1] Dr. Sayles has found that the rolls of the king's bench, the rolls of the lord treasurer's remembrancer and certain chancery records tell us much about the parliaments of Edward I and Edward II. It is possible that later records of the same sort might at times give information about later parliaments.

session of the last was virtually a second parliament and was so treated on the statute roll, we may sometimes refer to it as the parliament of 1465.

Certain of these parliaments were less important and less typical than the others. Such was the Coventry parliament of 1459, which next year was declared void, its acts being repealed. Such, too, was the parliament of 1460, which, apart from the act of voidance and the settlement of the duke of York's claim to the throne, produced only one brief statute. The parliament of 1461 again was largely concerned with establishing a new royal house. Although each of the three supplied the parliament roll with items of interest, the proceedings of the parliaments of 1453-4, 1455-6 and 1463-5 were more normal and the recording rolls are more typical of the mid-fifteenth century. In these three rolls appear bills of the various types, characteristically entered. Several bills in each parliament were approved and most of these with slight adaptations became statutes. It will be pertinent at times to compare the parliament roll with the statute roll.

Considered broadly, the parliament roll recorded matter of two sorts. One sort was narrative in character, an account of what went on during the session or sessions; the other was legislative, the transcription of a series of bills, accompanied often by notes on the action taken regarding them. The bills themselves, of course, contained much narrative matter, especially in their preambles; and, indeed, from their contents the historian derives largely his knowledge both of the activities of any parliament and of its political and economic background. Essentially, however, they were bills, and in examining the structure of the parliament roll we should regard them as such. In the fifteenth century bills constituted by far the greater part of the roll; but in certain of the parliaments under consideration, the necessity of twice appointing a protector of the realm and defining his powers, the later transfer of power from one king to another, and the attainting of various nobles brought about an expansion of the narrative. This narrative we may discuss first and, since it tells us little about the enactment of legislation, somewhat briefly. But it does at times reveal something of the organization and competence of parliament.

The narrative portion of the parliament roll concerned itself first with the calendar. This recorded the appointed day of meeting, a day often postponed. It told the length of the first session, if there was more than one session, by giving the date of prorogation. Often coupled with this date was a later one on which, it was explained, the king desired that parliament should renew its deliberations. The adjournment and the date of reassembling were announced by the chancellor, whose briefly recorded speech often touched upon the causes of adjournment and thanked the king's subjects for what they had done. Sometimes the day appointed for reassembling proved unsatisfactory and the announcement of another was often accompanied by the letters patent which authorized it. If, after a second session, there had to be a third or more, similar entries were made. Finally, the chancellor adjourned parliament, although the record of this was at times omitted.

The calendar, when it had occasion to describe successive sessions, was not always revealing as to what happened at each. The narration of adjournments and the letters patent authorizing them were sometimes entered toward the beginning of the roll, while bills which may have been presented and accepted at different sessions were enrolled later on. The so-called " communes petitiones," which usually embodied the essentially legislative work of the session, were grouped together at the end of the roll, regardless of the session in which they were offered. Although there may have been paramount reasons for such grouping, it does, nevertheless, obscure the sequence in which bills were considered and passed by both houses.

The enrolled record of the parliament of 1449-50 illustrates perhaps better than those of the following parliaments the way in which the calendar may fail to reveal the business done in various sessions.[2] At the beginning of the roll we are told that there were three sessions. The first lasted from 6 November to 17 December with a transfer in the midst from Westminster to London; the second extended from 22 January to 30 March; and the last, held at Leicester instead of Westminster, from 29 April to the latter part of May.[3] Immediately after the calendar is noted the grant of a subsidy which was confessedly not conceded until the last session. Thereupon follows a lengthy indictment of the duke of Suffolk together with an account of his appearance before the lords and his final banishment by the king. These events seem to have occurred between 22 January and 17 March, hence in the course of the second session. The remaining activities of the parliament are undated but are described together under the caption " Petitiones Communes." The most important of them, a request for the resumption of crown property, can be dated as belonging to the early days of the April-May session, if not to an earlier time.[4] Hence, as enrolled, the parliament's principal activities — the grant of a subsidy, the indictment of Suffolk and the presentation and approval of the bill of resumption — are related in a sequence different from the order of their occurrence. The illustration makes clear that in examining the rolls of fifteenth-century parliaments, the sequence of events has in each instance to be coordinated with a more or less isolated calendar. Sometimes,

---

[2] *R. P.,* V, 171-203.

[3] Stubbs says, without reference, that the session closed on 17 May (*op. cit.* III, 155). A letter of 13 May written to John Paston probably in 1450 suggests that parliament was sitting at Leicester (*Paston Letters,* I, no. 96). Royal letters patent were still dated at Leicester on 4 June (*C. P. R., 1446-1452,* p. 387); but this may not be conclusive.

[4] Certain revenues resumed were assigned to the household in a household act which was to become effective on 7 May, 1450 (*R. P.,* V, 174-5). When manors of the duchy of Cornwall were taken into the king's hands, the issues from them accrued to him as from 6 Nov. 1449, the first day of the parliament (P. R. O., Lord Treasurer's Remembrancer, Foreign Accts. 88). This suggests that the act of resumption may date from one of the earlier sessions.

however, as in the roll of 1453-4, shortly to be described, several of the transactions of the parliament were recorded with due reference to sessions which are described at intervals throughout the roll, not in a short narrative at the beginning. Yet, even when the roll was thus articulated, the " communes petitiones " at the end were unrelated to the sessions in which they were considered.

After an initial calendar item the narrative portion of the parliament roll proceeded to the chancellor's speech. Whether quoted or paraphrased, this stated in general and pious terms the reasons for the summons of parliament and directed the commons to choose a speaker. As a further sign of organization for business, the appointment of receivors and triours of petitions was noted. Thereupon followed the commons' announcement of whom they had chosen to be their speaker. After these narrative items, the entries were likely to be grants of subsidies or provisions for defence. The first assumed the form of indentures, the second usually the form of bills. The series of bills once begun straightway became the main concern of the roll, and bills of various sorts were enrolled. The narrative was henceforth resumed only when transactions were carried on which did not lend themselves fully to incorporation in indentures or bills.

An illustration of the resumption of narrative may be drawn from the roll of the parliament of 1455-6. The record of the first session from the 9th to the 31st of July, after the usual introductory matter, including this time the appointment of certain committees, consists of an official bill pardoning the duke of York and the earls of Salisbury and Warwick, the transcript of an oath taken by several lords to the king, and a bill of general pardon. The record of a second session, begun on 15 November, after recording the letters patent which named the duke of York lieutenant, falls into narrative. " It was shewed to the Duke of York, the Kyng's Lieutenant . . . and to the Lordes Spirituelle and Temporell by the mouthe of Burley [not the speaker] accompanyed with notable nombre of the Communes in name of all the Communes" that a protector and defendor should be appointed. There had been grievous riots in the West Country. The chancellor assured them that York and the lords would deliberate. Two days later Burley and his fellow commoners appeared again with the same request and were given the same assurance. After they had gone the chancellor asked the lords what should be done since "it is understood that they [the commons] will not ferther procede in matiers of Parliament to the tyme that they have answer to their desire and request." The lords straightway agreed that there should be a protector and that the duke of York, in view of "the polletique rule had in this land" when he was last protector, should again take upon him the charge. After modest protest the duke complied. Perhaps because this decision was not promptly conveyed to the commons, Burley and his fellows a third time appeared in the lords insisting on their original request and enlarging on the disorders in the West. A protector should be appointed at once and should ride to the West Country. Parliament might well be prorogued, especially as Christmas was near. The third visit was effective. On the same day the chancellor "declared unto the Communes being in theire house accustomed" that the king with the assent of the lords had named the duke protector. Protector and lords would be diligent in subduing the riots, and adjournment would take place as might be "most behovefull and expedient." The duke, thus nominated, accepted, but only after the lords had assented to six "articles," which he desired read and enrolled. Three days later his stipend was fixed and his appointment consummated.[5]

This account of the negotiations between commons, lords and the duke of York fills not more than three pages of the printed parliament roll. Yet it is unusual to find so long a piece of narrative intruded in the midst of the customary series of bills. There is no further narrative for this parliament and there is little in the records of the parliaments of 1453-1465

[5] *R. P.,* V, 284-289.

except in that of 1460.   In the parliament of 1453 the oral
request of the commons for a council, the endeavours of a
committee of lords to get a response from an invalid king, and
the first choice of York to be protector are told in a narrative
of two printed pages.   Semi-narrative matter is further embodied in two series of " articles " stipulating conditions on
which York consented to act respectively as protector and as
governor of Calais.[6]   On the parliament roll of 1459 there is
record of the reading in the lords of " a Cedule of a forme of
an Oath," which oath the lords proceeded to take in evidence
of their loyalty to the king.[7]

Only on the roll of 1460 is there narrative as extensive as
that of 1455.   And in both instances the subject matter is
the same — the position of the duke of York relative to the
throne.   In 1455 it was a question of his acting as protector
during the king's illness; in 1460 it was necessary to determine his status after his victory at Northampton.   Hence on
16 October his council brought to parliament a " writyng,"
which recounted his claims to the throne.   The treatment of
this by the lords is told at length.   They decided that it should
be read; they sent it to the king for his learned comment, since
he " had seen and understouden many dyvers writyngs and
Cronicles "; they referred it to the justices, who replied that
they could only " determyne such maters as com before theym
in the lawe betwene partie and partie . . ."; they twice and
insistently requested the assistance of the king's sergeants and
the king's attorney, but without avail; they themselves offered
objections to York's claim, which he in turn satisfactorily
answered; they finally brought about a concord between king
and duke whereby the duke and his heirs were to succeed the
king after his death.   The concord and various oaths support-
ing it are recited.   After which the roll proceeds to the enrollment of the bills of the session.[8]

[6] *Ibid.,* pp. 240-242, 254-256.
[7] *Ibid.,* p. 351.
[8] *Ibid.,* pp. 375-381.

The parliament roll of 1461 contains two brief bits of narrative appropriate to the occasion. The first is an appreciation of the bravery and beneficence of the young Edward IV presented to him by the commons in the form of a schedule which they desired enrolled. The second is almost unique, the transcript of a speech from the throne. At the close of the session Edward thanked the commons for their assistance in recovering his right and title, assuring them that "yf Y had eny better good to reward you withall then my body ye shuld have it, the which shall alwey be redy for youre defence.[9] Apart from these two items the roll has no narrative other than the usual calendar and the connecting sentences. The roll of the parliament of 1463-5 confined itself even more closely to the record of bills considered. The contents of the rolls of a half dozen parliaments of the middle of the fifteenth century thus demonstrate how comparatively inconsiderable was the narrative with which the clerk bound together his record.

One reason for this paucity of narrative is that foreign affairs as such received little attention on the parliament roll. Since it was not the business of parliament to direct negotiations with foreign powers, the dispatch of embassies and the conclusion of treaties were recorded elsewhere. Insofar, however, as the conduct of war involved the securing of money through the grant of a subsidy, an explanation of the foreign or military situation might be vouchsafed to parliament as an incentive to generosity. In this case the chancellor might incorporate the explanation in his speech, or he might devote a special speech to the subject. More often, however, the foreign situation was revealed in the preambles to subsidy bills or other bills. In the rolls of the years 1453-1465, when foreign policy turned largely upon the defense of Calais and of the sea, such explanation of it as was offered is to be found in the bills relating to these subjects. In 1453 the indenture for a subsidy on wool specified that twenty shillings of the amount paid

[9] *Ibid.,* pp. 462, 487.

on each sack, or nearly one-half of the entire subsidy, be expended on the wages and food of the soldiers at Calais;[10] and at the same time provision was made for the protection of the coast by the appointment of five lords to guard the sea, the income from tunnage and poundage being put at their disposal.[11]   In the earlier parliament of 1444 some account of the negotiations for a truce with France was given by Suffolk in a declaration of his recent services; and later in the same parliament the lords, through the mouth of the chancellor, disassociated themselves from any responsibility for the negotiations in question.   When in 1450 the commons brought charges against Suffolk in a series of articles, many of these touched upon his activities in France.[12]   References like these to foreign affairs were, however, more or less incidental to the immediate business of parliament; and in general it may be said that the recording of negotiations with foreign powers did not concern the parliament roll except so far as such negotiations might be introduced as explanatory to certain bills or to indictments preferred against responsible statesmen.

The mention of indictments brings us to the last sort of subject matter which occasionally found place in the narrative portion of the parliament roll.   This was the administration of justice.   Since Maitland edited the roll of 1305 all writers on the early history of parliament, especially Professors McIlwain and Pollard, have emphasized this aspect of parliamentary activity.   The latest investigators, Messrs. Richardson and Sayles, are even more emphatic in declaring that the parliaments of the three Edwards functioned primarily as sessions of a court.[13]   So convincing is the evidence adduced that the case may be regarded as proved.   Usually the grant of some form of financial or military assistance was expected by the

[10] *Ibid.*, p. 229. Similar conditions had been attached to the grant of the wool subsidy in 1447 (*ibid.*, p. 146).

[11] *Ibid.*, p. 244.

[12] *Ibid.*, pp. 74, 102, 177-181.

[13] McIlwain, *op. cit.*, ch. III; Pollard, *op. cit.*, ch. II; Richardson and Sayles, *Bull. Inst. Hist. Research*, V, 133; VI, 78; IX, 2.

king in return for the justice which he administered in parliament. Yet this was not essential and justice was dispensed when no subsidy was conceded.[14] The commons were not at first party to judgments pronounced in parliament; but when, from the early fifteenth century, private bills came to be submitted to them for approval they did indirectly share in administering justice.[15]

All sorts of requests for justice were not heard in parliament but only those for which other courts did not offer suitable remedy. In 1372 the chancellor defined a grievance suitable for parliamentary consideration as one " qe ne poet estre amende ne redresce en nul des Places le Roi mes en Parlement . . . ; " and in 1373 the commons gave the same definition in asking " qe les Petitions de chescuny Droit dont remedie ne poet estre suy en nul autre Court mes en Parlement " be heard then and there.[16] The history of early parliaments becomes, therefore, largely a description of the kind of justice which could be got in them and could not be got elsewhere. Yet during the fourteenth century, as it happened, private appeals came to be referred more and more to other courts. Fewer and fewer came to be considered appropriate for parliamentary action. Appeals of the commonalty, on the other hand, could be suitably heard only by parliament. By the fifteenth century the consideration of the requests of the commons had come to be the principal business of parliament.

[14] As, for instance, in 1305.

[15] In 1399 the commons " monstrerent au Roy qe, come les juggementz du Parlement appertiegnent soulement au Roy et as Seigneurs et nient as Communes sinoun en cas qe s'il plest au Roy de sa grace especiale lour monstrer les ditz juggementz par ease de eux, qe nul Record soit fait en Parlement encontre les ditz Communes q'ils sont ou serront parties as ascuns juggementz donez ou a doners en apres en Parlement." In this statement the chancellor at the command of the king acquiesced, adding, " Sauve q'en Estatuz a faires ou en Grantes et Subsidies ou tiels choses a faires pur commune profit du Roialme, le Roy voet avoir especialment leur advis et assent." (*R. P.,* III, 427). Cf. below p. 377.

[16] *R. P.,* II, 309, 318. Maitland pointed out than an order from parliament might greatly expedite a case elsewhere (*op. cit.,* p. lxix).

Both private and public appeals were, however, then embodied in the form of petitions or bills and hence did not fall within the narrative part of the parliament roll. Was there, however, no administering of justice other than that comprised in the responses to private or public bills? Were no cases as between parties ever enrolled and therefore accorded a description other than that of bill and response?

The answer is that such cases occur but are few in number. Attainders, which were in a sense judicial and which could be pronounced only in parliament, took the form of bills passed by both houses. The case against Suffolk referred to above was presented in the form of two commons bills. The first was read before the lords, was referred to the justices for advice, and was finally approved to the extent that the duke was ordered to " come to his answere." The second contained many articles, to which he made answer before the lords. Since he did not put himself " uppon [his] Parage " but submitted himself to the king, the conclusion of the case was a royal sentence of banishment without further parliamentary action.[17] Later condemnations of nobles usually took the form of official bills. Such was the attainder of the duke of York in 1459 and the attainder of many lords in 1461.[18] If the commons took the initiative this was likely to be in the form of a petition that certain misdoers appear before the common law courts on penalty of being convicted and attainted of high treason. Such was the purport of a commons bill of 1461 against John Waleys and six associates.[19]

Occasionally, however, action on a charge of treason or violence was recorded on the parliament roll merely as narrative without quotation of the bill of indictment. In 1454 the roll relates that the earl of Devonshire was arraigned in parliament before the steward of England on an indictment of high treason. Whereupon " by his Peeres the noble Lordes of

[17] *R. P.,* V, 177-183.
[18] *Ibid.,* pp. 346-351, 476-483.
[19] *Ibid.,* p. 483.

this Royaume of England being in this . . . Parlement [he] was acquited of all things conteigned in the seid enditement." This is all that we learn about the trial, there being no indication even that it was initiated by bill. The account may have been enrolled in order that the duke of York, who thought his own loyalty to the king brought in question, might make formal record of good faith. From the same month of March, 1454 there comes a brief enrollment of further action taken in the lords, this time semi-judicial in character. Lord Cromwell asked that the duke of Exeter be required to give surety for keeping the peace toward him. The request is said to have been expressed in a bill which after approval was sent on to the commons. But the bill itself was not enrolled, only the narrative of its acceptance and dispatch.[20] Thus it appears that, in the middle of the fifteenth century, judicial proceedings, whether they were initiated by bill or not, might occasionally be recorded in narrative fashion. Under Richard II suits in parliament were often recorded in a combination of bill and narrative.[21]

Another sort of judicial action in parliament was also sometimes enrolled as narrative. It related to the privileges of members and is well illustrated by the case of Thomas Thorp. At the opening of the parliament of 1453 in March, Thorp was chosen speaker of the commons. In this capacity he served throughout the two sessions of the spring and summer. During the vacation which lasted from 2 July, 1453 to 14 February, 1454 he took, it seems, certain chattels belonging to the duke of York from the house of the bishop of Durham. For this he was consigned to the Fleet. On the re-convening of parliament the commons through certain of their members asked the king and lords to release him, citing the customary and ancient privileges of men coming to parliament. The appeal was apparently oral. Next day the duke of York in the lords advanced reasons why Thorp should be left in prison.

[20] *Ibid.*, 249, 264.
[21] See below, p. 342.

He had been pronounced guilty in the court of the exchequer, his offence had been committed since the opening of parliament, he had been arrested not in " Parlement tyme" but in tyme of vacation. If he should be releasd the duke would be without remedy against him and could not collect damages, which had been assessed in court at £1000. The lords "not entendyng to empeche or hurt the Libertees and Privilegges" of the commons "but egally after the cours of lawe to mynystre justice" referred the case to the justices. The latter replied that it was not for them to determine the "Privelegge of this high Court of Parlement" but rather for the lords. They indicated, however, that it was the usage of the lower courts to give members of parliament liberty to attend sessions if the arrest were not for "treason or felony or suerte of the peas or for a condempnation hadde before the Parlement." To this principle the lords assented, affirming that "accordynge to the lawe" Thorp must remain in prison and telling the commons that another speaker must be chosen.[22]

Had Thorp's case been initiated by bill, the record of it would perhaps have been the enrollment of the bill. But the case had been brought before the lords orally. A reason for this lay in the need of haste. Thorp was not only a member of the commons but he was their speaker. Their affairs could not be dispatched without him or without someone chosen in his stead. Just as their presentation of a new speaker was always oral, so now their immediate need of a speaker led them to ask orally for Thorp's release. Yet even had the case been initiated by bill, the action of the lords would have had to be told in narrative, unless the reference to the justices and their reply had been incorporated in a cumbersome answer. The preference of the clerk for narrative at the moment is evinced by his casting the next request of the commons in that form. This referred to a council which had been promised them at the beginning of the session. Perhaps eagerness

[22] *R. P.,* V, 239-240.

to have a prompt response here too dictated recourse to an oral rather than to a written petition. At any rate both instances show that the circumstances of the moment probably had much to do with the occasional departure from the customary method of recording parliamentary action by the enrollment of bills alone.

How relatively small was the part of a fifteenth century parliament roll devoted to narrative has now become apparent. The calendar describing the time and place of the session or sessions was little more than a skeleton, even when it was expanded by a summary of the chancellor's speeches. Unusual circumstances like the choosing of a regent during the king's mental collapse or the replacement of one king by another might impel the clerk to relate such action. Foreign affairs got from him scant attention. Even the judicial activities of parliament, original and important as they were, cloaked themselves in the guise of petition and response, except in occasional brief narrations of trials for treason or of pronouncements on the privileges of members of the commons. The greater part of the parliament roll was not a chronicle but a body of bills. The bills might themselves indulge in narrative, as they sometimes did, rather extensively. But this was in support of the appeal which they proffered; it was not narrative for its own sake. We may therefore turn from the narrative portion of the parliament roll to the more extensive, more important and more interesting part of it, the record of recorded bills and their answers.

The bills of the parliament roll belonged to one or another of the types which have been described in the preceding chapter. They were private bills, some addressed to the king and introduced in the lords, some addressed to the commons and introduced in that body; or they were public bills, some originating with the government or the lords, some with the commons. Had the clerks of parliament developed what seems to us a logical procedure, they would have enrolled bills in accordance with these categories. Unfortunately they did not do so; and, in so far as they introduced captions indicating categories, these are misleading.

Since the parliament roll of 1453-4 has more than once been quoted, it may be referred to again to illustrate the order or lack of order in which it recorded bills of the four principal types.[23] As it happens, the calendar of this parliament was better articulated than was that of the parliament of 1449-50 described above; for to some extent it related bills to the session in which they were passed. To the first session, held at Reading from the 6th to the 28th of March, were ascribed two subsidy bills and a declaration made by the speaker of the commons. The former granted tunnage and poundage, a fifteenth and tenth, and a poll tax on aliens; the latter offered to the king 20000 archers. The indentures were of the usual sort, the declaration was oral.[24] On the 28th the chancellor, and this time the king as well, thanked the commons and prorogued parliament to 25 April, the next session to be at Westminster.

We must assume that the reassembling took place as ordered and that the following entries recorded the work of the second session, although the roll tells us neither of these things. What it did was to enroll six bills. The first was an official bill, remitting 7000 of the archers; the second was a "billa indentata," a variation of the usual indenture schedule, and a statement of how the commons would supply the remaining 13000 archers; the third was a second official bill postponing the levy for two years. The three other bills related to Calais. One took the form of a private petition of the duke of Somerset asking repayment of £21648, 10s., due him for the wages of himself, his captains and his soldiers while he was captain of Calais; the second was an official bill providing for repair of the works at Calais; the third was a second private bill in

[23] *Ibid.*, pp. 227-271.

[24] *Ibid.*, pp. 228, 230. "Declaravit etiam idem Prelocutor nomine Communium predictorum qualiter ipsi de assensu Dominorum Spiritualium et Temporalium . . . concesserunt . . . Regi . . . Viginti Milia Hominum Sagittariorum. . . ."

which the treasurer and victualler asked that assignment be made them from the wool custom in behalf of the soldiers. Following the six bills is an indenture presented in the lords on 2 July and granting to the king an additional half-fifteenth and half-tenth. Only the fourth and the sixth of the bills have sentences introducing them and other sentences at the end telling of their approval. The first and the fifth are enrolled without comment of any sort. The second and the third are without concluding information, but do have introductions, one brief, the other longer. The brief one is valuable for introducing us to a "billa indentata"; the longer one explains the postponement of the levy of 13000 archers. The king conceded this because he had learned that the commons in return would grant an additional subsidy. Thus indirectly is explained the concession of a half-fifteenth and half-tenth on 2 July.

To judge from the enrolled record it would thus seem that the only business considered in the two spring sessions of the parliament of 1453 was the grant of money and of men and the provision for Calais. This may possibly have been the case; for such business was important enough. But it is unlikely that the commons were willing to give so generously without return. At the end of the parliament roll are enrolled ten so-called commons petitions of which all were granted. Whether any of them was presented and agreed to in the spring sessions cannot be determined. If none was, then all must have belonged to the session of 1454 which began at Westminster on 14 February and dealt with a greater variety and a greater quantity of business than did the sessions of 1453.[25] No closing of this session is recorded, the last date mentioned in connection with it being 17 April.[26]

The initial records of the third session are narrative in character and have already been in part quoted. Such were

---

[25] The date set for the reassembling of parliament had at first been 12 November and later 11 February, and the place Reading (*ibid.*, p. 238).

[26] *Ibid.*, p. 247.

the oral requests of the commons for the release of Thomas Thorp, their speaker, and for the council promised in the preceding year. Next we are told of the mission of a committee of lords to the king at Windsor to secure his assent to the naming of a council and of a chancellor. When the committee returned without recognition from the king, the lords chose York to be protector. The articles on which he made his acceptance of the post conditional and the lords' responses to them follow. Thereupon a series of bills begins, to be interrupted only twice in the remainder of the roll. One interruption was the brief narrative of the trial of the earl of Devonshire and of York's protestation of loyalty already quoted. The other was a second list of articles submitted by the duke for acceptance by the lords if they desired him to act as governor of Calais.[27]

Over against the seven printed pages of narrative in this session stand twenty-nine printed pages of bills of various sorts. All the types of private and public bills described above appear. There were five private bills addressed to the king, four private bills addressed to the commons, sixteen official bills and four commons bills. The first and third groups were the sort originating in the lords, the second and fourth the sort originating in the commons. In the first two sessions of the parliament, as we have seen, in addition to the commons' concurrence in two subsidy indentures and in a " billa indentata " for 13000 archers, two private bills and three official bills, all originating in the lords, had been passed. The total number of bills enrolled for the entire parliament thus became two subsidy bills and a closely related *billa indentata,* seven private bills originating in the lords, four private bills originating in the commons, nineteen official or lords bills, and four commons bills.

Before we examine these bills it should be noted that many private bills, though approved by king and parliament, were not enrolled at all. Occasionally the same fate befell an official bill or even a commons bill. An illustration of an omis-

[27] *Ibid.,* pp. 254-256.

sion of each of the latter sorts is furnished by this same parliament of 1453-4. When the commons presented a petition asking that all who had assembled on the field of Dartford against the king in 1450 should forfeit any royal grant made them since the beginning of the reign, the king assented. But in the following parliament another commons petition asked for the repeal of this act on the ground that it brought into "doubte and ambiguitiee" the loyalty of many of the king's liegemen and might thereby cause "greet and perilouse division" among certain lords and others. The royal approval of the second bill annulled the first.[28] What is unusual is that neither bill was enrolled. The reason may have been in part the desire to appease passions which possibly were roused by the first bill and a feeling that since a contentious act had been so promptly repealed, no record of it need be made. But it seems to have been occasionally true, however, that acts repealing other acts, especially if the latter were at once superseded by new regulations, were thought unworthy of enrollment. In 1453-4 an official bill repealing the household act of 1450 on the ground that it was now "otherwise purveied for the said Householde" was not enrolled.[29] Acts repealing other acts, therefore, and even the acts repealed, if passed shortly before, sometimes did not appear on the parliament roll.

We may now return to a consideration of the bills of 1453-4 which were enrolled. A casual reader of fifteenth-century rolls of parliament would speedily reach the conclusion that on each roll there was at least a simple division between commons bills and all other bills. On nearly every roll the last group of bills enrolled was introduced by a caption which seems clearly to imply this. We have already met with it on the parliament roll of 1509 and have discussed its significance there.[30] On the roll of parliament of 1453-4 it ran, "Item

[28] *Ibid.*, pp. 329-330. The first bill is known only from its recital in the second.

[29] *Ibid.*, p. 272.

[30] See above, pp. 30-33.

diverses Communes Petitions feurent baillez en mesme le Parlement par les Communes d'icell, les tenours des queux ovesque lour Responses cy ensuent." [31]   As a result of our examination in the preceding chapter of the enrolled form assumed by the four usual types of bills, we are now in a position to discover whether the ten bills grouped under this caption in 1453-4 were really commons bills. And, as it happens, the survival of all of them in their original form enables us to test our conclusions.[32]

It quickly appears that not more than four or five of the ten bills actually originated with the commons. Only five of them as enrolled begin with " Prayen the Communes," then ask the king to grant a request with the advice and assent of the lords and finally are answered, " Le Roy le voet." Of the ten only five in their original form bear the inscription characteristic of bills originating in the commons, " Soit baille as seigneurs." Four of the latter are four which are recognizable in their enrolled form as commons bills. The fifth is a private bill addressed to the commons and sent on to the lords, bearing the same inscription as did the commons bills. The four amply certified commons bills related respectively to the attainder of Jack Cade, the removal of ambiguities in the act of resumption of 1450, the renewal of a statute of 1442 limiting the scope of outlawries pronounced in Lancashire against non-residents of the county, and, lastly, the remission for denizens of certain customs imposed in this very parliament. A sixth bill, which from its enrolled form appears to be a commons bill, is misleading and is unusual in being so. It related to the attainder of Sir William Oldhall and began " Prayen the Communes . . . that it please youre Highnesse by th' avys and assent of youre Lordes. . . ." The original bill, however, bears the inscription, " A cest bille les Comyns sount assentuz," a clear indication that the bill was an official

[31] *R. P.*, V, 265.
[32] C., P. & C. P. 29/9-10, 12-16; A. P. 1360-1362; *R. P.*, V, 265-271.

one. Reference has already been made to occasional bills couched in the phraseology of commons bills but actually official in origin. In this instance the explanation may be that bills of attainder were supposed to originate with the commons and, even when official in origin, were sometimes drafted in phrases which would imply this.[32a] Disregarding the deceptive attainder of Oldhall, we find that of the ten so-called " communes petitions " of 1453-4 only four were genuine commons bills.

Of the remainder, four, apart from the Oldhall attainder, were official bills. As enrolled, two of them began with a " forasmuch " clause and all of them asked the king to grant their respective requests with the advice and assent of the lords and *of the commons* or with the authority of the present parliament. All were answered, " Le Roy le voet." In their original form all bear not only this inscription but also the revealing one, " A ceste bille les communes sont assentuz." They were, further, official in content. One imposed penalties for ignoring a summons to appear before chancery or council on charge of riot or oppression, another limited the jurisdiction of the wardens of the Scottish marches, another protected at sea or in port strangers who had the king's safe conduct, and the fourth enforced a statute of Henry IV that farmers of the ulnage of cloth must have their royal letters patent warranted by the treasurer of England. There is little of the nature of commons petitions about these four bills. All were as clearly official as if they had been frankly so designated.

Along with the five official bills and the four commons bills was enrolled the one private bill already mentioned. It was addressed " To the worshipful and discrete Comones," requested that " please it youre wyse discretions . . . to pray the Kyng . . . by th' assent of his Lordes . . . and his Communes . . . to ordeyn . . ." and was answered, " Soit fait come il est desire en toutz pointz." The original bill bears the

[32a] See above, pp. 67-69; below, p. 115, n. 62.

inscription, "Soit baille as seigneurs." It related at length the rape of Dame Johane Beaumont, asked in the name of her son the punishment of her ravisher and his band, and concluded with an appeal that in all such cases a remedy be provided by writ out of chancery. The address, the appeal, and the response show that the bill cannot properly be called a commons petition.

We are now face to face with the most important aspect of the structure of the parliament roll. It is that the so-called "communes petitions" [33] following upon what seems a revealing caption were not necessarily commons petitions or bills at all. They might be such or they might not. They might equally well be official bills or they might be private bills. The discovery that the caption is a misnomer greatly enlarges the field in which we may henceforth look for official and private bills. They may be found after as well as before the caption. At once we ask, is a complementary inference also true? May we expect to find in that part of the parliament roll which precedes the "communes petitions" not only private and official bills, which we already know were enrolled there, but commons bills as well? The answer of the roll of 1453-4 is on the whole that we may not. Two or three oral requests of the commons were recorded on this part of the roll but no commons bills. It was otherwise, however, as we shall see, with other parliament rolls. On some of them an occasional commons bill was at times enrolled before the caption "communes petitions" was reached but such bills were never numerous. A first generalization thus emerges. In the middle of the fifteenth century, while nearly all commons bills were enrolled as commons petitions, all bills enrolled after this caption were not commons bills.

Preceding the caption "communes petitions" there were enrolled on the roll of 1453-4 official bills and both sorts of private bills. The former, including the three official bills

---

[33] This is the usual French spelling in the captions, and will be henceforth adopted.

of 1453 numbered fourteen. Private bills addressed to the king, including the two of 1453, were seven and private bills addressed to the commons were three. It will be seen that the only type of bill appearing before but not after the caption was the private bill addressed to the king. Examination of the rolls of other parliaments shows that even this type occasionally appeared after the caption as well as before it. A second generalization, therefore, is that official bills and both sorts of private bills were enrolled both before and after the caption " communes petitions." It does not follow that this was done indiscriminately. What we shall have to discover is a principle which guided the clerk in enrolling bills of all sorts after a caption which seems applicable to only one of them. The principle obviously was not inherent in the words of the caption.

Before seeking the principle it will be well to glance at the contents of the bills enrolled before the caption " communes petitions." The private and the official bills of the sessions of 1453 have been described. There were six of them and they related to a levy of archers and to the maintenance of Calais. In the session of 1454 three private bills, in addition to the bill touching Dame Beaumont, were introduced in the commons, five in the lords. The former were purely personal. One asked a confirmation of the status, titles and lands of the king's half-brothers, the earls of Richmond and Pembroke; another the confirmation of the transfer of the manor of Hukcote, Bucks. by the earl of Wiltshire to the Hospital of St. Thomas of Acre in London; a third the payment from customs revenue of money due to the earl of Shropshire for services done in past years. The three might quite as well have been addressed to the king and introduced in the lords. None of them had popular features which would elicit the commons' favour. They looked only to the ratification by the commons of certain titles and of a lien on the customs.[34] Of the five

---

[34] C., P. & C. P. 29/6; A. P. 1358; *R. P.*, V, 250, 257, 263. Of the last no original survives.

private bills introduced in the lords in 1454, three were very similar to those just described. One asked that estates in three northern counties, once the duke of Bedford's but now in the king's hands, be bestowed on the earl of Richmond; another that the title of a chantry established by Thomas Romayn be strengthened; a third that the merchants of the staple be repaid from the proceeds of a clerical tenth 10000 marks loaned by them. Two other bills were of wider scope. One was a composite petition from the staplers asking not only for the payment of the debt mentioned above but for restraint of export licences and for the rejection of two important commons petitions just presented (touching the prices of wool in England and the partition of profits at Calais). The fifth bill was described but not recorded. It was lord Cromwell's request that the duke of Exeter be bound to keep the peace.[35]

Two comments may be made on the private bills presented in this parliament. The first is that no difference in character is perceptible between those introduced in the commons and those introduced in the lords. The choice of address, appeal and presentment seems to have been a matter of personal preference. So it was, too, in Richardson's day. In this the fifteenth century anticipated the seventeenth. A second comment is that two of the bills, those presented by the staplers, were what we have suggested should be called group bills. They represented the interests not of an individual but of a group. In the records of the parliament of 1453-4 they were not treated differently from the larger category of private bills to which in form they belonged. In other parliaments group bills were at times enrolled after the caption " communes petitions." In 1453-4 one of the two staplers' bills had no title to such treatment. The request for the payment of a debt was like a similar request on the part of an individual. There would have been some excuse, however, for enrolling the staplers' composite petition with the commons petitions.

[35] *Ibid.*, pp. 253, 258, 248, 256, 264. Only one original survives, that of Richmond's bill (C., P. & C. P. 29/7).

It succeeded in preventing the passage of two commons bills which, had they been accepted, would have been enrolled along with other commons bills.[36] It succeeded also in having the recently imposed surtax on exported wool remitted and the remission took the form of a commons bill. Logically it might have been enrolled with the commons bills, since it affected a wide range of interests. Elsewhere group bills were so enrolled with less justification. Since this one, however, was in conflict with two commons bills which might have been enrolled, it would have been awkward to record that the commons asked for a favour and, at the same moment, for a rejection of their request.

Eleven official bills presented in the session of 1454 were enrolled before the caption " communes petitions " in addition to the five already described as enrolled after it. Three of them concerned the royal family. One, creating Edward prince of Wales, was presented only to the lords, who in token of their assent affixed their signatures. Two were " cedulae," making changes in the queen's dower. Two other bills affirmed the appointment of the duke of York as protector and fixed his stipend. The king's household claimed attention in two bills, one of which repealed a former household act, while the other made new provision for household expenses. Two other bills provided for the safekeeping of the sea, one by appointing five lords as its keepers, the other by instituting a levy of money on certain ports in anticipation of customs payable in each. Lastly, a bill authorized the collection of fines pledged as security that Robert Poynyngs would keep the peace; and another penalized lords who failed to attend parliament.[37]

Brief as are these indications of the content of the eleven bills, they disclose that all of them were not only official in form but official in character. The bills aimed to meet par-

---

[36] They are printed, *R. P.*, V, 274-277.

[37] *Ibid.*, 242-263. Originals survive for the stipend of the duke of York, the household bills, the appointment of lords to guard the sea and the levy of the Poynyngs fines. (C., P. & C. P. 29/3, 4, 5; A. P. 1187 B and *R. P.*, V, 272).

ticular needs of the court or of the administration. Some of them were of importance, far surpassing in this any of the commons bills. Such especially were the appointment of York to be protector, the setting apart of revenue for the royal household and the provision for the safeguarding of the sea. Similarly important in the earlier sessions of 1453 were the provision for Calais and the levy of archers. Not only were such bills more responsive to the pressing needs of the moment than were the commons bills but they were more important than any of the five official bills which we have seen grouped as "communes petitions," except the bill punishing disregard of summons to appear before chancellor or council.

It thus becomes clear that the division of the parliament roll between bills which were described as commons petitions and those which were not did not arise from the significance of the bills themselves. A second criterion has failed to explain the facts. Neither the importance of the bills nor the contrast between commons bills and non-commons bills led the clerk to construct the roll as he did. We may, therefore, turn to a criterion which proved not inadequate in explaining the roll of 1509. This was, it will be remembered, the prospect which a bill had of becoming a statute. In 1509 bills which appropriately became statutes were grouped at the end of the roll as "communes petitiones," those which were unfitted to be such were enrolled before the caption.[38] If we consider the roll of 1453-4 from this point of view, we shall find that of its ten "communes petitions" nine appear on the statute roll as nine statutes. No other bills whatever became statutes.

The explanation which accorded well with the structure of the roll of 1509 thus seems to accord with the testimony of the roll of 1453-4. A possible perplexity might be the fact that one so-called commons petition of 1454 did not become a statute. This was the attainder of William Oldhall. But attainders were not appropriate subject matter for statutes. To be sure, Oldhall's attainder was preceded on the roll by a somewhat

[38] See above, pp. 17, n. 7, 30-33.

similar bill against Jack Cade which did become a statute. This bill, however, was actually different in that it provided that all Cade's "tirannie, actes, dedes and fals opinions be voied . . . And all such Enditementes . . . made under the power of his tirannie also be voidet. . . ." Such provisions had general import as perhaps affecting many men who may have been compromised during the days of Cade's triumph. Nothing of the sort characterized the bill against Oldhall, which confined itself to condemning him and pronouncing forfeiture of his property.

There remains the question why the bill against Oldhall should have been enrolled after rather than before a caption which, we seem to see, introduced prospective statutes. Why should it not have been enrolled earlier along with the somewhat similar bill about Robert Poynyngs? A possible answer is that it was closely associated with the bill against Cade and the clerk may have wished that the association be perpetuated in enrollment. The instance, however, forces us to modify the hypothesis that all bills grouped as commons petitions were destined to become statutes. Instead of all, we must say, nearly all. We shall sometimes find on other parliament rolls after the caption "communes petitions" bills like that against Oldhall which, although approved, did not become statutes. We shall also find so grouped bills which were refused. Thus the generalization that "communes petitions" in the fifteenth century were bills which were to become statutes is only approximately established. We may even find that it was more consistently characteristic of the second half of the century than of the first half. Nonetheless it is the generalization which seems better than any other to explain the facts.

The explanation, however, remains only a formal one unless we can discover what characteristics of a bill fitted it to become a statute. A close examination of this question would bring us to a study of the statute roll, an undertaking which must be postponed.[39] To guide us at the moment, however,

[39] See below, ch. XI.

we may hazard the surmise that the applicability of a bill to many people, in other words its general import, was what strengthened its candidacy for the statute roll. The bill against Cade became a statute for this reason. So with all other bills grouped as "communes petitions" on the roll of 1453-4. Whether they were genuine commons petitions or official bills or even private bills, all had in them an element of general applicability. To be sure, one commons bill referred to outlawries valid only in Lancashire, one official bill to the powers of the wardens of the Scottish marches and another official bill to the improper farming of the ulnage. Still the persons affected by each were considerable sections of the nation. More open to question might be the private bill asking remedy for the violence done to Dame Johane Beaumont. But the request was extended to provide a remedy "in all suche cases" and the bill thus became one of general applicability. There can be no doubt about the general applicability of the remaining four bills. Ambiguities in the act of resumption of 1450, remission for denizens of a surtax on wool, penalties for disregarding the summons of great or privy seal, and punishments for violations of safe conducts might affect many people. The requirement, therefore, that a bill which aspired to become a statute must have general applicability or at least applicability to some group within the nation was met by the nine "communes petitions" of the roll of 1453-4 which eventually found themselves on the statute roll.

If nearly all bills following the caption "communes petitions" were of general applicability, is it equally true, as our hypothesis would demand, that no bill preceding the caption had this characteristic, at least in a noteworthy degree? We have seen that several of them affected persons at court or at best lords who absented themselves from parliament. But several also were concerned with the defence of the country whether by a levy of archers or by the safeguarding of the sea or by the strengthening of Calais. Surely such measures were of wide import. It is true that they were, but also true that they were primarily administrative measures. They were to be carried out by the action of the administrative organs of the government, and particularly of the central government, not to be observed as rules of behaviour by the nation at large or by some fraction of it and to be enforced locally. No advantage would have been gained by transforming them into statutes which might become widely known. Even the penalization of lords who might fail to attend parliament was a bill of limited scope, clearly designed to increase the efficiency of the upper house. The statutory character of a bill arose largely from its being a modification of the law of the land, which henceforth the courts would apply. The nine bills which in this parliament became statutes possessed it, the other bills, official and private, did not. One of these might seem an exception, the repeal of the household act of 1450. Since, however, the act repealed was, because of its administrative character, not a statute, no statute was necessary to make it void. What the parliamentary records of 1453-4, therefore, seem to disclose is that the structure of the parliament roll was principally determined not by the grouping together of bills of the same technical sort but by attending to whether a bill was or was not of a certain character. Bills which were of general applicability and modified the law in a way cognizable by the courts were, regardless of their type, nearly always enrolled at the end of the roll under the caption "communes petitions"; bills which had not these characteristics but were of special application or were primarily administrative were, regardless of their importance, enrolled before the caption.

Deductions of such scope cannot, however, be made from the records of a single parliament. Is it true of other parliament rolls, as it is of that of 1453-4, that bills of various types were enrolled under the caption "communes petitions," that most of these became statutes, and that no bills of general applicability and hence anticipatory of statutes were enrolled before the caption in question? To test this hypothesis we may turn to the records of other parliaments of the years 1453-1465.

On the parliament roll of 1455-6 seven bills were enrolled as " communes petitions." [40] In point of fact only three of them were really commons bills. Two were official and two were private, one of the latter addressed to the commons, one to the king. The appearance among the seven of a private petition addressed to the king is for us a new but not an unexpected phenomenon. If a private bill addressed to the commons could be enrolled in a manner which suggested that it might become a statute, as happened in 1453-4, a private bill addressed to the king might presumably fare in the same way. The appearance of one here completes the four types of bills which might be enrolled as commons petitions. All of the seven so-called " communes petitions " of 1454-5 regardless of their type became statutes. The distinction was attained by no other bill of this parliament.

The content of each of the seven was of general import, although sometimes of not very wide import. The private petition to the king of the abbot of Fountains Abbey for protection in the local courts of northern counties might seem entirely personal. But the privilege of appearing in these courts by attorney was asked for, and the petitioner declared that this was a right secured him by " the commen lawe of England." Various irregularities in the administration of local justice were complained of and the bill concluded with the request that " every man who will sue [against offending bailiffs] mowe have a writt of Dett " to recover from them £20 to be divided between himself and the king. In two respects, therefore, the bill reached beyond the immediate interests of the abbot. Four of the other bills were of an application somewhat but not entirely restricted. They applied to particular classes of the population or to the inhabitants of particular counties. A private bill of the silk-women of London asked protection against the imports of Lombards and was granted

[40] *R. P.,* V, 322-327.

for five years. A commons bill urged that makers of malt in Kent be maintained in their industry and was also granted for five years. Another commons bill looked to the limitation of the number of attorneys in Norfolk and Suffolk on the ground that the attorneys resident there were too numerous and were altogether mischievous. An official bill repealed a statute of the preceding parliament which protected non-residents of Lancashire against indictments there and substituted for it a prescribed form of jury trial. Only two of the seven bills were of national scope. One was a commons petition directed against extortionate fees exacted by exchequer officials from sheriffs and other accountants, who in turn were led to exact "outerageous" fees from the king's liege people. The other was an official or perhaps a lords' petition that servants who despoiled their master's property after his death be held answerable in court to the executors of the estate. Although, therefore, the legislation embodied in the seven bills was not very important and although some of it was restricted to specified groups or communities, all of it was of wide enough import for the courts to take cognizance of its violation. For this reason it was permissible to group it as " communes petitions " which were convertible into statutes.[41]

The portion of the parliament roll of 1455-6 which preceded the caption "communes petitions" contained an unusual amount of narrative matter, much of which has been described above. It recorded, further, a general pardon also already referred to.[42] Finally, it enrolled four official bills, one private bill to the king, and one commons bill. Two of the official bills were concerned with the bestowal upon the young prince of Wales and duke of Cornwall of the lands respectively pertaining to these titles. Another set apart £4000 of revenue for the expenses of the household. A fourth provided for the pay-

---

[41] Another commons bill was granted but it was not enrolled and did not become a statute. It recited and repealed the limited act of resumption passed in the preceding parliament (see above, p. 87).

[42] See above, p. 38.

ment from the customs of a large sum due the staplers for loans advanced by them to pay the soldiers at Calais. The private bill to the king was also in favour of the staplers. It was a request that £2000 recently received by them from the victualler of Calais in fulfilment of a certain contract should be credited them since the soldiers at Calais had seized wool of this value and much more. All five bills, it is obvious, were concerned either with the affairs of the court or with the administration of Calais.[43] None was adapted to become a statute.

Most interesting and unusual of the bills preceding the caption " communes petitions " was the commons bill. On the preceding parliament roll no commons bill was so placed and verbal logic would frown on so placing one. If, however, the caption meant not that everything following it was a commons bill but rather a bill suited to become a statute, it would be logical and indeed requisite that a commons bill not suited to become a statute should be enrolled before the caption. The commons bill here in question was of this sort. It was a bill for the resumption of alienated crown property.[44] Primarily an administrative measure, it affected the exchequer on the one hand and on the other certain beneficiaries of royal favour. The latter were not the nation at large or any considerable fraction of it or any class. The bill did not modify the law of the land, nor would cases normally arise under it which would be brought before the common law courts. Once enforced, it exacted no new compliance with its provisions. Although so completely non-statutory in character it was nevertheless a measure which might properly originate with the commons. Since 1449 it had been current belief that a successful resumption of crown property would maintain the household and relieve the exchequer of a charge which at the time it was endeavouring to meet from other revenues. In 1449-50 a first bill of resumption and in 1451 a second one had been ap-

[43] R. P., V, 290-295, 297-300, 320.
[44] Ibid., pp. 300-320. Internal evidence shows that it dates from 1456.

proved. On both occasions the clerk of parliament, impressed with the fact that the petitions were commons bills, had enrolled them as such after the caption " communes petitions." But they had given rise to no statutes. Recalling this fact in 1456, the clerk now enrolled a third bill of resumption before the caption.[45] At best, the situation was anomolous. The bill was a commons bill but unlike most commons bills it was not to become a statute. So it was perhaps more logical to enroll it before rather than after the caption. In later parliaments there were other bills of resumption but by that time they had assumed the form of official bills. No longer was there doubt as to where they should be enrolled. Always they appeared, as did the one of 1456, before the caption, which, in any event, was no longer descriptive of them.[46] The two new features, therefore, which distinguished the parliament roll of 1455-6 from that of 1453-4, the enrollment of a commons petition before the caption and the introduction of a private bill to the king after it, confirm rather than weaken our generalization about the structure of the parliament roll. The caption did not divide commons bills from official and private bills. Before it and after it every sort of bill was enrolled. What determined the enrollment of a bill relative to the caption seems to have been its suitability to become a statute; and this in turn seems to have depended upon its being not of a purely personal or administrative character but of such general applicability to the nation or to a part of the nation that a violation of it might bring the offender before the courts.

The rolls of the four other parliaments of the years 1453-1465 largely confirm this generalization which has been based on the records of the first two of them. Most nearly in conflict with it are certain features of the roll of 1459. Since the proceedings of the parliament of that year were afterwards annulled and none of its acts enrolled on the statute roll, its " communes petitions " had no future. Of these there were

[45] *Ibid.*, pp. 183-199, 217-224, 300-320.
[46] *Ibid.*, pp. 514-548, 572-613.

six, of which four were commons bills, one an official bill and one a private bill to the king.[47]   The last two and one of the commons bills were of the sort which we have been led to expect to find in this part of the roll; but the other three bills were of such limited range that they seem scarcely the material from which statutes were made.

The private bill to the king was a group petition from all sheriffs asking that they be not penalized for continuing in office somewhat longer than a year, as a statute of 1445 provided they must not, and that the election of knights of the shire held by them during the prolongation of their term be valid.   Though a group petition, this had general import as validating the qualifications of many members of the commons. The official bill annulled letters patent granted to the king's enemies after the battles of St. Albans, Bloore Heath and Ludford, and this too was of general import.   Of the commons bills one voided letters patent which granted to sheriffs and other officials in Chester and Wales estate for life in their offices, maladministration being charged against them.   This bill, also, affected many people.   The three other commons bills, however, were of such limited range that we should not expect them to aspire to be statutes.   One favoured five esquires "with other" who had opposed the king at Ludford but had afterward sued for pardon, substituting fines for forfeiture of estates.   Another provided for the apprehension and punishment of twenty-five men charged with being notorious robbers and oppressors.   The third was an attainder of lord Stanley and failed to receive the king's assent.   Two of these bills affected few people, and the third only one person.

The explanation of this inclusion of bills of limited scope under the caption "communes petitions" must be that the caption still had some literal validity.   All commons bill would still normally be enrolled under it unless there was good reason for not doing so.   The only commons bill hitherto noted which was not enrolled after the caption is the bill of resump-

[47] *Ibid.*, pp. 366-370.

tion on the roll of 1455-6. There it was regarded as an administrative measure not to be embodied in a statute. But on the roll of 1449-50 a bill of the same sort had been enrolled as a commons bill although the resultant act did not become a statute. Very similar was the treatment of the attainder of lord Stanley. As a judicial procedure affecting one man its appropriate place was before the caption "communes petitions." An official bill of attainder against the duke of York and others on this same roll of 1459 was so enrolled. But the attainder of Stanley was in origin a commons bill and the clerk saw fit to put emphasis on this aspect of it in his record. The two other bills of limited scope likewise enrolled after the caption were also in essence judicial measures which would more properly have been enrolled before it. Yet the clerk preferred to regard them with technical accuracy as commons bills. We learn, therefore, from the roll of 1459 that commons bills not suited to become statutes might still be enrolled in the part of the roll which was set apart for bills likely to become such. The caption which introduced this part of the roll might still be followed by commons bills of every type, whether of general or of limited import.

Most petitions of limited scope on the roll of 1459 appear correctly enough before the caption. Here were enrolled an oath taken by loyal lords, five official bills and two private petitions to the king.[48] One of the latter was the request of Prince Edward for confirmation of his inheritance of the duchy of Cornwall and the other was the petition of the prior and convent of Sheen for confirmation of the gifts of Henry V. The most important of the official bills was the lengthy attainder of York and his supporters. Of the others, one arranged an exchange of lands between the king and queen, and two confirmed the gifts and privileges enjoyed respectively by the king's colleges of Eton and Saint Nicholas. A fifth bill, appointing new feoffees for the duchy of Lancaster, had, as enrolled, all the characteristics of an official bill but yet was said

[48] *Ibid.*, pp. 346-366.

to have been presented by the commons.[49]   Hence it presents an early and unusual instance of an official bill introduced in the commons rather than in the lords.   In all other respects the bills preceding the caption "communes petitions" were normal.   All of them were limited in scope or were primarily administrative in character or were both.   Thus the roll of 1459 accords with the generalizations which have been hazarded regarding the structure of the parliament roll.   Its only innovations are an official bill introduced in the commons, and three commons bills (including a bill of attainder) which asserted their right to be called "communes petitions" although they were limited in scope and unsuited to be statutes.   Which acts of this parliament might have become statutes we cannot tell since no statutes were ever enrolled.

The roll of the next parliament, that of 1460, differs from its contemporaries in not being divided into two parts by the caption "communes petitions."   It does, nevertheless, record at least two bills which could have been placed after such a caption since both became statutes.   One was a commons bill, the other a private bill to the king.[50]   The former requested that the parliament of 1459 and all its acts be void.   The second, after explaining the refusal of livery of the lands of Isabell Nevyll to herself and her husband and the necessity imposed on the two to give recognizances for £1000 to have livery, asked that women of fourteen years of age at the time of the death of their ancestors have henceforth prompt livery of their lands and that the recognizances given in this instance be void.   The petition is an interesting illustration of a private bill expanded into a request of general import.   The bill for the annulment of a parliament was of course of general import.   Why the two were not isolated as bills suitable to become statutes is not clear.   Perhaps it was because the bill of annulment had to be placed at the beginning of the roll in

---

[49] *Ibid.,* p. 352.   " Item quedam Cedula exhibita fuit . . . Regi . . . per Communitates Regni Anglie. . . ."

[50] *Ibid.,* pp. 374, 387.

order to give logical consistency to what followed. The bill
for livery of lands was, to be sure, entered at the end of the roll,
but it may have seemed curious to introduce a single private
bill by the caption " communes petitions."

The roll, as it happens, records two commons bills other than
the bill of annulment.[51]   If the usage of the parliament of
1459 had been followed, these might have been grouped under
a caption " communes petitions."   One of them, however, was
almost as unsuited to such grouping as were the three commons bills of 1459 which were of restricted scope.   With a
view to procuring ready money for the government's expenses,
it asked that all revenues of the duchy of Lancaster be turned
over to the exchequer and that all assignments on them made
before Halloween, 1460, be deferred for two years.   This was
primarily an administrative measure, although it did imply
relief from taxation.   The other bill requested the liberation
during the session of an imprisoned burgess entitled to the
privileges of the commons.   In earlier parliaments commons
bills touching the privileges of members were enrolled as such
and this one might well have been here.   But neither it nor
the revenue bill was suited to become a statute.   And this
unsuitability may have influenced the clerk to omit the caption " communes petitions," since only the private bill of Isabell Nevyll remained to be entered more or less appropriately
after it.

The other bills of this parliament were official bills and none
of them was of wide applicability.   One recorded the acceptance by the king of the agreement whereby the duke of York
and his heirs were to succeed him.   Another stipulated for the
duke and two of his sons an income of 10,000 marks yearly.
A third provided that sheriffs and other officials should attend
upon the duke, who would shortly ride to various parts of England and Wales to suppress disorder.   Two others related to
the duchy of Lancaster, one cancelling the recent creation of
new administrative offices and the other appointing new

[51] *Ibid.*, pp. 374, 383.

feoffees for a part of the duchy.[52]   Since all of the five were administrative in character, their enrollment without suggestion of their becoming statutes was appropriate.   The parliament roll of 1460 was therefore normal except insofar as it failed to make the usual division between bills of wide import and those of restricted import.

The roll of the first parliament of Edward IV held in 1461 resumed the usage of dividing its record by the caption " communes petitions."   To be sure only three bills were enrolled after this and only two of these became statutes.[53]   But the third like the other two was of general import and failed to become a statute through its rejection by the king.   It provided for the relief of the counties by the removal of certain existent charges upon the sheriffs' farms.   Of the other two, one required sheriffs to bring indictments made at their tourns before justices of the peace instead of themselves imprisoning and fining the accused.   The other affirmed at length the validity of all administrative, legislative and judicial acts of the three Lancastrian kings.   All were commons bills.   The harmony between the caption and the matter recorded under it was complete.

There were, however, two commons bills which were enrolled before the caption, a practice thus far noted only in the case of the bill of resumption of 1456.[54]   One of the two was a petition that three esquires, two gentlemen and one yeoman, who were not yet submissive to Edward IV, appear before the king's bench on penalty of being attainted of treason.   The bill was not essentially different from the three commons bills of the parliament of 1459 which were of limited scope and judicial in character yet were enrolled after the caption.   That this one was enrolled before it shows closer logic in separating bills of limited import from those of general import regardless of whether they were commons petitions or not.   The other com-

---

[52] *Ibid.*, pp. 379-387.
[53] C., P. & C. P. 52/8/1, 35/1, 2; *R. P.*, V, 489-495; *Stats.*, II, 380-391.
[54] C., P. & C. P. 52/8/9, 52/7; *R. P.*, V, 483, 463-475.

mons bill which appears on the roll of 1461 before the caption
could not well have been entered elsewhere. It asked that the
king's title to the crown be "accepted and reputed true and
rightwise"; and it thus served as an introduction to the work
of parliament by giving it validity.

Although phrased as a commons petition and sent on to the
lords with the usual superscription, this bill was in essence an
official one. A trace of official form crept into its phraseology.
Instead of beginning "Prayen the commons," it opened with
"Forasmuch" clauses and only later stated that the commons,
now having no doubt about the king's title, requested king
and lords to establish it. This tendency to put official bills in
the mouth of the commons is shown in an attenuated degree
by another bill of this parliament. In form it was an official
bill providing for the attainder of Sir John Skydmore. Yet
the original bill bears the superscription, "Soit baille as seigneurs," showing that it was introduced in the commons and
sent on to the lords.[55] We may readily explain this as appropriate treatment of an attainder, which by preference should
originate with the commons. Yet in the parliament of 1459
we have seen another kind of official bill, the appointment of
feoffees for the duchy of Lancaster, introduced in, or as the
roll has it, "presented by," the commons. Although the line
between commons bills and official bills was still sharp enough,
we may, none the less, expect to meet occasionally with an
official bill which was introduced in the commons, or even with
a commons bill which was very official in content and not
without a touch of official phraseology.

The remaining bills of the parliament of 1461 which were
enrolled before the caption "communes petitions" were of the
sort which belonged there. Three of them were official bills,
one was a private petition to the king, and two were private
petitions to the commons. Of the official bills one was the
attainder of Henry VI and certain of his supporters, another
the creation of an annuity for Cicily, duchess of York, and

[55] C., P. & C. P. 52/8/10; *R. P.,* V, 483.

the third a voidance of judgments of Henry IV and Henry V against the king's grandfather and other lords. Of the private bills, the one addressed to the king asked that judgment of treason against Sir Ralph Lumley be revoked and that his cousin Thomas inherit his lands. The private bill addressed to the commons by Sir James Strangways, Sir John Conyers and their wives begged for the restoration of certain manors in Ireland which had fallen into the king's hands through the forfeiture of one Sir Thomas Bathe to whom they had leased them. The third private bill, also addressed to the commons, was the request of the men of North Wales that, unless a certain David ap Jeũn Eynyon and his companions who had seized Harleigh castle and were taking over property delivered themselves up to the king's justice, they should be attaint of high treason.[56] The feature common to the six bills is the narrowness of their interests. Although the attainder of Henry VI and his supporters and the appeal of the men of North Wales touched the fortunes of small groups, even these bills were primarily administrative and scarcely fitted to become statutes.

At the end of the parliament roll of 1461 occurs a novel entry which is neither primarily narrative nor does it take the form of a bill. It is a declaration of the will of the sovereign pronounced without regard to the assent of lords or commons. Its enacting clause runs baldly "the Kyng . . . chargeth and commaundeth. . . ." It forbade the giving of liveries beyond certain limits, the maintenance of misdoers, the playing of cards by servants or in taverns, and it bade "almanere of men" to consider it their duty to bring criminals to the king's gaol. It ended with a warning that, if anyone whom the king has pardoned should prove disloyal, no second pardon would be forthcoming. This curious and unusual document was described by the chancellor in a speech proroguing parliament as certain "articles" which the king had all lords spiritual and temporal swear to observe and which he had publicly pro-

[56] C., P. & C. P. 52/8 nos. 11, 8, 6, 3, 5, 4; *R. P.*, V, 476-486.

claimed throughout the realm.[57]   The "articles" follow close
upon and are clearly somewhat related to another unique record of this parliament to which reference has already been
made.   This is a speech from the throne.   Apparently the
speech and the articles were expressions respectively of the
young sovereign's gratitude to his people for their welcome
and support and of his desire to restore order and right living.
Neither was repeated in later rolls and neither affected the
general structure of the roll.   In all other respects the roll of
1461 was a normal one, resembling the rolls of 1453-4 and
1455-6 and emphasizing their characteristics.

The second parliament of Edward IV consisted of two sessions separated from each other through repeated adjournments by two years.   The first extended from 29 April to 7
June, 1463; the second from 21 January, 1465 to a date not
indicated.   Contrary to usage the "communes petitions" of
the first session were enrolled before the record of the second
session was begun.   Since the description of each session is
complete in itself, it will be better to consider them separately.

Under the caption "communes petitions" there were enrolled as belonging to the first session two private bills addressed to the commons, and three commons bills.[58]   All
became statutes except a part of one of the commons bills.
Both of the private bills were group bills and hence of the sort
which were of general enough import to warrant enrollment
under the caption.   One was a petition of the silk-women of
London very like the earlier one of 1455-6, which had asked
for protection against the new imports of aliens and which had
been granted for five years only.   The bill of 1463 requested

[57] *Ibid.*, 487.   No original is preserved.

[58] A. P. 1411, 1412; C., P. & C. P. 35/5, 6, 7; *R. P.*, V, 501-507.   All the
originals survive except one membrane of the first bill.   On this was probably written the "Soit baille as seigneurs" which is found on commons
petitions, but is not on the second membrane.   That this membrane was
attached to another is clear from two perforations on the margin.   On the
first membrane was the bill about woolen cloths, on the second the bill
about wool.   The two were enrolled as one bill, the second beginning, "And
over this. . . ."   But to each a separate response was made.

a continuance of the protection, and to this king and lords assented. In the second private bill various artisans asked similar protection against the importation of a great variety of merchandise, whether the importers were aliens or denizens. Adding four provisos the king agreed.

One of the commons bills, too, was directed against imports, this time of wheat, rye and barley. It provided that none of these grains should be brought into the realm until the price exceeded 6 s. 8 d., 4 s. and 3 s., respectively. Another commons bill revived and extended ordinances restricting the kind and the costliness of apparel, complaining of the " inordynat Aray" of all classes. The third commons bill was in two parts, each virtually an independent bill. One part asked that during three years all exported wools except those grown in northern counties be taken to Calais, that no alien export them, that one-half of the money received from their sale be brought into England (any plate or bullion being coined at Calais), that they be not mixed with inferior wool and that they be exported in the ships of denizens if such provided adequate carrying capacity. The other part related to the making of woolen cloths. It specified the length and breadth of various sorts, provided for the appointment of ulnagers to seal them, stipulated that cloth workers be fully paid in money and given wool of proper weight and, finally, prohibited the sale of woolen cloths of foreign manufacture. All of these commons bills, as well as the two group bills, were obviously of general import. It was appropriate that they should be enrolled as they were under the caption which introduced bills of this sort. It was appropriate, too, that they should become statutes. In point of fact all of them did except the cloth bill.[59] As it happened, this was recast in the session of 1465 and in its revised form appeared on the statute roll along with the other statutes of the later session.

The only enrollments preceding the " commons petitions " in the record of the session of 1463, apart from a rather

[59] *Stats.* II, 392-407.

lengthy calendar, were a subsidy indenture and an official bill modifying it in two respects. Since both were what we should expect to find here, we may pass at once to the second session of this parliament, that of 1465.

Under the caption "communes petitions" in this part of the roll were enrolled twelve bills. Two of them were refused by the king but all of the others became statutes.[60] If the ten were worthy of this distinction, they should, according to our thesis, have been bills of general import. Of the twelve, seven were commons bills, two official bills and three private bills. The last were group bills, two of them addressed to the commons and one to the king.

The group petition to the king was from the mayor and commonalty of Dover asking that the town might have a monopoly of all traffic from Kent to Calais except the passage of soldiers and of merchants carrying merchandise. Of the group petitions to the commons, one from the horners of London requested that the materials from which horns were made should not be sold to aliens, and one from the patyn-makers of the same city begged that a statute forbidding them to make their wares from "tymbre of aspe" be repealed. The three were of as wide import as group petitions usually were. The two official bills were of interest to traders throughout the realm. One imposed penalties for the shipment of wool, other than wool of the northern counties, from Newcastle to ports other than Calais; the second made easier for alien merchants the giving of surety that they would expend money received from the sale of their wares in buying commodities of the realm.

Of the seven commons bills one was a slightly expanded form of the bill of 1461 which had asked for the cancellation of certain charges upon the sheriff's farm, a request now as then refused. Another bill refused was an appeal for the

[60] All survive in their original form and all bear the usual inscriptions. C., P. & C. P. 35/14-23; A. P. 1421, 1422; *R. P.,* V, 561-570; *Stats.* II, 403-418.

removal of obstacles to traffic on the river Severn, whether these were weirs and mills or whether they were the requisitions of owners of the banks of the stream. While two commons bills were refused five were granted. The first was the revised cloth bill of the earlier session already referred to. Another prohibited cordwainers and cobblers in or near London from selling shoes or boots on Sundays and on certain feast days, and from making them with a pyke longer than two inches. Two other bills were concerned respectively with the buying and shipping of wool. To protect clothmakers against shortage of wool arising from "subtiell bargeyns made in biyng of Wooles or that the Shepe that beren it be shorn," it was asked that none except clothmakers might during three years be permitted to buy unshorn wool earlier than St. Bartholomew's day. And to insure that all wool save that of the northern counties and that which would pass through the straits of "Marrok" be shipped from the customs ports to Calais, a bill requested that surety be furnished by shippers that they would do this in future and further that they present certificates got at Calais that they had done so. Finally, a commons bill looked toward retaliation against the duke of Burgundy. Since the duke had forbidden the sale of English cloth or yarn in his lands, it was asked that no Burgundian merchandise be admitted to England, Wales or Ireland until the duke withdrew his prohibition. This was as close an approach to the regulation of foreign affairs as the commons ever made. Its justification, of course, was the disaster wrought in English industry by the exclusion of English cloth from a profitable market.

Nearly all the "communes petitions" of 1465, whether private bills, official bills or commons bills, which received the king's approval and became statutes, were concerned with industry or trade. To be sure, two rejected commons bills related to the burden of the sheriffs' farm and to impeded traffic on the Severn and one approved bill touched upon passenger traffic between Dover and Calais. But of the other approved bills three related to London crafts, three to the clothmaking industry, two to the wool trade and one to alien traders in England. If we are correct in thinking that "communes petitions" were bills of general import intended to become statutes, it is clear that, insofar as general legislation was sought and secured in the 1465, it was concerned almost exclusively with industry or trade. Much the same was true of the legislation of 1463. Two of the five "communes petitions" of the year came from artisan groups, one touched the wool trade, and a fourth protected growers of English corn. Only the last and the bill regarding apparel were not industrial or commercial. Bills of general import in the parliament of 1463-5 were, therefore, very largely bills for the regulating or protecting or fostering of industry or trade.

In the session of 1465 the bills enrolled before the caption "communes petitions" comprised a subsidy bill in the form of an indenture, four private bills and three official bills. Of the private bills, all of which were addressed to the king, one asked that Henry Wentworth inherit the lands forfeited through the attainder of his father, another that an attainder pronounced against the earl of Oxford in the time of Henry IV be void, a third that the king confirm documents bestowing lands upon the monastery of Sion, and a fourth that the annual rent paid by the borough of Plymouth to the priory of Plympton be reduced by some £12. All of these requests affected few persons except the petitioners. Of the three official bills one was similar in content to a private bill in that the king restored to Anne, duchess of Exeter, the lands of her husband, who had been attainted. Another was the attainder of the duke of Somerset and of certain other adherents of Henry VI, who, although pardoned after a first attainder, had proved disloyal to Edward IV. The third was a long bill of resumption.

The last differed from the three bills of resumption which have already been referred to in being an official bill. We have noted that the first two bills of this sort, adopted in the parliaments of 1449-50 and 1451 respectively, were commons bills and, although they were not made into statutes, were enrolled after the caption " communes petitions "; and we have seen that the next bill of resumption, adopted in 1456, was similar except that it was enrolled before the caption.[61] In the last instance the clerk, in changing from one method of enrollment to another, shifted the emphasis from the origin of the bill as a commons petition to its administrative features. With the fourth bill of resumption in 1465 the official origin of the measure as well as its administrative character at length divorced it from commons bills.   Inasmuch as royal grants made since Edward's accession were the subject of the resumption, it looks as if the act was a means not so much of recovering sources of income as of forcing recent grantees to compound for the retention of their grants.   The lists of provisos attached to two of the earlier bills exempting certain persons from their provisions formed precedents for a new series of exemptions.   So far as the place of the bill on the parliament roll is concerned, nothing could be more normal than that an official administrative bill should be enrolled as it here is.   Divested now of all features of a commons bill, it appeared appropriately in advance of the caption under which commons bills were usually grouped.   Later bills of resumption resembled this one in their official character and in the manner of their enrollment.   It turns out that we have unwittingly followed the transformation of bills of resumption from commons bills into official ones.   Under no circumstances were they commons bills of a sort which could be enrolled with a prospect of becoming statutes.   Although the earlier of them had legislative aspects, as an endeavour of the commons to lessen the burden of taxation, they were essentially administrative measures and, when this aspect of them became fully revealed, they ceased first to be enrolled as commons bills and then to be drafted as such, assuming at length all features of administrative measures.

[61] See above, p. 100.

The enrolled record of both sessions of the parliament of 1463-5 thus confirms conclusions first derived from an examination of the parliament roll of 1453-4 and strengthened by an examination of the four intervening rolls. These may be briefly recapitulated. The normal parliament roll of the middle of the fifteenth century was divided into two parts by a caption which declared that what it introduced were "communes petitions." The caption, which was not a recent one, pointed to a time when all or nearly all of the petitions following it were probably commons bills. By the years 1453-1465 this was no longer the case. It was then true, to be sure, that nearly all commons bills were enrolled after the caption. The only exemptions which we have noted were a commons bill of resumption in 1455, a petition at the beginning of the first parliament of Edward IV that his title be affirmed, and a bill in the same parliament attainting Sir John Skydmore. The first was essentially an administrative measure and was in later parliaments enrolled as such; the second could not well have been recorded except at the beginning of the roll; the third was a kind of bill which, like the bill of resumption, was in process of changing from a commons bill to an official bill.[62] Although practically all commons bills were enrolled after the caption appropriate to them, other bills which were not commons bills were also enrolled there. This is perhaps the most important revelation of our study of the parliament roll; for, while it need not greatly surprise us that private bills which were really group bills should be enrolled along with commons bills, it is surprising to find official bills so enrolled. Even if the official bills be looked upon as lords

[62] In the parliament of 1453-4 the attainder of Cade was a commons bill, but that of Oldhall an official bill couched in commons' phraseology. In 1459 the attainder of the duke of York was an official bill, that of lord Stanley a commons bill. In the parliament of 1463-5 attainders were official bills. In the parliament of 1461, while the attainder of Henry VI and his supporters was an official bill, that of Sir John Skydmore was still phrased as a commons petition but somewhat illogically was not so enrolled (*R. P.*, V, 476, 483).

bills which in virtue of acceptance by the commons were presented to the king as commons bills, the caption would be misleading; for it makes no mention of approved bills originating
elsewhere and declares that what follows were commons petitions, implying that they originated with the commons. This
grouping of official bills with the commons bills was thus in
disregard of the caption and perhaps of tradition. Official bills
could readily have been enrolled and often were enrolled before the caption. Some potent motive determined the clerk's
practice. An examination of the content of all the bills of
1453-1465 grouped after the caption, of whatever type they
may be, points to the conclusion that the guiding principle was
an endeavour to group together bills of general import the
provisions of which would have to be widely observed. The
commons bills, the private bills and the official bills introduced
as " communes petitions " were bills affecting either groups of
some size or the nation at large.[63] They were seldom merely
administrative measures or bills of special application but were
suitable for drafting and proclaiming as statutes. In fact
nearly all of them became statutes. In these years only those
which did not receive royal approval, together with the bill
for Oldhall's attainder and the bills for resumption in
1450 and 1451, failed of this distinction. The clerk in
making up his roll seems to have disregarded the origin of
bills and to have looked only to their future. In later parliaments, to be sure, especially in those of Richard III and
Henry VII, when official bills came to predominate over commons bills, we shall find that a few of the former, although
enrolled as " communes petitions " and enacted as statutes,
affected rather few persons or were primarily administrative
in character.[64] Occasionally, too, commons bills, although of
very narrow application, became statutes.[65] Thereby it appears that our explanation of why an approved bill, whether a

[63] The marked exception was the bill for the attainder of Oldhall.
[64] See below, pp. 139, 147, 153.
[65] See below, pp. 131, 132, 146.

commons bill or an official one, was thought suitable to become a statute has not complete validity. On the whole, however, it is subject to comparatively few exceptions—not to more than are most generalizations of wide scope; and it further accords with what was thought in the fourteenth century to be one of the characteristics of a statute.[66]

[66] See below, pp. 385-86.

CHAPTER VI

COMMONS BILLS AND OFFICIAL BILLS IN THE SECOND HALF
OF THE FIFTEENTH CENTURY

THE prolonged study of the structure of the parliament roll undertaken in the last chapter would scarcely have been warranted, had it merely added to our knowledge of diplomatics. Even its most important outcome, the discovery of what sort of bills were grouped as " communes petitions " and why they were so grouped, would be of little more than antiquarian interest if it had no application. As it happens, however, this discovery has a bearing upon a significant aspect of parliamentary history; for it may be utilized to estimate the influence of the house of commons upon late fifteenth-century legislation. So long as we are misled into thinking that all " communes petitions " were commons bills and that the legislation resultant upon their acceptance was legislation initiated by the commons, we are likely to overestimate the influence of that body. When we realize, on the other hand, that only a part of the " communes petitions " were commons bills and that only the statutes arising from this part originated with the commons, we are in a position to estimate at its true value the commons' contribution to statutory law. We may, therefore, attempt an application of our new-found criterion to the records of the parliaments of the second half of the century. It will be permissible to disregard that part of the parliament roll which precedes the caption " communes petitions " unless, as rarely happens, it records a commons bill or some other type of bill which became a statute. Since private bills were for the most part enrolled here, they will be automatically neglected. Official bills, on the other hand, whether enrolled before or after the caption, will demand close attention; for, if legislation arising from them should prove to be more important than legislation arising from commons bills, we shall be face to face with a significant relation between the commons, on the one hand, and the king, the council and the lords on the other. Our concern in this chapter, therefore, will be the influence of the commons upon legislation in the second half of the fifteenth century as revealed by such of their bills as became statutes after acceptance by king and lords and, in contrast, the prevalence and importance of the official bills of king, council and lords which, when accepted by the commons, likewise became statutes.

The legislation of the second half of the fifteenth century, in so far as it was enacted from 1453 to 1465, we have already surveyed. A word may be permitted in summary of the part of it which arose from commons bills and of the part which arose from official bills. Equally pertinent to an estimate of the influence of the lower house is a consideration of such commons bills as were presented to king and lords but were rejected. The originals of certain rejected bills have survived and some of them have been printed by the editors of the *Rotuli*. All will furnish data for our inquiry.

Of the nine statutes enacted by the parliament of 1453-4 four arose from commons bills. Of these, one was the attainder of Cade, another removed ambiguities in the act of resumption of 1450, a third limited the scope of judgments pronounced in Lancashire against non-residents of the county, and a fourth remitted for denizens certain new increases in the customs rates.[1] The last was perhaps the most noteworthy of four rather insignificant statutes. Yet in this parliament the commons had presented five important bills, all of which had been refused.[2] One of the latter, noting the scarcity of money within the realm, asked the king that it be lawful for his "liege peple to sette at werk" silver mines in the four counties of the southwest, rendering to king, prince and owner of the soil the

---

[1] Ten shillings the sack added to the wool subsidy, and the extension to denizen cloths of 12 d. the £, which constituted poundage.

[2] C., P. & C. P. 29/19-22, 24; *R. P.*, V, 272-277.

fractional part of the output which was appropriate for each. The refusal must have been due to a wish to retain the control of the silver mines and the profits arising therefrom in the monopolistic hands of the duchy of Cornwall, to which most of them belonged. A more important bill, also refused, was directed against the alleged misuse of fifteenths and tenths. It asked that anyone purchasing or accepting any assignment or letters patent on the lay fifteenth just granted or on the clerical tenth recently granted, except in return for money lent, should forfeit a sum equal to the assignment; and further that collectors of the subsidies should account promptly at the exchequer without being subjected to a demand for fees by exchequer officials. Since the government was unwilling to enact a remedy for the serious abuses alleged, the implication is that it was inclined to override protest against its own shortcomings.

Three other bills presented by the commons and likewise refused involved the interests of the staple. It will be remembered that the staple itself presented to the king a private bill divided into six parts each formulating a request.[3] Two of these requests, relating respectively to the safeguarding of Calais and to the payment of a debt of 12000 marks, were satisfactorily answered by official bills. A third, asking the remission of ten shillings recently added to the wool subsidy, was also embodied in a commons bill, which, as has just been noted, was approved. The three other requests of the staplers were closely connected with the three commons bills which were refused. One request was that all wool save that passing through the straits of Marrok be shipped to Calais, implying that no royal licence should be granted to ship wool elsewhere. The king's reply was that he would grant no licence without the advice of his council. The corresponding commons bill, which was refused, formulated the same request at much greater length, attacked directly the granting of licences and provided specific penalties for anyone who might secure

[3] See above, p. 9; R. P., V, 256.

such a licence. It thus appears that the commons could put forward as their own a bill devised in the interests of the staple. But it is also clear that the government was unwilling altogether to forego the granting of licences which it undoubtedly found profitable. The last two requests of the staple were openly directed against commons bills which, the authors say, had been presented in this parliament. One was a bill fixing the prices at which wool intended for export should be bought in various wool-growing counties. Inasmuch as these prices were, for the buyer, minimum ones, their enactment would have been a burden upon the staplers. The bill was in the interest not only of wool growers but also of cloth workers, since it provided that wool intended for the manufacture of cloth at home might be bought for less than the specified prices. Whereas in the bill against licences the staplers were not successful in overcoming government resistance, in securing the rejection of this bill, as they did, they scored a triumph over the clothworkers. The last of their requests was directed against a commons bill which provided that at Calais anyone selling wool should make partition of his profits among all wool merchants of the realm there. To this request the lords replied that on the advice of the justices they had given consideration to an act of partition passed in 1429 in accordance with which partition of profits at Calais was to be made only among wool merchants of the same county as the seller. This arrangement the king and the lords wished continued. A third commons bill, therefore, was rejected both because the staple appealed against it and because the lords pronounced for the continuance of the accustomed usage.

This brief consideration of commons bills rejected in the parliament of 1453-4 has disclosed points of interest. The five so rejected were more important for the welfare of the realm than the four commons bills which were approved, unless it be that one of the latter ranks with them. Three of the five — those touching the working of silver mines, the remedy of abuses in collecting subsidies and the restraint of licences for shipping wool elsewhere than to Calais — were contrary to the interests or at least to the inclinations of the government and were probably rejected for this reason. The two others, which concerned the supply of wool for cloth workers and looked to the more extended sharing of profits at Calais, were in conflict with the interests of the staplers, who apparently had influence with the government or with the lords. We must conclude, therefore, that, if a commons bill in 1453-4 ran counter to the inclinations of the government or to the wishes of the powerful body of staplers, it had slight chance of passage, the former influence taking precedence of the latter. Only where the commons' requests were innocuous or relatively trivial were they approved and enacted as statutes.

The parliament of 1455-6 showed striking similarities to its predecessor in the character both of the commons bills which it approved and of those which it rejected. The former were few and comparatively insignificant; the latter were numerous and important. It will be remembered that of the seven statutes enacted by this parliament three arose from commons bills.[4] Two of them were distinctly restricted in their provisions, protecting makers of malt in Kent and limiting the number of attorneys in Norfolk and Suffolk. The third strove to correct an administrative abuse, the exaction by exchequer officials of fees from sheriffs, escheators and other ministers and of other fees for enrolling pleas and entering pardons or writs. A petition of the preceding parliament had noted the same extortion relative to collectors of subsidies and had been rejected. The bill of 1455-6 was grudgingly granted. It was to become effective only if the council took no other "direction" in the matter before Michaelmas and then only for five years. This limited concession was the only one of consequence secured by the commons in 1455-6.

Eleven commons bills were at the same time rejected.[5] Two of them were of limited scope but several of the others were

---

[4] See above, pp. 98-9.
[5] C., P. & C. P. 30/7, 9-17, 20. All are printed in *R. P.*, V, 328-336.

wide-reaching. Of the two, one asked for the imprisonment of Sir William Bonville until tried by a commision of oier and terminer on the ground that his factiousness was disturbing the peace of the southwestern counties; the other fined and punished Thomas Thorp and William Joseph for alienating the king from the duke of York and the earls of Warwick and Salisbury. Three other bills embodied the peculiar interests of the staplers and were closely related to bills of the preceding parliament. One asked that the remission of ten shillings from the recently increased wool subsidy which had been granted in the preceding parliament for five years might continue "duryng the tyme of the said graunte"; [6] a second changed the request, vainly made in 1453-4, that there be no further issue of licences to ship wool elsewhere than to Calais into a request that anyone who since 1441 had shipped wool in virtue of such licences or had shipped wool in the king's name or who should in the future do either of these things should pay four marks for every sack so exported; [7] a third bill applied the last provision to John Ward, who had recently exported 1226 sacks of wool in the king's name, by requiring that he now pay therefor four marks the sack. As a matter of fact the increased rates of subsidy mentioned in the first of these bills was never collected.[8] But the government's unwillingness to limit its prerogative to grant licences for the shipment of wool elsewhere than to Calais remained unchanged. To this extent the commons failed to secure for the staplers the coveted monopoly.

Six other commons bills rejected in the parliament of 1455-6 looked to the relief of larger sections of the population. Two of them aimed at the increase of the royal revenue by a recovery of alienated sources of income, thereby relieving the king's subjects of taxation. In one case it was income from the

[6] Likewise the remission of the 12 d. the £ on cloth exported by denizens, an extension of poundage granted in 1453-4 and at the same time remitted for three years (*ibid.*, pp. 269, 331).

[7] *Ibid.*, pp. 273, 330.

[8] The enrolled customs accounts show that it was remitted.

shires, such as dues from liberties, hundreds and leets, alienated since the beginning of the reign; in the other it was the king's profits from wardship and marriage which had been transferred to others since 1449 without adequate payment. Of both bills it is recorded that the lords as well as the king disapproved, the second being designated by the lords as unreasonable.[9] Probably by the approval of either bill they would have sacrificed perquisites which they had secured.

Two proposed bills would have protected the industrial population, especially against alien merchants. One of them, attributing the low price of wool to the purchase of it by woolpackers acting for alien merchants, whereas they should have been impartial judges between buyer and seller, limited the purchases of each packer to four sacks. The other, declaring that alien merchants travelling freely through the realm exploited its poverty by buying cloth or having it made at a low price, stipulated that henceforth such merchants purchase cloth only at Winchester or at the ports which the galleys frequented. In the preceding parliament the clothmakers' bill, safeguarding their supply of wool, had been rejected because of the protest of the staple. The present bill conflicted with the interests of alien merchants, who must have acquired influence with the government or with the lords comparable with the influence of the staple; for they now secured the rejection of two bills by which wool-growers and cloth workers respectively strove to protect the prices of their products.

Two of the rejected bills of 1455-6, finally, aimed to protect the population at large by the reform of judicial procedure. One asked that justices of the peace be empowered to secure release on bail and later to hear the case against a person accused, it would seem maliciously, of felony and therefor detained in gaol. The other was directed against criminous clerks who were said to put aside money "to be dispended for their purgation." It requested that a criminous clerk, once committed to the ordinary and by him discharged and then

[9] *R. P.,* V, 328, 330.

again indicted of felony, be held for high treason, elaborate provision being appended for identifying him as the perpetrator of the second offence. Why the first of these bills was refused is not clear. The government may have disliked the implication that its sheriffs and other ministers were party to the accusing and imprisoning of people maliciously. The second bill by denying to a clerk a second trial before the ordinary would have diminished the privileges of the church. Clerical influence may have accounted for its rejection.

The outcome of our examination of the twelve commons bills rejected in the parliament of 1455-6 reveals that most of them were considerably more significant than were the commons bills which were approved. Whereas little more than the restraint of exchequer officials was granted the commons, there was denied them, apart from favours asked for staplers, a reduction of taxation through a recovery of alienated sources of royal revenue, a measure of protection against what was thought to be the capitalistic oppression of alien merchants and finally a better administration of justice both as regards possibly unjust detention in prison and as regards the eventual punishment of insolently criminous clerks. Even more than in the parliament of 1453-4 commons requests were disregarded. Later we shall have to inquire what attention was given to commons bills in the first half of the fifteenth century. So far as concerns these two parliaments of the middle of the century, both largely under the influence of the duke of York, it is clear that the commons, although far from silent in voicing their requests, were given little satisfaction.

For the four other parliaments of 1453-1465, the activities of which as recounted on the parliament roll we have examined with some care, no rejected commons bills survive other than those enrolled. From these, however, we can ascertain in a measure what requests the commons made and which of them were acceded to. Of the four commons bills granted in the inconsequential Coventry parliament of 1459, three were directed to the punishment of offenders, many of whose names were given and whose offenses were largely political. A fourth touched upon maladministration in Cheshire and Wales. Even had any of them become a statute and had not the proceedings of the parliament been annulled, the bills would have shown little more than the government's utilization of the commons to punish political opponents.[10]

Government influence again, we have surmised, lay behind one of the commons bills approved in the parliament of 1460. It was the bill annulling the acts of the Coventry parliament. Of the two other commons bills of the parliament of 1460, one requested and secured the temporary release of an imprisoned member of the house. The other, though seemingly an administrative measure, would have been to the advantage of the nation had it been unconditionally approved. It provided that all income from the duchy of Lancaster be made available for two years at the exchequer to remedy somewhat the existing dearth of revenue. The total net income of the duchy amounted to upwards of £5,000, but at least three-fifths of it had been alienated to a group of feoffees. On the part not alienated annuities and part of the queen's dower had been assigned.[11] The king, replying to the petition, agreed to it " savyng alway that it extend not to enything of the seid Duchie . . . put in feoffement." By this exception the intent of the bill was largely nullified so that it was reduced to little more than the suspension of a few assignments. Thus limited in application it added little to the government's annual revenue. In this parliament, therefore, as in those of 1453-4 and 1455-6, what was of moment to the commons was practically refused, while minor petitions were granted.

In 1461 commons bills ostensibly fared better. Of the five which were technically such, only one was rejected. Of the two, however, which were enrolled before the caption usually introducing commons bills, one was of very restricted scope

---

[10] A commons bill accusing and impeaching lord Stanley was, however, rejected (*ibid.*, p. 369).

[11] Accounts of the receiver-general of the duchy, P. R. O., D. Lanc. 28/5.

(demanding the appearance of six men in court) and the other affirmed the title of the king. A third bill, looking to the validation of the administrative, legislative and judicial acts of the Lancastrian kings, could scarcely have been rejected. Of the remaining two, that which transferred certain jurisdiction from sheriffs to justices of the peace was the outstanding concession to the commons; for a fifth bill, which requested relief for the counties by the cancellation of burdensome charges on the sheriff's farms, was rejected. Actually, therefore, the balance between what was granted the commons in 1461 and what was refused them was not very uneven.

In the parliament of 1463-5, the records of which we have already examined, three commons bills were approved in the first session and five in the second, while in the second session two other commons bills were rejected.[12] The approved bills looked largely to the protection of certain agricultural, industrial and mercantile elements of the population. One forbad imports of grain when prices fell below specified figures; one required good cobbling of shoes; one formulated regulations touching the manufacture and sealing of cloths and the payment of clothworkers; one forbad the purchasing of futures in wool except by clothworkers during a period of three and one-half years; one prohibited the importation of Burgundian merchandise so long as Burgundian markets were closed to English cloth; two succeeded, where bills of 1453-4 and 1455-6 had failed, in insisting that wool be shipped to Calais, but avoided the delicate subject of royal licences; finally, approval was given to a bill limiting the costliness of apparel, which was presented on the ground that " excessive Arayes " impoverished the realm, enriched strange realms and destroyed husbandry. Of the bills rejected one asked the removal of obstacles to navigation on the Severn, the other the cancellation of certain charges on the sheriff's farm, which greatly

---

[12] See above, pp. 109-12. Another commons bill, not enrolled, repaired the omission of the exemption of Yarmouth in the current grant of a fifteenth and tenth. It is wrongly printed as of 1474 (*R. P.*, VI, 166).

reduced its possible contribution to the revenue. The last bill had in simpler form been refused in 1461. Apparently the charges in question could not be shifted to other revenues and the government felt that it could not in good faith to the beneficiaries cancel them. Probably the same respect for vested rights lay behind the refusal to legislate against owners of the banks of the Severn. Apart from the rejection of these two bills the attitude of the king and lords in 1463-5 was distinctly favourable to the requests of the commons. A half dozen measures of considerable importance to large classes of the population were enacted and were duly proclaimed as statutes.

Before leaving the parliaments of the years 1453-1465 we may profitably inquire whether there is discernible in their proceedings any tendency to replace commons bills by official bills as a basis for legislation. One step suggesting this has already been noted. We have seen that in 1465 the act of resumption of the year was for the first time drafted as an official bill, not as a commons bill, which had been the form assumed by its three predecessors.[13] The next bill of resumption under Edward IV, that of 1467, was also an official bill; and the parliament roll carefully records that it was taken to the commons who assented to it in the words, "A toutz les Actez et Provisions desuis escriptez les Communes sount assentuz."[14] After this all bills of resumption were official bills. The commons no longer took the initiative in proposing them but acquiescently recorded their approval. Such a transformation in the character of so important a series of bills suggests that under Edward IV official bills may have tended in a measure to supersede commons bills as the basis of statutes. Since the change, however, in the case of acts of resumption, did not occur until 1465, it may not, if it did extend to other bills, be particularly apparent before that date.

As a matter of fact, the official bills which were enrolled as

---

[13] See above, pp. 113-14.
[14] *R. P.*, V, 572-613.

"communes petitions" in the parliaments of 1453-1465 and afterward became statutes were not numerous or significant. Although several official bills were enrolled before the caption on one parliament roll or another and were important administrative measures, they did not give rise to statutes and were not in this rivals of commons bills. Of the official bills which did become statutes, the parliament of 1453-4 furnished four, that of 1455-6 two, that of 1459 none, the next parliament and the first session of the next none and the session of 1464-5 two. All told there were eight of them in contrast with the twenty commons bills which, we have seen, were enacted as statutes in the same parliaments. Nearly all of the eight, being concerned with the execution of the law, originated appropriately enough with the government. Those of 1453-4 provided that the appointment of farmers of ulnage be not for life or term of years without the approval of the treasurer of England, that wardens of the northern marches summon to their courts only inhabitants of the counties over which they had authority, that violators of the king's safe-conduct be answerable in chancery and that disregard of a summons to appear before chancellor or council render the offender liable to further summons and to loss of titles, privileges and property.[15] One of the two official bills of 1455-6 made liable to summons before the king's bench servants who riotously despoiled their master's property at the time of his death; and the other repealed a commons bill of the preceding parliament touching the jurisdiction of the palatinate of Lancaster. Finally, of the two official bills of 1465, one forbad the shipment of wool, except the inferior wool of northern counties, from Newcastle to any port except Calais; and the other modified in favour of alien merchants the security which they were obliged to give that they would purchase commodities of the realm.

Of these eight bills the only ones which could be looked upon as belittling the commons' influence on legislation were the repeal of a commons' measure relative to the county of

[15] *Ibid.*, pp. 266-268.

Lancaster and the relaxation of the demands made upon alien merchants, to whom the commons were usually hostile. The forbidding of the smuggling of northern wool might have been prompted by the staplers, although the provision for the punishment of the riotous servants may well have originated in the lords. Most important of the non-commons bills were those directed against contempt of the king's authority — the violation of safe-conducts and the disregard of writs of great and privy seal. The last reflected earlier and foreshadowed later official legislation against insolence and disorder. But in general there was no marked tendency to supersede commons bills by official bills as a source of statutory legislation. So far as the legislative authority of the commons was concerned, the most serious threat to it during the years 1453-1465 lay in the rejection of several commons bills in the parliaments of 1453-4 and 1455-6 and in the transference to the government in 1465 of the initiative in introducing bills of resumption. In 1463-5 statutory legislation still for the most part originated with the commons; and, although considerable of it reflected the interests of wool exporters and clothworkers, some of it was of national scope and importance.

During the remainder of the reign of Edward IV the stream of legislation shrank as it had never done during so long a period in the fifteenth century. Not only were few commons bills and official bills approved by parliament but few were introduced. The commons bills rejected, so far as they survive, were scarcely more than a half dozen and these largely from the parliament of 1467-8. Commons bills approved from 1467 to 1483 were twenty-six, four of them being passed in the parliament of 1467-8, nine in the parliament of 1472-4, nine in 1478 and four in 1483. Official bills approved in the same four parliaments numbered respectively two, seven, one and two. Of private or group bills which gave rise to statutes, three were passed in the first of these parliaments, one in the third and two in the fourth.

What interests us most is the character of the commons bills.

In the parliament of 1467-8 eight such were introduced but only four were approved.[16] Of the four, three were of local or transient import. One extended the powers of the wardens of the worsted workers in Norwich and Norfolk, first conferred in 1444 and directed toward bettering the quality of worsteds; [17] one pardoned sheriffs who had continued in office for longer than a year in the troubled period, 1461-1464; and one appointed a committee of lords and commons to examine a charge against the master of the mint since the commons themselves had not time to consider it. The fourth bill prohibited the exportation of woolen yarn and unfulled cloth. None of the four was of national import and only the first and the last affected a group as large as the cloth-workers.

On the other hand three of the four rejected commons bills were of considerable scope. If it would perhaps have been extreme to declare that theft of sacred vessels from churches was high treason, as the fourth rejected bill asked, the three other requests were not unreasonable. One of them had already been granted in 1464 — a prohibition for three and one-half years of the purchase of futures in wool except by cloth-workers. Now the continuance of this regulation until the next parliament was refused, clearly a rebuff to the cloth workers and an encouragement to the wool dealers. The two other rejected bills had been introduced in earlier parliaments, on which occasions they had likewise been rejected.[18] One would have given to justices of the peace power to release on bail men held in gaol on questionable suspicion of felony.[19] The other requested the cancellation or at least the investigation of certain charges upon the sheriff's farm, since these, it was

[16] Ibid., V. 619-622, 629-635.

[17] This might well have been a group bill. It was like another bill of this parliament which regulated the length and breadth of cloths in Norfolk, Suffolk and Essex and was introduced as a group bill (ibid., p. 629).

[18] The first in 1455-6, the second in 1461 and in fuller form in 1465 (ibid., pp. 332, 494, 568).

[19] It extended the provisions of the earlier bill by authorizing justices of the peace to name a coroner to hear the testimony of " provers," accused men giving evidence against others accused (ibid., pp. 332, 620).

alleged, were borne indirectly by the king's poor subjects. Both involved administrative reforms which the government in 1467-8 was still indisposed to undertake; and the two embodied what were perhaps the most significant requests of the commons in this parliament.

The parliament, however, enacted a statute of some moment based on an official bill. Like a companion official bill, which became a statute and annulled a clause in letters patent conferring on London magistrates jurisdiction over felons in Southwark, the bill was administrative in character. It imposed heavy penalties for the giving and the receiving of liveries and for continued maintenance, encouraging anyone to make complaint against offenders by accepting his information on oath in lieu of presentment by jury. It enjoined the observance of earlier statutes against liveries and was in direct continuance of the policy enunciated in the official bill of 1453-4, which imposed penalties for the non-observance of writs of great or privy seal issued to bring men charged with rioting and oppression before the chancellor or the council. It leaves us with the impression that the government was acting as it had come to act in the earlier bill and in Edwardian bills of resumption — was itself drafting measures of first-rate importance. And this, of course, was more feasible when the interests of the government and of the commons coincided, as they did in these bills.

In the next parliament of Edward IV, that of 1472-4, there were few bills of any sort which could claim to be of first-rate importance, although several were passed.[20] Of the nine commons bills which were enacted as statutes, four had reference each to a transient condition. One annulled the acquittal of certain Welshmen at a session of gaol delivery at Ross, transferring the indictments to the king's bench; one released an imprisoned member of parliament for the duration of the session; one prolonged the period during which certain tallies and letters patent might be renewed; one excused sheriffs for

[20] *Ibid.*, VI, 154-164; *Stats.*, II, 431-451.

returning writs during the period between the expiry of their term and the assumption of office by their successors. Two other bills renewed earlier statutes which had expired. One of them authorized the reappointment of commissioners of sewers as they had been created and continued under Henry VI; the other, reciting the provisions of Magna Charta and of later statutes touching the removal of kiddles and weirs from rivers, reaffirmed them and provided for their execution. Finally, three bills touched upon new subjects which were at the same time of more general interest. One made void all letters patent which gave to others than the governors of towns the survey of victuals therein. One, lamenting the decay of archery and attributing it to lack of bows, required alien merchants to bring in four bowstaves with every " tuntight " of merchandise imported. A third, blaming escheators who farmed their offices to oppressive deputies, stipulated that henceforth no one be appointed escheator or deputy escheator who had an income of less than £20 a year.

If these commons bills, with the possible exception of the last, were not very impressive, the seven official bills which became statutes in this parliament were not much more so. Two of them protected in their legal rights men who might accompany the king in his voyage oversea. One directed the export of shorlings and morlings from the northern counties to New Middleburgh but another changed the destination to Barowe. One ruled that, despite the statutes, the prince of Wales might give liveries. One affirmed all statutes of earlier date than 1461 against breakers of truce and safe conduct. Finally, in order to check smuggling, a bill provided that imported cloths must be sealed before being sold, that exported cloths must be viewed in port and that the penalty for smuggling be no longer merely the payment of double subsidy but instead the forfeiture of the smuggled goods. This bill, together with the commons bills touching the maintenance of archery and the qualifications of escheators, was the most substantial contribution of this parliament to the legislation of the

reign. But in view of the number of bills passed and the
length of time which had elapsed since the last parliament
(some four years), the contribution was slender.

The next Edwardian parliament, called in 1478 after an
interval of three years, was scarcely more prolific of noteworthy statutes. Of the eight which arose from commons
bills, four contributed little to the welfare of the nation.[21]
One annulled the acts of the parliament summoned by Henry
VI in November, 1469. Another protected a member of the
house of commons from action for debt during the session.
Another amended the act of the preceding parliament which
extended the authority of retiring sheriffs. A fourth laid down
regulations to be observed by tilers in making tiles. Four
other statutes were of somewhat wider scope. Two of them
enacted sumptuary legislation, one by prohibiting certain
games in order that men might the rather turn to archery,
the other by instructing sheriffs and justices of the peace to
proclaim frequently and to inquire into the observance of the
statute of apparel of 1463, which, the preamble declared, had
not been executed. A seventh statute limited the competence
of courts of piepowder to contracts made at fairs. Finally, the
most important measure of the parliament had to do with the
conservation of the money of the realm. It provided that no
Irish money be legal tender in England (since the small coins
were untrue and counterfeit); that no coined money, plate,
bullion or jewels be exported; that no goldsmiths melt coin
to make gold or silver vessels; that the gold vessels which
they might make be 18 carets fine and the silver vessels of
the fineness of sterling; that the goldsmiths of London, whether
alien or native, be under the supervision of wardens of the
craft and inhabit open streets; and that alien merchants expend the money which they received for their wares upon commodities of the realm. Some of these regulations were not
new, especially the last, which not only conserved the supply
of coined money within the realm but protected the market for

---

[21] Ibid., pp. 452-467; R. P., VI. 183-192.

exportable commodities. The other regulations of the bill might well have been of official origin. Their proposal by the commons shows that, whenever the interests of the nation and the interests of the government coincided, it might still be a matter of indifference whether a remedial measure was a commons bill or an official bill.

Only one official bill was enacted by this parliament. It related that the king had suffered loss from the ulnage act of 1465, an act, by the way, of commons' origin. To remedy this, cloths of the length and breadth specified in the earlier act were henceforth to be sealed with wax instead of with lead (save in London and Bristol) and in particular the treasurer might in the future let to farm the subsidy and ulnage of cloth as had been the custom before 1465. This administrative measure retained the earlier provisions which were of most interest to the commons, the specifications about the length and breadth of cloths. That the ulnage was put to farm should have mattered little to them since the fee for sealing cloths was fixed by law; but there may have been less upright collection at the hands of farmers than at the hands of appointed officials. Apart from this questionable point the official bill was more or less dwarfed by the commons bills of the session or at least by the elaborate coinage bill.

Edward's last parliament, held in 1483, was still more jejune in legislation than its predecessors had been.[22] Its statutes, apart from two based on the private bills of the silk-workers of London and the burgesses of Berwick, were derived from four commons bills and two official bills. Of the commons bills one endeavored to protect the fullers of hats and caps by forbidding the use of a newly invented " Fullyng Mille" which accomplished more in one day than did eighty men. Another returned to the encouragement of archery, this time by providing that no bow should be sold for more than 3s. 4d. A third specified how salmon, herring and eels

[22] *Ibid.*, pp. 220-225; *Stats.*, II, 468-476.

should be packed and in barrels of what size. A fourth, declaring that earlier statutes of apparel had not been executed, repealed them, and substituted for them a more concisely worded new one in which minor changes were made. This, despite its lack of originality, was the most important bill of the parliament; for the two official bills merely provided that no one might keep swans unless he had lands to the yearly value of five marks and that areas in the king's forests in which trees had been cut might be hedged about for seven years instead of for three in order to give the young trees time to grow. Apart from protecting the consumers of barrelled fish and from renewing the attempt to check " inordynat aray " the parliament undertook no legislation of moment.

If now we glance at the legislation of the three decades 1453-1483 as a whole, we shall be able to formulate certain generalizations about it. In the first place it appears that the commons bills which received the approval of king and lords were for the most part bills of no great moment to the nation at large. Foremost among them were two bills which protected the staplers by forbidding shipments of wool elsewhere than to Calais and by remitting a recent increase in the subsidy on wool; four bills which protected clothworkers by retaliating against the Burgundian ban on English cloth, by specifying standard lengths and breadths for different sorts of cloth, by forbidding the purchase of futures in wool and by prohibiting the exportation of yarn and unfulled cloth; one bill which protected agriculture by prohibiting imports of wheat, barley and rye whenever prices fell to a certain minimum; three bills which apparently with little success attempted to restrain extravagance in dress; three bills which strove to encourage the practice of archery; one bill which restrained the cupidity of exchequer officials; and, finally, a bill which protected the supply and quality of coin within the realm. Although these were measures of some consequence, especially for staplers and cloth workers, they did not constitute an impressive legislative achievement on the part of the commons during a period of thirty years.

Still less are they impressive when they are contrasted with commons bills proposed but rejected. And this brings us to a second generalization, namely, that rejected commons bills especially in the years 1453-1467, when we know most about them, were on the whole rather more important than the bills which were approved. To appreciate this we have but to recall how a deaf ear was turned to the commons' requests when they appealed in behalf of various groups. Interceding for the staplers, they were refused the cessation of the granting of licences to export wool elsewhere than to Calais. Interceding for the cloth workers they were refused the fixing of favourable prices for wool, the prohibition of the purchase by merchants of futures in wool (although this had for a time been granted), the limitation of wool packers' purchases and the restriction of alien buyers to ports of shipment. Finally, interceding for the nation at large, they were refused the exploitation of silver mines, the better collection of fifteenths, the recovery of certain royal revenues, the lightening of charges on the sheriff's farm, the release on bail of men questionably imprisoned and the diminution of privilege of clergy. Although most of these rejected bills dated from the parliaments of Henry VI, certain of them, like those relieving the sheriff's farm and the one providing bail for men imprisoned, belonged to the first decade of Edward's reign. Later fewer bills were rejected, but also fewer of importance seem to have been introduced.

A final generalization relates to official bills which were enacted as statutes. On the whole not many of these were introduced and passed during the three decades under survey. Of those which were, however, some were important. Punishment for smuggling, for the violation of royal safe-conducts and for the disregard of summons to appear before chancellor or council was essential to good administration. Bills providing it were appropriately enough of official origin. Apparently the Yorkist government was becoming conscious that bills of this kind might in a measure be made to supersede commons bills. The most noteworthy illustration of such an attitude on its part was the substitution in and after 1465 of official bills of resumption for commons bills of resumption. Inasmuch as bills of this sort seem to have been the principal parliamentary concern of the period, the change was significant. Although such bills never became statutes, other bills destined to the distinction may have been influenced by the change which these underwent. Before 1484, however, legislation based on official bills was only beginning to supersede legislation based on commons bills. In and after that year, on the contrary, the change was so intensified that by the end of the century nearly all significant statutory legislation was of the newer sort.

The parliament summoned by Richard III in 1484, to which we may now turn, bears eloquent testimony tó the change in question.[23] It is not that we find commons bills rejected as they had been thirty years before; for, so far as we know, no commons' request made in this parliament was rejected. Nor were the commons bills which were approved altogether insignificant. Of the four which became statutes one, to be sure,

[23] *Stats.*, II, 477-498. With the reign of Richard III the *Rotuli Parliamentorum* cease to print the " communes petitions " except occasionally a bill or two. The editors explain that the end of the parliament roll " consists of Acts of Parliament which are entered upon the Statute Roll of this Year, the Titles whereof are as follow " (*R. P.*, VI, 263). The original " statute rolls," however, practically end with the reign of Edward IV (below p. 390). The editors of the *Statutes of the Realm,* finding themselves bereft of such had to turn to other sources for the statutes of Richard III and Henry VII. These they found in an exchequer MS., which they refer to as Liber Scacc. Westm. XI, but particularly in the manuscript rolls of parliament. The latter they quoted verbatim, giving, therefore, the form assumed by bills as they were introduced. They thus did what the editors of the *Rotuli* failed to do. For our purpose this is fortunate since in their original forms bills reveal their character as private, commons or official. The originals of no " communes petitions " survive from the two reigns. The text quoted henceforth will therefore be that printed from the parliament rolls in the *Statutes of the Realm.* (See above p. 18, n. 8 and below p. 150, n. 37.)

did no more than prolong until the next parliament a statute of 1478 touching the competence of courts of piepowder. But of the other three, one recited elaborate regulations for the making of cloth, another required that tuns of imported wine or oil be of full measure, this to be testified by gaugers at the ports, while the third restrained the activities of Italian merchants throughout the realm.[24] Similar anti-foreign sentiments were echoed in three group bills which also became statutes. One continued the protection already granted to the silk-workers of London against the competition of imported stuffs; another initiated similar protection for the makers of girdles, glass, scissors, buckles, candlesticks and like small wares; a third was the bowyers' repetition of alarm expressed earlier by the commons about the dearth of bows and a requirement that importers of Tyre or Malmsey bring into England ten good bowstaves along with every butt of wine. With such a record of anti-foreign legislation we cannot say that the voice of the commons was not lifted or listened to. Yet the narrowness of interests is noteworthy; and this appears the more striking if we glance at the subjects touched upon by the official bills of this parliament. For now at length bills of this sort became distinctly more numerous and more important than commons bills.

Of the nine official bills of 1484, four, to be sure, were limited enough in scope. One divested Richard, as king, of feoffments to uses made to him as a private person; another recovered for king and queen alienated rights of wardship and marriage in the duchy of Lancaster; another annulled all letters patent and acts of parliament which had been made in favour of Elizabeth Grey, late queen; a fourth protected col-

---

[24] They might not sell in gross, must expend their money on commodities of the realm, might not be hosts to men of other nations, might not give out wool to be manufactured, might not traffic in wool or woolen cloth within England, might not drape cloth there, might take no apprentice or servant except each man his own children, and might not be handycraftsmen except as servants to denizens. One half of the penalties imposed should go to whoever would sue, the other half to the king.

lectors of clerical tenths accounting at the exchequer from suits brought there against them in matters not touching their account.   Five other official bills, however, were of considerable significance.   One was an assurance on the part of the king that the commonalty would no longer be charged with benevolences, an assurance which might well have been asked for in a commons bill and which showed Richard apparently eager to anticipate the commons' wishes.   Another bill showed him ready to grant on his own initiative a measure which had already been twice presented without success; for it was an official bill which finally empowered justices of the peace to release on bail persons imprisoned on questionable charge of felony.   Richard's three other bills also looked to improvement in the administration of justice.   Since false indictments were made at sheriff's tourns by persons of no substance, bailiffs in future were to empanel only freeholders having an annual income of 20 s. or copyholders having one of 26 s. 8 d. Since titles to property had often become doubtful through secret feoffments to uses, all feoffments and all recoveries should in future be valid against the seller or feoffor.   Lastly, that final concords might no longer suffer from the operation of a statute of non-claim but might stand in great strength, those levied in the court of common bench should be there read three times during the year following the engrossing and a copy, sent to the shires in which the transferred lands lay, should be read there by justices of assize and by justices of the peace in four yearly sessions.   Claims against such fines must, unless the claimant was a minor or temporarily incapacitated, be pursued within five years, after which period the concord became unassailable.

Anyone of these five bills might appropriately have originated with the commons.   The relief extended by each was of wide scope and the need for it must have been widely felt. In contrast with the industrial protection sought by the commons bills and the private bills of this parliament, the four judicial bills disclosed on the part of their framers a certain divorce from class interests and a concentration on the needs of the community at large. Since the commons of 1484 seem not to have been generous enough in interests or perhaps not bold enough in spirit to rise to this detached zeal, it was left for the king, the council or the lords to take the initiative. In the assumption of leadership in framing bills which were likely to become statutes, Richard's government was almost epoch-making. It took as its own the task which the commons had for at least twenty years been disregarding and which Edward IV's government had taken up gingerly and intermittently. Henceforth the new practice was to prevail. To the parliaments of Henry VII there was to be presented a greater number of official bills than of commons bills and the content of the former was to be more significant than the content of the latter. The government was largely to replace the commons as the initiator of statutory legislation.

Bacon, who wrote eloquently of the legislation of Henry VII, declared that his exposition of it constituted the most original part of his biography.[25] Nowhere does he speak as if this legislation was proposed to the king by the commons and accepted by him. Always the king is pictured as the devisor of beneficent statutes. What Bacon attributed to Henry, perhaps in exaltation of his hero, is abundantly borne out by the parliamentary records of the reign. The tendency to legislate by means of official bills appeared in the king's first parliament and found its full development in the succeeding parliaments of 1487 and 1489. Of precedents so convincingly established later parliaments were observant and the reign of official bills had begun.

In the parliament of 1485 certain private bills were enacted into statutes of some moment.[26] Although the silk-workers of London were granted continued protection against foreign

[25] F. Bacon, *A History of the Reign of King Henry the Seventh*, ed. J. R. Lumby (Cambridge, 1902), p. 74.

[26] All the bills of this parliament are printed from the parliament roll in *Stats.*, II, 499-508.

competition, Italian merchants secured a repeal of the statute of Richard III which had reiterated and extended the unpalatable regulation of their activities. On the plea that the navy would be strengthened, English mariners, and perhaps masters of ships, secured a ruling that until the next parliament no wine should be imported from Gascony save in English, Irish or Welsh ships. Lastly, certain persons interested in limiting the jurisdiction of the courts of the staplers got a bill passed to this effect.

Rather less important than the private bills were two of the three commons bills of the parliament. One of them, re-enacting a bill of 1423 which drew a line of demarkation between the crafts of tanners and cordwainers, demanded good workmanship from both. Another allowed complaints against men who hunted in forests in disguise, especially in Kent, Surrey and Sussex, to be brought before the council as well as before justices of the peace. The third commons bill, however, was important. Bacon conjectured that it was put by the king into the mouth of the commons, a not improbable surmise.[27] It was enrolled on the parliament roll before the " communes petitions " and it did not become a statute. It provided that " the Inheretance of the Crounes of . . . England and of France . . . be, rest, remaine and abide in the . . . person . . . of King Harry the VIIth and in the heires of hys body . . . perpetuelly. . . ."[28] In its purport and in its place on the parliament roll this act followed the precedent set by Edward IV, except that the earlier act had been prefaced by the grounds for the change of sovereign. The commons in accepting Henry made no such explanations, perhaps for the reasons which Bacon ingeniously attributed to that prince.

Although the crown was barely placed on his head, two at least of Henry's four official bills in this parliament looked beyond his immediate interests. As a matter of course his adherents were pardoned for acts of violence committed

[27] Bacon, *op. cit.*, p. 15.
[28] *R. P.*, VI, 270.

against the adherents of Richard.[29]   As a provision against smuggling and consequent loss of royal revenue, alien merchants, even though they had been made denizens, were told that they still must pay alien custom rates since they had been shipping the wares of other aliens as their own.   Both of these measures were to the king's immediate advantage.[29a] But another official bill, directed to the reformation of priests, authorized bishops and ordinaries to imprison them for "fornicacion, inceste or eny other flesshely incontinency"; and a fourth bill, in order to assist a plaintiff who might wish to bring suit but because of feoffments created often did not know against whom to bring it, declared that he should have action against whoever received the profits of the lands or tenements in question.   These last bills with their breadth of outlook were premonitory of the type of legislation which was to characterise Henry's parliaments of 1487 and 1489.[29b]

In the parliament of 1487 the dominance of official bills over commons bills was fully established.   Eleven of them, all important except three, became statutes, whereas only four commons bills were approved, one of these being a re-enactment and another local in application.[30]   The commons bill which prolonged a statute — one of 1478 itself not novel — required alien merchants to expend the money received from sales of their merchandise on commodities of the realm and

[29] In addition to this pardon, there are among the approved bills which do not appear as "statutes" not only an official bill which attainted several Yorkists but also two official bills, two commons bills and some forty-four private bills which annulled existent attainders or adverse judgments (*ibid.*, pp. 273-88, 290-99, 304-34).

[29a] So too was a private bill presented by Italian merchants and virtually annulling the statute of Richard III which regulated their activities (see above, p. 125).   Penalties accruing to anyone who might sue were now repealed; and, although the king might enjoy seizures and penalties, he might also grant safe-conducts.   The resultant act must have facilitated bargaining between merchants and king at the expense of the latter's subjects (*Stats.* II, 507).

[29b] Neither of them is mentioned by Bacon, *op. cit.*, pp. 17-18.

[30] The text of all these bills is printed from the parliament roll in *Stats.*, II, 509-523.

to give security to collectors of customs that they would do so. The commons bill of local application was the annulment of an ordinance of the mayor and aldermen of London, which forbad citizens of that city to buy and sell at fairs held outside its precincts. The two other commons bills were of general import. One, to check the abuse of making deeds of gift to defraud creditors, provided that such deeds made to the use of the person making them should be void; and the other, to penalize a defendant who after judgment had been given against him might sue a writ of error to delay execution, declared that if the writ should prove erroneous, the plaintiff might recover costs and damages for delay and vexation.

In contrast with these four commons bills were the eleven official bills which became statutes.[31] Of the three which were of minor importance, one re-enacted a commons bill of 1483 forbidding the selling of bows for more than 3 s. 4 d., but reduced the penalty for so doing from 40 s. to 20 s.; another required licences from merchants who transferred their merchandise in coastwise trade from one port to another; and the third revised the statute of 1484 which enabled justices of the peace to release on bail persons accused on light suspicion of felony by requiring that two justices rather than one act in each instance.

Of the eight official bills which embodied the most substantial legislation of this parliament one, Bacon surmised, may have been prompted by the fears of the chancellor for his personal safety.[32] It authorised the inquiry by jury of the household whether any member of it under the state of a lord had conspired to murder the king or any lord of the realm or

---

[31] Two official bills, although enrolled as commons petitions, did not become statutes. One of them attainted John Spynell and some eighty other rioters who threatened to kill the king's great officials and others of his council while the king was sitting in parliament on 15 December, 1487. The other summoned Thomas Keneston and others of Shropshire to appear before the king's courts or be outlawed as felons (*R. P.*, VI, 402-403). The parliament roll closed with an official act of resumption (*ibid.*, pp. 403-408).

[32] Bacon, *op. cit.*, p. 63.

any member of the king's council or the steward, treasurer or
controller of the household, such offense to be deemed a felony.
This making of "the will in . . . case of felony . . . the
deed" was, Bacon noted, close to an invasion of ancient liberties, but its justification, apart from its limited application,
lay in the king's desire to protect his great officers and councillors.

The seven other official bills were directed to the protection
of the liberties of all the king's subjects. Two of them aimed
at financial protection. Earlier statutes regarding the exchange of money were henceforth to be observed and only
men deputed by the king were to make exchanges. Unlawful
chevisaunces and usury were forbidden, while brokers guilty
of either were to be disqualified for the further practice of
brokerage. Contracts made in accordance with the "newe
chevesaunce," such, for example, as paying £120 for merchandise worth £100, were to be void. Three bills related to
the better administration of justice. One provided that suits
brought by feoffees in trust "to the use and behofe of other
persones then of themselves," i.e., in behalf of feoffees to uses,
should not be suspended to the hurt of the latter by any outlawry, attainder, or conviction of the former. One branded
the taking away of a woman against her will as felony. A
third, since private appellants in case of murder were "of-
tymes slowe and also aggreed with and by thend of the yere
all ys forgoten," authorised the arraignment of an accused man
at the king's suit within a year and a day (instead of after that
period) and, even though he was acquitted, authorized his continued imprisonment or release on bail that he might be
answerable during the year and the day to private appeal.
Finally, two bills strove to repress disorder. One declared
that officials of royal lordships, manors and forests might not
retain any person and might not themselves be retained or
suffer anyone dwelling on the estate to be retained, and might
not with anyone so dwelling attend unlawful assemblies.
Going to the heart of the matter the most famous of the bills

of the parliament gave to an afforced committee of the council, in time to be known as the court of the star chamber, power
to summons before it by writ of privy seal sheriffs guilty of
making untrue returns and men guilty of maintenance, bribery
of juries or complicity in riot.   The bill was a fitting crown
to the legislation of a parliament which, even more than its
two predecessors, marked the transition from legislation primarily by commons bills to legislation primarily by official
bills.

Henry's third parliament, held in 1489, adopted and thereby
confirmed the new usage.   Of its twenty-four statutes, two
arose from private bills, seven from commons bills and fifteen
from official bills.[33]   The private bills were directed to the
removal of London butchers without the city walls and to the
maintenance of the quality of imported gold-thread used by
London embroiderers.   Two commons bills were quite as limited in scope.   One forbad the keeping of boats, nets or
engines which might destroy spawn of fish in the haven of
Orford, Suffolk; the other extended the powers of the mayor
of London as conservator of the river Thames to newly-made
tributory creeks.   Three commons bills re-enacted or extended
earlier statutes.   One prolonged commissions of sewers for
twenty-five years; another continued for twenty years the
prohibition of the export of coin and plate as enacted in 1478;
a third enlarged the scope at the same time that it prolonged
the term of a group bill of 1484 by forbidding the importation
from Gascony of woad as well as of wine in ships other than
those of England, Ireland, Wales and Calais and by extending
the prohibition to exported merchandise of denizens if at the
time of shipment sufficient denizen ships were in port.   Only
two commons bills having new provisions affected the commonalty at large.   One, by fixing the maximum price at which
hats and caps could be sold, presumably protected the community from a craft which practiced extortion; the other, declaring that "actions popular," though usually beneficent,

[33] *Stats.*, II, 524-548.

were being abused, enabled a plaintiff to aver that a defendant was using "covyn" in having such an action brought against him to bar an antecedent action.[33a] This bill and the ones touching hats and caps and denizen ships were the noteworthy contribution of the commons to the legislation of this parliament.

In contrast were the fifteen official bills. Three of them, to be sure, dealt with minor matters. One gave legal protection, as had been done in 1474, to men who would accompany the king on his voyage over seas; another recalled the appointments of the keepers of the royal forest of Inglewood, alleging negligence; a third provided that official documents in the earldom of March should no longer be sealed with the special seal of the marches but only with the "brode seale of Chauncery." Two other bills were somewhat narrowly administrative — the cancellation of the exemptions of abbots and priors from collecting or paying clerical tenths and the warning to yeomen of the crown and of the king's chamber who might not be dutiful in attendance that henceforth their letters patent would be held at the king's pleasure.

Ten of the official bills of the parliament, however, were of considerable moment and elicited Bacon's praise. Two protected clothworkers as commons bills of the time of Edward IV had striven to do. Woolpackers, whose purchases of wool a bill of 1455 limited to four sacks,[34] were now forbidden to buy any wool whatever for aliens. The purchase of futures in wool, prohibited in 1465 but again permitted in 1467, was now once more forbidden. Both measures of protection were to endure for ten years. Two famous bills constituted the initial effort of the government to protect husbandry and to maintain a sturdy peasantry capable of defending the country. One

---

[33a] Bacon explains an "action popular" as the "practice that was grown in use to stop and damp informations upon penal laws by procuring informations by collusion to be put in by the confederates of the delinquents to be faintly prosecuted and let fall at pleasure; and pleading them in bar of the informations which were prosecuted with effect" (*Henry VII*, p. 73).

[34] See above, p. 124.

of these, lamenting the depopulation of the Isle of Wight through the consolidation of agricultural holdings, prohibited anyone from having after Michaelmas, 1490 a farmhold there of more than ten marks yearly value. The other, pointing to the decay of houses and the employment of land for pasture instead of for tillage in the country at large, required owners of houses which with twenty acres or more of arable had been let to farm within three years to maintain the houses and the arable and to do the same if they had taken the houses and lands into their own hands, the penalty for non-observance being the forfeiture of one-half of the yield of the land to the immediate lord. In the interest of all consumers the drapers and tailors of London were forbidden to sell cloth above certain prices — 16 s. the yard for woolen cloth of scarlet grained or other cloth of any colour grained and 11 s. for woolen cloth of any colour "out of graine" or for fine russets. In the interest, too, of the entire population two bills protected the currency. One declared that the counterfeiting of foreign coins, as well as that of English coins, should be considered treason. The other forbad refiners of gold and silver to alloy these metals, required that they be sold only to masters of the mint or to goldsmiths, specified standards of fineness for silver and instructed goldsmiths that they use silver only for making of "Amells for diverse Werks of Goldsmythry and for the admendyng of plate."

Four bills, finally, concerned themselves with the better administration of justice. One, censuring the remissness of justices of the peace, required them to proclaim four times yearly an appended proclamation which enjoined execution of their commissions and authorized appeals against any one of them to a neighboring justice of the peace or to a justice of assize or even to the chancellor or the king. Another, enjoining observance of a privision of the statute of Marlborough against fraudulent feoffments, declared that the heir of *cestui que use* holding by knight's service should, if within age, be in ward or, if of age, should pay relief and have action of waste.

Another, the virtues of which Bacon expounds,[35] was in fact a re-enactment of the statute of Richard III already described. It provided for the reading of final concords in the court of the king's bench in the three terms following the engrossing, omitting the reading by justices of the peace prescribed in the earlier statute, and like its predecessor limiting to five years, except in a few instances, the period during which claims against the fine might be pursued. A fourth bill, as Bacon phrased it, "began . . . to pare a little the privilege of the clergy.[36] Henceforth full benefit of clergy should be allowed only once "to persons lettered" but not "within orders"; on the occasion of a second offence the offender should be branded on his left thumb before being delivered to the ordinary.

The number and importance of these official bills is in contrast with the paucity and slightness of the commons bills approved at the same time. Apart from such of the latter as re-enacted earlier statutes or were extremely local, the commons asked and secured only a possibly wider use of denizen ships, a limitation of the prices of hats and caps, and a remedy for an abuse of "actions popular." The official bills, on the other hand, turned to various shortcomings in the government of the realm and proposed judicious reforms. Whether it was the protection of the wool supply of the cloth-workers, or the endeavour to restore a decaying husbandry, or the safeguarding of the currency, or the defining of judicial procedure, or the strengthening of local justice, or the restraint of criminous clerks, it was not the commons but the king and his council, perhaps supported by the lords, who proposed the remedy. In this parliament as in its predecessor, the reliance upon official bills as the basis of legislation was so pronounced that it may correctly be thought of as an accepted procedure.

Henry's next parliament, held in 1491, legislated little, nor were either its commons bills or its official bills of much mo-

---

[35] Bacon, *op. cit.*, p. 70.
[36] *Ibid.*, p. 64. Wrongly attributed to 1487.

ment.[37] Five of each became statutes. Two of the commons bills prolonged earlier statutes — one protecting young fish in the harbour of Orford, Suffolk, the other providing that outlawry pronounced in county Lancaster should be ineffective in other counties.[38] Of the other three, one expedited the conduct of suits in London by abolishing the challenge *Riens Deyns le garde*;[39] another increased the duty on wine payable by Venetian merchants, since the Venetians were taxing Malmsey wine bought in Candia by English merchants; the third provided that standard weights and measures be sent to every city and borough and that from them all weights and measures within the shires be reformed. Only the last of these statutes was of widespread interest.

The five official bills were of equally limited range, some of them being war measures. One extended legal privileges to men serving with the king overseas. Another enjoined all Scots to depart the realm within forty days. Another stipulated that captains beyond seas should have full contingents and should pay their men promptly, while desertion on the part of the latter was pronounced felony without benefit of clergy. A fourth repealed, as soon as it was enacted, the statute touching the jurisdiction of the palatinate of Lancaster. Lastly, a fifth declared that abbots, priors and their tenants should be no further relieved by letters patent from contributing to fifteenths and tenths than they had been under Edward IV. The fact that practically all statutes of the par-

---

[37] The " communes petitions " which were enacted as statutes, along with two commons bills preceding the caption are printed in *Stats.*, II, 549-554, 567. The editors of the *Statutes* also print from the parliament roll fourteen other acts, of which one is the grant of a subsidy, the others private bills or official bills. All of the fourteen were enrolled before the " communes petitions " and should not be thought of as giving rise to statutes. (See above pp. 18, n. 8, 138, n. 23.)

[38] The second was first enacted in 1442, was made perpetual in 1453 but had been repealed in 1455.

[39] The challenge presupposed the residence in each ward of four persons each with a livelihood of 40 s. the year and it was proving difficult to get four such to appear.

liament were of transient or local import stamps it as a war-
time parliament, unready to undertake serious legislation.

With the return of peace the parliament of 1495 reverted to
the task so laudably initiated by the parliaments of 1487 and
1489. No fewer than twenty-seven bills, including a private
bill of the upholsterers, were enacted as statutes.[40] Eight of
the number were commons bills, eighteen official bills. Half
of the commons bills repealed or extended earlier statutes.
One, annulling a statute of 1406, permitted worsted weavers
in Norwich to take as apprentices children whose parents did
not have lands or rents to the annual value of 20 s. and added
that no one might shear worsteds unless apprenticed for seven
years. Another re-enacted and extended the specifications of
the statute of the preceding parliament which ordered standard
weights and measures sent to cities and towns. Another, in
order that there might be full panels of twenty-four men at the
sheriff's tourn, reduced until the next parliament the qualifications set by the statute of 1484 for jurors there, cutting in
half the value of lands and rents which each must possess and
even allowing the summons of men who had less than this. A
fourth bill, declaring that the statute of 1487 against usury
was obscure, repealed it and substituted for it a penalization
of the offence, which was now defined as taking anything in
payment of a loan above the money lent (except compensation
for non-payment), or selling merchandise to repurchase it for
a smaller sum within three months, or giving over lands and
tenements with the income from them during the term of the
loan. Of the commons bills with new subject matter one, taking the standpoint of those who had paid their contributions
to a benevolence recently granted the king, ordered proclamation that those who had not paid must do so within three
months or be committed to gaol without bail. The interests
of shearmen were consulted in a bill which, explaining that
imported fustians were useful for doublets, stipulated that they
be not shorn by new and ruinous "irons" but by the "brode

[40] *Stats.*, II, 568-635.

shere." Only the two remaining commons bills proposed legislation of broader scope. One, endeavouring to stamp out riots,
provided that rioters, whether accused by private appeal or by
public indictment, might be summoned by justices of the peace
to the next general sessions at which, if they appeared, they
might be released on bail until tried or, if they did not, might
be adjudged guilty and be imprisoned or fined. If the riot
involved forty persons or, being a " heynous " one, a smaller
number, the case should go to the council. Finally, a commons
bill facilitated the bringing of actions by poor persons. At the
discretion of the chancellor writs might be issued in their
behalf without payment and, both in the preparation of the
action and after the return of the writ, learned counsel and
attorneys might be assigned them. These two bills were on
the high plane of public interest. To a degree they qualify a
generalization which on the whole seems justified, namely, that
commons bills under Henry VII usually dealt with the re-
enactment or revision of earlier statutes or with matters of
minor importance.

The complement of the generalization, namely, that in
Henry's parliaments the most important legislation was introduced by official bills, is pretty well sustained by the procedure
of 1495. Of the eighteen official bills, four confirmed or revised earlier statutes and four were narrowly administrative,
but the ten others were of more general import. Of the first
four, one modified a statute of 1394 by assigning vagabonds
to the stocks rather than to gaol and added that beggars not
able to work should go to their own hundreds and that apprentices should not play games except at Christmas. A second
modified a statute of 1472, which had ruled that woolen cloths
before export be packed in the presence of the collectors of
customs, by allowing them to be packed elsewhere so long as
the duties were paid. A third rephrased but did not change
a statute of 1485, which exacted from aliens who had letters
of denization the customs rates paid by aliens, since they were
in the habit of importing the merchandise of the latter as their

own. A fourth bill, reciting the statute of 1483 on the proper barreling of fish, added the fees to which gaugers were entitled.

Of the four official bills which were narrowly administrative, one reminded those who held gifts, offices, fees or annuities of the king that they were, with the exception of specified officials, bound to attend him when he went to war in person. Another, reciting that freeholds in Calais which had been granted by Edward III to certain lords on the tenure of finding watch now seldom performed the service, declared them forfeit if the charge was neglected for a year and a day. A third incorporated North and South Tyndale in the county of Northumberland, and a fourth ordered the removal of weirs and fishing " engynes " from Southampton harbour.

In contrast with these administrative measures were ten bills of increasingly wider purport. Beginning with penalties for poaching or for hawking with certain birds and with a prohibition of the exportation without licence of horses and mares worth more than 6 s. 8 d., the series proceeded to the penalizing of widows for alienating any part of their dower and to a comprehensive fixing of maximum wages for artificers and for servants of husbandry. One measure, the subtlety of which elicited Bacon's praise, promised that, if anyone should serve in war whoever might be king, he should not thereafter be attainted of treason for this service.[41]   Five bills turned to judicial reforms and to the repression of lawlessness. Sheriffs were warned not to enter complaints against defendants other than those made by plaintiffs (their opportunity of collecting 4 d. for each non-appearance being thereby restricted), and defendants were to be warned of complaints preferred against them. Jurors in London were required to have lands and rents worth forty marks and sometimes more. If anyone felt himself aggrieved by their verdict, twenty-four men of substance should be empanelled to inquire into the truth or falsity of it,

[41] Bacon, *op. cit.*, p. 134. He noted, too, the illusory character of the latter part of the act, which declared that future acts contrary to it should be void (*Stats.*, II, 568).

and, even if it was found true, they might inquire into the possible corruption of the jurors. If it was found false every guilty juror should forfeit £20 or more. By a similar bill to be in force until the next parliament anyone in the realm aggrieved by a verdict on an issue which "concerneth not the jopardie of mannys lyfe" might by writ of attaint secure a jury of twenty-four men to inquire into the guilt of the petit jury, the qualifications of the attaint jurors and the fines to be imposed on guilty jurors varying as the stake had been greater or less than £40. A fourth bill required a justice of the peace before admitting a panel of inquests of office to see it and at his discretion to reform it. If anyone complained before him of perjury in inquests, induced by unlawful maintenance, this complaint should be passed on to the chancellor, who with the treasurer, the two chief justices and the clerk of the rolls should examine the person accused and punish him if guilty. Finally, justices of the peace or justices of assize might even without presentment by jury proceed to hear and determine offences against any statute. The professed purpose of this bill was the securing of a better enforcement of statutes against riots, unlawful assemblies, extortions, embracery, the giving and receiving of liveries, the taking of excessive wages, the playing of unlawful games and the wearing of inordinate apparel. Like its four companions it aimed to restore the administration of justice, declared to be so perilously in decay.

The official bills of the parliament of 1495 thus carried further the concern for the public weal shown by two of its commons bills. All of them together advanced by specific steps the royal purpose so clearly enunciated in 1487 by the strengthening of the court of the star chamber. Just as the intention of the government to suppress disorder of various sorts by the summons of offenders before the highest officials of the land was there apparent, so here a commons bill and an official bill provided respectively for similar reference to the council or to great officials of cases of riot and of the perjury of jurors due to unlawful maintenance. The distrust of the veracity of jurors manifested by the provisions for testing their verdicts and by the powers given to justices of the peace to proceed directly against suspected violators of the statutes reveals the same realistic and energetic attitude. That nearly all of this legislation emanated from the king or his council or possibly from the lords has become clear from our consideration of the type of bill in which it was embodied. The third of the important legislating parliaments of Henry VII thus takes its place besides those of 1487 and 1489 as likewise dominated by official bills.

The parliament of 1497 did little more than supplement the work of its predecessor.[42] One interesting private bill, to be sure, became a statute. In answer to the complaint of the merchant adventurers dwelling outside London that the mercers and other merchant adventurers of the city exacted initial fees of £20 for trading in the marts of the Low Countries, it was enacted that these fees be only ten marks. Of the two commons bills of the parliament, one extended to worsted workers of Norfolk the privilege of freely taking apprentices, granted the year before to the worsted workers of Norwich; and the other suspended until the next parliament penalties which in accordance with the statute of 1484 might have been incurred by cloth-workers in the making and draping of cloths. Three of the official bills of the parliament likewise were concerned with recent statutes. One prolonged until the next parliament four statutes of the last parliament, all enacted to endure only until the parliament which followed and "not yet put in force."[43] Another, admitting that weights and measures sent out as enjoined in the last parliament were defective, provided for their replacement. The third bill repealed the statute of the last parliament which fixed the wages of

---

[42] *Stats.*, II, 636-647.

[43] These were the commons bill against rioters and the official bills restraining over-zealous sheriffs, authorizing writ of attaint against juries, and conferring upon justices of the peace and of assize power to proceed without indictment of jury against the violators of statutes.

artificers and servants of husbandry. And a fourth, passing
to new ground and declaring guilty of petty treason a certain
James Grame who had murdered his master, refused to any
lay person who should murder his master any benefit of clergy.
It was the only bill of the parliament, apart from the bill of
the merchant adventurers, which introduced a new subject,
this being a kind of second step in "paring the privileges of
the clergy."

The parliament roll of the last parliament of Henry VII,
held in 1503-4, omits the caption "communes petitions" and
distributes throughout its record the bills which were to become statutes. Most of them, to be sure, were grouped together, interrupted only by the introduction of three private
bills and an official bill of attainder. But four other private
bills, contrary to usage, were enrolled after them and two official bills which became statutes preceded them at an interval.[44]
The enrollment was irregular in these respects; for the parliament roll of 1509 resumed the custom of introducing most of
its prospective statutes as "communes petitiones." [45]

The bills of the parliament of 1504 which became statutes
of the accepted sort numbered, apart from one group bill of
the pewterers of London and York, eight commons bills and
fifteen official bills.[46] More than in preceding parliaments they
were based upon antecedent statutes and in consequence new
legislation of importance was not extensive. Of the commons
bills one prolonged until the next parliament the statute of
1495 which had reduced the property qualifications of jurors
at the sheriff's tourn; another, explaining that the statute of
1487 which enabled a defendant to recover damages if a writ
of error sued against him should prove unwarranted was as
yet not enforced, provided that it be put in execution; another,

[44] R. P., VI, 542-555, 525, 529.

[45] See above, p. 29.

[46] The editors of the *Statutes of the Realm* printed, as they did for three
earlier parliaments of Henry VII, all the bills of the parliament roll as if
they were statutes (II., 648-694).

responding to the appeal of the shearmen of Norwich who declared that in consequence of the act of 1495 the shearers of worsteds in the city were choosing wardens and acting independently of the larger craft, repealed the act so far as it required seven years of apprenticeship; another, quoting the expired statute of 1437 which required the approval of justices of the peace or of the governors of cities for the ordinances of crafts, gilds and fraternities, enacted that henceforth this approval must be got from the chancellor, the treasurer and the chief justices, or three of them, or from justices on circuit and that no such ordinance restrain anyone from bringing suit in the king's courts. A fifth bill, noting that earlier statutes had forbidden cordwainers to be tanners and tanners to be curriers, now forbad cordwainers to be curriers; and a sixth bill, relying upon a statute of 1431 which provided free passage of the river Severn, imposed penalties upon royal officials in the city of Worcester and the town of Gloucester for exacting impositions. Of two commons bills which were new in content, one forbad officials of any town except London to take scavage from denizens; and the other, more far-reaching, extended legislation already noticed which tended to regularise the growing practice of alienating to a feoffee to uses. Lands enjoyed by *cestui que use* were now made liable to the execution by the sheriff of judgments for debt or trespass, while the relief and heriot due at the death of *cestui que use* for lands held in socage were to be paid by his heirs as the statute of 1489 had directed should be done in the case of lands held by military service. Since earlier legislation touching the responsibilities of *cestui que use* had been enacted through official bills,[47] it is curious to find this extension of it initiated by a commons bill. The new measure, however, responded to the needs of trade by preventing the evasion of an action for debt, and this probably explains the procedure. By its enactment the commons achieved at least one satisfactory item of new legislation in 1504.

[47] See above, pp. 140, 148.

The official bills of this parliament, like the commons bills, were so largely concerned with the repeal, prolongation, amendment or amplification of earlier statutes that nine of the fifteen were of this sort. One of them extended the scope of a bill of 1495, which required holders of office to attend upon the king when he went to war in person, to men who held by letters patent honours, castles, lordships and manors, failure to attend entailing voidance of patents and martial law thus being assisted by law of parliament.[48] One prolonged until the next parliament the statute granting writs of attaint in the case of false verdicts, enacted in 1495 and already once extended. One repealed an act of 1489 which forbad burgesses of Calais to be factors for wool merchants, since the act had resulted in the depopulation of the town. One modified the statute of 1495 against vagabonds by lessening the punishment of the vagabonds but also by increasing the penalties imposed on negligent officials whose conduct might, it was now declared, be investigated by the highest officers of state. One continued the series of acts forbidding the importation of silken stuffs, but for the first time distinguished silks which might be imported from those which might not be. Two, striving as their predecessors had to maintain archery with the long bow, abolished until the next parliament the duty on bowstaffs of 6½ feet " or above " and forbad anyone except lords and men of wealth to shoot with the rival crossbows. Finally, two statutes dealing respectively with riots and retainers were expanded. Whereas in the act of 1411 against riots the qualifications of jurors were not set down and no punishment was indicated for the embracery of juries, these shortcomings were now repaired; and, touching the giving of liveries, earlier statutes were affirmed, the fine for persisting in the offence was increased, and elaborate provisions were added for discovering the offender.[49] The added provisions of this bill were perhaps

---

[48] Bacon, *op. cit.*, p. 195.

[49] The fine was increased from 100 s. the month to 40 s. the day. Bailiffs of hundreds and constables of townships should give evidence before sub-

as significant as any other legislation of this parliament.

Of the six new bills two related to minor matters. One declared that no statute hitherto made touching merchants' wares should be prejudicial to the Hansa and the other provided that shire courts in Sussex be held alternately at Lewes and at Chichester. Of the four remaining official bills one forbad the setting of nets for deer or the stalking of deer in a park without licence from the owner and also the taking of herons except by hawking or by a shot of the long bow. Another bill, encouraging the recoinage of groats and pence, specified the gold and silver coins which should be legal tender within the realm and prohibited the exportation of bullion, plate or coin to Ireland. A third, noting that delays arose in " accions of the case " in the king's bench and the common bench, provided that henceforth there be like process in these actions as in actions of trespass or debt. Finally, " since privileged officers [were] no less an interruption of justice than privileged places," a bill declared all gaols, except those held by inherited right, to be in the keeping of sheriffs, at the same time imposing fines for negligence in allowing the escape of prisoners. This bill, together with the expanded provisions of the bills touching riots and maintenance, constituted the government's final enactments to repress disorder. As a whole the legislation of this parliament was not as significant as that of the parliaments of 1487, 1489 and 1495. In those characteristics which for the moment concern us it did not differ from them. Its commons bills were fewer than its official bills and in general were distinctly less important.

With the parliament of 1504 we may close this epitome of

stantial jurors empanelled by the sheriffs before the justices of the peace. Justices of the peace should examine anyone suspected and report all such to the king's bench on penalty of £100. Anyone might sue or complain to the chancellor in the star chamber or to the king's bench or to the king and council and he would receive a reward if the accusation should prove true. Chancellor, justices or council might without suit or information summon by writ of subpoena or writ of privy seal anyone suspected (*Stats.*, II, 658-60).

the legislation of the second half of the fifteenth century. It has been cursorily surveyed with a definite purpose in view. Since a preceding chapter supplied us with a clue to the form assumed respectively by commons bills, official bills and private bills, including group bills, it became possible to ascertain what share the commons took in formulating the legislation of the half-century; for their immediate contribution to legislation lay in the bills which they proposed. Insofar as their bills were rejected, their unfulfilled aspirations are also revealed. What then have we discovered?

Relative to the half-century as a whole it has become apparent that the share of the commons in legislation was not great. In the parliaments of 1453-4 and 1455-6 several serious measures of reform which they proposed were rejected, while only bills of minor moment were approved and became statutes. In the reign of Edward IV, apart from certain bills of the parliament of 1463-5, the statutes which originated as commons bills referred largely to the interests of particular groups, especially to the interests of the staplers and the merchant adventurers. A tendency was appearing for measures of national interest to assume the form of official bills. Under Edward IV such bills did not as yet surpass commons bills in number, although they sometimes did in importance. With the single parliament of Richard III the palm passed to them in both respects. At length they outnumbered commons bills and they embodied nearly all constructive legislation which had national scope. What was an innovation under Richard became an established custom under Henry VII. For the energetic, well-considered and beneficent measures of the early parliaments of this king, especially those of 1487, 1489 and 1495 the official bill was the chosen instrument. Throughout the reign commons bills were relatively few in number and only occasionally contributed remedies for the disorders with which the government so energetically coped. Bacon attributed to Henry in person the far-sighted measures of the reign. Some of them were probably formulated by the council and some may have originated with the lords, although there is little evidence of this. At any rate the impulse did not come from the commons.[50] Whether the commons had been dis-

[50] It would, however, be rash to maintain, as Professor Pollard seems to, that official legislation was passed without the assent of lords and commons. "Certain formulae," he writes, "about the advice and consent of Lords and Commons had come into use; but they had not yet been stereotyped and were by no means essential to the validity of statutes made in Parliament. Many of Henry VII's Acts, indeed, begin 'Prayen the Commons'; but many others 'The King, remembering' without the least indication of advice or consent by anyone else." (*Reign of Henry VII*, I, p. xxxi). In point of fact the normal phraseology of the statute roll of Henry VII for official acts is, "Il est ordeigne, establie et enacte par ladvise des seignours espirituels et temporels et lez comens en le dit parliament assemblez et par auctorite del mesme qe . . . (e.g., *Stats.*, II, 500). In a following statute this phrase is sometimes abbreviated to "de ladvise, assent et auctorite suisdictez," the implication of "suisdictez" being clear (*ibid.*, p. 513). Frequently, however, we read only, "il est ordeigne . . . par auctorite du dit parliament qe. . . ." Since one of these phrases always occurs, it must have seemed to Professor Pollard that the last of them implies "without the least indication of advice or consent by anyone else." It is true that there is mention only of authority and not of advice and consent. In a contracted formula, however, it would not be unnatural to suppose that the second and more authoritative part of a customary phrase implied the first part of it. What seems to assure us that it did is the manner in which statutes employing the abbreviated phrase are, except in Henry's last parliament, enrolled. All of them on the parliament roll, of which the printed statute roll is virtually a transcript, are introduced by the caption, "Item, diverse Communes Petitiones exhibite fuerunt . . . Regi in parliamento predicto, per Communitates Regni Anglie . . . quarum tenores cum suis responsis hic inferius annotantur" (*ibid.*, pp. 402, 418, 426, 456, 508, 513). Although we have seen that all petitions following this caption were not actually commons petitions, it is not likely that there would be enrolled as such bills to which the commons had not assented. It is unfortunate that few original official bills of the reign survive to give us complete assurance on this point. But since no original official bill which we have from this reign or from many decades before it is without inscription of the commons' assent, it seems safe to conclude that, when under Henry VII a bill was said to have been enacted with the authority of parliament, it had received the assent of lords and commons.

Nor is Professor Pollard convincing when he says further that "in 1504 Henry was empowered by parliament itself to repeal Acts of Attainder on his sole authority" (*op. cit.*, p. xxxii). The statute in question recites that, because this parliament "draweth so nere to the ende" and the king does not wish to call another and certain named suitors, who have asked annul-

placed from a position which they may once have held as authors of bills destined to become statutes must be left for later consideration. Two aspects of the evidence before us point in that direction. In the parliaments of the fifties the bills accepted and rejected were nearly all commons bills, official bills being very few; and throughout the half-century bills destined to become statutes, even official bills, were grouped under the caption "communes petitions." The latter usage suggests a time when it was expected that all or nearly all legislation would originate as commons bills. To test this inference we shall have to turn to the legislation preceding 1453, and examine it much as we have examined the legislation of the following fifty years. If the inference is sustained, it will be true that the later period witnessed a decline in the influence of the commons upon legislation. But such a generalisation is scarcely warranted as yet.

Before approaching the legislation of the first half of the century we must, however, complete our survey of that of the second half; for the latter may be approached from yet another point of view. It may be admitted that in and after 1484, if not indeed before, official bills predominated over commons bills, but it may be added that perhaps the commons exerted an influence upon official bills by amending them. Conversely it would be pertinent to discover whether throughout the half-century commons bills were to any degree altered by amendments added by the king or the lords. Legislation in the fifteenth century may not in short have sprung

ment of attainder against them or their ancestors would be aggrieved by delay, the king, with the assent of lords and commons, is empowered to annul these attainders and any others made during his reign or the reign of Richard III. The statute, therefore, was equivalent to a repeal of certain acts but not to authorization to repeal any acts of attainder which the king might wish to invalidate. The decision of the judges touching another act cited by Professor Pollard and holding that an attainder passed without the assent of the commons was invalid correctly represented existent law and usage. That Henry used pressure to get his measures accepted is likely, as Sir Robert Plumpton's correspondent testified; but it is unlikely that such assent was not got.

from a single source any more than does legislation today. A
bill originating with one house may have been altered, perhaps
in essential features, by amendment in the other before it became a statute. It is appropriate, therefore, to extend our
investigation of the influence of the commons in the second
half of the fifteenth century by an inquiry into the amending
of bills during that period.

CHAPTER VII

THE AMENDING OF BILLS IN THE SECOND HALF OF THE FIFTEENTH CENTURY

THE amending of a bill was only one stage in its passage through lords and commons and, indeed, a stage which was often omitted. What necessarily took place, however, in dealing with any bill which was to have a future was its introduction in each house, its reading or readings in each, its possible commitment, the probable debate, and the final acceptance of it by both houses before it was submitted to the king. These were the stages which Richardson so carefully described in the seventeenth century and which the journals of the sixteenth century reveal in a casual way. For the description of them in the fifteenth century our records are very unsatisfactory and are naturally more so in the fourteenth century. The rolls record little more than set formulae and the original bills do not add a great deal. Touching commitment to committees there seems to be no information at all; touching the number of readings there is a little; and touching debate only a formula. But something can be ascertained about amendments, not, to be sure, about the way in which they were formulated but about who added them to the bills to which they were respectively appended. The information about readings and debate, moreover, relates to the lords and can be applied to the commons only by inference.

What we are told about the reading of a fifteenth-century bill can be briefly related. From the beginning of the reign of Henry V several private bills bear on their faces written in a hand different from that of the bill the inscription *leg^{ur}*, or *leg^{ur} coram dnis*, i.e., *legitur coram dominis*. In the reign of Henry VI the briefer inscription appears on commons bills as well and is expanded to *lg^{ur} et r^e*, abbreviations for *legitur et respondetur,* as one or two instances reveal.[1]   These inscriptions appear often on later bills but not always.   In their absence the enrolled record supplies a few descriptions of the reading of bills.   The earliest seems to be an account of the way in which the lords on Saturday, 9 March, 1454, received a petition of lord Cromwell that surety to keep the peace be required of the duke of Exeter.   The bill was a private one and the text of it is not given.   But an instructive narrative runs as follows: " . . . whereof the seid Lord Cromwell put in a Bille to the Kyng and to the seid Lordes, which was too tymes radde the same day; and it was thought by the seid Lordes that sueerte ought to be had and founde; but as to the grete paynes conteigned in the seid Bille the seid Lordes seyde they wolde be advised and deliber theruppon unto Moneday or Tuesday then next commyng.   And aftirward, the xx day of Marche then next ensuyng, the seid Bille was aggreed and assented unto by the seid Lordes; and so the xxii[ti] day of Marche next folowyng the seid Lieutenaunt commaunded that the forseid Bille shuld be sent unto the Commons and so hit was doon."[2]   Important characteristics of later procedure are here revealed.   Two readings occurred at so brief an interval that there can have been little or no debate after the first; a part of the bill was accepted on second reading; there was debate on and postponement of another part of it with agreement only after eleven days; and there was possibly a third reading before dispatch to the commons two days later.   It would seem that procedure in the reading of a bill in the lords in 1454 was much the same as it was in 1509.   Although a third reading is not mentioned, the acceptance after debate following upon second reading accords closely with the essential features of a third reading.

For a long time after this we have no precise information about the reading of a bill.   The parliament rolls continue to note relative to most bills which were recorded before the

---

[1] See below, pp. 375, 302.
[2] *R. P.,* V, 264.

" commues petitions " that each was *lecta et plenius intellecta,*
but they are content with this trite formula. Finally in 1491
there was added the adverb *sepe* or *sepius*. In 1495 this became precise. A bill was *trina vice lecta* or *ter lecta,* the latter phrase finding favour also in 1497 and 1504.[3] It seems
likely that the custom of reading bills twice or oftener was
hardening into the custom of reading them three times.

Any debate to which a bill may have been subjected was
concealed rather than described by the rolls in the stereotyped
plenius intellecta or *mature intellecta.*[4] The original bills tell
us no more, either about debate in the lords or about it in the
commons. Regarding the final passage of a private bill or of a
commons bill, too, there are obscurities. Usually it is not possible to differentiate between the action of the lords and that
of the king or whoever acted for him. Endorsed on such bills
we find merely one of the phrases which the king is said to
have affixed with the advice and assent of the lords. It is
either the affirmative *Le Roy le voet* or *Soit fait come il est
desire* or it is the negative *Le Roy s'advisera*. On a few rejected bills of 1455, however, there is written on the left margin " Respectuatur " or " Huic bille Domini non concenserunt,"
the king's refusal being as usual on the dorse. Once this information is given a little more verbosely but not so clearly.
On the dorse of one of the bills of this year we read, " Memorandum that it is thought to the Kyng and to all the Lordes
that this Bille is unresonable and therefore the Kyng woll that
it be leyd aparte." [5] Although the attitude of the lords here
is not differentiated from that of the king, the memorandum
is of value as embodying what was probably the lords' phrase
of disapproval. The phrase in its affirmative guise appears
clearly on an unprinted private bill addressed to the commons

---

[3] *Ibid.,* VI, 451, 452, 460 (*persepe*), 490 (*plerique*), 492, 493, 512, 530.

[4] *Ibid.,* 217, 219, 449, 462, 416 (*ad summum intellecta*), 418 (*summarie
intellecta*), 460 (*ad plenum intellecta*), 465 (*efficaciter percepta*).

[5] C., P. & C. P. 30/7, 10, 11, 20, 9; *R. P.,* V, 328-331. The editors have
failed to note the inscription on the commons bill against John Wodde
(p. 335).

probably soon after April, 1450. While the commons sent this bill on to the lords with the customary "Soit baille as seigneurs" and while the dorse bears the approval "Le Roy le voet come il est desire," there was also written below the text "This bille is thought resonable." [6] In the light of the memorandum, there can be little doubt that these were the usual words in which the lords gave their "advice and assent" to the king. The bill, unfortunately, seems to be almost if not quite alone in bearing three inscriptions which recorded its reception by commons, lords and king respectively. The absence from nearly all bills of any separate expression of the lords' opinion, like the one written on this bill, involves us in perplexity; for it does not permit us to distinguish whether a rejected bill owed its rejection to the disfavour of the lords or to that of the king and his immediate advisors.[7] We have, however, evidence to show that the action of the lords was distinguished from that of the king at least as early as 1379. To a private bill of that year in which the University of Cambridge asked confirmation of its privileges as against the townsmen the response was a dual one as follows: "Si plest au Roy, semble as Seigneurs de Parlement qe ce lour est a granter pur cynk ans . . ." and "Il plest au Roy depuis qe les Seigneurs de Parlement l'ont ordeyne." [8] Though this bill was probably not submitted to the commons and though it tells us nothing about the procedure regarding commons bills, it does at least differentiate the action of lords and king at an early date.

In addition to the formal record of the king's approval on the dorse of a bill, there came to be often written on the face of it his personal signature in the form of a sign manual. On documents of the second parliament of Edward IV in 1463-5 this appeared as R. E. written above exceptions made to the

---

[6] A. P. 5838.

[7] For a lord's amendment, see below, p. 187, n. 59.

[8] *R. P.*, III, 68. The bill was enrolled at the end of the parliament roll following upon the commons petitions. After the lords' approval is the signature "W. de Beauchamp."

act of resumption and above certain private bills.[9]   After this it recurs often, being found on the commons bills of 1472-4.[10] It is doubtful whether Henry VI approved bills in this way and the original bills from the reigns of Richard III and Henry VII are so few as to give no reliable information.[11]

Turning now to the amending of bills in the second half of the fifteenth century, although we cannot tell whether this was usually done by commitment to a committee or by the entire house, we can at least tell something about the results. The subject naturally has to be approached from two points of view; for the amending of commons bills had a history longer than and different from the history of the amending of official bills.   Private bills, too, were amended; and it is possible that some of the amendments to them may throw light on the general subject.

The amending of early commons bills will be examined at length in a later chapter.[12]   It began with the emergence of such bills in the early fourteenth century.   We shall see that commons bills, once they had gained favour, came to supersede officially formulated measures as the basis of legislation and that from the middle of the fourteenth century to the middle of the fifteenth nearly all statutes enacted in parliament were based on commons bills.   During this time the amendment of them took place in a simple and uniform manner.   Since they were petitions which required an answer, the answer might be an unconditional assent or a conditional one. If it was unconditional, there was no amendment and the bill was likely to become a statute, undergoing the necessary

---

[9] A. P. 1414, 1417, 1418, 1419; *R. P.,* V, 530 (le Vulre), 541 (R. Suthwell), 548 (H. Wentworth), 551 (Sion nunnery).

[10] C., P. & C. P. 36/8-11, 37/5, 38/17-20, 22, 23; *R. P.,* VI, 154-162 (nos. 1-5, 8-13).

[11] On the dorse of two commons bills of 1437 and of one group bill adopted by the commons, a sign manual of some sort follows the royal response. It may be that of Henry VI; but the non-recurrence of the inscription tells against this. See below, p. 276.

[12] See below, pp. 261-85, 310-23.

verbal adaptation. If, however, there was a condition which took, as it always did, the form of a reservation, a limitation, an exemption, an exception, an added provision or even an explanation, this became an amendment. At first the answers to all commons petitions presented in a parliament were written down together in a series as was appropriate in answering the different articles of a single comprehensive petition; but from about 1439 they were usually inscribed each on the dorse of the bill which it answered.[13] This practice was still the accepted one in 1453 and it is in the answers endorsed on commons bills that we usually find whatever amendments were made to them. Since the answers often introduced the conditions which they imposed by "purveu," the term provision or proviso came to be a customary designation for an amendment and continued to be so during the remainder of the century.[14]

In the hundred years and more which preceded 1453, the amending of commons bills underwent other changes than the inscription of the answers on the back of the bill. In general, amendments became briefer and less numerous. They came to confine themselves usually to limiting the duration of the act which the approved bill became, or to reconciling it with existent law, obligations or the royal prerogative, or, finally, to exempting certain persons or groups from its operation. It will appear, too, that the commons in and after 1415 claimed the right to ratify or reject amendments which changed the intent of their bills and that for a time at least their claim was admitted. But it is not certain that amendments of the simpler sort which did not alter the intent of a bill were always submitted to them. Our problem for the moment, therefore, is to ask whether the amendments to commons bills from 1453-1503 are to be found on the dorse of the bills to which they respectively belong, whether they were submitted to the commons for approval and whether they greatly altered the purport of the bills which they amended.

To the first of these questions the answer is that a part of the royal response to a bill was throughout the half-century always endorsed on the bill, but that this part did not necessarily include the amendment. What we always find on the back of an approved commons bill is the formal "Le Roi le voet." [15] To these words might be added the amendment, if there was one, or, instead, some such phrase as "ovesque le provision a cest bille annexe." In the earlier years it was the amendment, as had been the practice for some time before; but later the second usage came to prevail. Although there were premonitions of this in 1439,[16] what was practically its first appearance was in connection with the ponderous bills of resumption, the first of which belongs to the spring of 1450. Since it was practically impossible to inscribe on the dorse of such bills the numerous exceptions made to them, the provisos were written on small parchment membranes which were filed with the bill. Some of these survive for each of the commons bills of resumption approved respectively in 1450, 1451 and 1456.[17] Small membranes were the accepted vehicle for exemptions from the somewhat similar bill of 1461 which established the claims of Edward IV, and they there protected many from what might have been sweeping confiscations of the new king.[18]

[15] Or some slight variant of this phrase. For group bills the inscription was, "Soit fait come il est desire."

[16] The response to a commons bill of 1439, asking that no one be appointed a justice of the peace unless he had lands and tenements yielding annually £20, was written entirely on a separate membrane. It ran, "Le Roy le voet Purveu toutz foitz [that, if there were none such in the county, the chancellor might appoint others]" (C., P. & C. P. 24/2; R. P., V, 28). The response to another bill of the same year, asking that citizens be not made collectors of fifteenths in the counties unless they had an income from lands there of 100 s. or more, was written both on the dorse of the bill and on a separate membrane (C., P. & C. P. 23/14; R. P., V, 25).

[17] See below, p. 187, n. 59, and A. P. 6372, 5177 (R. P., V, 186, 218), exemptions for the wardens and scholars of Merton College and of Pembroke Hall respectively.

[18] C., P. & C. P. 52/7; R. P., V, 463-475.

It was now only a step to extend this practice of inscribing amendments on separate strips of parchment to cases where bills were of the usual sort and provisos were few.

An early instance of such extension is from 1461, when a commons bill, asking that indictments hitherto corruptly made before sheriffs be heard by justices of the peace, was answered with the endorsement " Le Roy le voet," but also with a proviso on a separate membrane guaranteeing fines and amercements granted by letters patent before December 10th.[19] The usage reappears in the king's acceptance of a tunnage and poundage indenture of 1465. The indenture made the grant dependent upon the royal assent to certain measures, which it outlined, for the defense of Calais. How the king accepted the conditions but added two provisos, one by his own hand, the other by the hand of his attorney has already been related.[20] What should be added is that the two provisos were written on two strips of parchment, which were attached to the indenture and survive in this form.[21] Although subsidy indentures were not commons bills, this one had certain features of a commons bill and the new usage as applied to its amendment is instructive. A commons bill of 1465, asking for the suspension of imports from Burgundy, offers us a curious combination of the two methods of amending a bill. The burden of the amendment, refusing the penalties asked and imposing a time limit was written on the back of the bill. But the exemption of the Hansards, which is enrolled as a final royal proviso, does not appear there. The explanation is found on a separate membrane, not now affixed to the bill but outlining instructions for the clerk of parliament as follows: " Be it remembred unto my maister the Clerk of the parlement that the provision made by the Kyng for the Marchauntes of Almeyn be entred of Recorde aswele upon the act of the graunte of the Subsidie made to the Kyng by the Communs

[19] C., P. & C. P. 35/1; *R. P.*, V, 493-4.
[20] See above, p. 42.
[21] C., P. & C. P. 35/9; *R. P.*, V, 508.

of this parlement as upon the actes of Resumption and Re-
streint of merchaundises of the Duke of Burgoynes land
etc." [22]   The instance shows how flexible was the amendment
written on a separate membrane in that it could be applied
to more than one bill if desired.   But it also shows that the
older method of amending was still in 1465 the favoured
one.[23]

Not until 1478 does the new method seem definitely to have
supplanted it.   The important commons bill of that year,
which regulated the coinage and the work of goldsmiths, forbad the export of coin, plate and bullion, and required alien
merchants to expend their money on commodities of the realm,
contained, when it was presented by the commons, four provisos; but it was subjected by king and lords to two others,
which protected respectively the monastery of St. Peter,
Westminster and the king's free chapel of St. Martin le Grand.
Each of the two was written on a separate membrane and the
two membranes were and still are attached to the bill.   In
consequence, the inscription on the dorse of the bill ran, " Le
Roy le voet ovesque les deux provisions en les deux cedules a
cest bille annexes." [24]   The same method of recording an
amendment was used for the bill of this parliament which
forbad unlawful games.   Two provisos were written on separate membranes which were once attached to the bill, while
on the dorse was recorded the king's assent in the words, " Le
Roy le voete avek les cedules et provisions a ce annexes." [25]
Although the method of amending these two bills was the
same, the clerk of parliament enrolled the amendments differently.   Those of the first bill were made to follow the words
of the endorsement as they logically should; but those of

[22] C., P. & C. P. 35/18, 23; R. P., V, 565.

[23] A group bill, enrolled as a commons petition, was amended in the old
way in the parliament of 1463-65, by having four provisos written on
the dorse as part of the response (A. P. 1412; R. P., V, 506-508).

[24] C., P. & C. P. 39/8; R. P., VI, 183-187.

[25] C., P. & C. P. 39/10; R. P., VI, 188. There are marks of stitching on
the left margin of the bill.

the second were made to precede it, and the endorsement itself was abbreviated to " Le Roy le voet." Although in substance it mattered little to contemporaries whether the provisos were enrolled before or after the king's approval, it matters considerably to us. For the second method prevents us, if we have only the enrolled record, from distinguishing a proviso added by king or lords from one which was inherent in the bill, having been put there by the commons themselves. Since it was the method perhaps sometimes adopted in the parliament rolls of Henry VII and since from this reign we have almost no originals of commons bills, it becomes difficult to determine which provisos to the commons bills of 1485-1504 were inherent and which were added by king and lords. The difficulty does not arise in connection with a bill of Edward IV's last parliament in 1483, one which related to the restraint of costly apparel and was amended on a separate membrane to which the endorsement referred in noting that the king accepted the bill "ovesque cest exception." As enrolled, the amendment correctly followed upon these words.[26] It will be noticed that the term "exception" has appeared beside "proviso," although there seems to be no essential difference in the kind of limitation imposed by each.

Amendments to commons bills, therefore, which were usually known as provisos or exceptions and which were written on separate strips of parchment, became usual at the close of the reign of Edward IV and seem to be one of its innovations. When we have the originals of them or when they were carefully enrolled, we are able to distinguish between provisos which were amendments of king and lords and provisos which were inherent in the bills themselves. The former now differed scarcely at all in appearance from the amendments which Richardson described as characteristic of the seventeenth cen-

[26] C., P. & C. P. 53/9; R. P., VI, 220. Another amended commons bill of this parliament was enrolled in the same way; but no original survives to guarantee that the amendment was written on a separate membrane (ibid., p. 221).

tury.   In two respects, however, some doubt still enshrouds amendments to commons bills under Richard III and Henry VII, and cannot be dissipated in the absence of originals. One is whether a brief response, such as the limitation of the duration of a statute or the safeguarding of the king's pre- rogative, was as yet inscribed on a separate membrane rather than on the back of the bill; [27] and the other is whether some provisos which are enrolled before the response " Le Roy le voet " may not after all be amendments rather than inherent provisos, as the brief response would strictly imply that they were.

A second question to be asked about the amendments to commons bills in the second half of the fifteenth century is whether they were submitted to the commons for approval. The question has an antecedent history, as will be more fully explained elsewhere.[28]   As early as 1415 the commons claimed that no amendment which altered the purport of the " termes " of one of their bills could rightly be made to it and become part of a statute without their assent.   A bill to insure this claim was approved but the resultant act does not appear on the statute roll.   In the parliaments immediately following, amendments to commons bills were enrolled with the state- ment that they had the commons' assent; but after a little the statement no longer appears.   The status of the question is next partly revealed in connection with three bills — one a private bill of 1441 addressed to the king and presented to him by the commons, the others commons bills of 1439 and 1444.   The first begins with the declaration of John, lord Scroop, that he had in 1425 petitioned the commons to inter- cede with the king to restore to him the forfeited lands and

---

[27] An approved commons bill of 1483, forbidding the fulling of hats and caps by a newly invented " Fullyng Mille," has its last sentence, which restricted its duration to two years, added in a different ink and probably in a different hand.   This suggests that a brief amendment might appear in a third way — might be added on the face of a bill rather than on the dorse or on a separate membrane (C., P. & C. P. 40/7; *R. P.*, VI, 223).

[28] See below, pp. 261-85, especially p. 281.

other possessions of his brother Henry on the ground that
they were entailed. The petition, he continued, had been approved and the bill had been endorsed with the royal assent.
But "ensuyingly uppon which endossement was added a
clause of Purveu," which "facta fuit de avisamento Dominorum Spiritualium et Temporalium et Servientium Domini
Regis ad legem." "Whereby," the petitioner now maintained,
"hit appereth openly that the seide clause of Purveu was made
withouten knoulech or assent of your seide Communez and
ayenst the Statuit in suche cas made in tyme of the seide
Kyng your noble Fader; of the whiche Estatuit a copy ys
annexed to this Bille." Unfortunately the annexed "statute"
does not survive but it was probably a copy of the act of 1415.
Scroop went on to explain that, as a result of the "clause of
Purveu," which authorized the king to retain any lands of
Lord Henry held in fee simple, he had been disturbed in his
possession through inquisitions recently held by the king's
escheator in Yorkshire. He now petitioned that he be no
longer troubled, advancing as reasons his age and long service
but particularly the fact that the king would not by that
"clause of Purveu" recover any lands, since all had been
granted to various persons at the time of forfeiture. Possession should now be allowed him, "the seide clause of Purveu . . . notwithstanding." [29] It will be noted that the petition, although seeming to impugn the proviso on the ground
that it had not received the assent of the commons, yet did
not rest its argument primarily on this. It even asked security of possession *notwithstanding* the proviso, a phrase
which went half way toward admitting the validity of the latter. Thus the bill, while asserting the commons' right to
approve an amendment of king and lords admitted that such
amendments sometimes were not submitted to the commons
and did not altogether deny the validity of them when they
were not.

[29] E 175, 4/10; *R. P.,* V, 41-42.

An amendment to a commons bill of 1439, already noted as written on a separate membrane,[30] testifies more convincingly to the commons' claim to ratify amendments not of their own making.   In this instance the bill asked that no citizen be made a collector of a fifteenth in a county unless he had there lands and tenements to the annual value of 100 s.   The king's response granted the request, rephrasing it at length but making practically no change in it.   The response survives and shows three interlinings and six erasures.   Below it is written "a ycest cedule les communes sount assentuz."[31]   It is clear, therefore, that in 1439 a response was still sometimes submitted to the commons for their approval.   The same thing happened in 1444.   Among the commons bills of that year is one which tells of murder and robbery following upon attempted rape committed by one John Bolton, who none the less had secured a charter of pardon through becoming a "provour" (giving evidence against others) and through the king's ignorance of the seriousness of his crime.   The petition asked that the crimes constitute treason and that in the future no charter pardoning them be valid at law.   No response is enrolled but one was made and inscribed on a separate membrane.   It consigned Bolton to perpetual imprisonment as a felon, but refused the general request.   Below it was written "a cest cedule les Communes sount assentuz."[32]   Of the amendments to these two bills the first detracted little from the commons' request; the second refused a vague generalisation but granted what was immediately asked.   Both of them could be submitted to the commons with reasonable assurance that they would be approved.   What we still need is evidence that, in the middle of the fifteenth century and later, important amendments to commons bills were submitted to the commons for their approval.

[30] See above, p. 170, n. 16.
[31] C., P. & C. P. 23/14; R. P., V, 25.
[32] C., P. & C. P. 26/5, 6; R. P., V, 111.   No response whatever was enrolled.

So far as our records go, we do not get it. No amendment to a commons bill, important or otherwise, survives from 1444 to 1503 inscribed with the commons assent. To be sure, we have few original amendments to commons bills of these decades save the exceptions granted to bills of resumption and like personal exemptions from the operation of other bills. For these, it is clear, the commons assent was not asked. Perhaps other amendments were withheld from the commons in the same way, the pretext being that they lay within the scope of the prerogative. If so, the extent to which the commons' influence on legislation was restricted depends upon the importance of the amendments themselves, and to this question, which is the third one of interest touching these amendments, we may now turn.

As soon as we ask how far commons bills of the second half of the fifteenth century were diminished in their content by amendments of king and lords which were added either with or without the commons assent, we are face to face with a widely accepted thesis. It was formulated by Stubbs and has been mentioned above in connection with the origin of the term bill.[33] The passage in his history which has been quoted tended to advance as an ascertainable conclusion what was really little more than a questionable hypothesis. Relying upon the occurrence in Ruffhead's *Statutes* of the phrase "petitio . . . formam actus in se continens," he inferred that it indicated a significant change from what he called procedure by petition to procedure by bill and marked the commons' triumph in getting their bills enacted without a tampering with the text. The change, he thought, occurred toward the end of the reign of Henry VI, hence at the beginning of the half century which we are studying.[34] Professor Pollard refers to the same phrase but more cautiously. "In the fifteenth century," he says, "the practice was extended, if not also begun, of drafting petitions in the form of acts and we

[33] See above, p. 46.
[34] Stubbs, *op. cit.*, II, 608-609.

have frequent references to a bill or petition 'in se formam actus continens.'" The acts which he cites are of 1485, 1489 and 1495.[35] Elsewhere he remarks: " . . . to the end of the Tudor period procedure by bill [as distinguished from commons petition] was thought to trench on the royal prerogative." [36]

Despite the wide acceptance of this hypothesis, pointing, Stubbs fhought, to an increase in the influence of the commons, it is inherently exposed to question. In the first place it was curious to assume that petition meant one thing and bill another when throughout the century and earlier the terms were used on the parliament roll as synonymous. In the second place it was not shown that before the later years of Henry VI commons petitions were considerably changed before they became statutes but that after that time they were very little changed. To establish such a thesis would have involved a study of the answers made to commons bills before and after the middle of the fifteenth century, since it was through the addition of these answers to the content of the various petitions that the statutes were formed. In the third place, although Stubbs may not have been conscious of how much the stream of commons bills was dwindling in the second half of the fifteenth century, the results of our study of them in the preceding chapter must make us chary of accepting an inference that the influence of the commons was increasing when it is clear that the number and importance of the bills presented by them was diminishing. Lastly, Stubbs did not give attention to the sort of bills to which the supposedly innovating phrase was attached, did not in short inquire whether it was used in connection with commons bills or only in connection with private bills and official bills. It may, therefore, not be amiss to reconsider the evidence touching the phrase, "billa formam actus in se continens."

What seems to be the first occurrence of a phrase of this

---

[35] Pollard, *Evolution of Parliament*, p. 130.

[36] *The Reign of Henry VII from Contemporary Sources*, 3 vols. (London, 1913), I, p. xxxiv.

sort was in 1461. In the parliament of that year the act for
the attainder of Henry VI and certain Lancastrian lords was
recorded on the parliament roll under the caption, "Item,
quedam Cedula, formam Actus in se continens, exhibita fuit
prefato Domino Regi in presenti Parliamento sub eo qui sequitur tenore verborum." [37] Again in Edward's next parliament
of 1463-5 an act of resumption was introduced in almost the
same words: "Memorandum etiam quod quedam Cedula in
pergameno exhibita fuit coram Domino Rege . . . formam
cuiusdam Actus in presenti Parliamento fiendi in se continens. . . ." [38] Finally, Edward's second act of resumption in
1467 was described as "quedam Cedula formam cuiusdam
Actus Resumptionis in se continens. . . ." [39] The three
cedulae were drafts of official bills and were duly sent to the
commons and lords for approval. This we learn both from
the phraseology of each and from the endorsement which is
enrolled at the end of each. The enacting words, for example,
of the act for the attainder of Henry VI are, "It is declared
and adjudged by th' assent and advis of the lordes Spirituelx
and Temporelx and Commyns . . ."; and at the end of the
act is the fuller description: "Qua quidem Cedula Communibus . . . transportata fuit. Cui iidem Communes assensum
suum prebuerant sub hiis verbis, A cest Acte les Communes
sount assuntuz. Quibus quidem Cedula et assensu in Parliamento predicto lectis . . . , de avisamento et assensu Dominorum Spiritualium et Temporalium . . . respondebatur eisdem sub hiis verbis, Le Roy le voet." [40] Similar words follow
the two enrolled acts of resumption.[41]

Until 1483 the phrase "formam actus in se continens" was
used only in connection with what were called "cedulae." [42]
But in that year there was enrolled "quedam Billa formam

[37] *R. P.*, V, 476.
[38] *Ibid.*, p. 514.
[39] *Ibid.*, p. 572.
[40] *Ibid.*, pp. 478, 482.
[41] *Ibid.*, pp. 517, 576.
[42] *Ibid.*, VI, 134.

cuiusdam Actus sive Ordinationis [providing for the expenses of the household] in se continens . . ."; and in the next year, "quedam Billa cum duabus Cedulis eidem annexis formam cuiusdam Actus Conviccionis et Attinccionis diversarum personarum in se continens.[43] Both, being official bills were sent to the commons and received their assent. Later under Henry VII bills were often said to be presented in the form of acts.[44]

All "cedulae" and bills thus far noted as cast in the form of acts were official in character. It was natural that official bills should be so described and they might well have been long before 1461. Stubbs noted that two royal bills of 1439 touching the household, while not said to be in the form of acts, virtually were so.[45] Close also to the form which they were to assume as statutes were three official bills which appeared on the parliament roll as early as 1414. Although the caption, "formam actus in se continens," is wanting, the bills were phrased, not as petitions with answers but in the words of the statutes which they became. One provided for the punishment of Lollards, another for the enforcement of a statute against unlawful assemblies, a third for the capture of felons.[46] In each of the last two it was stated that divers and grievous complaints had been made to the king in the present parliament as a result of which he now ordained remedy with the advice and assent of the lords and "a la requeste des ditz Communes." To put an end to the congregations and insurrections of the Lollards he also ordained punishments "a la priere des ditz Communes." The mention of the request and prayer of the commons might lead us to think that the ordinances were framed in response to commons petitions. But the justification for the phrase lay perhaps in the various rumours and complaints which must have come to the king at the moment. Relying on these he inserted in an

---

[43] *Ibid.,* pp. 198, 244.
[44] E.g., *ibid.,* pp. 275, 444, 462.
[45] *Op. cit.,* II, 480, n. 1.
[46] *R. P.,* IV, 24-26; *Stats.,* II, 181-187. See below, pp. 260, n. 128a, 278-79.

official ordinance a phrase usually reserved for legislation based on commons petitions.

If official bills were cast in the form of acts, confessedly in and after 1461, and actually as early as 1414, was the practice at any time extended to private and commons bills? Examination of the parliament rolls reveals that it was eventually extended to the former but apparently not to the latter. In the parliament of 1488 "quedam Billa formam Actus in se continens per William Comitem Marescallum et de Notyngham . . . exhibita est . . ."; and in the parliament of 1492 "quedam Billa formam cuiusdam Actus in se continens . . . per Communitates Regni . . . exhibita fuit . . . Regi . . . ex parte Thome Lovell, Militis, . . ."[47] After this, similar occurrences of the phrase in connection with private bills are not unusual.

The type of bill to which the phrase "formam actus in se continens" was not applied during the fifteenth century was the commons petition. The closest approach to anything of the sort was in 1504 when the parliament roll noted, "Item, quedam alia Billa in Parliamento predicto formam Actus in se continens exhibita est Domino Regi per Communitatem Regni Anglie. . . ." After recording the bill and the king's assent the roll added, "Soit baille as Seigneurs."[48] Pretty clearly the bill was introduced first in the commons and thence sent to the lords. Equally clearly, however, it was not a normal commons bill. It was not enrolled on the roll along with the other bills which became statutes, resembling in this two official bills destined to become statutes, and in the same way enrolled apart. It was not couched in the phraseology of commons bills. Instead of beginning "Prayen the commons," it began "For as muche as"; and instead of asking the king to grant its request with the assent of the lords, it proceeded "Please it, therefore, the Kings Highnesse, the Lordes Spirituell and Temporelle and the Communes . . . to establishe,

[47] *R. P.,* VI, 411, 452.
[48] *Ibid.,* p. 532.

ordeyne and enacte. . . ." Finally, the content of the bill scarcely proclaimed it a commons' request. It asked that men who would shortly be obliged, when the king's eldest son was created prince of Wales, to take upon themselves the order of knighthood and who thereby would be disabled in suits and actions which they might be pursuing should be able to maintain their suits as if they had not received the order and that this rule should always apply under similar circumstances. From all these characteristics it becomes clear that the bill was a group bill, or possibly an official bill, introduced in the commons. Like other group or official bills it could in 1504 be described as "formam actus in se continens"; and the custom confining this descriptive phrase to private and official bills remained unbroken. Up to the reign of Henry VIII the phrase was not applied to a commons bill.

This circumstance alone is altogether damaging to Stubbs' hypothesis and reveals the attempt to make a distinction between petition and bill as futile. It forces us to the conclusion that the new phrase of 1461 was merely a succinct description of a carefully drafted official or private bill to which the king's assent was assured, although he might naturally add to it a proviso.[49] To such bills the assent of the commons had, of course, to be got. But if the commons wished to amend an official bill or a private bill addressed to the king, they would after 1461 have done so, just as the king did, by adding a proviso, which would not have altered the phraseology of the original bill.[50] Hence the phrase "billa formam actus in se continens" would still have been an appropriate description of it.

This last consideration suggests that, although Stubbs' hypothesis has to be rejected as based on inadequate and misunderstood evidence, there lay behind it a justifiable belief that the adoption of the new phrase in and after 1461 reflected

[49] He did this, for example, in 1495 (*ibid.*, pp. 459, 462, 468).
[50] They did so in 1495 on behalf of the prince of Wales (*ibid.*, p. 471).

some real change in the drafting of bills — that there was developing at this time a closer correspondence between many bills and the statutes which arose from them than there had been before. What this was we have already discovered. It was the increasing tendency to draft a condition attached to the acceptance of a bill as a proviso, to inscribe this proviso often on a separate membrane and finally to enroll it distinctly as a proviso rather than as an undifferentiated part of the answer. These changes were not momentous and they did not affect unamended bills, to which the new phrase was primarily applied. But they did give flexibility to the handling of bills by the two houses and they marked a step in the evolution of bill and amendment. If the phrase did not have the significance which Stubbs attached to it, it did at least synchronize with a minor change.

Now that we have perhaps been disillusioned as to any strengthening of the commons' influence on legislation through the supposed adoption of their bills without change, we may resume our inquiry as to the extent to which commons bills actually were amended between 1453 and 1504. It is the third question which we have asked relative to the amending of such bills. May it not be that, although the phrase " formam actus in se continens " did not apply to them, they were, nevertheless, amended little or not at all? If they were not, this need not surprise us, since, as we shall see, at least one-half of all commons bills throughout the preceding half-century were accepted without amendment and a large part of the other half with only slight change.[51]

As a matter of fact the usage of preceding decades was pretty closely followed. About the commons bills of the reigns of Richard III and Henry VII we cannot draw precise conclusions, since by that time amendment had come to be by proviso and we cannot always distinguish on the enrolled record (which is practically our only source) provisos which

---

[51] See below, pp. 310-29, 332-33.

were inherent in the bills from provisos which were added by king and lords. In the parliaments of 1450-1483, however, thirty-three of the fifty commons bills which were passed were approved without amendment. Of the remainder, four were subjected to amendments which limited the duration of the resultant statute, five to amendments which reconciled the bills with the prerogative or with existent obligations, and eight to exceptions in favour of designated persons or groups. Only two of these last exemptions together with two other amendments materially changed the purport of the bills to which they were respectively attached.

Of the amendments which imposed a time limit, one applied to the bill touching the extortion of exchequer officials, one to the bill protecting malt-makers in Kent, one to the remission for denizens of newly imposed subsidies on cloth and wool, and one to the restraint of imports from Burgundy.[52] In the case of the first three the limitation was for five or for three years, in the case of the last it was the king's pleasure. To the last two bills other conditions were added as well.[53]

An amendment which protected the prerogative was appended to a bill that appointed a committee of officials and "persones of the Comen House" to examine a charge of maladministration of the mint.[54] Three amendments evinced concern for existent obligations. One of them permitted a reduction of the number of superabundant attorneys in Norfolk and Suffolk only "if it be thought to the Judges reasonable"; one stipulated that a bill for transferring indictments corruptly made before sheriffs to the justices of the peace should not be prejudicial to anyone having a grant of fines or of franchises by letters patent dated before 10 December "of this present

[52] C., P. & C. P. 30/4, 30/5, 29/16, 35/18; R. P., V, 323, 324, 269, 565.

[53] The remission of the subsidy on wool was made to apply not only to shipments to Calais, as had been asked, but also to shipments through the straits of Marrok. Other conditions attached to the bill touching imports from Bungundy are noted below.

[54] Ibid., p. 634.

mone"; and the third limited the enactment of regulations
for the packing of fish by declaring it without prejudice to
anyone having forfeiture of felon's goods and by assuring to
holders of franchises the income from the penalties imposed.[55]
The amendments to a composite commons bill which was presented to Edward IV in his first parliament also sought to
reconcile its requests with the situation of the moment. The
bill, which comprised twenty-six articles each answered separately, looked toward securing guarantees that all grants, acts
and legislation of the three Lancastrian kings as well as of
Edward himself be valid. One article, touching corrodies was
refused and one guaranteeing royal obligations to the staple
was "respited." Ten were agreed to without change but the
remaining fourteen were amended in one way or another. In
general the amendments touched upon minor matters and were
most concerned that none of the king's enemies profit by the
articles, especially no one attainted in the parliament then in
session.[56]

[55] C., P. & C. P. 30/6, 35/1; *R. P.,* V, 326, 493-4; VI, 221. No original of
the last survives. The second amendment was enrolled in what is probably a misleading manner. Along with another proviso it was made to
precede the king's assent ("Le Roy le voet") as if it were, as the other
actually was, a proviso inherent in the bill. We have noted a similar misleading enrollment of provisos added by king and lords to a bill of 1478
(see above pp. 172-73). The date of the bill about false indictments is 1461
and it differed from the later one in that the endorsement made no reference to a proviso, whereas the bill of 1478 did. The origin of the proviso
of 1461 is, therefore, not altogether clear. Although it is written in a hand
different from the hand of the bill to which it is appended, it may have
been an afterthought of the commons themselves; or it may, as is assumed
above, have originated with the lords or with the king.

[56] When it was asked that grants of titles and estates be valid, the
response promised this and added new grants of annuities. To a similar
request for the validity of liberties, privileges, and franchises, there was
assent and a promise of confirmations from chancery. Salaries of justices,
barons of the exchequer, sergeants at law and the king's attorney were not,
however, to be affirmed by parliament, as requested, but were to be at the
king's pleasure. Pardons, licences and livery of ecclesiastics' temporalities
were to be valid "so that any such Advowson apperteyne not to the
Coroune." Assignments of dower were confirmed, an amendment guaran-

Of the eight commons bills, the provisos to which consisted in the exempting of certain persons or groups from their operation, the most noteworthy were the bill of resumption of 1456 and the bill conferring the crown on Edward IV. The effectiveness of the bill of resumption, like that of its predecessor of 1450, was seriously impaired by the number and scope of the provisos attached to it.[57] In this it resembled later acts of resumption which were official bills. There is no evidence that the provisos appended to any of these bills were submitted to the commons for acceptance. The phraseology of the response of 1456, which guards the prerogative, suggests, although it does not affirm, that the exemptions arose naturally out of an exercise of the prerogative. It ran: " Wherefor the Kynge, by th' advise and assent of the Lordes . . . resumeth into his hondis all maner thyngis conteyned in the seid Petition . . . , the penaltee in the seid Petition conteyned except, . . . alwey his Prerogatiff reserved. Forseyn alwaye that all such provisions and exceptions as been by his Highnesse by th' advice of the seid Lordes . . . made and agreed . . . be goode and effectuell, the seid Act notwithstondynge, for the egalte and reason that the Kynge aught to doo to his peo-

teeing that of the duchess of Bedford. If lands or other property had been granted to the late kings to be by them re-granted " of amortysment," the re-grants should remain in force, provided no crown property had abeen given in exchange. Benefices and prebends for life should not be invalidated so long as the grantee had not been attainted in the present parliament and had not " been oute with the Kynges Ennemyes." Livery of lands falling due since 4 March should be carried out unless they were affected by any attainder of the present parliament. Grants made since 4 March should be in force unless prejudicial to other grants made since the same day to certain specified officials. Lands held by the late king as feoffee to uses should not be affected, provided that no person attainted in the present parliament receive any advantage thereby. In general no one now attainted should enjoy any benefit from the operation of any of the articles (*ibid.*, pp. 489-493).

[57] C., P. & C. P. 30/1; *R. P.*, V, 300-320. On the parliament roll we read, " the tenours of which provisions and exceptions hereafter folowyn." But on the original bill this sentence ends " been conteyned in certeyne cedules thereto filed."

ple. . . ."[58]   The process by which such exemptions were
secured we know from documents which survive.   A petitioner
asked for and drafted a proviso in a private bill to the king,
and the king thereupon authorised it.[59]   Very similar to these
exceptions were the numerous provisos added to the commons
bill which conferred the kingship on Edward IV.   They were
important in serving to protect several persons and groups
from the dispossession to which they might otherwise have
been exposed.[60]

Far less numerous and important than the personal "exceptions" to these two bills were those added to each of six
other bills.   The latter were the attainder of Oldhall, the annulling of certain appointments to office in Cheshire and
Wales, the prohibition of imports from Burgundy, the regulation of cordwainers, the protection of the coinage and the
restraint of costly apparel.[61]   Only in the prohibition of imports from Burgundy could any of the exceptions have seriously affected the ends which the commons as petitioners had
in view.   Since, however, it was the Hansards who secured

---

[58] *Ibid.*, p. 303.

[59] E.g., Ancient Petitions, 1365-1384. One of the series is interesting as
showing how the lords amended a proviso which the petitioner framed.
The petition ran: "To the Kyng: Please . . . to graunt . . . by thavis and
assent of the Lordes . . . unto Maister William Hatclyff, youre phisicien,
that in the Acte of Resumpcon . . . a provision be made . . . : Provided
also that this Acte extende not nor be prejudiciall unto Maister William
Hattecliffe, Doctour in Medicyns and Phisicion sworn for the saufte of oure
person, of xl li. yerely by us unto hym graunted. . . ." Below, however,
is written in another hand, " xx li. yerely parcel of the xl li. yerely by us unto
him graunted," the words which were finally enrolled. The explanation is
to be found in the inscription on the dorse of the petition: "The lordes
spirituelx and temporelx ben aggreed that Maister William Hatteclyff be
provided for xx li. and that the " Kyng take and resume in his handes that
other xx li." (A. P. 5824; *R. P.*, V, 314).

[60] C., P. & C. P. 52/7; *R. P.*, V, 463-475.

[61] C., P. & C. P. 29/10, 35/18, 35/20, 39/8, 53/9; *R. P.*, V, 265, 366, 565, 566;
VI, 183-7, 220. No original for the bill annulling appointments in Cheshire
and Wales survives. It is possible that the exceptions added to a bill of
1459, which fined certain rebels, were not inherent, as the response implies,
but were added by king and lords (*ibid.*, V, 368).

exemption from this prohibition, there may have been a noteworthy diminution in its effectiveness.

Still other clauses in the amendments to the bill of resumption and to the bill prohibiting imports from Burgundy were of some significance; for they disallowed penalties which had been asked for. The response to the former bill, already quoted, spoke of " the penaltee in the seid Petition conteyned except "; and, where the latter bill would have imposed a penalty of forfeiture of goods and chattels on denizens or aliens who after 1 February might accept from the king a licence to import, the amendment ran, " The Kyng agreeth to this Bille except the penaltee . . . laid upon the Denysen or Alien." [62] Thereby the door was left open for the issue of licences, which, if sufficient in scope or numbers, might have thwarted the intent of the petitioners. Finally, a weighty amendment to a commons bill of this period has been noted in the preceding chapter in connection with the legislation of 1461. When in that year the commons strove to increase the revenue available for the government by recovering the income from the duchy of Lancaster, then cumbered with annuities and with a heavy feoffment, the response to their bill accepted the reform in general but exempted the feoffment, which amounted to about three-fifths of the income of the duchy.[63] In importance the amendment ranks with those appended to the bill of resumption and to the bill prohibiting imports from Burgundy. But the three stand alone in modifying in any noteworthy way the commons bills of 1453-1483.

The outcome of our inquiry into the importance of the amendments to which commons bills were subjected in the second half of the fifteenth century may now be summarized. About amendments of the reigns of Richard III and Henry VII little can be said since they cannot always be clearly distinguished. Regarding those of 1453-1483 we have discovered

[62] Ibid., pp. 303, 566.
[63] Ibid., p. 383. See above, p. 126.

that they were appended to only one-third of the commons bills approved during those years. Other approved commons bills were left without change. Of the amendments added, moreover, only those attached to three bills were of serious import. To be sure, the three — the bills for the resumption of crown property, for the temporary exclusion of Burgundian merchandise and for the recovery of the revenues of the duchy of Lancaster — were bills of first-rate importance. Since it happened that they touched closely the interests of the crown or of its dependents or of the lords, it is not surprising that they were amended. In the case of the other amended commons bills the provisos attached confined themselves to limiting the duration of the proposed act or to reconciling it with existent obligations or to exempting a few persons from its operation. Such amendments were not serious and had been characteristic of the preceding half-century, as will be shown later. It had been characteristic of the preceding half-century, too, that a few important amendments should be added to commons bills, but only a few. In no way, therefore, did the amendments of the second half of the century differ from those of the first half — neither in frequency of occurrence nor in importance. The difference between the half-centuries as we shall see, lay not in the diminution of the content of commons bills by amendment but in the number and importance of the commons bills introduced and accepted.

From the amendment of commons bills we may now turn to the amendment of official bills; and the questions to be asked differ a little from those which have been asked about the amending of commons bills. In the first place we must be assured that the commons presumed to amend official bills at all. If they did, were the amendments on separate membranes? And lastly were they of much significance? If they were, the commons' influence on legislation flowed into a new channel.

In our examination of the characteristics of official bills we discovered that one of these was the appearance below each bill of a phrase indicating the commons' approval. Throughout the half century few originals of official bills which survive are without the inscription, "A cest bille les communes sount assentuz." The custom of thus registering assent dates from the first half of the century. During this earlier period, however, official bills which became statutes were few, although many which did not become statutes were also presented to the commons for their approval. The latter sort of official bill was also characteristic of the second half of the century; and we may at this point appropriately enlarge the scope of our inquiry to include bills of both sorts. The influence of the commons, if exerted to amend an official bill, was just as noteworthy in one instance as in the other.

To discover from the enrolled record alone whether a proviso was added to an official bill by the commons is more difficult than to discover whether a proviso was added to a commons bill by king and lords. As we have seen, the latter sort of proviso when enrolled followed upon the king's assent, at least until 1478, and was thus clearly distinguishable. But the enrollment of it before the endorsement in one of the bills of that year was an ominous sign which impaired for us the value of later enrolled records; for, after 1478, it was not always possible to be certain that a proviso enrolled before the king's assent was an inherent one, as it hitherto had been, or whether it was added by king and lords, as was the one of 1478. A difficulty not unlike this confronts us in regard to amendments to official bills. These were of three sorts. Some provisos were inherent in the bills themselves, so appearing on the original bill and on the parliament roll. Some were added to the bill by king or lords and were written on separate membranes before they were sent along with the bill to the commons. Lastly, some were commons amendments, written either on the original bill or on separate membranes and returned along with the bill to the king and lords. The difficulty lies in distinguishing the last sort from the other two,

and this sometimes even when we have the original bill. Three
or four illustrations from bills of 1453-1461 will make clear
these types of amendment.

In 1453-4 an official bill which imposed penalties for disregard of a summons which enjoined appearance before chancellor or council ended with three paragraphs each introduced
by "Provided that." They included material for rather more
than three provisos, and one of the restrictions was to the
effect that "noo matere determinable by the lawe of this lande
be by this Acte determined in other fourme than after the
cours of the same lawe in the Kynges Courtes. . . ." Below
the bill and the provisos was inscribed, "A cest bille les
Comyns sount assentuz," and on the back of it, "Le Roy le
voet." Only the latter inscription was noted on the parliament roll.[64] The bill illustrates the treatment of inherent
provisos, although, if we had merely the enrolled record, we
might from such a restriction as that quoted conjecture that
perhaps one or more of the provisos had originated with the
commons. The bill was enrolled as one of the "communes
petitions" and became a statute.

In 1460 an official "Cedula sive Billa," which did not become a statute, assigned to the duke of York and his sons
an annual income of 10000 marks, the yield of specified estates.
It concluded with an inherent amendment protecting the king's
interests in the duchy of Lancaster. The parliament roll then
relates, "Item due alie Cedule exhibite fuerunt in Parliamento
predicto et Cedule sive Bille predicte annexe. . . ." The two
annexed schedules, which were provisos, protected the interests of the bishopric of Exeter and of the nunnery of Sion
respectively. After reciting them, the roll continued, "Que
quidem Cedula sive Billa et due alie Cedule predicte transportate fuerunt et deliberate Communibus Regni Anglie . . .
quibus iidem Communes assensum suum prebuerunt sub hac
forma, A cest Bille et a les Cedules a ceste Bille annexes les

---

[64] C., P. & C. P. 29/12; *R. P.*, V, 266-7.

Commyns sount assentuz." Bill, schedules, and commons' assent were now read in the lords and approved by the king with "Le Roy le voet." At the same time, however, the king "quasdam provisiones et exceptiones in dicto Parliamento deliberat quas super istis premissis inactitari mandavit." Four other provisos followed, protecting respectively the interests of the duchess of Bedford, of the duchess of Suffolk, of lord Stanley and of the manor of Hawardyn.[65] Three sorts of provisos thus appear in connection with this bill, none of them originating with the commons. One was an inherent proviso, two were provisos on separate membranes sent with the bill to the commons and four were provisos added by the king after the bill had passed both houses and added apparently without the assent of either house.[66] The last were probably on separate membranes, although in the absence of the originals we cannot be certain of this. We can be certain of it, however, in the case of another official bill which had a single amendment made to it in much the same way as the four provisos were added to the duke of York's bill. This other bill was the attainder of Henry VI and many of his adherents in 1461. It was duly inscribed with the commons' assent, was, the parliament roll tells us, then read in the lords, and with their approval was endorsed, "Le Roy le voet." But a proviso excepting John Neuburgh was enrolled after this sentence and the endorsement of the original bill explains what had occurred. It ran, "Le Roy le voet ovesque cest provision a cest bille annexe"; and to the bill had been duly attached the proviso, as we now have it, on a separate membrane.[67] It would seem, therefore, that even after an official bill had been approved by both houses, the king might attach

---

[65] *Ibid.*, pp. 380-2.

[66] The same three sorts of provisos were added to a private bill of the preceding parliament which gave to Prince Edward the duchy of Cornwall; and the commons' assent to the officially appended schedules was in the words quoted above (*ibid.*, pp. 356-63).

[67] *Ibid.*, pp. 476-83; C., P. & C. P. 52/8/11.

to it a proviso on a separate membrane without getting the assent of either house.[68]

A third official bill or "cedule," this time from 1454 and concerned with the appointment of certain lords to guard the sea, illustrates the addition of amendments both by the drafters of the bill and by the commons. But we learn this only through the preservation of the original which reveals that some provisos were written in one hand and some in another. All the amending is done on the original bill, none of it on attached membranes. The addition made by the hand that drafted the bill defined more closely one clause of it. Where the bill referred to the subsidy of tunnage recently granted to the king, there was written in, "cloth oonly excepte for the terme of III yer." It was an exemption granted in another bill of this parliament, perhaps after the introduction of the bill to guard the sea. Two other changes were inserted in the hand which inscribed at the end of the bill, "A cest cedule lez Communes sount assentuz." Since this hand must have been one which gave expression to the will of the commons, changes written in it were commons' amendments. The first of them was the insertion of the clause, "ne that the said act bee preiudicial to eny personne or personnes for whom eny act is in this parliament made for paiement of the wages of Caleys"; and the second was the addition of the last sentence, "and that this Acte be not prejudiciall to eny persone or persones whiche by auctorite of an nothir Acte in this present Parlement made shall lenne M li. or eny parcell thereof toward the kepyng of the See. . . ." The bill was further changed in two ways but we cannot tell by whom. Three paragraphs were altogether elided and do not appear at all on the roll

---

[68] Three provisos were thus attached to a household bill in 1454 (A. P., 1187, 1187A; *R. P.*, V, 246-7). One proviso was in the same way attached to an unprinted official bill of 1453 which annulled a grant made in 1444 to the duke of Suffolk of the wardship and marriage of the young duchess of Somerset. The amendment, which was a single line on a strip of parchment, protected anyone "having title or interesse in any of the premisses by force of the king's letters patent" (C., P. & C. P. 29/17).

of parliament.   The first would have given to the five lords for three years as great "power, authoritee and jurisdiction" as the admiral of England had and would have exempted them and their men from the admiral's jurisdiction; the second would have permitted them "to make patisment in any place or Cuntrey upon the Kyng's enemyes . . . without any enpechement of the Kyng or any other persone therfore," provided this was not prejudicial to the captain of Calais or his lieutenant; and the third would have excused them for the subsequent loss of "any place or fortresse" which they might have captured.[69]   Since all of these elisions diminished somewhat the authority and privilege given to the five lords, they may have been the work of the commons who, pretty clearly, added two cautious provisos.   If they were, it shows this body acting vigorously in changing an official bill; if they were not, the commons added at least two minor amendments.

These illustrations show that amendments to an official bill, when they were not inherent, might originate with king and lords either before or after the bill had been sent to the commons or they might originate with the commons themselves.   In order to estimate the commons influence on legislation we should like to know how often the latter sort occurred.   From the first half of the fifteenth century, when, as we shall see, few official bills were enacted as statutes, there come one or two early instances of commons' amendments to such bills.   In 1429 an official bill touching the misuse of judicial records had attached to it a schedule on which was noted, "Les Communes sount assentuz a la bille a cest cedule annexe parissint qe les forsprises en cest cedule comprisez soient affermez come parcelle de la bille."   The proviso follows and was incorporated in the enrolled form of the bill.[70]   Another and earlier instance was less clearly expressed but at least by inference is as authentic.   In 1406 a bill was drawn up by the

---

[69] C., P. & C. P. 29/4; *R. P.*, V, 244.
[70] C., P. & C. P. 19/16, 17; *R. P.*, IV, 354.   See below, p. 308, n. 37.

prince of Wales and the lords temporal and spiritual instituting new measures against Lollards, including the bringing of the accused before parliament. No original of it survives and it did not give rise to a statute. But an introductory clause tells us that it was presented in parliament by the speaker of the commons. " [He] pria en noun des ditz Communes qe mesme la Petition purroit estre enactez et enrollez en Rolle de Parlement et tenuz pur Estatuit tanq'al proschein Parlement. Quel prier le Roy de l'advys et assent des Seigneurs en Parlement graciousement ottroia." It is unusual to find at so early a date a lords bill thus submitted to and sponsored by the commons. Of immediate interest, however, is the discovery that in the bill itself there is no intimation that its duration was to be limited. What we have, therefore, is a lords bill which the commons had been induced to support and present but which they accepted with the important amendment that the legislation endure only until the next parliament.[71] The amendment incidentally is of interest relative to the commons' attitude toward anti-Lollard legislation.[72] But it seems to be the first instance of a commons' amendment to a lords bill.

If we now return to such amended bills as are preserved between 1453 and 1503, it quickly appears that we find very few of them. The bill for the appointment of lords of the sea just cited seems to be the only original bill preserved. Among those enrolled we find, apart from many bills with inherent provisos, a considerable number amended much as was the bill for the duke of York. Provisos were added on annexed membranes before the bill was sent to the commons. The parliament roll reveals this by using the phrase " billa et cedule transportate fuerunt communibus," thereby making clear the implications of the inscription which stated that the commons had assented to the bill and to the annexed schedules. In the reigns of Richard III and Henry VII we

[71] *R. P.*, III, 583.
[72] See below, p. 276, n. 173.

sometimes find the commons inscribing their assent on the appended membranes as well as on the bill. This happened, for instance, in 1484 and 1485.[73] Whenever, therefore, we find either the *transporta* clause or the commons' assent inscribed on the annexed proviso, we can feel assured that the provisos were not commons' amendments. There are a few cases, however, in which we have neither of these assurances. One or more provisos appear on attached membranes without any inscription on them and there is no *transporta* clause. The commons' inscription on the bill records, as did the one on the duke of York's bill, that the commons assented to bill and to annexed schedules. Normally we should infer that this was an abbreviated record of what occurred in the case of that bill and that the schedules to which the commons assented were official ones. But there is one bit of evidence which suggests that there may sometimes have been concealed behind the commons' inscription, when there is no *transporta* clause, one or more commons' amendments.

The evidence occurs in connection not with an official bill but with a private bill of 1465. In that year the nunnery of Sion asked the king to confirm with the assent of lords and commons their existent privileges, reciting charters of 1421 and 1461 and adding the confirmation which they desired. The parliament roll, implying that the bill was sent to the commons, explains what there befell it. "Cui quidam Petitioni ac *cuidam Cedule per Communes* Regis nostri Anglie in dicto Parliamento existent[es] *dicte Petitioni annexe* iidem Communes assensum suum prebuerunt sub hiis verbis; A cest Petition et a la Cedule a ycelle annexe les Communes sount assentuz." Although the inscription is like that written on the duke of York's bill, the schedule to which it referred had in this case not been appended when the bill came to the commons but was appended by them. It reserved rights which any of the king's lieges might have in the nunnery's posses-

---

[73] *R. P.,* VI, 251, 273.

sions and which the mayor of London had in supervising the river Thames. Petition, schedule, and assent were, as usual, read in parliament before the king, who with the approval of the lords answered, "Soit fait come il est desire." [74]

If testimony like this of a private bill were repeated in connection with official bills and repeated not once only, we might conclude that some of the provisos annexed to official bills and referred to in the commons' inscription were actually commons amendments. But such testimony does not recur touching either private or official bills. The instances, too, in which the commons' inscription is ambiguous, since unattended by the "transportata" clause, are relatively few. Nor was the content of the amendments in these cases usually such as to imply that they emanated from the commons. Even if some of them did, these were not of a character greatly to enhance the repute of the commons as contributing to legislation. Most of them belonged to the year 1474. Two were appended to private bills which asked the king to restore estates forfeited through outlawry or treason, and protected persons who had drawn profit from the estates when they were in the king's hands. The others were added to official bills. One qualified the settlement of the Warwick lands upon the dukes of Clarence and Gloucester and their wives by a proviso that they might alienate the lordship of Chesterfield and Scarnesdale to the king, as they might not alienate any other part of the inheritance; another protected several beneficiaries of acts of parliament from a preferential assignment of £600 on the customs now made to the earl of Douglas; another included within a bill requiring velvets and cloths of silk or gold to be sealed by the collectors of poundage such of these stuffs as being within the realm might be offered for sale after Michaelmas, while a second amendment exempted from the bill's further requirement that all exported cloths be surveyed and pay subsidy

---

[74] *Ibid.*, V., 551-555; A. P., 1419 B, 1419 A. The schedule was attached to the bill by four stitches. The bill itself bears the king's sign manual above the text.

anyone who had the king's licence to ship cloths and retain the subsidy on them; still another declared that no prejudice to any of the king's lieges should arise from a bill which enabled anyone accompanying the king on his "Viage" overseas to appoint attorneys, have livery of lands and be able to transfer estates; finally, the many provisos to an act providing income for the king's household were special protections for many people.[75]   All of these amendments, save perhaps that safeguarding parliamentary beneficiaries against the earl of Douglas' assignment and that guaranteeing to exporters of cloth their licences, were of the kind which usually appeared as official amendments.   It is unlikely that they were commons' amendments here.

It thus appears that there is little ground for thinking that the commons amended official bills to an appreciable degree in the second half of the fifteenth century.   The right to approve such bills along with any amendments which might already have been attached to them they consistently exercised.   Amendments of their own which are discoverable reduce to two appended to a bill of 1454 which appointed five lords to guard the sea.   The identification of these is possible through the hand in which they were written.   Two commons' amendments also were made to a private bill of the nunnery of Sion submitted to the king in 1465.   This is clear from the description of the parliament roll.   Whether, further, certain

---

[75] A. P. 1452 B and A; C., P. & C. P. 38/13, 38/1, 37/3, 4, 36/9, 38/23, 40/2; R. P., VI, 129-131, 100, 132, 154-5, 162, 198-202. The last instance differs slightly from the others in that the bill is said to have been carried (*transportata*) to the commons, while nothing of the sort is said about the provisos. Precisely what provisos are referred to in the commons' inscription is uncertain. The original bill has only one attached. Of the many which are enrolled after the inscription several begin, "Provided alwey that thys Acte or eny other Acte in thys present Parlement made . . ." and several others, "Provided alwey that nother thys Acte of Resumption nor noon other Acte made. . . ." Since the household act was not an act of resumption, it seems that these personal exemptions were blanket ones secured to guard their beneficiaries against any possibly confiscatory acts. Pretty clearly they did not originate with the commons.

provisos of 1474 were commons' amendments depends upon what inference is to be drawn from the inscription which the commons wrote upon them. This may have implied what it did in the private bill of 1465; or it may have implied what it did in other official bills about which we have more information. Even if we adopt the former interpretation where it seems appropriate, the commons' influence in amending official bills during this half century was slight, so slight as to be negligible. At most it was confined to protecting in a few instances existent obligations which conceivably might have been infringed by the provisions of a proposed bill.

This conclusion is an answer to a part of the inquiry undertaken in this chapter. We set out to ask whether the commons bills and the official bills of the second half of the fifteenth century which were examined in the preceding chapter were to any degree amended — the former by lords and king, the later by the commons. Through difficulty in interpreting the enrolled records of the reigns of Richard III and Henry VII our answer has to be based largely on the bills of 1453-1483. During this period, the commons, it is clear, amended official bills little. The king and lords amended commons bills much more often but usually in no very significant way. Their provisos in general confined themselves to limiting the duration of a proposed statute, to reconciling it with existent law and obligations or to exempting certain persons or groups from its operation. In some three instances their provisos went beyond this and diminished the substance of what was asked for — notably the amendments to a bill of resumption, to one suspending imports from Burgundy and to one asking the utilization of the revenues of the duchy of Lancaster. This attitude of king and lords toward commons bills was very much the one which they had taken during the preceding half-century. One-half or one-third of such bills they accepted without reserve; to the remainder they added what were usually minor restrictions or changes. Although, therefore, the king and lords amended commons bills more often than the commons amended official bills, the outcome of all the amending of the half-century need change little the conclusions of the preceding chapter. If anything, these conclusions are emphasised. The commons were playing a continually decreasing part in the legislation of the period, while the authors of official bills were playing a continually increasing part in it. Further negative evidence which has emerged in the course of our inquiry, the doubt whether the commons were given an opportunity to ratify most of the amendments made to their bills by king and lords, an opportunity granted them at times in the first half of the century, fortifies this conclusion.

While the half-century thus witnessed a tendency to substitute in every way legislation initiated by king and lords for legislation initiated by the commons, it witnessed also a change in the technical handling of amendments. Whereas at the beginning of the period amendments were usually a part of the answer made to a bill and usually were endorsed on it, they came during the reign of Edward IV to be written as provisos on separate slips of parchment, which at once or eventually were attached to the bill. Since provisos made in the house in which a bill originated were drafted in the same way, it becomes difficult at times to distinguish one sort of proviso from another. Despite this, the new technical device takes its place beside the increasing dominance of official bills over commons bills as a legislative innovation of the period.

CHAPTER VIII

EARLY COMMONS BILLS

THE caption "Communes Petitions," so often referred to in the preceding chapters, has frequently seemed illogical in including many bills which were not commons bills. An explanation of this anomaly has been deferred with the hint that the history of earlier commons bills might supply it. The time has come to examine this possibility. When and in what form, we may ask, were such bills first drafted and how were they enrolled on the parliament roll?

Commons bills, in the sense of petitions offered by the body which came to be called the house of commons, rarely appear among the records of the earliest parliaments.[1] They were almost unknown to the parliaments of Edward I. On the roll of the parliament of 1305, which Maitland estimated to be about one-fifth of the preserved rolls of the reign and which, as we have it, records some 500 petitions, there is scarcely more than one deserving the name of commons bill. Maitland, to be sure, points to three, each of which is noted in the margin as presented by the "communitas Anglie." In each instance, however, the text of the petition shows that the petitioners included earls and barons, while once the bishops and abbots were added. In two of the bills, the subject matter, the collection of scutage, concerned the nobility rather than knights of the shire and burgesses.[1a] It is clear that the marginal "communitas Anglie" in the time of Edward I connoted all classes in parliament.

One petition of the parliament of 1305, however, had the

---

[1] On the earliest commons bills, see Richardson and Sayles, Parliaments of Edward III in *Bull. Inst. Hist. Research*, IX, 7-13.

[1a] Maitland, *Memoranda*, pp. xxiv, 122, 126, 313. A fourth petition is similar (*ibid.*, p. 54). The four are also printed in *R. P.*, I, 166, 167, 178, 161.

characteristics, although not the name of the later commons bill. It began "ad petitionem pauperum hominum terre Anglie" and went on to complain of two evils to which the commons were often to recur — the corruption of jurors and the encroachments of ecclesiastical courts.[2]   The complete isolation of the petition and its unobtrusive designation show more clearly than anything else the novelty of commons bills in the parliaments of Edward I.   The response made to this one — a reference of anyone aggrieved to the appropriate writs — indicates, too, that it was not differentiated from the numerous private bills in the midst of which it was recorded.

Commons petitions like that of the *pauperes homines* in 1305 were not to appear frequently in parliaments of the two following decades.   For the reign of Edward II the rolls of parliament record four such in 1314 and three in 1320.   In the seven the petitioners were now "la Communaute d'Angleterre" or the "Communitas Regni" and there is no indication that they included lords or clergy.   Their appeals, too, were typical of later commons appeals.   They requested that conspirators might not serve on assizes, that charges of trespass brought to exact fines from defendants be not lightly permitted, that there be no increase of tolls at the passage of the Humber, that justices should not protect felons, that violators of the peace be more effectively tried and punished by the justices, that men indicted for murder or other felonies be not released on bail and that ecclesiastical courts should not appropriate common pleas.[3]   What is noteworthy about the seven, however, as it was about the petition of the *pauperes homines,* is that the responses were like those made to private

---

[2] Maitland, *op. cit.,* p. 305.

[3] *R. P.,* I, 289, 290, 291 (bis) (duplicates pp. 299, 319, 324), 371, 372 (the same in slightly different phraseology, p. 374), 375.   A petition of 1330 from the king's "bones gentz de sa ligeance" asked that the statute giving the Templars' lands to the Hospitallers be repealed; yet the context shows that the petitioners were not the commons at large but men to whom the lands would otherwise have escheated (*ibid.,* II, 41).

bills. Redress was promised by instructions to be given to officials, and future complainants were referred to chancery or to the common law courts. Although the grievances brought forward in some of the seven might have furnished a basis for statutes, no statutes arose from any of them. Commons petitions which were to be so honoured were to be presented in a somewhat different way. Although in later parliaments bills like these embodying a single request might be presented and occasionally were, they were infrequent; [3a] and the course of development was to lie, not through them, but through *the* commons petition.[4]

The commons petition of early parliaments was, strictly speaking, not one petition but several petitions. It reconciled the plurality of its contents with its designation, which was not plural, by a simple device. It was a petition of several articles. Although each article was in itself a petition and demanded its own response, there was a certain appropriateness in enumerating in a series the commons' requests of any session and calling the series the commons petition of that session. It is what might be expected from a period when the "common house" was itself taking form. Instead of preparing several bills to be presented to the king, the inchoate house of commons found it wiser to present a single bill in which divers requests might be briefly stated. We shall, henceforth, for want of a better name, call such a bill a comprehensive commons petition.

The emergence and superior importance of the comprehensive commons petition is indicated by the response made to a group petition of c. 1320. It was a request from archbishops, bishops, abbots, priors, earls, barons and all others who claimed to have fines, amercements, issues and chattels of felons by charters of the king's ancestors that they might have such without interference of the exchequer. To this request

---

[3a] See e.g., below p. 259, notes 125, 126, 128.

[4] On the importance of the earliest commons petitions, see Pollard, *Evolution of Parliament*, pp. 119-128.

the response, written on the dorse of the bill, ran: "Responsum est in communi in quadam petitione exhibita coram Rege et consilio que continet materiam istius petitionis et plures alios articulos tangentes communitatem Regni. Et remanet illa peticio in custodia W. de Herlestone." [5] A private or group bill, therefore, needed no specific response because the grievance of which it complained was, together with others, provided for in the response to a petition of several "articles" which touched the commonalty of the realm. A similar but less definite reply was made to a similar group bill perhaps of the same year. When the clergy of London asked for allowance at the exchequer of amercements of their tenants and of chattels of felons as granted by their franchises, the reply was, "Alia est petitio generalis in communi pro communitate regni." [6] Probably the reference was to the commons petition indicated in the first reply. We may, therefore, inquire whether from the reign of Edward II there is further and fuller evidence about comprehensive commons petitions.

There is such evidence from the reign, but the characteristics of comprehensive commons petitions may perhaps best be ascertained from a glance at two of them which survive from the early years of Edward III. The first, which dates from 1333, is a single membrane about twelve inches wide and nineteen inches long on which a series of seventeen brief articles, numbered in the margin, note the commons' requests. On the dorse is a series of answers similarly numbered. Following the answers is the inscription, "Peticio communitatis exhibita coram Rege et consilio suo in parliamento tento apud Eboracum in Octabis sancti Hillarii anno regni Edwardi terti

[5] A. P. 3926. William of Herleston was one of the two clerks who were receivers of petitions in the parliament of 1320 (*R. P.*, I, 365). I am indebted for reference to this petition to Dr. G. O. Sayles, and likewise for reference to A. P. 169, 4273, 13584, quoted below.

[6] A. P. 169. A. P. 4273 is a duplicate printed in *R. P.*, I, 380, and is endorsed with an order that a writ of chancery instruct the treasurer and barons of the exchequer to observe the charters of the clergy of London. Cf. *C. C. R., 1318-1323*, p. 306.

post conquestum sexto." The character of request and response may be understood from article IV which ran as follows: "Item prie la commune qe les Eschetours, viscountes, hundredours, Baillifs errauntz et autres ministres soient de meisme les countees ou ils serront en office eauntz suffisauntz terres en yceux solom les estatuz de ceo faitz au parlementz de Nicol et Westmoustier." To which the answer was: "Ad quartum petitionem tangentem Esceatores le statut de ceo autrefoitz fait suffit et soit garde." All the articles of the petition are in one hand and all the answers in another hand. It it clear that the petition was presented as a single complete embodiment of the commons' requests and was answered as a whole, the answer being an itemized reply to an itemized request.[6a]

The bill has left no trace of itself either on the roll of parliament or on the statute roll. The brief roll of the Hilary parliament of York in 1333 tells of the appointment of receivers and triors of petitions but records no petition of any sort. The king's business, it tells us, was considered by three groups — one consisting of six bishops and six lords, one of the remaining lords and clergy, and a third comprising "les Chivalers des Countez et Gentz de Commune," each group "par euxmeismes." Since there was not full accord about what the king ought to do, he turned for counsel to the pope and to the king of France. After the chancellor had announced the appointment of a guardian of the Scottish march and of an advisory council, the knights of the shire and the commons were given leave on the sixth day of the session to depart, the lords and clergy on the following day.[7] The significant item in the narrative is the deliberation of the knights of the shire and the commons by themselves. While this group was discussing

---

[6a] C., P. & C. P. 6/20. The MS. is in a bad state of preservation and is difficult to decipher. This roll and other early rolls will be printed by Messrs. Richardson and Sayles under the auspices of the Royal Historical Society with the title *Rotuli Parliamentorum Hactenus Inediti.*

[7] *R. P.,* II, 68-69.

the king's business, what could have been more natural than that they should formulate a petition embodying their grievances? Such was probably the origin of the petition before us.

The next comprehensive commons "petitio" which survives in its original form is one which probably belongs to 1337.[8] It begins "Ista petitio liberata fuit VIII die parliamenti" and it consists of nine itemized articles with replies to each inscribed on a second membrane. From the point of view of procedure its most interesting article is the last which ran, "Item prie la commune qe com plusours petitions ont este mys avant en parlement le queux ne ont mie estee responduz pleinement, pleise a . . . le roi qe tous les peticions mis avant en parlement [par les communes] soient totes responduz avant le lever du parlement." To this the reply was: "Quant au point touchant qe les peticions des communes seient respondues: Totes les peticions einz ces heures mises par la commune en parlement ount este respoundues pleinement devant le departir de ditz parlementz. Et quant as singuleres peticions ore bailez a yce parlement, . . . le roi voet qe les auditours ore assignez pur les trier les trient et terminent avant leur departir de mesme le parlement." To contrast

---

[8] A. P. 13584, 13587. The petition does not tell in which year it was presented. It refers to what the king granted at Nottingham, probably in the parliament of 1336, and to a statute for alien merchants recently made at York (in 1335). It speaks of the tenth and fifteenth granted to the king in "lan utyme" (1334) as fixed "a la somme dont le roi fust servi lan syme"; and the response calls this fifteenth "le tax derrainment grante." At the end, a note adds that the reply was made on Thursday the first week in Lent, the day on which the commons were given leave to depart. Of the parliaments which were held soon after 1336 and which met shortly before Lent, that of 1337 met on Monday after the feast of St. Matthias (3 March) and the first parliament of 1340 met on the octave of Hilary (Stats., I, 280; R. P., II, 107). If the petition belonged to the later year, it is likely that there would have been some record of it on the parliament roll, which survives; but there is none. If it belonged to the former year, its non-appearance in the Rotuli would be explicable, since no roll is preserved for the parliament of 1337. For the parliaments of 1336-1340, see Richardson and Sayles in Bull. Inst. Hist. Research, VIII, 79.

between the petitions of the commons and private petitions is sharply drawn.

This petition, like that of 1333, has left no trace on the parliament rolls or on the statute roll. Since the articles and the replies seem important enough to have been enrolled, the lack of record can best be explained, if it is correct to assign the petition to 1337, by the fact that no roll survives for the parliament of that year. Unsupported as this manuscript bill is by further record, it at least confirms the evidence of its predecessor of 1333. Together the two supply the key to the interpretation of other comprehensive commons petitions of the fourteenth century, which are like them but of which no originals have come down to us. For, as it happens, similar originals from the century are few. In any study of commons bills of the period we have to rely largely upon those which have been enrolled on the parliament rolls or have left some trace of their existence on the statute roll. Not that this is a great misfortune, now that we know what sort of document the clerk had before him when he made the enrollment. We are in a position to infer that his record most closely resembled the original petition when it grouped together the several articles and followed them by the series of responses. It departed a little from being a precise transcript when it transferred the responses and entered each after the article to which it pertained. The latter form came, in the course of the century, to be the approved one. Both forms appear in certain comprehensive commons bills which were earlier than those of 1333 and 1337 and which may now be described.

What is perhaps the earliest comprehensive commons petition of which we have knowledge is one enrolled on the close roll of 1309.[9] Although not describing itself as *the* petition of the commons, it begins in a sufficiently revealing manner as

---

[9] *R. P.*, I, 443-445; *C. C. R.*, *1307-1313*, p. 175. The original petition is A. P. 14698.

Messrs. Richardson and Sayles look upon this petition as one emanating not from the commons but from "the general body of suitors attending

" Les Articles souz escritz furent baillez a . . . le Roy par
la Communalte de son Roialme a son Parlement " at Westminster in the second year of his reign.   The articles embodied

parliament in contra-distinction to the king and council by whom the
petitions were considered." They associate it with similar petitions of
1325 and 1327 (described below) and see in the petitioners the " *communitas, commune* or nation at large." On the point they take issue with
Professor Pollard (*Bull. Inst. Hist. Research,* VI, 77, n. 2; IX, 8). Apparently they feel that the petitioners included the lords, as was the case in
the petitions of 1305, cited above.

But in 1346 the comprehensive commons petition was unquestionably
framed by knights of the shire, citizens and burgesses (below p. 338), and
before this year the terms *communitas, commune* and *communes* had
come, in connection with parliamentary bills, to be used to designate the
commons in contrast with the lords. The last two of them were clearly
so used in the comprehensive commons petition of 1343 (*R. P.,* II, 139,
nos. 3, 4). Likewise in the similar comprehensive bill of 1327 the first two
articles contrast " la bone Gent de la Commune," " la Comminalte " and
" la Commune " with the lords temporal and spiritual (*ibid.,* p. 7); and the
introductory phrase of the derived statute does the same (below, p. 217).
Again, the use of the terms " commune " and " communes " in the manuscript petitions of 1333 and 1337 described above is far from suggesting
that the lords are included; and the same is true of the " gentz de commune " who presented the petition of 1334 (*B. I. H. R.,* IX, 18). The
grievances voiced in these bills and in that of 1327 are like later commons
grievances. That restoration of temporalities to bishops and " a tute
Seinte Eglise " is asked for in 1327 (par. 5) is not surprising, since nearly
all later comprehensive commons petitions request observance of the liberties of Holy Church. In the reign of Edward II as well as in that of
his successor the terms *communitas* and *commune* seem to have been usually restricted to the commons. When petitioners so designated themselves
in brief petitions of 1314 and 1320 (above p. 195) there is no evidence that
any of them were lords and clergy, as had been the case in 1305. A writ
which describes a petition of 1314 from " Ercevesques, Evesques, Contes et
Barons " as the " querelam Archiepiscoporum, Episcoporum, Comitum, Baronum et *aliorum de Communitate Regni* " (*R. P.,* I, 295) employed the
last four words only as a shorter form of the phrase which we find in statutes of 1305 and 1309. There it is " aliorum nobilium et communitatum "
or " aliis nobilibus et communitatibus " (*Stats.,* I, 151, 152). In these
phrases of the statutes of 1305 and 1309, the commons are clearly distinguished from the lords, as they are in 1327 and 1343. The same distinction occurs in the statute of 1320 (below pp. 214-15). In 1309 the
description of the petitioners by themselves as " les bones gentz du Roialme " and by the answering statute as " des bones gents " (below, pp. 211-
212) is not one which suggests inclusion of the lords. In one article, which

the conditions upon which " les laies gentz " granted a twenty-fifth. In the summer at the parliament of Stamford the king gave answer — " ordena respons et remedie a meismes les

complains of inadequate measures taken to receive individual petitions in parliament, those who are aggrieved are " les Chavaliers, gentz de Citez e de Burghs e d'autres Villes qe sont venuz a son Parlement par son commandement." In all the articles of the petition the grievances are about matters which affected primarily the commons rather than the lords. The petition of 1325 (see below p. 203) about which Messrs. Richardson and Sayles especially differ from Professor Pollard has, like that of 1309, some of the earmarks of later commons petitions. The petitioners are always " voz liges gentz "; and once, as " les gentz de la Commune," they ask for observance of the privileges of London, a matter of no immediate concern to the lords. Some ground, therefore, exists for inferring that " la Communalte " of 1309 and the " liges gentz " of 1325 did not include the lords.

If, however, Messrs. Richardson and Sayles see in these phrases a designation of all men, except the lords, who happened to be present in parliament, both the representatives of shires, cities and boroughs and the unorganized group of individual petitioners, this interpretation, like the one just discussed, is unconvincing. The individual petitioners were interested, each primarily in his own petition and their petitions were received and considered differently from the comprehensive commons petition. Almost never was a private petition incorporated in the commons petition, although group petitions readily were (below p. 319-326). Since the latter were always so treated throughout two centuries, there is no reason for thinking that at the outset they were not promptly adopted by the representatives of the shires, cities and boroughs. Apart from group petitions there is no evidence that the unorganized group of individual petitioners interested themselves in the articles of a petition which touched the realm at large, or associated themselves with the official representatives of the commons in formulating them. The formulation must have been the business of these representatives and it is not unlikely that they had assumed it as early as 1309 and 1325.

It is true, however, that the word " commune " had throughout the fourteenth century a somewhat variable significance and sometimes was used in a way which distinguished the persons whom it connoted from the knights of the shire. In the description of the parliament of 1333 already quoted the group set over against lords and clergy was " les Chivalers des Countez et Gentz de Commune " (above, p. 205). But the fact that the two sorts of representatives deliberated together and were dismissed together suggests that, when the tie between them had become closer, one name would describe the entire group and the name would probably be the more generic one. As late as 1390 a bill for John Northampton began " A le Roy Supplient les Chivalers et communes de cest present parlement." But another and similar request for him was presented in the

articles . . . lesqueux sont cy dessouz escritz, c'est a saver apres chescun article le remedie qe y est ordene." On the close roll the recording clerk has transferred the responses so that, instead of being together as they were on the dorse of the petition, each appears after the article which it answered.

The articles and responses to this comprehensive commons petition numbered eleven and some of them were to have a future; for six were welded into a statute, the "statutum apud Staunford." In this form they were enrolled on the statute roll and thereby given a certain permanence. Indeed, the importance of this petition is due not only to its being probably the earliest comprehensive commons bill which we have but still more to its furnishing for the first time the subject matter of a statute. Up to this time statutes emanated from the king or at best from the king and his council. The first occasions on which the commons are mentioned as participating in legislation were at the parliaments of Westminster and Carlisle, four and two years earlier respectively than this statute of 1309. At Carlisle, in response to a petition presented by earls, barons, and "tote la Communaute de la terre" against the encroachments of the papacy, there was re-enacted a statute first enacted at Westminister in 1305 by

comprehensive commons bill, beginning "Item supplient les Communes" (below p. 231, n. 2). Despite the differing phraseology it is likely that both petitions came from the same source, the term "communes" being used more generically in the second request than in the first. In 1351 and 1353 the term "communes," as used at the beginning of the parliament roll, clearly embraced knights of the shire. In 1351 "chescun des Grantz et des Communs" who was present was told to tarry until Monday next. In 1353 there assembled in the White Chamber "le Roi, Prelatz, Ducs, Countes, Barons et les Communes." (R. P., II, 236, 246). Since Messrs. Richardson and Sayles incline to see the influence of the lords in early commons petitions, it is unlikely that they would eliminate the knights of the shire as participants in the formulation of them. Although, therefore, the formulators of the earliest comprehensive commons petitions cannot be identified with certainty, it is likely that they soon came to be, if they were not at the outset, the knights of the shires and the burgesses in parliament.

the king "de consilio Comitum, Baronum, Magnatum, procerum, et aliorum nobilium et regni sui communitatum." The re-enactment followed "post deliberacionem plenariam et tractatum cum Comitibus, Baronibus, proceribus et aliis nobilibus et communitatibus regni sui." [10] In the legislation of these years, therefore, the commons were associated with the lords, although the initiative probably lay with the latter.[11] In 1309, however, the petition which gave rise to the statute was more clearly the commons' own. The innovation was to be momentous for the future. Henceforth in place of officially drafted statutes legislation was to consist largely of commons petitions as modified by the responses made to them by king and lords. A comparison of the petition of 1309 with the resultant statute will illustrate the new procedure.

Since four of the articles of the petition related to encroachments of the king's purveyors and to pleas improperly heard by seneschals and marshals and since the responses declared that an ordinance of Edward I provided remedy for these abuses, it sufficed in part to re-enact certain "articles" of 1300.[12] The statute, however, next proceeded to enact new legislation in response to two other articles of the petition. It continued: "Et, quant a la requeste des dites bones gentz endroit des pledz trere et tenir a les portes des Chasteux le Roi, veut le Roi qe les Conestables de ses Chasteaux ne destreignent gentz a pleider devant eux nul plai de forein Conte ne deinz Conte autrement qe auncienement soleit estre fait." If now we turn to article ten of the commons petition we find it embodying a complaint that "common pleas of the king's bench in the counties" instead of being held in some "certein lieu" were drawn by constables before the gates of their castles. The

---

[10] *R. P.*, I, 219; *Stats.*, I, 151, 152.

[11] The preamble to the statute of provisors of 1351, however, says that at Carlisle Edward I heard the petition put before him and his council by the commonalty (*ibid.*, p. 316).

[12] *R. P.*, I, 444, articles 1, 4, 5, 7; *Stats.*, I, 154-156. "Les queux articles le Roy qe ore est a la requeste de ses bones gentz de son Roiaume . . . voet et commande qe desormes soient pleinement tenuz et gardez. . . ."

response is in precisely the words of the statute which follow "veut le Roi." The statute next responded to a commons' further request. This asked for the abolition of certain customs on wine, cloth and avoirdupois which, the petitioners declared, were enhancing the prices of commodities by one-third. The king's reply and the statute drafted from it are in almost identical words. The former enjoined that the customs in question "soit souztrete et oustee a la volente le Roy pur saver quel profit et quel avantage accrestera a li et a son poeple per cele souztrete et puis en aura le Roi Conseil selonc l'advantage q'il y verra, Sauve totes voies a . . . le Roy les auncienes prises et customes auncienement dues et approvees." The statute changed the first verbs to "cessent," inserted after "saver" the words "et estre avise," changed "per cele souztrete" to "par cesser de la prise de celes custumes" and made a few alterations in spelling. But in general the correspondence of statute with response is so close that we may safely say that the former was derived from the latter with insignificant verbal changes.

Only these two articles of the petition of 1309 as answered by the king gave rise to articles of the statute. The statute notes that "quant a les autres requestes qe les dites bones gentz fesoit au Roi" the king has granted them "bonement" and has charged the chancellor and his other ministers to guard them firmly. If anyone should still be aggrieved on any point contrary to the ordinances and the said articles, the chancellor will give remedy by writ. At the most, therefore, six of the eleven articles of the commons petition of 1309 were of a character to give rise to legislation. Four of these could be met by the re-enactment of an earlier ordinance and two of them elicited replies which became articles of a statute. For grievances enumerated in the others remedy could be got from the chancellor. The most significant feature of this legislation, of course, was the almost literal reproduction of two replies as two articles of a statute. More will be said later about the derivation of fourteenth- and fifteenth-century statutes; [13] but we may as well note at once that the expedient adopted in 1309, whereby some articles of a statute derived directly from the responses to commons petitions, was to mould legislation during these two centuries more than anything hitherto devised. The appearance of the usage in what seems to be the earliest comprehensive commons petition which survives coordinates from the outset such petitions with the influence exerted by the commons, as distinct from lords and clergy, upon statutory legislation.

From the reign of Edward II only one other comprehensive commons petition comparable with that of 1309 is recorded; and, with one exception, no statute of the reign other than the statute of Stamford was derived from such a petition. The other petition was that embodied in six articles presented by the commons in 1325 and enrolled under the caption, " Memorandum quod Petitiones subscripte concesse fuerunt." [14] That they were articles of one petition rather than six independent petitions is shown by the introductory words of all except the first, " Et auxint, prient voz liges gentz. . . ." Two added the address, " Sire," and two explained that the " gentz " were those " de la Commune." They gave rise to no statute. Since the replies to three of them referred the petitioners to remedies in chancery, the three were akin to those articles of 1309 which were referred to the chancellor without specific legislation. The reply to another article defined certain royal perquisites in honours which had come into the king's hands, perquisites which were being interpreted in a way prejudicial to tenants of the honours, as those possessed by lords before the honours escheated. It did not change custom and did not demand legislation. A fifth reply promised a hearing to petitions which had received no response and a sixth assured to London the observance of its franchises. From none of the six would legislation naturally have sprung.

The sixth petition, however, is noteworthy for a feature

---

[13] See below, pp. 216-21, 248 *et seq.*
[14] *R. P.,* I, 430.

which was to characterize many commons petitions of the future.   The commons besought that the citizens of London might enjoy their franchises as against the king's ministers, adding "pur ceo qe nostre commun recoverir est en la dite cite."   Normally the citizens of London would themselves have petitioned for their liberties and the petition would have been a group one, i.e., technically a private bill.   In this instance, however, the commons at large adopted the appeal, adding in explanation their general interest in the city.   There was, of course, some justification for incorporating in a commons bill the petition of a large group within the commonalty. But to do so introduces a distinct modification into our conception of a commons petition.   Henceforth we shall be prepared to find that one or more articles of such a petition may relate not to the affairs of the community at large but to some group within it.

The statute of Edward II's reign, which, like the statute of Stamford, was based on a commons petition, is often called the statute of Westminster IV.[15]   It dates from 1320 and comprises only two articles.   One of these provided that sheriffs and other ministers must not fail to acquit at the exchequer those from whom they had taken money, having given therefor a tally or other acquittance; the other declared that there must be no delay in impanelling juries of twenty-four men through waiting for recalcitrant jurors to appear.   As basis of this statute no original petition survives nor is any such recorded on the transcript of the parliament roll of 1320 printed in the *Rotuli*.[16]   This transcript, however, is imperfect; and on the original parliament roll, which has now been found, the petition is recorded in full.[17]   Thereby is justified the introductory phrases of the statute which explain that the two grievances were shown to the king "par pleinte de la Commune de son roialme" and add that the statute was made "par

---

[15] *Stats.*, I, 180.
[16] *R. P.*, I, 365-386.
[17] Exch., Parl. Ro., no. 23.   This information I owe to Dr. Sayles.

assent des Prelatz, Countes et Barouns et tote la Commune
de son Roialme."

While the reign of Edward II thus presents to us in enrolled
form only two statutes based on commons petitions along with
a third similar comprehensive petition from which no statute
arose, the reign of Edward III was prolific of comprehensive
commons bills. Those of 1333 and 1337, surviving in their
original form but not known to us in any enrolled or derived
form, have already been described. Much more important
than either is the commons petition of Edward's first parliament in 1327. Thus far we have known it only as it has been
somewhat carelessly printed by the editors of the rolls; but a
better version will soon be available.[18] Despite the imperfec-
tions of the text of the *Rotuli,* the general character of the
petition is clear. That the original was a single bill of some
forty articles is shown in three ways. At the end it is called
" ceste Bille endente "; each article except the first is introduced by the words " Item, prie la Commune "; and, lastly,
each response, instead of following the petition to which it
refers, is grouped with its fellows in a series which follows the
series of petitions. Without doubt the articles of the petition
were written on the face of the original bill, the responses on
the dorse or perhaps on a second membrane. The bill must
have been in appearance like that of 1333 or like that of 1337.

One other feature of the original seems to be implied in the
word with which the bill concludes.[19] The last paragraph
asked that writs be sent to the sheriffs and to the bishops bidding commons and clergy respectively swear, as their representatives had just sworn, to support the king's party — " de
meyntenir la querele." [20] Whereupon follows a disavowal: " et

[18] *R. P.,* II, 7-12. The carelessness on p. 7 is striking. The forthcoming
text of Messrs. Richardson and Sayles will correct that of the *Rotuli* in
the light of an almost contemporary version, C., P. & C. P., roll ii (cf. *Bull.
Inst. Hist. Research,* IX, 16).

[19] The last three printed articles were on an attached schedule.

[20] " querele " is used to indicate a political group in an earlier caption

si nul autre Bille soit bote avant en nom de la Commune nous
le disavowm fors qe ceste Bille endente." The only bill, therefore, authoritatively proceeding from the commons in this parliament was this bill which assumed the form of an indenture.
A similarity with later subsidy indentures is at once suggested.
If these implied, as presumably they did, bargains with the
king, so this first bill of Edward III's parliaments must have
been one side of a bargain in which the commons swore to support the young king's "querele." That other comprehensive
commons bills of the reign were indentured bills is not probable. Those of 1333 and 1337 were not. Later in the reign
there did not again arise the precarious situation which existed
in 1327, and at no subsequent time did the commons swear as
they then did to support the king's party.

Two features of the bill of 1327 affiliate it with comprehensive commons petitions already described. One is the inclusion of an article which was properly a group petition. We
have seen such an article presented by the commons for the
city of London in 1325. In 1327 the thirty-eighth article of
the commons petition instead of beginning "Item prie la Commune," as the preceding articles did, began "Item Prient les
Gentz dela Trente." It continued with a complaint against
a local official, the justice of the forests beyond Trent, alleging
that he had re-incorporated within the forest villages, lands
and woods excluded in the time of Edward I. A preceding
article, number thirty-one, voiced at greater length a similar
complaint against two recent justices of the forests this side
of Trent. The article began with the usual "La Commune
prie remedie" precisely as did the article of the petition of
1325 touching the city of London. The two articles of 1327,
both asking redress for similar abuses, show how short was the
step from a commons petition asking remedy for a group to a
group petition incorporated in a comprehensive commons bill.

of this parliament: "Petitiones pro illis qui fuerunt de Querela Thome,
Comitis Lancastre" (*ibid.*, p. 5).

The second feature of the commons bill of 1327 which affili-
ates it with an earlier petition is that several of its articles
along with the replies to them were transmuted into statutes.
It will be remembered that this occurred on a small scale in
1309. Four articles of the petition of that year gave rise to
the re-enactment of an ordinance of Edward I and the replies
to two others became articles of a statute. In 1327 this correspondence between the articles of the commons petition along
with their answers and the articles of the statute of the year
was greatly extended. Of the seventeen articles of the statute
all except one derive from certain of the forty-one articles of
the petition. The one article of the statute which has no such
counterpart was pretty clearly derived from a petition of the
clergy. It states that, whereas bishops, abbots and priors have
long been harassed with royal requests for "empensions, pro-
vendes, Eglises et Corodies" so that they cannot reward their
own friends, the king "ne voet desore prier mes la ou il
devera."[21] That the statute as a whole arose from the articles
of the petition is indeed proclaimed in its introductory phrase.
This runs: "le Roi . . . a la requests de la commune de son roialme per lor petitions mys devant luy et son conseil en le dit
parlement par assent des Prelatz, Countes, Barons et autres
grantz . . . ad graunte . . . a toutz jours les articles soutze-
scritz."[22]

The method by which the articles of the statute arose from
the articles of the petition can be pretty precisely ascertained
by a comparison of the two groups, including always the royal
responses to the articles of the petition. For brevity we may
henceforth refer to the articles of each group as statutes and
petitions respectively; for the responses themselves call each
article of the comprehensive commons petition a petition. The
principle upon which the statutes of 1327 were framed appears
to have been the simple one of joining petition and response,

[21] *Stats.*, I, 256, article x. The antecedent petition is wanting.
[22] *Ibid.*, p. 255.

the former on occasion being modified or even replaced by the latter. In the application of the principle we can, therefore, discern some six slightly different modes of procedure. If the response was a simple assent, the statute might become the petition in affirmative phraseology. If it was a simple assent, the statute in affirming the petition might, however, rephrase it so as to make it simpler and clearer. Thirdly, the response might define a penalty where the petition had merely asked for remedy and the penalty would, of course, appear in the statute. The response, again, might add a restriction, or a reservation, which would be incorporated in the statute. The response might refuse or postpone some part of the petition while granting the most of it. The response, finally, might so modify the petition that the statute would differ considerably from it and would thereby become the response rather than the petition. Of the sixteen statutes of 1327 which arose from commons petitions, the most were formed in accordance with the second method. But each method was used.[23]

The best illustration of a statute formed by merely affirming a petition is the last of the series, number 17. The petition, number 41, asked that indictments taken by sheriffs or bailiffs of franchises be entered on a " Roule endente," of which one part might remain with the indictors, the other with whoever held the inquest, the latter to be shown to the justice who might come to make deliverance. The object was to prevent embezzlement of the indictments. The response ran, " Il fait a faire "; and, since it introduced no modification and since the petition was clearly phrased, the statute followed it almost verbatim, changing an appeal to an imperative. Another statute which did little more than repeat a petition was the brief number 9. This assured to cities, boroughs and franchised towns their privileges " solonc ce qils deyvent avoir et soleyent." The words quoted were from the response to petition 14, whereas the petition had

---

[23] *R. P.,* II, 7-12; *Stats.,* I, 255-257. The illustrations of the following paragraphs are from these pages and will be referred to by the numbers of the respective petitions and statutes.

asked that the privileges might be "sauntz disturbance . . . nient blemies."

This instance is perhaps the simplest transition to some eight statutes each of which, while derived immediately from the petition, modified more or less the phraseology of it. A good illustration is statute 16 derived from petition 40. The latter ran: "Item La Commune prie sovereynement qe bones Gentz et leaux soient assignez en chescun Cunte a la Garde de la pees qe ne soient meintenours de mausbaretz en pays et q'ils eient power de chastier le mesfesurs solome ley et resun." The response was: "Quant a la Petition touchant la garde de la pees, Il fait a faire par Election du Conseil le Roi. Il plest au Roi." What the statute did was to weld the rambling request into a compact, well-formed sentence: "Item pur la pees meultz gardes et meyntener, le Roi veot qen chescun Countee qe bones gentz et loialx queux ne sont mye meyntenours de malveis baretz en pays soient assignez a la garde de la pees." The statute, somewhat irregularly, failed to add the phrase of the response which directed that keepers of the peace be chosen by the king's council. Other statutes which modified petitions much as this one did were longer and sometimes omitted explanatory phrases. For instance, statute 6, which rephrased petition 10, remedied grievances that arose when the king's subjects granted him an "eyde de lour biens." The petition more verbosely had spoken of the aid as "les deners paies a l'Escheker, ceo est asavoir de xv, xvi, xvii, x and xx." The abbreviating and recasting of the phraseology of a petition without changing its purport but making it imperative was the most usual procedure of this parliament.[24]

The incorporation of a specific penalty where the petition had vaguely asked remedy is illustrated by statute 11 based on petition 21. The grievance in question was that clerks or

---

[24] Statutes thus derived from petitions were numbers 3 (from pet. 7), 6 and 7 (from pet. 10), 8 (from pet. 12), 12 (from pet. 27), 13 (from pet. 30), 14 (from pet. 33).

laymen, indicted before sheriffs but delivered by the justices, thereafter sued in courts Christian those who indicted them, so that many men hesitated further to indict. " De qei la dite Commune prie remedie." The brief response, " Eient prohibition en Chauncellerie," was amplified in the statute to " Le Roy voet qe en tieux cas chescun qe se sent greve eyt sur ce prohibicion en Chauncellerie fourme en son cas." Incidentally the statute stated the grievance much more clearly than the petition had done.

How a brief addition or qualification in the response was incorporated in the statute is illustrated by statute 4 based on petition 8. The petition asked that debts due the king might be cancelled or payment of them deferred, the sheriffs and bailiffs of franchises to account on oath at the exchequer for what they could collect " sauntz abatement de la contenaunce del detour." The response granted the saving of the countenance of the debtor but limited debts deferable to those of less than 300 livres. The statute, rephrasing the petition with clarity, incorporated the limitation. Another illustration of an added limitation is statute 15 based on petition 36. The latter, declaring that many men had been forced to bind themselves by writing to appear armed at the king's summons on penalty of life and limb, asked that no one should be forced to make such writings in the future and that writings which had been made should be void. The response granted that none should be made henceforth but was more hesitant toward contracts which had been entered into in the past. These should be shown to the king in view of the chancellor and treasurer and the king would annul such of them as had been made against right and reason. The statute incorporated these limitations.

Instead of restricting the petition by a limitation, the statute might refuse or postpone a part of it while granting the most of it. Statute 1 derived from petition 3 was of this sort. It is a composite statute, confirming the great charter and the charter of the forest, providing that earlier perambulations of the forests be observed and that necessary new ones be ridden and charted, and finally assuring *housebote* and *heybote* to anyone who had wood within the forest. Comprehensive as this is, the original petition embodied other requests which have left no trace in the statute. One, asking for an addition to the charter of the forest, was answered by deferring the addition until the king should come of age; another, touching assarts, was answered by directing anyone aggrieved to present to parliament a private bill; a third, touching certain " ordenaunces," was granted by an order that these be examined and that the good ones among them be put in a statute. As a whole, therefore, the composite petition attained in half its requests to the state of a statute but in the other half did not. Similar is statute 2 based on petition 5. The part of the petition which asked for the restoration of bishop's temporalities which had been seized was granted and became a statute; but another part, which asked the annulment of certain judgments pronounced against the bishops in the matter of provisions, was referred to the consideration of prelates, nobles and men of law and came to nothing. A third part touching papal provisions was ignored completely by response and statute.

The parliament of 1327 furnishes lastly a single instance of a response so different from the petition that the resultant statute, neglecting the petition entirely, adopted the response. It is statute 5 enacted in response to petition 9. The petition asked that men might not be forced to go to war against their will " en les Terres " where they had no holdings, or " en les Terres " where they had, except in accordance with the terms of their tenancy, and that the " gentz de Comune " be not destrained to arm themselves at their own costs contrary to the provisions of the statute of Winchester or go outside their counties except at the cost of the king. The response declared that it pleased king and council that men " ne soient autrement charger de soi armer q'ils ne soleient en temps de ses Auncestres " or go outside their " Conteez " except in case of a foreign invasion when they should do " come ad este fait avant ces hures pur defens du Roialme." The statute, disregarding the petition, was in almost the words of the response. It departed little, to be sure, from the spirit of the request; but its less binding, though clearer, phraseology gave the crown somewhat wider latitude of action in the future.

All articles of the commons petitions of 1327, however, did not give rise to statutes. Only sixteen of the forty-one did so. Since the ratio is small, it might seem that a large majority of the commons requests were disregarded. Closer inspection of the responses made to the remaining twenty-five scarcely justifies such a conclusion. Only three petitions were pointedly rejected — one as being against the law, one as encroaching on the king's prerogative, one as being against the judgment of the council.[25] The remaining twenty-two were in general of such a character that they could be dealt with by a remedy less formal than a statute. Often it was sufficient to refer them to an earlier statute or to some provision made elsewhere.[26] Some petitions were concerned with individuals, two referring to members of the royal family and two to certain justices of the forest.[27] Three were set apart for later consideration,[28] and two were deferred until the king should come of age.[29] One was referred to the church.[30] Three, finally, which were concerned with the administration of justice, seem to have been considered so narrowly administrative that, although they were granted, they were not re-edited as statutes.[31]

[25] Nos. 13, 35, 18.

[26] Nos. 4, 6, 15, 28, 37. Reference to an earlier statute might sometimes amount to an evasion of the redress asked for, especially if new measures of enforcement had been proposed. See below, pp. 304-305.

[27] Nos. 23, 24, 31, 38.

[28] Nos. 17, 19, 32.

[29] Nos. 26, 34.

[30] No. 25.

[31] One (no. 11) provided for new inquests in case of false judgments; one (no. 20) asked that, in order to expedite suits, juries of 24 knights might be summoned by writ of *Nisi Prius;* a third (no. 22) requested that justices of assize make inquiry whether sheriffs, gaolers and other ministers had oppressed "apellours" with charges of false appeal.

This brief survey of the comprehensive commons petition of 1327 serves at least to show its significance. It was by far the longest petition of its kind which had ever been drafted. So far as we know, it had only three predecessors, the petitions of 1309, of 1320 and of 1325, two of which gave rise to statutes. It is, therefore, the fourth exemplar of what was to be for a century the most important of parliamentary documents — more important than subsidy indentures, private bills or records of jurisdiction. For it made clear that out of certain articles of comprehensive commons petitions legislation might arise, taking the form of articles of a statute. The innovation had been made in 1309 but in a timid, tentative way. Nor had it been more than perhaps once or twice imitated for nearly twenty years. Now, however, with the beginning of the new reign a statute of seventeen articles appeared, all of which except one arose directly from certain of the forty-one articles of a commons petition. The relation, too, was immediate. Although the articles of the statute usually rephrased the articles of the petition, this was merely to give them greater clearness and precision. The fundamental fact emerges that legislation was rapidly becoming the outcome of requests made by the commons, on the one hand, and replies to these made by king and lords on the other. The replies of 1327 were usually acquiescent, rarely introducing addition or change. Although many of the articles of the petition gave rise to no statute, the reason for this was usually revealed in the respective responses. Such articles were of less immediate import. The more important articles, together with the answers to them, were welded by a skillful hand into the legislation of parliament. Royal legislation like that of Edward I had now found a rival and seemed threatened with being superseded by what may henceforth with propriety be called commons' legislation. So far as this happened, statutory legislation was to become nothing other than commons bills assented to or modified by the king and the lords and made imperative.

To what extent and in what way this came to pass must now be considered.   In particular we must inquire about the development of the comprehensive commons petition of several articles into the "communes petitions" of the middle of the fifteenth century.   The latter, as we have seen, took the form not of a single bill but of several bills each sent separately to the lords, the response to each written on the back of it, while at times official bills, although they should have been excluded by the caption, were intruded among them.   Certain simple questions present themselves.   Did the presenting of a comprehensive commons bill become a characteristic feature of parliamentary procedure at once after 1327?   As soon as it did so, for how long did it continue to be the accepted vehicle for expressing the commons' wishes and at what time did it give place to separate bills such as characterised the second half of the fifteenth century?   Have we any evidence about the material from which it was drafted?   How much statutory legislation was derived from the requests of the commons as embodied in their petitions?   Finally, so far as statutes were derived from commons bills, were they greatly changed in the process?   The answers to the first three questions relate primarily to matters of procedure; the answers to the last two should reveal something about the influence of the commons upon legislation.

The comprehensive commons petition was destined to have at first a somewhat chequered but afterward a pretty consistent career for almost a century.   For it may as well be stated at once that the commons continued to express their wishes in parliament for the most part through the articles of a single bill until 1423.[32]   Unfortunately we have no original copies of these petitions save the bills of 1333 and 1337 already described.   Hence it is necessary to study all the others in the transcripts which the parliament rolls preserve.   In the same way in the absence of original copies of the statutes of nearly

---

[32] For exceptions, see below pp. 236-40.

all parliaments of the three Edwards,[33] it will be necessary in making comparisons to rely upon the statute roll. The following discussion of commons bills up to 1423, therefore, is based largely on these two series of enrolled records.

Although the comprehensive commons petition of 1327 was so extensive and so influential upon legislation as to suggest that succeeding parliaments could not afford to neglect it as a precedent, the series of similar petitions with similar reflection in legislation seemingly did not become continuous until after 1352. From 1327 to 1339 the rolls of parliament record no comprehensive commons bill. But the rolls are badly preserved, and there is other evidence that such bills were presented during the twelve years in question. We have already considered two of them in their original form, those of 1333 and 1337. Another, consisting of eighteen articles, belonging to 1334 has come down to us in an abbreviated sixteenth-century copy.[34] The one-time existence of three others is implied by the introductory phrases of the statutes of 1330, 1335, and 1336, which declare that they were enacted at the request of the commons.[35] Finally, in 1339 the roll records six brief articles, which are described in the margin as "La demand de la Commune";[36] and in 1340 and 1341 the commons presented petitions along with the petitions of clergy and nobles.[37]

It is from 1343, however, that the series of long, enrolled, comprehensive commons petitions begins. In the parliament of that year and in each of the ten succeeding parliaments such

---

[33] See below, pp. 392-93.

[34] *R. P.*, II, 376-377. The original is now Chancery, Parl. Ro. no. 4 and will soon be printed (cf. *Bull. Inst. Hist. Research*, IX, 17).

[35] *Stats.*, I, 261-265, 269-272, 275-277.

[36] *R. P.*, II, 105.

[37] In 1340 a statute arose from the requests of the four estates of the parliament of that year; and in 1341 another statute of six articles was based on three responses made to three separate petitions submitted respectively by "Clergie," "Grantz," and "Communes." In neither year was the statute the outcome simply of a commons bill. In 1340 the petitions did not appear on the parliament roll, although there was a promise that they would (*R. P.*, II, 112-113, 126-131; *Stats.*, I, 281-294).

a bill was presented and duly enrolled.[38]   Each bill comprised
from ten to fifty-five articles — usually more than twenty.
What is rather surprising, however, is that of the first six of
these comprehensive bills only one influenced legislation.
From the twelve articles of 1344 seven articles of a statute
were enacted.[39]   Why the five other comprehensive commons
bills, each of them more extensive than the bill of 1344, were
disregarded is not clear.   Perhaps it was owing to the political
and military situation of the forties.

Not until 1352 do two series of parallel records begin, that
of comprehensive commons petitions on the one hand and
that of statutes derived from them on the other.[40]   The instances of such parallelism which our records reveal somewhat
discontinuously in 1309, 1327 and 1344 at length evolved into
two fairly continuous series.   In 1352, 42 articles of a commons bill gave rise to 23 articles of a statute and in 1354, 41
articles of a bill resulted in a statute of 15 articles.[41]   To be
sure, the 17 articles of 1355 left no trace on the statute roll
and, owing to a gap in the rolls of parliament, we cannot tell
whether the statutes of the two following parliaments did or
did not arise from commons bills.[42]   But, in 1362, 24 articles
of the commons petition were answered by 13 articles of a

[38] *R. P.*, II, 139-143, 148-150, 160-163, 165-173, 201-203, 227-230, 238-243,
252-253, 257-262, 265-267.

[39] *Stats.*, I, 200-301.

[40] In 1351, although the commons petition of thirty articles resulted in no
statute, parliament did enact the statute of labourers and the statute of
provisors at the request of the commons (*R. P.*, II, 232-235; *Stats.*, I, 311-
318). In 1353 there was submitted to the commons for debate eight articles
of an " ordinance of the staple," which was later enrolled on the statute
roll. The ten articles of the commons petition of the year were not similarly honoured but, instead, a statute of eight articles was enacted which
seems to have been based on no commons petition (*R. P.*, II, 246-253;
Stats., I, 329-343).

[41] *R. P.*, II, 238-243, 257-262; *Stats.*, I, 319-324, 345-349. Articles 2, 11
and 15 of the statute of 1354 seem to have no antecedents on the parliament roll.

[42] *R. P.*, II, 265-267; *Stats.*, I, 349-353, 364-369. The statutes are said to
have been made with the assent of the commons.

statute and in the five succeeding parliaments the interrelation was similar.[43]   There was, however, a marked falling off of legislation in the four parliaments which followed, the last of Edward's reign.   In 1372 and in 1376 the numerous articles of the commons petitions (32 and 140 respectively) left no trace on the statute roll, while the 22 articles of 1373 were answered by only two articles of a statute, and the 61 articles of 1377 by only three.[44]

The reign of Richard II continued the precedents set during the preceding twenty-five years.   In the first place the series of comprehensive commons petitions as recorded on the rolls is continuous save for the year 1388; and in the second parliament of 1388 one must have been presented since the articles of the statute of the year were clearly in large measure derived from the articles of a commons bill.[45]   In the second place the articles of the petitions usually were numerous.   Of the twenty-one comprehensive petitions of the reign only four had fewer than ten articles, four others fewer than twenty-five, while the remaining thirteen had from twenty-five to sixty-nine articles each.   The statutes arising from the articles of the petitions, however, were sometimes relatively numerous, sometimes few.   In the first year of the reign eleven statutes were drafted from the sixty-nine articles of the commons bill apart from four others from the fourteen articles of the clergy's bill.[46]   In each of the four succeeding parliaments, on the other hand, only two or three statutes arose from the rather numerous articles of the commons petitions.[47]   In four of the parliaments of 1381-1383 statutes were again liberally drafted

[43] *R. P.*, II, 269-273, 276-280, 285-288, 295-297, 300-301, 304-308; *Stats.*, I, 371-376, 378-385, 388-393.

[44] *R. P.*, II, 311-314, 318-320, 331-372; *Stats.*, I, 395-398

[45] *Stats.*, II, 55-60.   This was the reforming parliament of Cambridge (Stubbs, *op. cit.*, II, 505).

[46] *R. P.*, III, 15-26; *Stats.*, II, 1-5.

[47] Consisting of 35, 29, 14 and 24 articles respectively (*R. P.*, III, 42-47, 61-66, 80-83, 93-96; *Stats.*, II, 6-16).

from the articles of the commons petition;[48] and this also happened in the parliaments of 1388-1394.[49]   It will be noticed
that these were the two periods of the reign during which the
nearest approach to popular government was attained.   During
1384-1385, when the king was attempting to establish a personal rule with the support of a court party, statutes were few
and unimportant;[49a] and in the years of his second tyranny
both petitions and the statutes based on them sank into insignificance.[50]

The records of Richard's reign, in conjunction with those of
the later years of Edward III, thus show that the second half
of the fourteenth century saw the comprehensive commons
petitions fairly entrenched as a characteristic phenomenon in
parliamentary procedure.   Usually it expanded into numerous
articles, each in fact a particular commons bill.   Nearly always,

[48] 9, 9, 5, 17 statutes from 30, 31, 9, 27 articles respectively (*R. P.*, III,
115-119, 137-141, 146-147, 158-164; *Stats.*, II, 17-23, 26-36).   The six articles
of the statute of 1382 did not arise from a commons petition but did receive the assent of the commons (*R. P.*, III, 123-125; *Stats.*, II, 23-26).

[49] 7, 15, 4, 9, 4, 7 statutes from 22, 25, 20, 25, 14, 27 articles respectively in
the parliaments of 1388 (Westminster), 1399, 1390, 1391, 1393, 1394 (*R. P.*,
III, 246-250, 265-273, 279-283, 290-296, 305-308, 318-323; *Stats.*, II, 43-55,
61-68, 76-77, 78-82, 82-87, 87-92).

[49a] In 1384 no statutes were drafted from the five petitions of the first
parliament and only five from the sixteen petitions of the second.   In
1385 the twenty-eight commons petitions gave rise to two statutes, one
of them embodying a serious limitation (pet. 1, stat. 1).   In 1386 fifteen
petitions brought only the statute creating a commission of reform (*R. P.*,
III, 173-174, 200-202, 210-214, 221-223; *Stats.*, II, 36-43).

[50] In 1395 there were four petitions and no statute; in 1397 three petitions and one statute.   Of the twenty statutes of Richard's last parliament in 1397-1398, several profess to have been enacted at the request of
the commons (nos. 2, 4-6, 9-11, 14); but these were political statutes,
annulling the acts of the commission of 1386 or strengthening the measures of 1397-1398.   They were put into the mouth of the commons by the
government, Speaker Bushy being an ardent supporter of the king.   No
comprehensive commons petition is recorded; but the parliamentary committee which sat after parliament had been dismissed answered a commons' appeal against the grant of export licences and one touching
obstruction in rivers (statutes 17-19).   (*R. P.*, III, 330, 344-345, 349-371;
Stats., II, 93 (art. 5), 94-110.)

too, some response to certain of the articles found place on the statute roll. How many articles might be so honoured seems to have depended largely upon the political situation of the moment. At certain times in Edward's later years (but not at the end of the reign) several articles of the commons petition became articles of a statute; again during the so-called constitutional years of Richard II this was the case. Under Henry IV the tendency, as we shall see, became practically a rule. In every parliament of his reign the commons presented a comprehensive petition of many articles,[51] and in each instance a statute of several articles was drafted in response.

Now that we have seen the comprehensive commons petition becoming a characteristic feature of parliamentary procedure at least from the middle of the fourteenth century, we may inquire into the length of time during which the commons were to embody their requests in the articles of a single bill. Actually, of course, each article was in itself a commons petition and in the usual parlance of the fourteenth century the articles were referred to as the commons petitions. In the middle of the fifteenth century we have seen that each took the form of an independent bill and that the group of them no longer appeared as the articles of a single bill. At what time did the change take place?

We are able to date it with precision. The first parliament of Henry VI in 1422 adhered to the old usage, the second one in 1423 adopted the new one. The change may be discovered both from the enrolled record and from the petitions in their original form. In the first place the caption which introduced the commons petitions on the parliament roll was, up to 1423, an appeal to the king or to his representative in some such phrases as, "A . . . le Roy . . . supplient les poveres Communes de votre Roialme d'Engleterre qe plese a votre tres graciouse Seigneurie par assent des Seigneurs Espirituelx et Temporalx en cest present Parlement . . . grauntier les Peti-

[51] From 15 to 68 (see below, p. 259, n. 128).

tions q' ensuent." [52]   In 1423 the introductory caption changed
from an appeal to a statement.   It now ran, " Item diverses
autres Communes Petitions furent baillez en le dit Parlement
par les ditz Communes, les tenours de queux ovec lour Responses
cy ensuent.[53]   The word " autres " might indeed suggest that the
usual invocation had been prefixed to other commons petitions
which preceded these on the roll.   Such, however, was not the
case; the word " autres " had reference only to certain preceding private and group petitions which the commons had sponsored.   To make the matter entirely clear the roll of the next
parliament, that of 1425, introduced its commons bills by the
bald statement, " Item diverses communes Petitions furent
baillez . . . par les ditz Communes, les tenours des queux
ovec lour responses cy ensuent." [54]   And in the rolls of all subsequent parliaments the phraseology is much the same.   What
the enrolled record suggests, therefore, is that before 1423 the
commons petitions were so grouped together that they could
be presented to the king with an introductory address, but that
in and after this year such may not have been the procedure.
If they were thus grouped, however, before 1423, it is likely
that this was done, as we know that it was in the early fourteenth century, by writing them on a single membrane as successive articles of a single comprehensive bill.

The phraseology of each request bears out this inference.
Before 1423 each article of the comprehensive petition usually
began, " Item priont les ditz Communes."   If, as occasionally
happened, the commons adopted a private or a group petition
as their own, the article embodying their request began, e.g.,
" Item suppliont les Communes pur John Brompton de Bev-
erley," or " Item priont les Communes pur les Marchantz de
Leyns, denizeins deins la Roialme d'Engleterre." [55]   In and
after 1423, however, the petitions which the commons adopted

[52] R. P., IV, 146, a. 1421.
[53] Ibid., p. 253.
[54] Ibid., p. 289.
[55] Ibid., pp. 83, 115.

for individuals or groups were enrolled just as they had been presented to the commons, beginning, e.g., " A les tres sages Communes . . . Suppliont . . . les Chivalers, Esquyers et les autres poveres Communes del Countee de Northumb'." [56] It is true that even before 1423 a private or group petition occasionally crept in among the commons petitions little changed.[57] But the instances are so rare as not to invalidate seriously the distinction just drawn.

In still another feature did the series of commons requests in and after 1423 differ from earlier series. Up to 1423 they were always couched in French, or rarely in Latin. In and after 1423 it is not unusual to find some of them in English.[58] It would seem that before 1423 the comprehensive commons petition was, so to speak, edited in order to give its parts a linguistic unity. In and after 1423, if a commons' request happened to be first written as a commons bill in English, no trouble was taken to translate it either on its presentation or at the time of its enrollment.

The evidence of the enrolled record that commons requests before 1423 were presented in parliament as the articles of a comprehensive petition but in that year and afterwards as a series of petitions each offered separately is confirmed by an examination of the bills in their original form. In 1423 we find for the first time original manuscripts of commons bills which were presented in the latter way; and from nearly all succeeding parliaments there are similar original bills. From the parliament of 1423, to be sure, the surviving originals are not numerous. As enrolled, the " Communes Petitions " of that year are numbered in the margin of the roll up to and including number " XII " but after that bear no marginal numeral. The twelfth and apparently the next two are petitions of more than one article each, the articles having separate

---

[56] *Ibid.*, p. 291.

[57] Beginning, e.g., " Please a les honurables et sages Communes d'ycest present Parlement considerer. . . ." (*ibid.*, p. 80, *a.* 1415).

[58] *Ibid.*, pp. 255-258, 289-294 *et passim*.

responses. The three refer to coinage, goldsmiths and the mint.[58a] After them come four commons' requests, the last four of the parliament[59]; and three of these are the ones of which originals survive.[60] As it happens, in the upper left-hand corner of each of the three membranes is a numeral; and the numerals seem to be XVI, XVIII, and XIX. These are precisely the numerals which according to the enrollment the three would probably have borne. It happens further that on the left of each membrane is a perforation, such as would have been made for the passage of a cord with which to tie the membranes together. The three membranes, therefore, suggest that they were the last of a group of nineteen, which were at one time strung together.

What is suggested by the fragmentary survivals of the commons bills of 1423 becomes a certainty from the more numerous survivals of the commons bills of the parliament of 1425. Of the sixteen "communes petitions" which the parliament roll of that year records,[61] fourteen survive. They constitute a valuable series, the first of their kind. In the upper left-hand of each is written a numeral and the numerals correspond surprisingly well with the order in which the petitions are recorded on the roll.[62] A single perforation on the left of each shows that they were tied together. To other characteristics

---

[58a] *Ibid.*, pp. 253-258.

[59] One is a group petition adopted by the commons, par. 57.

[60] C., P. & C. P. 15/10, 11, 12. They are enrolled as pars. 56, 58, 59 (*R. P.*, IV, 258-260).

[61] *Ibid.*, pp. 289-294.

[62] The fifth and sixth of the sixteen are missing. The numerals on the bills are I to XIV with IIII and V missing and with III occurring twice instead of III and IIII. The discrepancy between the sixteen of the roll and the fourteen of the originals arises in part because the first of the original petitions (no. 1) is enrolled as two petitions. Either the fifth or the sixth of the enrolled series must have been added to the series of originals after its members were numbered. The correspondence between the first four and the last nine of the two series is precise. In the order of the enrollment, the original bills are as follows: A. P. 1192, C., P. & C. P. 16/5; A. P. 6716, 1193, [one missing], 1194, 1196, 1195, C., P. & C. P. 16/6, A. P. 1197, 1198, C., P. & C. P. 16/7, 16/8, 16/9.

of these bills we shall return later; but the feature of commons petitions in which for the moment we are interested is convincingly illustrated by them. No longer are the requests of the commons presented as articles of a single comprehensive petition. Instead, separate commons bills have become the rule. Someone, perhaps the clerk of parliament, numbered them in a series and the order indicated was observed in the enrollment.

A passage in the minutes of the council for 1423, usually quoted in another connection, indicates that bills of all sorts passed in parliament were in this year individual documents. After the clerk of parliament had read to the council the acts of the last parliament, he was instructed to give those which were to be statutes to the justices of both benches that they might edit them, and to see that copies of other acts touching governance by the council be given to the clerk of the council. Finally, all acts were to be enrolled in chancery as was the custom.[63] It was of course possible to turn over to the justices a comprehensive commons bill and the replies to its articles that they might edit such articles as were to be statutes. But the phraseology of the minute implies that the several acts of parliament were written on separate membranes and that only certain of these were to be given to the justices. It is not unlikely that the instructions of the council minute arose from the fact that individual commons bills were an innovation of the year, necessitating new instructions to the clerk of parliament.

While it is clear enough that commons petitions were no longer presented in parliament after 1422 in the form of a comprehensive bill, is there proof from original documents that up to that time they were presented in this manner? Only two comprehensive commons bills have been described in their manuscript state, the bills of 1333 and 1337. Inasmuch as these were respectively ninety and eighty-five years earlier

---

[63] See below, p. 389, where the text is quoted.

than the supposedly last appearance of such bills in 1422, might we not expect to find survivals of the many others which appeared in the interim? Numerous private bills and group bills survive from the period, both those enrolled and those not enrolled.[64] In view of this it is undoubtedly surprising not to find in the records, as we do not, a single original comprehensive commons petition from 1337 to 1422. We are, it is true, assured by the parliament roll of 1353 that the commons petitions of that year were presented in " une Roule contenante si bien l'Eide q'ils avoient ordeine . . . come les Petitions touchantes la Commune de la terre." [65] We have, too, one small roll recording the responses to the articles of 1368; but this can do no more than tell us that the responses were, as they had been in 1337 but had not been in 1333, written on a separate membrane.[66] It does not prove that the petitions of the year were a series of articles; for in 1425, when they no longer were, the responses were not written on the backs of the separate petitions but were recorded elsewhere, presumably on a membrane by themselves. That so extensive and important a series as the comprehensive commons petitions of ninety years should have completely disappeared is extraordinary. It is as if the clerk of parliament after entering on his roll any one of them and the responses to it had intentionally destroyed the originals.[67]

Surprising as it is that no original comprehensive commons bills survive from 1337 to 1422, it is equally true that, during the same interval scarcely any commons bills like those of

[64] See above, pp. 37-8.

[65] *R. P.*, II, 237. In 1346 they were presented as one petition (below, p. 338).

[66] C., P. & C. P. 8/12; *R. P.*, II, 295.

[67] Dr. Sayles tells me that on the parliament rolls up to 1343 the articles of the commons petition were entered with a space left after each in which the king's response was later written in another hand and sometimes with evidence of crowding, but that after that year articles and responses were entered in the same hand and presumably at the same time. Yet it is still not clear why all original comprehensive commons petitions and nearly all the membranes of replies have disappeared.

1423 and 1425 are to be found.[68]   In view of the considerable
number of such originals which appear at the moment when
the captions of the enrolled record would lead us to expect
their existence, the complete absence of anything of the kind
before 1423 is significant.   If separate commons bills had been
usual before that year, certainly a few of the great number of
commons' requests recorded in the rolls would have survived
in this form.   While, therefore, it is not easy to explain the
disappearance of a series of original comprehensive commons
petitions, it would be more difficult to account for the disappearance of a far larger number of separate commons bills.
What is at best an unsatisfactory state of our records is more
easily explained, although not well explained, on the supposi-
tion that only comprehensive commons bills, fewer in number
than their constituent articles, existed before 1423.   The sup-
position has good ground for support in the captions of the
parliament roll and in the phraseology and language of the articles of the commons' requests before 1423, as contrasted
with the captions, phraseology and language after that date.
With this inference, strongly supported as it is, we shall, in the
absence of documentary evidence, have to rest content.

With the reasonable assurance, therefore, that commons'
requests for a century after their origin took the form of comprehensive petitions, have we any evidence touching the preparation of these documents?   Does anything survive in the
form of drafts of the articles, such as, it would seem, must have
been in the hands of whoever drew up the comprehensive bill?
The evidence touching this question is somewhat difficult to
interpret.   In the first place we must be on our guard against
later copies of any article.   A copy may usually be detected by
the fact that, if the response is given, petition and response
are in the same hand.   The second article of the commons
petition of 1399, along with the response to it, survives on a
strip of parchment some 13 inches wide by 4½ inches long.

[68] See below, pp. 237-47.

Although it might at first glance be taken for an original commons bill, the response, written in the same hand as the petition and suspiciously not on the dorse but immediately after the bill, reveals that the document is a copy.[69]

Nor should we be misled by the discovery of original commons petitions which are in all respects like the articles of a comprehensive petition save that on the parliament roll they are enrolled separately and precede or follow the comprehensive bill. The occasional appearance of such on the roll furnishes, of course, a presumption that an original might now and then be found. On the parliament roll of 1406, long before the series of commons petitions is reached and immediately after the grant of a subsidy, there is record of a commons' request which begins " Et priont les Communes " and proceeds to ask that aliens, with certain exceptions, be expelled from the realm. No response is recorded. What seems to be the original in this petition survives in a wide, short strip of parchment with apparently nothing written on the back of it.[70] Why the petition was not incorporated with the other commons petitions of the parliament is not clear. Its position on the roll suggests that it was closely connected with the grant of a subsidy. At the end of the parliament roll of 1380 and separated by intervening group petitions from the comprehensive commons bill is recorded an ordinance, which was the king's response to a commons petition of which we have the original. It renewed an ordinance of 1369 touching the enjoyment of captured castles and lands in France.[71] The petition might well have been an article of the comprehensive commons bill.

[69] C., P. & C. P. 13/2; R. P., III, 439. It is true that some early responses were written below the petitions but, of course, not in the same hand. See below, p. 295.

[70] C., P. & C. P. 13/15; R. P., III, 578.

[71] Ibid., III, 87; A. P., 5471. The petition runs: " A nostre tresredoute . . . Roi supplie humblement touz ses liges de son roialme denglterre qe vous plese de radefier et confermer . . . un ordenance [of 43 Edward III] touchant conquest en votre Roialme de Fraunce a toutz ceux qe voillent peyne et travailler en votre querell et en recoverer de votre dit droit et heritage . . .

Since we occasionally find the originals of isolated commons petitions which appear on the parliament roll either before or after the articles of the comprehensive petition, we shall not be surprised to find similar commons petitions which do not appear on the roll at all. And this although they were not always refused but were at times granted. Of such there are a half dozen examples from the reigns of Richard II and Edward III. The editors of the rolls have printed four from Richard's reign, of which two belong to 1389. One of them, beginning "A . . . le Roy supplient ses lieges Communes en ceste present Parlement," asked that castles which had served sheriffs as prisons be restored to them; the other, beginning "A le Roi . . . et a lez Seigneurs de cest present Parlement suppliount touz lez povres Communes de la Roialme," asked that in the present parliament no bill be endorsed without the assent of the commons which exempted from the lay subsidy lands in the town of Oxford acquired by clergy and colleges. To the second bill there is no sign of assent, although the first received the king's approval in the endorsement, "Le Roy le voet." [72] Similar is a petition of 1383, which asked that the leaders of the late rebellion who were put to death without being attainted and whose heirs were now demanding their lands be declared felons. The petition began "A . . . le Roy et son . . . Consaill en cest present Parlement supplient les Communes de son Roialme . . . ," and it received the king's assent that the traitors "soyent tenuz com felons convictes." [73] Again in 1397 a commons bill, beginning "A . . . le Roy et a lez Seigneurs . . . suppliont les Comunes . . ." asked remedy for the escape of villeins from their manors to market towns, whence their lords could not recover them. The bill was re-

soit affermez et tenuz pour Estatut. Et le Roi voet qe sur ceste Ordinance chescun eit Patente en especial s'il le vorroit demander." On the back is written, "Le Roi le voet bien." In essence this was a group petition.

[72] A. P. 1029, 1032; *R. P.*, III, 275.

[73] A. P. 970; *R. P.*, III, 175.

ferred to a committee of lords and no response is recorded.[74]
Of the four bills two at least were answered favourably.

From the reign of Edward III there survive two other commons petitions which were not incorporated in comprehensive
commons petitions and were not enrolled. One, badly injured,
begins "A . . . le Roi et a son conseil prie la commune de sa
terre " and complains of the misdoings of sheriffs and escheators. It is endorsed " Coram Rege," just as many contemporary
private bills were.[75] The other, also badly injured, beginning
" A . . . le Roy et a son consail prie la communaulte de sa
terre . . . ," seems to ask remedy in cases where bailiffs and receivours cannot get accurate accounts from executors without
writs of account. On the dorse is the double inscription
" Coram magno consilio " and " Non est adhuc Lex ordinata in
hoc casu." [76] What is striking about the two bills is not only
the appeal from the commons but the character of the response. The endorsements of both, like the endorsements of
numerous contemporary private bills, merely dispatched the
petitions to the king or to the great council. Since the articles
of a comprehensive commons petition were never dispatched
in this way, it is clear that the two bills were in the tradition
of the isolated commons petition which we have already
noticed as antedating the appearance of the comprehensive
commons bill.[77]

[74] A. P. 1070; R. P., III, 448. For the dating and other characteristics
of this petition see below, pp. 324-325.

[75] C., P. & C. P. 7/11. The catalogue assigns this to 14-34 Edward III.

[76] Ibid., 8/22.

[77] See above, pp. 195-196. A third bill from Edward's reign came not,
to be sure, from the commons but from the " king's people." Beginning
"A . . . le Roi et a son conseail mustre seon peuple," it asked remedy for
unwarranted charges made by ordinaries for receiving proofs of wills and
was endorsed, " Si quis senserit se gravatu[m] adeat canc[ellario] et ibi
habeat remedium " (C., P. & C. P. 8/20). A fourth bill of the reign came
from the poor men of the commons. Beginning "A . . . le Roi et al Coun-
sail de Parlement monstrent lez Poures de la Comune," it begged that
clothworkers might sell their cloths before they were fulled without paying
the subsidy of 1353, but that this be paid by whoever sold the finished
cloth (A. P. 6708). There was no response. Despite the slightly anom-

In the reign of Edward III and Richard II, therefore, we find occasional isolated commons bills which were either enrolled apart from the comprehensive commons petition or were not enrolled at all. An interesting light on the relationship of such bills to the comprehensive commons petition is thrown by certain petitions of late Edward III and early Richard II. All are isolated commons bills, not enrolled; but they differ from those just described in that the responses refer the petitioners "elsewhere" and sometimes to "les communes petitions." The first of them, which is later than 1362, begins "A Roi et son Conseil prie la comune," and declares that, whereas according to the statute of 1362 purveyors for the household should pay in cash or otherwise, they now take provisions without payment. Remedy for the abuse is requested. The endorsement, which is fragmentary, begins "Cest responduz aill. . . ." [78] In the "elsewhere" a reference to some other response is at least suggested.

What is here only a clue becomes entirely definite in the answers given to two petitions of 1377. One of them, beginning "A . . . Roy et son . . . conseil supplient la commune . . . ," asked that the possessions of alien priories in the king's hands be leased not to alien priors or to secular men but to "diosesans" who would appoint English monks to guard them. On the back of the bill is written, "Cest bille si est responduz entre les communes petitions." On turning to the enrolled commons petitions of 1377, we find that article 50, which was an appeal for the expulsion of all aliens, was answered with a long conditional assent, the last part of which related to the lands of alien priories in the king's hands and provided that under certain circumstances they be leased "as autres suffisantz gentz de Seint Esglise." [79] The answer to the particular bill was to be found in the answer to a similar re-

olous form of the address, the first of these two bills was in essence a commons bill, the second a group bill.

[78] C., P. & C. P. 8/5.
[79] A. P. 5052; *R. P.,* III, 22.

quest which was an article of the commons petitions. Precisely like the endorsement of this bill is that of another isolated commons bill of the same year, viz, " Ceste bille est respondu entre les communes petitions." The second bill, beginning " A . . . Roi monstrent plusours de sa commune . . . ," complained that chyrographers who engrossed fines violated the statute of Westminster by taking fees greater than four shillings and asked that whoever did this should suffer a penalty "pluis grendre" than that contained in the said statute. On turning to the comprehensive petition of 1377 we find that the thirty-seventh article recites the same abuse of the chirographers, asks that they be obliged to pay any complainant "dys fois atant" as in the statute of jurors, and receives the response, " Il y ad Estatut ent fait lequel soit tenuz et gardez." [80]   The circumstance that in this bill as well as in that touching the lands of alien priories there is no verbal correspondence between the text and the text of the corresponding articles of the comprehensive commons petition makes it clear that the latter arose independently. In the parliaments of Edward III and Richard II, therefore, we occasionally find along with the "communes petitiones" presented as a single bill an isolated commons petition, the answer to which referred the petitioners to the comprehensive commons petition.

Is there, however, at any time close enough verbal correspondence between isolated commons bills and certain articles of the comprehensive commons bills to warrant our thinking that the latter may have been built up from various commons petitions presented in a parliament. In other words, may not the comprehensive bill have been derived from isolated commons bills instead of coming into existence along beside them, as it seems to have done in the instances just cited? Verbal correspondence does indeed exist but it is pretty well confined to bills of a certain sort. These are what we have come to know as group bills, i.e., petitions presented

[80] A. P. 5055; *R. P.,* III, 20.

by groups but often adopted by the commons as bills of their own. We have seen them numerous at the end of the fifteenth century and have noted that already two of them appeared as articles of the comprehensive commons bills of 1325 and 1327 respectively.[81] From this time to 1423 they occur with increasing frequency as articles of comprehensive commons bills. Of the eighty-five articles of the commons petition of 1402, seven were group petitions.[82] Since such petitions must first have been presented to the commons for adoption rather than drafted by the commons themselves, it would not be surprising to find certain of them preserved in their original form. As a matter of fact a few do survive and may be examined both as presented and as rephrased after adoption.

In 1382 the Lombard merchants begged that an ordinance of the last parliament forbidding exchanges between merchant and merchant be repealed. Their appeal began, " A nostre tres rodote seigneur le Roy et a touz les graciousez seigneurs et tres bone comune du parlement Supplient humblement lez marchantz Lumbardz demurantz en Engleterre." The commons, adopting the petition made it one of their own. In so doing they rephrased the introductory words so that these became "Item prient les Communes et les Marchantz Lumbards en Engleterre. . . ." The body of the petition was left as it had been in the original with changes in only two or three words and occasionally in the spelling. In the last sentence one phrase was omitted.[83] What took place was merely the substitution of one form of address for another, the new one being appropriate in a series of requests.

A group petition in the first parliament of Henry IV underwent the same transformation in being adopted by the com-

---

[81] See above, pp. 120, 123, 130, 214, 216.

[82] *R. P.*, III, 494-511. Pars. 34, 42, 53, 54, 68, 74, 75.

[83] A. P. 966; *R. P.*, III, 138. In the original the last sentence ran: " Sur qoy plese a notre tresgraciouse seigneurie et tressage conseil ent ordine due remedie . . ."; in the enrolled form this became, " Par quoy plese ent ordiner due remedie. . . ."

mons. It was a request from the city of London for the repeal of a statute 1353 which penalised it severely for disorder and bad governance. The original bill began "A . . . notre tres redoute seignur le Roy Monstre[nt] . . . voz tres humbles liges les maire, viscountz, Aldermans et la communaltee de votre citee de Londres . . . qe come par estatut . . ." and requested "Qe plese a votre regalie de votre grace tresbenigne en ceste present parlement et par auctoritee dicell ordeigner qe le dit estatut soit casseez. . . ." As enrolled on the parliament roll in the midst of the articles of the comprehensive commons petition the opening sentence was abbreviated to "Item priont les Communes qe come par Estatut . . . ," and the request to "Qe plese a votre Hautesse graciousement graunter en cest present Parlement qe le dit Estatut soit cassez. . . ." In the original the response, written on the dorse and of a grudging character, began "Le Roy de lassent de seigneurs espirituals et temporelz et de les communes esteantz en cest present parlement voet et grante qe. . . ." This, too, was abbreviated in the enrollment to "Le Roy voet qe. . . ."[84]

Sometimes the commons in adopting a group petition explained explicitly that they were doing so. In 1407 the inhabitants of Stoke and other villages in Hampshire presented a bill beginning "A . . . le Roy . . . supplie . . . les hommes de Stoke . . ." and, after the recital of the grievance, continuing "Please a votre . . . Seigneurie grantier. . . ." As enrolled among the commons petitions of the parliament of the year the bill began "Item priount les Communes pur voz lieges les gentz de les Villes de Stoke . . ." but the remainder of it, including the words of the appeal, remained unchanged. The endorsement of the original was like that of a private bill, "Le Roi de ladvis . . . des Seigneurs . . . en parlement ad octroiez ceste peticion." As enrolled this was abbreviated to "Le Roy le voet."[85] The transformation of a group peti-

---

[84] A. P. 1068; R. P., III, 442.
[85] A. P. 1115; R. P., III, 620.

tion into an article of a comprehensive commons petition was thus simply and correctly achieved by the statement that the commons appealed for the group.

If the commons not infrequently made a group petition their own, might they not with equal appropriateness incorporate a private bill among the articles of their comprehensive petition. They might and occasionally did, but clearly not with equal appropriateness; for, whereas a group bill affected a considerable number of the commonalty, a private bill was fundamentally in contrast with a commons bill. A method simpler and better than incorporation was devised from the end of the fourteenth century for expressing the commons' approval of a private bill.[86] But until this method was established, the commons occasionally made a private bill their own. In 1399 the reinstated archbishop of Canterbury presented a bill beginning "A . . . le Roy Supplie Thomas Ercevesque de Cantirbirs" and asking that he recover the issues and profits of the see recently taken from him. The commons, adopting the petition, introduced it among the articles of their petition with the words, "Item priont les Communes pur lour tres Reverent Piere en Dieu Thomas Ercevesque de Cantirbirs," precisely as they had adopted the petition of the Hampshire towns. The enrolled response, too, like that to the Hampshire bill, was abbreviated. Instead of, "le Roy ad grantez ceste petition en toutz pointz de ladvis et assent des toutz les seigneurs espirituelx et temporelx esteantz en cest present parlement," it became, "Le Roi le voet."[87] Instances like this of the commons adopting a private bill as their own are rare and were confined to the end of the fourteenth century or to the early fifteenth.[88] On the other hand, the adoption of group petitions was long continued.

[86] See below, pp. 344-6, 348 *et seq.*

[87] A. P. 1067; *R. P.,* III, 434.

[88] The original of a bill of about 1390 began "A le Roy Supplient les Chivalers et communes de cest presente parlement" and asked that John Northampton recover his lands and goods. One article of the compre-

One type of original bill supplying the subject matter for articles of a comprehensive commons petition we have therefore found. Group bills survive which the commons adopted and then adapted to the form of their articles. Even a private bill might be so adopted. But have we also any commons bills in their original form which were adopted verbatim and became articles of the comprehensive commons bill? The question is closely related to the thesis that until 1423 commons bills were presented in parliament very largely as articles of a comprehensive petition; for, if we should find several original bills which are in precisely the words of the enrolled articles, it might seem that they and others like them, rather than comprehensive petitions were the original commons bills of the period. The non-survival of any comprehensive commons bill for nearly a century would fortify such a conclusion.

There do survive three isolated commons bills which are very like certain enrolled articles. From 1376 comes an original bill which begins " A . . . le Roi supplient ses communes de sa terre " and proceeds to ask for a limitation, or at least for a definition, of the jurisdiction of the seneschal and marshal of the household. Among the articles of the enrolled commons petition of this year is one which is in practically the words of this bill, save that it begins " Item prie la dite Commune." The enrolled response, too, is the response written on the dorse of the original. It defines the jurisdiction in question.[89] Similar in every way is an original commons bill of 1377 and the manner of its enrollment. This bill, beginning " A . . . le Roy humblement supplient les communes," requests that the bishop of Winchester be included in

---

hensive commons bill of 1390 began " Item supplient les Communes pur Johan Northampton " and asked for the repeal of judgments against him. Since the requests in the two bills differ there is no connection between them other than an attempt to benefit John Northampton. No private petition of John Northampton himself survives. (A. P. 5072; *R. P.,* III, 282).

[89] C., P. & C. P. 8/16; *R. P.,* II, 336.

a general pardon recently granted by Edward III. As enrolled the introductory words are changed to "Item supplient
les Communes." The response, which is written on the back
of the original bill and is like the enrolled form of it, is in
this instance illuminating about procedure. It explains that the
king himself gave answer in full parliament: "Le Roi en sa
propre persone de sa bouche demesne de commune assent et
avys des Prelatz, Ducs, Countes, Barons et autres Grauntz en
plein Parlement assemblez ad graunte ceste Peticion. . . ."[90]
The emphasis upon the king's oral response suggests that such
personal attention was not usually given to a bill. Clearly this
particular bill was considered apart from others. If so, it must
have been submitted by itself and its inclusion among other
commons bills was a later step. Finally, from 1380 comes a
petition which begins "A . . . le Roi et as tresages Seigneurs
du parlement monstre la communalte dengleterre. . . ." It
asks that the drowning of a sailor of a ship while in port be
no longer occasion for the forfeiture of the ship, the so-called
"deodand." This petition as enrolled in the comprehensive
commons petition of the year is introduced by the words,
"Item prie la Commune." The enrolled form follows the
phraseology of the original until it reaches the concluding
words where it changes "en relevacion du dit communalte et
salvacion de la navie et en oevre de charite" to "en relevacion
du dit Navie." But the greatest divergence between the original and the enrolled form lies in the absence of any response
written on the back of the former.[91] Since a response of some
length was enrolled it must have been recorded elsewhere,
probably along with the responses to other articles of the comprehensive commons petition, as happened in 1368.[92]

These three petitions are not of quite the same sort. The
second was clearly the special case of a bill which received
the king's verbal assent in full parliament. The first was like

[90] C., P. & C. P. 9/2; *R. P.,* III, 24.
[91] C., P. & C. P. 9/13; *R. P.,* III, 94.
[92] See above, p. 234.

commons bills of the middle of the fifteenth century or like the occasional isolated ones of the fourteenth. The third underwent a verbal change in becoming an article of a comprehensive commons petition. If we had preserved a considerable number like the first, there might be some reason for thinking that the comprehensive commons petition had been superseded before 1423 by commons bills of the later type. Since, however, it stands alone, or at best supported by the somewhat unusual second petition, it is better to look upon the two as akin to the isolated commons bills which first appeared along beside early comprehensive petitions and which were occasionally enrolled on the parliament roll throughout two centuries. The two differed from these in being incorporated each in a comprehensive commons petition. But the incorporation may have occurred only on enrollment; for the two differed from the third in apparently having been answered before they were incorporated. The third, with no response inscribed on the dorse and with its phraseology changed in its enrolled form, was pretty clearly incorporated before it was answered.

The inference to be drawn from the three and from the form which they assumed on enrollment is that behind the comprehensive commons petition there were at times antecedent isolated commons petitions which became the articles of the comprehensive one. Such a petition might itself be considered separately in parliament, might have the response written on the dorse and was perhaps made an article of the comprehensive petition only on enrollment. Sometimes such an antecedent petition was virtually a draft one, which, on acceptance by the commons, was incorporated in their comprehensive petition before its presentation and enrollment, undergoing slight changes. In general, however, the articles of the comprehensive commons petition probably did not appear individually drafted, as did these three bills. Several of them or all of them may have been drafted together. We have what may possibly be such a composite draft. An original bill of 1388 consists of four articles. The first is introduced by " Item priont les Communes," the others by " Item " only. After each article has been left a blank space sufficient perhaps for the insertion of a new draft or of an answer. But no answers have been written in, nor are there any on the dorse. In their enrolled form the articles follow precisely the phraseology of the original, while after the first, second and fourth of them answers have been added.[93] Although the original membrane may, of course, be a copy of the enrolled articles, the blank spaces between the articles suggest that it may have been a preliminary draft; for the introduction of each article by " Item " shows that it was not an isolated petition addressed by the commons to the king.

This completes the rather unsatisfactory evidence as to what lay behind the comprehensive commons petitions of 1327-1423. Most of the commons bills of the period which survive in their original form and show similarities with the enrolled articles of comprehensive commons petitions have been cited. It will be noticed that nearly all of them date from the reign of Richard II or from the later years of Edward III. From the reign of Henry V there are none like them, and from that of Henry IV only three group bills. Although relatively few, these commons bills do, nonetheless, show not only that group petitions and even private petitions, when adopted by the commons, were incorporated with slight changes as articles of the comprehensive petition but also that certain articles were derived from antecedent commons bills. That commons bills might sometimes be presented individually was not un-known to the fourteenth and fifteenth centuries. Bills so presented were, early in the fourteenth century the precursors of the comprehensive commons petition and their continued appearance is not surprising. In the late fourteenth century they were enrolled before or after the comprehensive petition or, following upon presentation and answer in parliament, as an

---

[93] C., P. & C. P. 12/1; *R. P.*, 248-250.

article of it.   Since our evidence for this latter usage is from the late fourteenth rather than from the fifteenth century, the usage seems to have been a declining one.   If so, most articles of the comprehensive petition were probably prepared by the commons without regard to antecedent bills.   Just how they were prepared we do not know.   They may have been drafted individually, like the " deodand " bill; or the draft may have been composite like the four articles of 1388 (if, indeed, they were a draft).   But up to 1423 the articles were in some way edited and given a certain uniformity.

From the obscure subject of how comprehensive commons petitions were prepared before 1423 we may turn to two aspects of them about which more can be learned.   Both concern their relation to statutory legislation.   To what extent, we may inquire, did legislation from 1327 to 1423 arise from commons petitions; and whenever it did, to what degree did the statutes derived from commons petitions change or modify the petitions?   The extent to which commons petitions gave rise to statutes is most easily ascertained by contrasting statute so originating with statutes which originated otherwise.   It will be found that the former far outnumbered the latter.

Up to 1362 the evidence does not admit of precise conclusions.   From 1327 to 1362, as we have seen, the only parliaments, the statutes of which may be compared with the commons petitions of surviving parliament rolls are those of 1327, 1344, 1352 and 1354.   Although there are statutes from several other years of this period and parliament rolls from still other years, no other group of statutes is synchronous with any other group of petitions.   In the four parliaments for which comparison is possible all statutes were derived from commons petitions except one in the first and two in the last.   In 1327 seventeen statutes arose from forty-one articles of the comprehensive commons bill; in 1344 seven from the twelve articles of another; in 1352 twenty-three from the forty-two articles of a third and in 1354 thirteen from the forty-one articles of a fourth.[94]   Regarding the statutes belonging to years from which no parliament roll survives, the preambles to those of 1330, 1331, 1335, 1336, declare that they were enacted " a la requeste de la Communalte," but the preambles of those of 1337, 1351, 1357 and 1360 refer merely to the assent of the commons.[95]   Whether any emphasis should be put upon this varying phraseology of the statute roll is doubtful; for, when in and after 1362 statutes and petitions can again be compared, nearly all of the former arose from the latter, although the preambles sometimes mention merely the commons' assent.[96]

It has just been noted that two statutes of 1354 had no prototype in the articles of the commons petition.[97]   In this they departed from what was, so far as we can judge, fast becoming the established usage of the reign.   The explanation of the divergence inheres in the nature of the two statutes themselves.   One provided that the lords of the Marches of Wales should be attached to the crown of England as they and their ancestors always had been and not to the principality of Wales.   This was clearly an administrative or official measure, although it may have arisen from a group petition of the Lords Marchers themselves of which we know nothing.   About the official character of the other statute there can be no doubt. After reciting how alien merchants complained of robbery as they passed through the land, it noted that the king considered their coming and abiding profitable for the realm and proceeded, "le Roy . . . ad ordene et establi par assent de tout son parlement [that there be extended to them the protection of the statute of Winchester]."   No other statute of the parliament was said to be ordained by the king with the

[94] *R. P.*, II, 7-12, 148-150, 238-243, 257-262; *Stats.*, I, 255-257, 300-301, 319-324, 345-349.

[95] *Ibid.*, pp. 261, 265, 269, 275, 280, 311, 349, 364.

[96] *Ibid.*, p. 383. Sometimes the preamble does not refer to the commons although the statutes were derived largely from commons petitions (*ibid.*, p. 388).

[97] *Ibid.*, pp. 345, 347; Statutes 2 and 11.

assent of parliament. Nearly always the enacting phrase was
"accorde est et establi." What we have, therefore, is a royal
ordinance not derived from any article of the commons petition. In view of the usual attitude of the commons toward
aliens we can scarcely expect that they would have requested
protection for them. Two statutes, therefore, of the parliament of 1354 were of official origin in contrast with thirteen
of commons origin; and we may repeat that in the parliaments
of 1327, 1344 and 1352 all statutes, except one of 1327, were
of commons' origin.[97a]

How the commons of the middle of the fourteenth century,
when not themselves suggesting in their petitions the material
for statutes, yet co-operated with royal officials in enacting
them is demonstrated by the way in which two famous statutes
and one elaborate ordinance of the period came into being.
The statutes were those of labourers and provisors, the ordinance that of the staple. While the Great Pestilence was
still raging immediate provision for economic dislocation was
made by the ordinance of labourers of 1349, promulgated
while no parliament was in session. In 1351 the commons,
declaring that it was ill-observed, requested remedy; and in
response to the request the ordinance was erected into the
more comprehensive statute of labourers.[98] In the same parliament the equally famous statute of provisors was enacted
in much the same way. The commons in general terms petitioned for remedy and a statute was officially drafted in response.[99] In one case the commons had asked that a provision
already officially made should be continued; in the other that
a new law should be enacted along general lines which they
suggested.

Two years later the ordinance of the staple was enrolled on
the statute roll. The procedure by which this came about is

[97a] One statute of 1327 arose from what was probably a petition of the
clergy.
[98] *Ibid.*, pp. 307-308, 311-313; *R. P.*, II, 227, 233-235.
[99] *Ibid.*, pp. 228, 232-233; *Stats.*, I, 316-318.

significant. In the White Chamber before lords and commons the chief justice explained that the king had transferred the staple for wool, hides and lead from foreign to home ports, and that with the assent of prelates and lords he had ordained for its governance " ascuns pointz " which he therefore had read before lords and commons to secure their assent. The commons instead of assenting demanded a copy of the said points. One copy, therefore, was given to the knights of the shire, one to the citizens and burgesses. " Et ils, apres grande deliberation eue entre eux monstrerent au Conseil leur Avis en escrit; quele escrit lue et debatue par les Grantz si furent les Ordinances de l'Estaple faites en la forme qe s'ensuit." [100] Thus the commons debated and amended and possibly formulated the ordinance of the statute roll. In its preparation they apparently participated more immediately than they had done in the formulation of the statutes of labourers and provisors. In all three, however, the co-operation of commons with lords and king is apparent. If the commons did not take the initiative in preparing legislation, as they did in their petitions of 1327, 1344, 1352 and 1354, they adopted or suggested or amended proposals of the king and lords.

As soon as our records of petitions on the one hand and of statutes on the other assumes a satisfactory parallelism, as it does from 1362, we find the procedure of 1354 almost always repeated. Nearly all the statutes of a parliament arose from the articles of the commons petition, but a few did not. The number of what may be called commons statutes in contrast with the number of what may be called official statutes was, in 1362, 12:3; in 1363, 17:2; in 1364, 12:4; in 1368, 10:1.[101] They arose respectively from 24, 30, 18 and 10 articles of commons petitions.

---

[100] *R. P.*, II, 246-251; *Stats.*, I, 332-343. Cf. *Bull. Inst. Hist. Research*, IX, 13, n. 4.

[101] *Stats.*, I, 371-376, statutes 13-15 being official; pp. 378-383, statutes 7 and 19 being official; pp. 383-385, statutes 9-12 being official; pp. 388-390, statute 11 being official.

Some of the official statutes, although not technically derived from commons petitions, were yet said to respond to the wishes of lords and commons or of the king's " people." The three statutes of 1362, for example, which were technically official began respectively: " Item par la grevouse pleinte qe le Roi ad oie de son people de ses Eschetours . . ."; " Item par ce qe l'entencion des Seigneurs et de la commune est declare en cest present parlement . . ."; " Item pur qe monstre est soventfoitz au Roi per Prelatz, Ducs, Counts, Barons et tout le comune. . . ." On the parliament roll the three were enrolled at the end of the commons petitions and practically as a part of them. Their official character was more nominal than real and scarcely detracted from the popular character of the legislation of this parliament as a whole.

In the same way the four official statutes of 1364, which, as it happens, amended or extended earlier ones, employed in two instances the enacting words " est assentu "; and the other two declared that " pur la diversete des opinions de pluseurs il plest au Roi." What they enacted was the outcome of agreement between commons and king and for this reason they were enrolled on the parliament roll, as were the official statutes of 1362, immediately after the commons petitions. They, too, in substance if not in form were popular statutes.

The official statutes of the parliaments of 1368 and 1363, while referring less pointedly to the co-operation of the commons, nevertheless gave evidence of an immediate regard for commons' interests. The single official statute of 1368, declaring that " pluseurs gentz ont este desheritees et subduitz " because names of inquest jurors were not announced sufficiently long before the inquest, provided that sheriffs array the panels four days before the sessions of the justices and constitute them of substantial and trustworthy men. All this obviously was in the commons' interest and might well have arisen from a commons petition. Of the two official statutes of 1363, one regulated the work of goldsmiths, while the other re-enacted and extended an ordinance touching the theft of hawks. The former at least was not a matter of indifference to the commons.

The official statutes of the parliaments of 1362, 1363, 1364 and 1368 are seen, therefore, on closer examination to differ from the far more numerous statutes of the same parliaments in form rather than in substance. Nearly all of them suggest that they were occasioned by a commons' complaint or received the commons' assent or interpreted the commons' interests. They fortify rather than weaken the impression made by the legislation of the parliaments of the middle of the fourteenth century as a whole. Nearly all of this legislation arose directly from commons petitions. Such statutes, however, as did not grow directly out of commons appeals nevertheless reveal the co-operation of the commons or an effort to protect their interests. The triumph of the representative body of parliament in initiating legislation was nearly complete. Most legislation had come to rest directly upon their petitions and the remainder indirectly upon their needs.

The triumph of the commons in initiating or determining legislation, seemingly won by 1368, did not remain unclouded in the following decades. Certain parliaments of these years continued the newly-established usage but several others showed tendencies to revert to official legislation. This was to be expected from the character of the three decades, rival political influences being then at work. Whenever the attention given to the wishes of the commons was slight, few statutes were drafted and these were not always the outcome of commons petitions. Whenever, on the other hand, popular interests triumphed in parliament, many commons petitions and the responses to them were drafted into statutes. Broadly considered, the last eight years of the reign of Edward III (1369-1377) and the first four years of the reign of Richard II (1377-1381) were of the former character, as were also the years 1384-1385 and 1395-1397. In contrast, the years 1382-1383 and 1386-1394 were periods of popular legislation.

The six parliaments of the last eight years of the reign of Edward III enacted only nineteen statutes, although in them

299 articles of commons petitions were presented. Of the nineteen, moreover, only thirteen arose from commons petitions. Some of the thirteen, too, were of little importance. The one of 1369 pardoned, with certain exceptions, past trespasses of the forest laws.[102] The four of 1371 respectively confirmed the charters, re-enacted a statute prohibiting weirs in rivers, responded to the complaint of lords and commons about ecclesiastical demands for tithes on full-grown trees cut and sold, and forbad further impositions on wool, wool-fells and hides without the assent of parliament.[103] The two of 1373 reiterated the statutory lengths and breadths of English cloths and fixed the value of the Scottish groat.[104] Finally, the six of 1377 respectively confirmed the charters and the liberties of the church, rehearsed the king's general pardon of his jubilee year, forbad the transfer of tenements and chattels to evade payment to creditors, prohibited the exportation of unfulled cloths and excepted Irish friezes from the subsidy and ulnage on cloth.[105] In view of the number of commons petitions presented, this was not an impressive legislative showing.

Of the remaining six statutes of the period, two were in answer to clerical petitions[106] and four were technically official. The latter reflected in a measure the influence of the commons and were somewhat more important than the thirteen commons' statutes just described. In 1369 a relaxation of the prohibition of the import of Gascon wines by Englishmen was enacted at the request of the Black Prince and would have been a complete abrogation of the prohibition had this not been debated by lords and commons, and opposed by them. Another statute of 1369 transferring the staple for wool from Calais to England was made by " saying and showing " to lords and commons that this should be done and by getting their assent.[107]

[102] R. P., II, 301; Stats., I, 392.
[103] R. P., II, 304-305, 308, pars. 14, 18, 23, 42; Stats., I, 393.
[104] R. P., II, 318; Stats., I, 395.
[105] R. P., II, 364-372, nos. 1, 6, 34, 38, 54; Stats., I, 396-398.
[106] R. P., II, 373; Stats., I, 398, nos. 4, 5.
[107] R. P., II, 301; Stats., I, 390-392.

A third statute, directed against the extortion of the king's butler, although official, was enacted because lords and commons had made complaints.[108]   The fourth of the official enactments, however, regulated the composition of the commons and was, so far as we know, prompted by no complaint from that body.   It was an ordinance of 1372 declaring that men of law practicing in the king's courts and sheriffs during their term of office were not eligible to be members of Parliament.[109]

Viewed as a whole the statutes of the last eight years of Edward III's reign were not so much insignificant or devoid of commons' co-operation as they were few in number. The greatest contraction came in the last two years of the reign. From the 140 articles presented by the commons in the Good Parliament of 1376 no statute was drafted and from the 61 articles presented in 1377 only six statutes. Since no years of the reign witnessed more vigorous activity on the part of the commons than did these two, it is clear that the crystallizing of the commons' will into legislation had not yet become easy or usual. In this thwarting of their wishes we may perhaps see clear testimony to the reactionary character of the régime which was so roundly condemned in 1376.

In the first parliament of Richard II the voice of the commons was heard in legislation but somewhat feebly.   From the 69 articles of their petition eleven statutes were drafted, while from fourteen articles of the clergy's petition four other statutes arose.[110]   In the next four parliaments, the commons, although vocal to the extent of presenting 102 articles in their petitions, secured in response only ten statutes.[111]   At the same time six official statutes were enacted.[112]   In the parliament

---

[108] *Ibid.*, p. 392. But no complaint is enrolled on the parliament roll.

[109] *Ibid.*, p. 394; *R. P.*, II, 310.

[110] *R. P.*, III, 15-25; *Stats.*, II, 1-5.

[111] *R. P.*, III, 42-49 (pars. 44, 60, 74); pp. 61-67 (nos. 1, 20); pp. 80-84 (nos. 1, 7, 12); pp. 93-97 (nos. 25, 23); *Stats.*, II, 6-11 (nos. 6, 8, 1); II, 12 (nos. 1, 2); II, 13-15; II, 16.

[112] *R. P.*, III, 48 (pars. 75-78); *Stats.*, II, 8-11 (nos. 2, 3, 4, 7, 5); p. 12 (no. 3). There is nothing antecedent to the last two statutes on the parliament roll.

of November, 1381 the tide began to turn. Nine statutes were drafted in response to four of the thirty commons petitions presented and three others were based on recommendations of the merchants. But four other statutes were official; and the five "ordinances and establishments" of the spring parliament of 1382 were entirely official.[113] The irresponsiveness to the wishes of the commons, characteristic of the later years of Edward III, was not dissipated in the early years of Richard II.

In the Michaelmas parliament of 1382 the traditions of the sixties were more fully restored. From the thirty-one articles of the commons' bill nine statutes were formed. Along with them four others constituted the response made to a petition of the mayor, aldermen and commonalty of London, a group petition of the sort often adopted by the commons and here enrolled on the parliament roll at the end of the commons bill. There were no statutes of official origin.[114] In the parliament of the following spring the responses to the petitions of the commons were with like generosity five statutes, although three of them were drafted in response to one petition.[115] Still greater deference attended the wishes of the commons in the parliament of October, 1383, when no fewer than sixteen statutes answered the twenty-seven articles of the commons bill.[116] The legislation of these three parliaments constituted the first popular successes of Richard's reign.

With the assumption of authority by the young king in 1384, however, a somewhat chill wind blew upon popular legislation. In the spring parliament at Salisbury, at which for the first time Richard opposed his councillors, the five petitions of the commons were in part referred to earlier statutes and there

[113] *R. P.*, III, 115-121; *Stats.*, II, 17-28. Nos. 1, 9-16 were based on petitions; nos. 2-4 on recommendations of the merchants; nos. 5-8 were official and appear on the parliament roll before the commons bill.

[114] *R. P.*, III, 137-143; *Stats.*, II, 26-30 (nos. 1-8, 13, are from petitions 1-4, 9, 11, 17, 19, 22).

[115] *R. P.*, III, 146-147; *Stats.*, II, 30-31 (nos. 3, 4, 5 from petition no. 6).

[116] *R. P.*, III, 158-165; *Stats.*, II, 32-36. Of the remaining statute of this parliament, no. 15, there seems to be no precursor on the parliament roll.

was no new legislation whatever.[117]   In the November parliament of the year five statutes were promulgated in response to
seventeen petitions, nearly all of them concerned with the administration of the common law.[118]   In the autumn parliament
of 1385 the popular statutes derived from twenty-eight petitions dropped to two and beside them were enacted three official statutes of a judicial character.[119]   Next year, when the
movement to control Richard gained headway, it found expression in a statute which was the answer to one of the fifteen petitions presented by the parliament of October.[120]   The statute
was of high importance, for it created a commission of lords
and officials to amend the shortcomings of the king's government and of his household.   Answers to the other commons
petitions may have been deferred until the commission should
act.   The movement against Richard completed its triumph
early in 1388 in the "merciless parliament."   In reply to the
twenty-five commons bills there presented seven statutes were
enacted.[121]   One of these affirmed the action of the preceding
parliament against the lords who were supposed to be associated with Richard's tyranny, and four additional ones, apparently not directly of commons origin, supplemented it in making
provision for the confiscation of the estates of the attainted
lords.   No parliament roll survives for the parliament held by
the lords appellant at Cambridge in the autumn, but the sixteen statutes of the statute roll suggest in their content a commons' origin.[122]

The popular control of legislation begun in 1382, interrupted
for some two years (1384-1385) by Richard's first assumption
of control, but resumed with the overthrow of his supporters

---

[117] *R. P.,* III, 173-174.

[118] *Ibid.,* pp. 200-202; *Stats.,* II, 36-37.

[119] *R. P.,* III, 210-214; *Stats.,* II, 38-39.

[120] *Ibid.,* pp. 39-43; *R. P.,* III, 221-224.

[121] *Ibid.,* pp. 246-251; *Stats.,* II, 43-55 (nos. 1, 6-11).

[122] *Ibid.,* pp. 55-60.   Although the sentence which introduces them says
nothing about the initiative of the commons, the same silence had come
to characterize the introduction to statutes which did originate with the
commons.   It, therefore, tells us nothing.

in 1388 was to be continued, although in a somewhat modified manner, until 1395. In the first five parliaments held during the years of the king's constitutional government (1390-1394) a fair amount of legislation followed upon commons petitions; but at the same time each parliament saw the enactment of several official statutes. The ratios of popular to official statutes in these parliaments were 15:9, 5:7, 11:1, 4:2 and 7:6, while the popular statutes themselves were in response to 25, 20, 25, 14 and 25 articles of commons petitions respectively.[123] In the last two parliaments of the reign, when the king again asserted himself, there was a decline in popular legislation. In the first parliament of 1397 three commons petitions were answered by one statute to which five official statutes were added, while in the second parliament of the year seven statutes were official in contrast with two which arose from private bills, two or three from commons bills, and eight from royal ordinances said to be framed in response to commons' requests but pretty clearly prompted officially. Naturally the latter were not enrolled as parts of a comprehensive commons petition.[124]

The revolution of 1399 directed against Richard's tyranny should logically have had an influence on the popular control of legislation. As a matter of fact the influence was very marked indeed. The accession of Henry IV ushered in the complete triumph of a movement which had had only discontinuous success during the preceding half-century. Throughout his reign and that of his son practically all legislation arose from commons petitions. In his first parliament, to be sure, two official statutes were enacted but they were in contrast

---

[123] *R. P.*, III, 265-273, 279-282, 290-296, 305-308, 318-323; *Stats.*, II, 61-92. No statutes at all arose from the four commons petitions of 1395 (*R. P.*, III, 330-331). The statutes arising from commons petitions in the five parliaments were respectively nos. 1-12, 14, 17; nos. 8, 9, 10, 12; nos. 1-7, 10, 11; nos. 1-4; nos. 1-7.

[124] *R. P.*, III, 344-385; *Stats.*, II, 92-110. The statutes arising from private bills were nos. 16 and 18; from commons bills, nos. 1, 17 and 19; from requests officially put into the mouth of the commons, nos. 2, 4-6, 9-11 and 14 (cf. above, p. 228, n. 50).

with eighteen which arose from commons petitions.[125]   In his second parliament two of the twenty-four statutes were of official origin, but they stood in contrast with twenty-two derived from commons bills.[126]   In the remaining seven parliaments of the reign the only statutes which did not arise from commons petitions were one of 1404 and two of 1411. The first answered an appeal of alien merchants. The second confirmed an earlier statute of the reign prohibiting the circulation of " Galy halpenies " and foreign coins, while the third empowered justices of the peace to arrest and deal with rioters.[127]   The last was primarily administrative in character, and the second confirmed a statute enacted in response to a commons' request. Only the first was probably displeasing to the commons, annulling, as it did, a statute made shortly before at their request. In contrast with these three official statutes, the seven parliaments enacted respectively 35, 15, 3, 18, 8, 8 and 5 statutes in response to commons petitions.[127a] Such petitions were numerous in every parliament of the reign, numbering usually from 24 to 85[128] and the statutes which responded to them were

[125] *R. P.*, III, 425-446; *Stats.*, II, 111-119. One of the official statutes (no. 7) was the important one touching liveries, while the other (no. 2) provided that no one who in aid of Henry IV had assisted in the pursuit of Richard II should be impeached. Of the commons petitions, seven were enrolled on the parliament roll before the comprehensive commons bill and three of these were answered by statutes which respectively repealed the parliament of 1397, restored the lords there condemned and affirmed the parliament of 1388 (nos. 3, 4, 5. cf. *R. P.*, III, 425).

[126] *R. P.*, III, 464, 468-479; *Stats.*, II, 120-131. One of the popular statutes was based on a commons petition enrolled before the comprehensive commons bill (no. 4, cf. *R. P.*, III, 464). Of the two official statutes, one (no. 2) amended a statute of the preceding year and modified the requirements there made upon those who would enjoy royal grants (cf. *R. P.*, III, 458); the other forbad the use of foreign coins, especially those of Flanders and Scotland. There is no trace of the latter on the parliament roll.

[127] *Stats.*, II, 150, 168-169; *R. P.*, III, 553. Nothing touching either of the last two is enrolled on the parliament roll.

[127a] *Stats.*, II, 132-169.

[128] In the nine parliaments of the reign the articles of the comprehensive commons bills numbered respectively 67, 68, 85, 30, 15, 39, 28, 32, 24 (*R. P.*, III, 431-446, 468-479, 494-511, 538-544; 554-557, 591-603, 613-621, 634-645,

from this point of view not too many. But what was significant was the disposition to regard them and them alone as preliminary to legislation.

This attitude remained unchanged under Henry V. In the nine parliaments of his reign all statutes were drafted in response to commons petitions except that four arose from private petitions and one was official.[128a] Since the four private petitions had themselves been addressed to the commons and had been sponsored by that body, they too testify to the commons' control of legislation.[129] The official statute forbad the counterfeit of money.[130] Not only were practically all of Henry V's statutes derived from commons petitions but the number of them was not ungenerous in comparison with the number of commons' requests preferred. Apart from the five just noted they numbered sixty-seven and were in response to one hundred and forty-seven articles of the commons bills. Under Henry IV 397 articles of commons bills had elicited 132 statutes; and under Richard some five hundred had resulted in 143 statutes.[131] The ratio of commons statutes to antecedent commons petitions, therefore, increased from less than one-third to one-third, and then to more than one-third during the three reigns.

More significant than the increase in the attention given to commons petitions, which after all had become considerable

659-666. Nine isolated commons petitions, enrolled before the comprehensive commons bill, became ground for statutes (*ibid.*, pp. 425, 464, 580, 585, 626-628).

[128a] For four statutes, all of 1414, we have no commons petitions. Quite irregularly they appear on the parliament roll as statutes said to be made at the request of the commons. Although they were enrolled among the commons petitions, it is perhaps best to look upon them as official (see above, p. 180; below, pp. 278-80.

[129] *R. P.*, IV, 74, 131, 143; *Stats.*, II, 194 (no. 5), 206-208 (nos. 7, 8, 9).

[130] *Ibid.*, p. 208 (no. 11); *R. P.*, IV, 130.

[131] We do not know how many commons petitions were presented at the parliament of Cambridge in 1388, when 16 statutes were drafted apparently from commons petitions. The articles of commons bills of all other parliaments of the reign numbered 470.

under Edward III and Richard II, was the fact that under the first two Lancastrian kings almost no statutes were enacted that did not arise from commons bills. This had not been true of the reigns of Edward III and Richard II except in the case of a few parliaments. It is not true of parliaments of the last half of the fifteenth century, as we have already discovered. Pretty clearly the accession of the Lancastrians accelerated and completed an already existent movement toward the triumph of popular legislation, a triumph which, however, was not to endure long after 1450.

Yet it by no means goes without saying that, because statutes were drafted in response to commons requests, they embodied the wishes of the commons. The figures just given are impressive as far as they go. It is possible, however, that the answers given to commons petitions may so far have departed from the implied or expressed wishes of the petitioners that the resultant statutes were virtually official statutes rather than popular ones. This brings us to the last question which was posited earlier in this chapter, viz., to what extent did the statutes drafted in answer to commons petitions depart from the remedies asked for in the petitions themselves? We have seen from a consideration of the petitions and statutes of the parliament of 1327 that the latter incorporated the answers given to the former and sometimes were modelled on the answers rather than on the antecedent petitions. It is obviously important to discover to what extent this took place during the years which we have been considering. If the answers and resultant statutes actually disregarded the remedies proposed and urged, the statutes did not constitute popular legislation properly so-called. If the answers, on the other hand, assented to the proposals made and if the statutes registered this assent, the legislation was genuinely popular.

Some light on this subject seems to be promised by a commons petition of 1414, which runs in part as follows: "Our soverain Lord, youre . . . lieges that ben come for the Commune of youre lond bysechyn . . . That so as hit hath evere be thair liberte and fredom that thar sholde no Statut no Lawe be made oslasse than they yaf therto their assent, Consideringe that the Commune of youre land, the whiche that is and evere hath be a membre of youre Parlement, ben as well Assentirs as Peticioners, that fro this tyme foreward by compleynte of the Commune of eny myschief axkynge remedie by mouthe of their Speker for the Commune, other ellys by Petition writen, that ther never be no Lawe made theruppon and engrosed as Statut and Lawe, nother by addicions nother by diminucions by no maner of terme ne terms the whiche that sholde chaunge the sentence and the entente axked by the Speker mouthe or the Petitions biforesaid yeven up yn writyng by the manere forsaid withoute assent of the forsaid Commune.   Consideringe, our soverain Lord, that it is not in no wyse the entente of youre Communes . . . But that evere it stande in the fredom of your hie Regalie to graunte whiche of thoo that you luste and to werune the remanent." [132]

The commons thus recited what they claimed to be one of their privileges and requested observance of it in specific manner.   The privilege was that no statute be made without their assent; and, although they did not say — what we have learned to be true — that at this time it was customary to enact practically no statute except in response to their petitions, they assumed this and proceeded to ask that no additions to or diminutions from the content of their petitions be made without their assent.   It would seem that the privilege was one for which they were contending and which had not always been observed.   In the reply the king granted that henceforth "nothyng be enacted to the Peticions of his Comune that be contrarie to hir askyng, wharby they should be bounde withoute their assent, Saving alwey to our liege Lord his real Prerogatif to graunte and denye what him lust of their Petitions and askynges aforesaide."   Lawful procedure for the future was thereby formulated.   The king's prerogative permitted him to grant or reject commons petitions.   But if he granted

[132] *R. P.,* **IV, 22.**

them he might not change their purport and thereby enact a statute without the commons' assent. It may be not without significance that such a petition was advanced not very long after the commons had brought it about that statutory legislation almost never arose except in response to their petitions. A final step would be to secure that seeming assent to their bills should be real assent and that seeming control over legislation should be real control.

In itself the formulating of the petition of 1414 implied that in recent parliaments the requests of the commons had not met with complete acquiescence through the statutes drafted in response to them. Perhaps, too, it might imply that the greatest ground for complaint lay in the treatment of commons requests in the parliament immediately preceding. A glance at the commons petitions and the resultant legislation of 1413 is, therefore, an appropriate beginning for our inquiry.

In 1413 ten statutes were drafted and all of them were in response to commons petitions, of which the total number was twenty-four.[133] Three of these statutes reproduced the petitions to which they responded with practically no change other than the substitution of an enacting clause for a petitioning one. They were not statutes of great importance.[134] A fourth statute incorporated an exception stipulated in the response. The petition asked for the exclusion of all Irishmen from the realm but excepted graduates of the schools, sergeants and apprentices at law, persons having inheritance in England and " Religeouses professes." The response added to these exceptions Irish merchants of good fame and their apprentices dwelling in England and others to whom the king might wish to grant

---

[133] *R. P.*, IV, 8-14; *Stats.*, II, 170-174.

[134] Statutes 5, 9, 10 from petitions 10, 22, 24. Statute 10, which related to the measure of corn, added a clause forbidding the taking of anything for measuring corn. Statute 5, which required that there be added to the names of defendants in original writs of personal action their residence, estates and occupation, declared itself operative from Michaelmas next. Statute 9 annulled letters patent wrongly granting revenues and offices at Calais, as the petition had asked.

letters of dispensation. In incorporating these additions the statute did not greatly change the intent of the commons petition.[135]

The divergence between petition and statute was greater in the remaining legislation of the parliament. Two statutes omitted, in each case, a part of the commons' request. When the commons asked that knights of the shire be resident in the shire at the time of election and be elected by residents and that the election be in the presence of the sheriff and "nemy par voice ne l'assent ne maundement de ceux qi sont absentz," the response granted the first two points but ignored the last two, as did also the statute.[136] The omission may have left open an opportunity for the exercise of extraneous influence upon county elections. When again the commons asked that sheriffs' deputies, clerks, receivours and bailiffs because of their extortions be not reappointed after a year's service until three years had elapsed on penalty of imprisonment and paying the king £40, the response and statute in acceding to the request omitted the penalty.[137] Obviously this omission took all sting from the prohibition. Two other statutes, instead of omitting the penalty asked for, modified it as the response directed. Where a petition against the forgers of false deeds asked that the person aggrieved recover double damages and that the person guilty be imprisoned for two years and "puis reintz a volunte le Roy," response and statute modified this by assigning to the plaintiff merely "ses damages" and by limiting the punishment of the guilty to "fyn et raunceon au Roy."[138] Another petition suggested redress against Welshmen who as late rebels had lost their property to lieges of the king but who were now annoying the latter in attempting to recover it. Although the petition asked that such offences be punished with

---

[135] Statute 8 from petition 21.

[136] Statute i from petition 1. The petition also asked and the statute enacted that representatives of cities and boroughs be resident.

[137] Statute 4 from petition 9.

[138] Statute 3 from petition 8.

loss of life and limb, the response and statute limited the punishment to payment of treble damages, imprisonment for two
years and payment of fine on deliverance.[139] To modify a
penalty as was done in these two instances showed about the
same disregard of the commons wishes as the omission of it in
the less serious reappointment of sheriff's officials.

Finally, two statutes of 1413 more or less neglected the principal point of the commons petitions from which they were
respectively derived.   One petition, reciting the annoyances
and losses arising from the increase of obstructions in streams,
such as mills, stanks and kydells, requested that the statutes
touching these obstructions be kept and that commissioners
be appointed to survey and remedy the situation by holding
sessions at which they should have the third part of the fines
imposed.   The response to this request contented itself with
a wish that the statutes be kept and a statute, repeating the
wish, said nothing about the commissions.[140]   The last of the
ten statues seems to have been equally disregardant of the
petition on which it was based.   The petition asked that there
be affirmation and execution of an ordinance of 1390 forbidding the holding of benefices by Frenchmen and mentioning
especially alien conventual priories.   The king assented to the
enforcement of the ordinance but exempted alien conventual
priors and all other priors who had been instituted and inducted,
provided they were catholics and would give security that
they would not reveal the counsel and secrets of the realm.
The exemption was embedded in the statute.[141]

Viewed as a whole the legislation of 1413 seems to have warranted the criticism implicit in the petition of 1414.   In the
case of six of the ten statutes enacted there was addition to or
diminution of the commons petitions on which the statutes
were based.   In some cases it was not very serious and may
have been warranted, as in the modification of certain penalties

[139] Statute 6 from petition 11.
[140] Statute 2 from petition 2.
[141] Statute 7 from petition 13.

proposed. But when penalties were altogether omitted or when the mechanism for giving effect to a reform was disregarded or when an exemption excepted many of the persons against whom the petition was directed, the change was serious. The irritation of the commons revealed in their petition of 1414 had, therefore, considerable justification. Divergence did exist between the statutes of 1413 and the petitions to which they were supposed to give satisfactory response. Was this divergence, however, a chronic phenomenon in the legislation of parliaments earlier than 1413, or was it an innovation against which the commons protested because it was new? To answer this we must turn to the practice of the later parliaments of Henry IV.

Of the last four parliaments of Henry IV that of 1406 enacted eighteen statutes, that of 1407 eight statutes, that of 1410 nine statutes, that of 1411 seven statutes, two of the latter not arising from commons petitions. Considering the four parliaments in reverse order, we find that in 1411 two statutes reproduced, with only necessary changes, the petitions to which they responded.[142] A third, which answered a petition asking for the re-enactment of a statute of 1384 which in turn defined who should be justices of assize, enlarged, as the petition did not, the definition at one point and protected the king's prerogative.[143] These additions were not at all far-reaching. Nor were those which appeared in a fourth statute of 1411. The commons asked that collectors of customs at the ports be men of substance and in particular be resident. The response incorporated in the statute, granted the request in general but modified the definition of residence. It was sufficient to be present when ships arrived or departed and to limit absence to three weeks unless engaged in the king's service.[144] The fifth statute of 1411, however, did not conform so closely to

[142] *R. P.*, III, 659-666; *Stats.*, I, 166-169. Statutes 1 and 3 from petitions 1 and 13. Statutes 6 and 7 did not arise from commons petitions.

[143] Statute 2 from petition 9.

[144] Statute 5 from petition 20.

the petition which gave rise to it. The petition, reciting the cloth statutes of 1406, 1407 and 1410, asked for the removal of ambiguity in them, the acceptance of a width of five quarters instead of six for cloths of ray (a privilege granted by the statute of 1407) and pardon for any penalties incurred for making cloths of this width. The response and resultant statute, re-enacting the first and last of the three statutes, disregarded the second of them. Since it was the second only in which the petitioners were interested, the statute virtually rejected the petition and enacted what the latter strove to avoid. In the parliament of 1411, therefore, while four statutes responded precisely or closely to the petitions which prompted them, a fifth failed to do so.

Of the nine statutes of 1410, two embodied commons petitions without change.[145] The seven others show, in comparison with the petitions from which they were derived, minor changes. Sometimes the change lay in the definition of a penalty. To the petition which forbad the playing of games on Sunday by servants and labourers and asked for penalties, the statute responded by specifying penalties. To another petition, which asked that " gali-halpens " be not legal tender and that all found in the realm be forfeit to the king, response and statute were acquiescent with the proviso that two months should first elapse and that all statutes regarding foreign monies should be kept.[146] Sometimes the change lay in the omission by the statute of some part of the petition. The request of one petition that justices of assize return to the exchequer every second year all records of pleas with no judgment altered was acquiesced in by a statute; yet a further request that the justices hold their assizes in the chief town of the county was disregarded. Another request that certain indictments recently

---

[145] *R. P.*, III, 623-628, 635-646; *Stats.*, II, 162-166. Statutes 1 and 2 from petitions 19 and 20. In this parliament the commons presented two comprehensive bills, one of 18 articles, one of 32. Statute 9 was derived from an isolated commons petition (*R. P.*, III, 628).

[146] Statutes 4 and 5 from petitions 25 and 28.

made at Westminster by jurors improperly summoned be revoked was answered in a statute, but the further request for
the punishment of those who had brought about the indictments, although granted in the response, was ignored in the
statute.[147] Sometimes, finally, the change lay in the making of
one or more additions to the petition. A long request for the
specification of the measurements of cloth and for the punishment of those who did not observe them and of delinquent
ulnagers was met by a statute which added a reward for any
who would sue and a guarantee to lords of their franchises.[148]
Another request that alien merchants pay custom and subsidy on cloths of grain, which they were exporting as non-
dutiable manufactured garments, was answered by a statute
which enacted this provision and extended the liability to other
woollen cloths similarly manufactured. A last request that exchanges with Rome conducted by the Lombards be not in silver
or plate but in commodities was embodied in a statute which
added provisions that the chancellor send to the exchequer
every fortnight estreats of the writs of exchange and that the
barons of the exchequer examine the collectors of customs
touching these matters.[149] As a whole the changes undergone
by the petitions of 1411 when they reappeared on the statute
roll were slight. Although several petitions were subjected to
definition or suffered omissions or additions, the legislation
derived from them was so nearly what was asked for that it
may be regarded as entirely popular legislation.

Of the eight statutes of 1407, as many as four reproduced
commons petitions in imperative form.[150] Two others granted

---

[147] Statute 3 from petition 22; statute 9 from petition on p. 628. The
ignoring of a part of the response in the statute was unusual; but in this
instance the pronouncement of punishment for a past offense was inappro-
priate in a statute.

[148] Statute 6 from petition 29.

[149] Statutes 7 and 8 from petitions on p. 626.

[150] *R. P.*, III, 613-621; *Stats.*, II, 159-161. Statutes 1, 3, 4, 5 from pars.
29, 38, 39, 48.

such petitions but abbreviated their phraseology.[151] A seventh, approving a request for the affirmation of statutes of Edward III and Richard II touching provisors, shortened it somewhat and added a proviso affirming the king's liberty and prerogative. Lastly, one statute departed somewhat from the petition on which it was based. To a request that no ulnage be paid on woollen cloths worth 13 s., 4 d. or less the dozen and that the king's ulnage be not let to farm the royal reply was the usual formula of refusal, "Le Roy s'advisera." Normally nothing more would have been heard of the petition. In this instance, however, a statute was enacted granting the privilege asked in the case of the cloths designated but disregarding the request that the ulnage be not farmed.[152] Viewed as a whole, therefore, only one of the eight statutes of 1407 showed serious divergence from the content of the commons petitions.

The parliament of 1406 was rather more prolific of legislation than its successors. It enacted eighteen statutes in response to forty-one commons petitions.[153] Of these, six merely substituted an imperative sentence for one of appeal.[154] Three others rephrased or shortened but did not otherwise change the petitions on which they were based.[155] Three others added minor provisos. In the case of two statutes which protected the beneficiaries of lands held by Percy and other traitors as feoffees to uses, there were incorporated, as there had not been in the petitions, provisos that the inherited lands of these lords be not within the scope of the statutes; and in the case of another statute that assured payment of annuities of long standing assigned on the issues of counties in preference to those recently assigned, there was added a proviso excepting, as was natural, proffers at the exchequer and grants to the queen and

---

[151] Statutes 6 and 7 from pars. 50 and 53.

[152] Statutes 8 and 2 from pars. 56 and 34.

[153] *R. P.,* III, 580, 585, 591-603; *Stats.,* II, 150-158. Two statutes, numbers 2 and 18, arose from commons petitions which on the parliament roll preceded the comprehensive commons bill.

[154] Statutes 1, 2, 10, 15, 17, 18 from pars. 104, 60, 129, 139, 141, 64.

[155] Statutes 4, 6, 8 from pars. 109, 113, 119.

to the sons of the king.[156]   Three statutes changed somewhat
the administrative provisions asked for in the petitions.   One
made responsible for inquiries into the making of well-hardened
arrow-heads not only justices of the peace but also the authorities in cities and boroughs.   Another substituted as officials
empowered to grant power of attorney in case of illness the
justices of either bench and the chief baron of the exchequer
for the justices of the king's bench and all justices of the peace.
The third, excusing men appointed to be commissioners and
fined for not acting although ignorant of the commission, left
the conduct of each case with the justices of the two benches
and the barons of the exchequer, disregarding the justices of
assize who in the petition were alternate with the former.[157]
One statute amplified a remedy asked for in general terms, securing, as it did, to merchants who visited London protection
against the claim that they must sell only to citizens.[158]   In one
instance a statute ignored a clause of its antecedent petition
which may have been of some moment; for, where the petition
asked that clerks of estreats make precise record of these to
avoid extortion and give over the copy of them if asked for,
the statute enacted briefly the request about the record but
ignored the provision about giving over the copy.   Instead it
enjoined the observance of a statute of 1368 which ordered
that estreats on payment be " tottee " — presumably checked
off the roll.[159]   In the case of only one statute, finally, does
there seem to have been serious divergence between it and the
petition which prompted it.   The latter, noting the non-observance of a statute of 1399 which fined the givers of liveries at
the will of the king, asked that anyone who should give liveries
in the future be fined £100 and that the men who should receive them be fined 40 s., the justices of assize and the justices
of the peace to inquire into cases of non-observance.   In reply

[156] Statutes 5, 12, 16 from pars. 111, 132, 140.
[157] Statutes 7, 13, 11 from pars. 115, 133, 130.
[158] Statute 9 from par. 127.
[159] Statute 3 from par. 108.   Cf. *Stats.*, I, 389.

to this petition the statute reaffirmed the statute of Henry IV and also one of Richard II, excepted crafts in towns from their scope, made them inapplicable to lords, knights and esquires serving in the wars, gave powers of enforcement only to justices of assize and, above all, as to penalties, provided that knights and men of lesser estates be fined only 100 s. for each giving of livery.[160] The latter modification, together with the ignoring of justices of the peace, went far to take the sting out of the legislation, although it might of course be argued that the imposition of moderate penalties upon men who were not nobles was more likely to be effective and was perhaps more just than the attempt to impose heavy ones. However this be, it is clear that the relatively numerous statutes of 1406 corresponded in general pretty closely with the wishes of the commons who asked for them. Half of them embodied their wishes practically without change, eight others introduced minor changes and only one or two went so far as to ignore a proposal of seeming importance.

We are at length in a position to answer the question propounded sometime since. Was the request of the commons in 1414 that no statute, made in answer to any of their petitions, should in the future show any addition to or diminution of the content of the petition prompted by the action of the parliament of 1413 or did it arise from the experience of several years? That the statutes of the parliament of 1413 in themselves gave ground for it has become clear. What we are now entitled to add is that the statutes of the last four parliaments of the reign of Henry IV scarcely did give ground for it. The total legislation of the four amounted to forty statutes derived from commons petitions along with two others of official origin. Of the forty, nineteen reproduced with only slight or necessary changes the phraseology of the petitions to which they gave answer. In eighteen others there were additions, omissions or changes which in no instance were of such consequence as to render the content of the statute very unlike that of the peti-

---

[160] Statute 14 from par. 137.

tion. Three statutes, however, each from a different parliament did diverge somewhat from the respective petitions which prompted them. The ratio of these to the thirty-seven petitions which were entirely or substantially granted was scarcely high enough to warrant the complaint of 1414. The latter, therefore, seems likely to have been due to the commons' displeasure at the treatment of their petitions in the parliament immediately preceding.

Yet it is scarcely safe to generalise about this important matter from an examination of the records of only five parliaments. There may have been disregard of commons petitions in the parliaments preceding 1406, the memory of which may have lingered on in 1414 despite intervening acquiescence in the commons' wishes. To make a comparison of all statutes earlier than 1406 with the commons petitions from which they arose — so far as they did arise from commons petitions — would be beyond the scope of this chapter. Inasmuch, however, as a comparison has already been made between the statutes and petitions of 1327, it may not be amiss to make similar comparisons relative to two parliaments of Richard's reign. Such will at least illustrate procedure toward the end of the fourteenth century. Since statutes based on commons petitions were comparatively numerous in 1383 and 1391 and since these were years when the parliamentary system of the reign was stable, the comparisons may well relate to the petitions then presented and the statutes then enacted.

In the parliament of 1391 twelve statutes were enacted in response to twenty-five articles of a comprehensive commons bill and two isolated commons petitions preceding it.[161] Of these statutes four reproduced with only a change to the imperative the petitions to which they responded.[162] Five others amplified the respective petitions to which they gave otherwise acquiescent answers. Where one petition asked that the stat-

---

[161] R. P., III, 285, 286, 290-296; Stats., I, 78-82.
[162] Statutes 1, 9, 10, 12 from pars. 26, 14, 40, 9. Statute 9 may be an official one.

utes against forcible entries and riots be kept, the statute, besides granting this, empowered justices of the peace assisted by the sheriff and men of the county to proceed to the place of forcible entry and to arrest and confine to gaol anyone persisting in it. Where another petition asked for a definition of the jurisdiction of the admiral, a statute defined this at length and precisely. To a petition that the statutory regulation of eight bushels to the quarter be observed in London (where the citizens were exacting more) a statute gave assent and added penalties for non-observance. In response to a petition that land given to the church for cemeteries be brought within the scope of the statute of mortmain, a statute granted not merely this but added that licences must in the future be got if lands were to be conveyed to towns corporate or to the use of the religious or of gilds and fraternities. Finally, a petition which asked that merchandise carried to Berwick be free of customs was assented to in a statute which also discharged any who had been detained for non-payment of such customs. In all of the five instances the statute, far from diminishing the content of the petition, was generous in fulfilling its intent.[163]

Three statutes of the parliament, however, viewed in comparison with the petitions from which they derived, showed omissions. While one of them acceded to a request that girdlers might, despite special charters granting the contrary, henceforth garnish girdles with white metal as they had been wont to do, it omitted the list of customary fees which the petition had detailed. Another, while repealing an earlier statute which had stipulated that all tin be exported from Dartmouth, granted the complete freedom of export asked for but only until the feast of the Nativity of St. John the Baptist, after which date tin, although it might be exported from any English port, must go to Calais. A third responded to a petition which, after reciting the evils which arose from the appropriation of benefices by spiritual patrons and emphasising the ruin of buildings, the neglect of divine service and of works of charity, the

---

[163] Statutes 2, 3, 4, 5, 7 from pars. 27, 30, 31, 32, 42.

non-promotion of the clergy and the export of money from the realm, requested in general terms a remedy. The answering statute, neglecting certain of the evils noted, provided that at the time of the appropriation of a church the diocesan of the place should ordain a suitable sum to be distributed annually to the poor of the parish and that the vicar should be adequately paid.[164] In the cases of the first of these three statutes the omission of a part of the petition was of little importance; in the case of the second and third it was more serious. Complete freedom in the exportation of tin was not granted after a certain date and all the evils arising from papal provisions were not remedied. In view, however, of the generous way in which ten of the twelve commons petitions were answered, the cautious responses to these two detract little from the popular character of the legislation of 1391. The commons in that year could scarcely have complained that their petitions had been subjected to additions or diminutions which changed them materially.

In the parliament of 1383 seventeen statutes were enacted, all of them except one derived from the twenty-seven commons petitions of the comprehensive bill.[165] Two of these statutes made no change in the phraseology of the petitions beyond what was necessary.[166] Three rephrased petitions without changing their purport.[167] Three others extended somewhat the remedies asked for. One of these, while granting a request for the appointment of attorneys, defined fully how the appointments should take place. Another, enacted for the relief of jurors summoned to an inquest and suffering through the delay of the latter, specified, as the petition did not, the procedure and the writs to be used. A third, in response to a petition asking the reaffirmation of an earlier statute which for-

---

[164] Statutes 11, 8, 6 from pars. 49, 48, 38.

[165] R. P., III, 158-165; Stats., II, 32-36. The rolls seem to record no petition upon which statute 15 is based.

[166] Statutes 1 and 2 from par. 26.

[167] Statutes 5, 6, 10 from pars. 28, 29, 31.

bad anyone to administer the benefices of aliens without the king's leave, granted this and added that if aliens took possession of their benefices in person without the king's permission they should suffer certain penalties, especially those imposed by the statute of 25 Edward III.[168] One statute changed somewhat a penalty suggested. Where the petition had asked that defective cloths sold in the market should be cut into three parts and returned to the seller, the purchaser recovering his money, the statute assigned one-third of the cloth to whoever would expose the defect, ordering the delinquent ulnager to make good this loss to the king.[169] Two statutes granted petitions save in cases where the king had given licence to the contrary. One of them forbade the use of lancegeys, the other the sending of food and arms to Scotland.[170] Finally, a statute, in response to a petition which asked for the repeal of recent statutes touching the sale of wines and fish in London, granted the repeal, but with a reservation to the king of forfeitures incurred under the recent statutes and with a declaration that the statute of wines of 37 Edward III remained in force.[171] All of these twelve statutes were alike in departing not at all or only in an insignificant degree from the intent of the petitions to which they responded.

Four other statutes of the parliament were not so acquiescent, since they either changed or disregarded a part of the petition. Where one petition asked that the sureties of a defendant be responsible for all his obligations and not merely for a fine to the king, the statute made them responsible only up to a certain limit determinable by the justices. Where another petition asked that juries of the forests be elected in county court and be not moved from place to place, the statute granted merely the latter part of the request, although affirming all earlier statutes of the forest. Where a third petition asked

---

[168] Statutes 14, 7, 12 from pars. 33, 38, 49.
[169] Statute 9 from par 32.
[170] Statutes 13, 16 from pars. 56, 59.
[171] Statute 11 from par 45.

that officials of the forest who wrongly imprisoned men be removed from office, the statute did no more than impose penalties on them. Finally, where a petition asked for the restraint
of purveyors of the king and of lords with inquiry by justices
of the peace, the statute granted the restraint but said nothing
about the justices of the peace.[172] In all these instances, except
perhaps the last, it is not so much evasion of the petition that
is apparent as it is modification of the provisions asked. The
four illustrate how far the legislation of the first half of Richard's reign might diverge from the commons' requests which
prompted it. Their not very serious reticences by no means
counterbalance the acquiescent tenor of the twelve other statutes enacted at the same time. It is doubtful whether the commons of 1383 would or conscientiously could have proferred a
bill like that of 1414 complaining of statutory additions to or
detractions from their petitions.

This examination of the legislation of two parliaments of
Richard II confirms what we have learned from similar surveys of the legislation of the first parliament of Edward III
and the last four parliaments of Henry IV. Although the
seven were few in comparison with the number of parliaments
held during the reigns in question, it is likely that their legislation represents not badly the usual treatment of commons
petitions. If it does, we may conclude that, while minor
changes, sometimes verbal, sometimes factual, were often incorporated in commons petitions which were enacted as statutes, serious changes were relatively few and often there was
no change whatever.[173] The complaint of 1414 touching the

<hr>

[172] Statutes 17, 3, 4, 8 from pars. 48, 60, 30.

[173] An unusual and important instance of legislation attendant upon a
commons petition but perhaps not altogether pleasing to the commons was
the famous statute of 1401, *de heretico comburendo*. Among the commons petitions of that year was a brief one asking " qe qant ascun Homme
ou Femme . . . soit pris et emprisone pur Lollerie qe maintenant soi mesne
en respons et eit tiel juggement come il ad deservie [in order that others
of the sect may cease from their preaching and hold to the Christian
faith] " (*R. P.*, III, 473). It is not altogether clear whether the intent
of the petition was to punish Lollards or to hasten judgment of such as

matter seems to have been based largely upon the legislation of 1413, which did diverge considerably from the commons' requests upon which it was based. It is likely, too, that if there had been ground for complaint earlier, some petition would have given voice to it. If, then, the complaint of 1414 was an expression of irritation on the part of the commons who had been accustomed to have such of their petitions as met with favour adopted with little change but felt that this had not been done in 1413, our next inquiry must be whether during the remainder of Henry V's reign the old practice was resumed or perhaps even became more favorable to them.[173a]

might be arrested. However this be, the king assented. In the same parliament a long petition of the clergy asked that diocesans be authorized to arrest Lollards, to imprison them in their prisons and, if the persons arrested refused to abjure or after abjuring relapsed, to give them over to the secular arm. The reply to this request, which adopted its proposals and expanded some of them, declared that the king acted " de consensu Magnatum et aliorum Procerum " but made no mention of the attitude or assent of the commons (*ibid.*, pp. 466-467). The resultant statute, however, which combined the clergy's complaint and the king's response, noted that it was enacted because " super quibusdam quidem novitatibus et excessibus superius recitatis prelati et Clerus supradicti ac eciam Communitates dicti Regni in eodem parliamento existentes . . . Regi supplicarunt ut sua dignaretur Regia celsitudo in dicto parliamento providere de remedio opportuno (*Stats.*, II, 126). The statement that the commons had asked for a remedy is perhaps justified in view of the petition quoted above; but there is no ground for inferring that the commons desired the drastic measures of the clerical petition and of the statute. Indeed, the statute goes on to say that the king enacted it "ex assusu magnatum et aliorum procerum," as the response to the clergy's petition had stated, but, as in the response, with no further reference to the commons. It is not unlikely, therefore, that the commons did not approve of the provisions of the statute. At any rate, in 1410 they petitioned for the repeal of the foremost among them, the arrest by the diocesan and the refusal of bail. The request was refused (*R. P.*, III, 626). The procedure of 1401 thus illustrates how a vague commons petition might be manipulated to enact legislation which responded to the desires of others than the petitioners. The attitude of the commons to the statute of 1401, together with their probable modification of another anti-Lollard petition in 1406 (see above, pp. 194-5), suggests that the form of anti-heretical bills under Henry IV should be closely scanned before pronouncing upon the commons' sympathy with such bills.

[173a] The opening pages of Professor J. E. Neale's valuable paper on " Free

One immediate outcome of the complaint of 1414 may have been an innovation which characterises the parliament roll of that spring.   Of the nine statutes then enacted four important ones appear on the roll among the commons petitions but most unexpectedly in the precise words of the statutes.   Instead of

Speech in Parliament " (in *Tudor Studies*, London, 1924, pp. 257-286), after defining such freedom in the commons as that body's being the " arbiter upon the conduct of members in parliament save only when treason or felony had been committed," proceed to " stress the fundamental distinction between the power of the commons in modern times and in mediaeval " (p. 258).   In explaining this distinction the author deprecates Stubb's statement that " never before and never again for more than two hundred years were the commons so strong as they were under Henry IV " (*Const. Hist.*, III, 73), and conjectures that " to the new historical school," with its interest in conciliar and administrative history, " Henry IV's reign will appear . . . as an episode in the mediaeval struggle between baronage and king for the control of the government " (*op. cit.*, p. 261).   Such influence as the commons seemed to have arose largely because they " were used by the lords as a body to initiate their requests " (p. 262).

Professor Neale's argument rests largely upon evidence drawn from the rolls of parliament for the reigns of Richard II and Henry IV.   It relies upon the deferential phraseology found in many protestations of the commons from 1378 to 1413 and upon the practice from 1373 to 1407 " for a number of lords to be assigned as advisers to the commons " (p. 262). The deferential statement, however, which carefully referred to lords as well as king, since petitions of the commons were addressed to both, and which asked that whatever seemed prejudicial or depreciatory in the commons' requests should be held for naught, was little more than the sort of remark befitting petitioners.   It should be compared with the petition of 1414 discussed above, in which the commons departed from phrases of obeisance and explained specifically what they conceived to be one of their privileges over against the prerogative of the king.

The assigning of lords to be advisers to the commons would, on the other hand, go a long way to support Professor Neale's argument if it could be shown to have been a usual practice and to have implied general influence on the commons' deliberations.   Our evidence for it, however, does not extend much beyond a decade and during that decade the advisory lords were chosen to consider a single kind of business.   The instance of 1407, when the commons asked for and secured "certeins Seigneurs de communer ovesque eux de certeines materes busoignables touchantz la commune bien et profit de tout le Roialme (*R. P.*, III, 610), is unusual, although, of course, at any time such a conference committee might be asked for.   What especially attracted Professor Neale's attention were the

the usual introductory " Item prient les Communes " the phrase
which introduces them runs, " le Roi . . . de l'advis et assent
des Seigneurs Espirituelx et Temporelx et a la requeste de ses
Communes . . . ad fait certeins Estatuitz, Declarations et

committees of lords which the parliament rolls of 1373-84 describe. As
described, these were named for a special purpose. They were " pur entrecomuner et conseiller avec mesme la Commune sur lour Charge a eux
donee . . ." (*ibid.*, p. 167). From the context we learn that in all instances
the " Charge " was the king's request for financial assistance. In Richard's second parliament in 1378 the " Charge " is distinguished from two
"Articles," which were likewise " given " to the commons by the king
(*ibid.*, p. 35). On this occasion we also learn considerable about the procedure. " Item ils [the commons] prierent qe cynk ou VI des Prelatz et
Seigneurs venissent a la Commune pur treter et communer avec eux sur
lours dites charges. Et a celle requeste les Seigneurs responderent, en
disantz qe ce ne devroient ne ne vorroient faire. Qar tielle affaire et
manere n'estoit unques veuz en nul Parlement sinon en les trois [should
apparently be four] derrains Parlementz prosch' passez. Mais ils diont
et confessont q'ad este bien acustumez qe les Seigneurs elisioient de eux
mesmes un certaine petite nombre de VI ou X et de les Communes une
autre tielle petite nombre de eux mesmes et yceux Seigneurs et Communes issint eslus deussent entrecomuner [after which each group should
report to its fellows]. . . . Et sur ce la Commune assenti bien de eslire cer-
taines Seigneurs et Communes en petite et resonable nombre par manere
come ent ad este usez d'ancienetee " (*ibid.*, p. 36). The usage, therefore,
at this time was that a small committee of each house deliberate together
on the grant which was to be made to the king. In the preceding three
[four] parliaments the request of the commons that lords should come
to them was an innovation which in 1378 the lords resented. Instead of
the request being an evidence of the weakness of the commons, the lords
thought it an impertinence. That the commons should ask at all for a conference on the subsidy bill the petitioners deferentially attributed to their
simple-mindedness. Actually there must have been behind it the wish
to get the lords' agreement to the bill which was sent up. The procedure
was the precursor to the later usage of submitting subsidy bills to the
lords. It was pretty clearly the one more briefly described in four parliament rolls which follow that of 1378 (*ibid.*, pp. 100, 134, 145, 167). There
is little evidence that the advising lords influenced to any degree the
formulation of the comprehensive commons petition; and the argument
of Professor Neale relative to the influence of the lords on the commons
in early parliaments rests, therefore, on a narrow base.

Doubtless there was often a baronial party which was friendly to the
commons and coöperated with them. The fraternization of the commons
with certain barons during and after the Good Parliament (*Anominalle*

Ordinances. . . ."[174]   As we have them, therefore, these four statutes show no evolution from petitions and we must assume that when first formulated or later they had the commons' full approval.

The five other statutes of the parliament, however, were derived from commons petitions in the usual manner. One of them followed the petition without change. One, touching felons in Tyndale and Exhamshire, shortened the petition but granted the substance of it. A third, in answer to a petition that surveys be made of the management of hospitals, instructed ordinaries to do this and to report to chancery or to make correction. A fourth, which responded to a petition that defendants in spiritual courts be given a copy of charges against them and that the spiritual judge forfeit £15 for refusal to do so, restricted itself to an order that "a quell heure la copie de le libelle est grauntable par la ley" the copy be given, and added no penalty for failure to do so. Lastly, a fifth statute, answering a petition that the statute of labourers be enforced, that justices of the peace have power to arrest and punish fugitive labourers and that an ordinance be made touching labourers' array and vesture, authorized the enforcement of the statute and the action by justices of the peace and added

Chronicle, ed. Galbraith, p. 94), is evidence of it. On critical occasions like this when both groups were striving for drastic reforms the coöperation extended to matters other than financial. Such fraternization or the more usual conference on money grants did not, however, necessarily imply that the commons were a mouthpiece for the lords. Since many enrolled late fourteenth-century bills clearly originated with the lords or with the government there was no technical reason as yet why the lords should act through commons petitions. The exceptional petition of the prince of Wales and the lords in 1406, which was sponsored by the commons and is cited by Professor Neale, was so sponsored with an important limitation (above pp. 194-5). Professor Neale's evidence in support of his thesis is very slight for the first half of the fifteenth century. Indeed, he is perplexed by Yonge's case in 1453. Stubbs' dictum, extended to include the Lancastrian half-century, may not perhaps be yet altogether antiquated.

[174] *R. P.*, IV, 19-26, 22; *Stats.*, II, 175-187, nos. 6-9. Statute no. 6 omits a part of what appears on the roll. See above, p. 260, n. 128ª.

several regulations, but disregarded the request about array and vesture.[175] As a whole the five statutes show as much acquiescence in the wishes of the commons as was usual before 1413. Apart from the four statutes enrolled among the commons petitions, however, it is not clear that especial consideration was shown to the commons' request, enrolled elsewhere on this parliament roll, that no changes be made in their petitions without their assent. Such consideration was reserved for the next parliament.

In the next parliament, which was held in November, 1414, six statutes were enacted. Five were based on commons petitions, the sixth upon a petition of the staplers sponsored by the commons.[176] Two of the six reproduced the respective petitions to which they gave satisfaction, one of them abbreviating slightly.[177] The responses to four other petitions introduced in each instance some change, which in turn was incorporated in the corresponding statute.[178] Such change made without the assent of the commons was precisely what the petition of the spring had declared represensible; and at the time promise of amendment had been made. Evidence that the promise was now kept appears in the opening words of each of the four responses which introduced the changes. They are: "Le Roy de l'assent de Seigneurs Espiritualx et Temporelx et des Communes . . . voet. . . ."[179] Such a preface to responses which amended petitions was a novelty. There can be no doubt that it reflected the change of attitude promised in the spring. That the disregard of commons' wishes had not been a tradition of the preceding decades does not seemingly detract from the commons' triumph. In 1413 the liberal tradition of earlier reigns had been disregarded and a prompt

---

[175] Statutes 2, 5, 1, 3, 4 from petitions 4, 8, 3, 5, 6.

[176] *R. P.*, IV, 49-54; *Stats.*, II, 187-190.

[177] Statutes 1 and 5 from petitions 6 and 11.

[178] Statutes 2, 3, 4, 6 from petitions 7, 8, 10, 13.

[179] The response to petition 8 even had " al priere de Communes," suggesting a commons amendment to a commons bill.

protest had elicited a written promise that the tradition would in the future be strictly observed. The introductory phrases of the responses of November, 1414 were the assurance that amendments to commons bills were now submitted to the commons for approval.

In the responses to the commons bills of the remaining parliaments of Henry V's reign, however, these phrases do not recur. In general, while there was a tendency to observe the promise made in the spring of 1414, the observation of it was rather in the manner of earlier reigns. As before 1414, many commons bills became statutes without change, relatively more than at any earlier time. On the other hand, there was a renewal of the practice of incorporating in the statutes minor amendments formulated in the responses. Nor was there any indication that the assent of the commons to these amendments was asked. The amendments themselves henceforth often took the form of limiting the period during which the statute should be effective. Sometimes the period was to be until the next parliament, sometimes for one, two or three years. It is possible that such limitation was looked upon as within the king's prerogative just as the right to reject a commons petition had in the bill of 1414 been admitted to be within the prerogative. After all, limitation of the duration of a statute was acceptance of a bill for a time and then rejection of it. There was no addition to or diminution of the bill which changed "the sentence and the entente" of it. Evidence for these generalisations may be briefly summarised as it emerges in the legislation of the last eight parliaments of Henry V.

In the parliament of 1415 only one statute was enacted and this reproduced a commons bill without change.[180] In the spring parliament of 1416 seven of the eight statutes arose from commons petitions.[181] Of these four reproduced four

---

[180] *R. P.,* IV, 69; *Stats.,* I, 191.

[181] *Ibid.,* pp. 192-196; *R. P.,* IV, 76-86. The other one (statute 5) reproduced without change a private bill which the commons had approved (*ibid.,* p. 74).

petitions without change.[182] A fifth, in reply to a petition that counterfeiters be tried before justices of assize, justices of the peace and on occasion before special commissioners, authorised justices of assize and of the peace to act on commission of the king but said nothing about special commissioners. The other two statutes imposed upon themselves a time limit, while for the most part granting what was asked. Both declared their duration to be a year and thereafter until the next parliament. One of them at the same time assigned to the king all of a penalty instead of half of it as the bill had proposed; and the other, which limited the fees to be taken for the probate of wills, added to the bill a regulation that executors render to ordinaries an account of the goods of testators.[183] As a whole the legislation of the parliament diverged little from the content of the commons petitions.

In the autumn parliament of 1416 eight statutes were enacted, all at the request of, or with the approval of, the commons.[184] One was a group petition sponsored by the commons; and another, like the four statutes of 1414, was enrolled on the parliament roll along with the commons petitions although it had already assumed its statutory form.[185] Of the other six statutes, all of which were derived from commons petitions, three reproduced the bills without change.[186] One imposed a time limit; another, while granting a bill that fletchers should be relieved of the competition of patyn-makers in securing their supply of " aspe," added that they should also sell their wares at a more reasonable price than they had been doing. Lastly, to a petition that, despite certain usages of the exchequer, sheriffs be discharged after rendering their accounts

---

[182] Statutes 1, 3, 4, 6 from petitions 1, 9, 12, 17.

[183] Statutes 2, 7, 8 from petitions 3, 19, 24.

[184] *Stats.,* I, 196-199; *R. P.,* IV, 102-105.

[185] Statutes 5 and 7 from pars. 21 and 31. The answer to the group petition extended the scope of it, but this was at the " prayer of the commons."

[186] Statutes 1, 5, 8 from petitions 1, 8, 9.

on oath, response and statute drew a distinction between annual farms, on the one hand, for which sheriffs should be responsible, and casual dues not susceptible of annual estimate, on the other, for which they should be credited and then discharged after taking oath.   The statutes of the autumn of 1416, therefore, show only minor divergences from the petitions which they answered.

The single statute of 1417 and the two of 1419 reproduced commons petitions without change.[187]   But the three statutes of 1420 were slightly less acquiescent.   One of them omitted an item of the petition, which, none the less, was touched upon by the remainder of it and by the derived statute.   Another modified the very severe penalties which a bill would have imposed for illegally gelding and silvering metal.   A third assigned to the king all of a certain forfeiture, whereas the petition would have left half of it to whoever might sue.[188]   Again the divergencies between petition and statute were of little moment.

In Henry V's last two parliaments, those of the spring and autumn of 1421, twelve and eleven statutes respectively were enacted.   Of the twelve, one was official and three were based on private bills which the commons had approved.[189]   Of the remaining eight, four reproduced commons petitions without change and one omitted introductory explanatory matter.[190]   Two other statutes introduced time limits, one of them also adding minor regulations which did not change the purport of the petition.   The last statute of the parliament, made in response to an extended appeal for repair of the bridge of Rochester, concerned itself with only the latter and more im-

---

[187] *Stats.*, II, 200-202; *R. P.*, IV, 115, 120-121, petitions 2 and 5.

[188] *Stats.*, II, 203; *R. P.*, IV, 124-126, pars. 7, 15, 18.

[189] *Stats.*, II, 204-209, nos. 11, 7, 8, 9 from *R. P.*, IV, 129-149, pars. 7, 22, 14, 15.   The statutes derived from private bills consisted largely of the responses made to them.   This substitution of response for petition had not the significance it would have had if the bills had originated with the commons.

[190] Statutes 1-4, 10 from petitions 7-10, 12.

portant part of the petition, namely, the validation of writs to be purchased by the wardens of the bridge.[191] The divergence of statutes from petitions in this parliament was, therefore, slight.

Of the eleven statutes of the autumn parliament of 1421 the first and the last made no change in the petitions which they answered.[192] The remaining nine, however, imposed upon themselves time limits, stating that they were to endure only until the next parliament or until the return of the king.[193] The restriction was natural in view of Henry's absence in France. One of them added regulations not in the petition and omitted a penalty. The commons had asked that the king establish exchanges in London and elsewhere to which bullion and plate might be brought as well as to the Tower and that coinage charges be always at a specified rate with a penalty imposed for asking more. Response and statute granted the exchanges "so far as the king conveniently could," accepted the rates as applicable at the Tower, but added other rates for money brought to the exchanges and stipulated that the coinage be done within eight days, while omitting the penalty for excessive charges.[194]

The instance shows how far a petition might in the later days of Henry V still be modified in being accepted as a statute. In the parliaments of the reign between 1414 and 1421 so much change was unusual. Nearly always an approved petition became a statute either with no change or with a time limit imposed. The promise of 1414 that the commons petitions should suffer no addition or diminution without the commons' assent had been on the whole well kept. Although the commons' assent to changes seem not to have been specifically got as it was in the first parliament after the promise had been made, the

---

[191] Statutes 6, 5, 12 from petitions 4, 13, 14.

[192] *R. P.,* IV, 154-157; *Stats.,* II, 209-212. Statutes 1 and 11 from petitions 2 and 15.

[193] Statutes 2-10 from petitions 3-4, 6-10, 12, 14.

[194] Statute 2 from petition 3.

changes were few in number, slight in substance and usually restricted to the fixing of a time limit for the duration of the statute. What was tending to become a custom before the reign of Henry V was re-established and emphasized. Statutes had come to follow commons petitions very closely. We shall later inquire to what degree the custom was continued during the first three decades of the reign of Henry VI.

This long survey of commons bills during the first century of their history has revealed certain of their characteristics. At the beginning of the fourteenth century a commons bill was of rare occurrence and differed from a private bill only in being an appeal of "la Communaute." In 1309, however, there was presented to the king a commons bill of several articles, each in fact a separate petition. This comprehensive commons bill was the precursor of a type which was to prevail for a century. Surviving only in isolated examples from the reign of Edward II and from the early years of Edward III, comprehensive commons bills became numerous from 1350 and continued to give expression to the commons wishes until 1423. Along with them occasional isolated commons bills presenting a single request appeared on the roll of parliament preceding the comprehensive bill.   The latter, however, demonstrated its importance by becoming in an increasing degree the basis of legislation. While at times a statute was derived from an official bill of the parliament roll, especially in the fourteenth century, the tendency was for all statutes to derive from those articles of the comprehensive commons bill which received the assent of king and lords. Under the first two Lancastrian kings scarcely any statutes were longer of official origin. Although legislation had thus come to be formulated in response to commons petitions, it did from the time of Edward III show verbal and other divergences from the articles of the comprehensive bill to which it responded. We have been at some pains to inquire whether these divergences were considerable. The testimony of one parliament of Edward III, of two parliaments of Richard II and of all the parliaments of 1406-1421 is on the whole surprisingly concordant. Apart from the statutes of 1413, the divergence of which from commons petitions apparently called forth protest in 1414, it seems clear that the general practice of the four reigns was to incorporate the substance of commons requests in the statutes which were framed upon them. A statute, of course, always also incorporated the response made to the petition by king and lords. Sometimes this was a brief assent, sometimes it was an amendment of a minor character, rarely it was an addition or a detraction of a serious nature. So greatly did the first two sorts of response predominate and find expression in the resultant statutes that it seems safe to say that not only did nearly all legislation of the four reigns originate with commons petitions but that nearly all of it reproduced commons petitions without marked change. Since this generalisation applies with greater force to the last two reigns than to the first two, it follows that the influence of the commons upon legislation, already great at times in the fourteenth century, was extended in the first two decades of the fifteenth so that it practically dictated the content of the statute roll.

CHAPTER IX

COMMONS BILLS UNDER HENRY VI

Now that we have examined in one chapter the characteristics of the "communes petitions" of the second half of the
fifteenth century and in another the characteristics of the comprehensive commons petition from 1327 to 1423 we are in a
position to compare the two. Presumably they should be alike
or nearly so. Both occupied the same place on the parliament
roll, both professedly voiced the commons' wishes, both formed
the basis of legislation. Actually there were differences. The
"communes petitions" were a group of bills, not the articles
of a single bill; and in their original form they survive as separate bills with responses written on the dorse; they comprised
not only commons and group bills but also official bills, as the
articles of the comprehensive petition never did; they bore
upon their faces, as the comprehensive bill probably did not,
appropriate inscriptions, despatching them to the lords if they
were genuine commons bills, or expressing the commons approval if they were official bills; they furnished the subject
matter of nearly all statutes, whereas the statutes of the earlier
parliaments, although largely derived from the articles of the
comprehensive petition, were occasionally based upon isolated
official, group or commons bills.

Between the "communes petitions" of 1453 and of later
years, on the one hand, and the comprehensive commons bill
of 1422 and of earlier years, on the other, lay the bills of the
first three decades of the reign of Henry VI. It was a period
of frequent and verbose parliaments, as the parliament rolls
testify. Fortunately original bills survive from these decades
far more extensively than from preceding years and considerably more extensively than from succeeding years. In the

light of these original records and of the manner in which they, and others which have not survived, were enrolled we may be able to answer certain questions. To what extent did commons bills and official bills assume under Henry VI the form which characterized them in the second half of the century? Was the tradition of the first two Lancastrian reigns followed both as to the predominance of commons bills over official bills and as to the slight degree to which commons bills were amended by king and lords? If the evidence should show that the bills of the three decades were increasingly modern in form and at the same time that commons bills with little change were the basis of the legislation of the period, we shall have discovered a time marked by technical advance in procedure and by a continued dominance of the commons in legislation. The first characteristic will affiliate the period with the latter half of the century, the second will differentiate it from that decreasingly democratic time. If it should further appear that few commons bills of importance were rejected by king and lords, the period will stand forth as one of markedly popular tendencies in legislation.

That the substitution of separate commons bills for the comprehensive commons bill of several articles took place in 1423 has already been explained; and it has been shown that the separate bills of the parliaments of 1423 and 1425 took the form of strips of parchment on which someone, perhaps the clerk of parliament, wrote numerals, which, as it happens, corresponded with the order in which the bills were enrolled on the parchment roll.[1] Perforations near the left-hand margins of the membranes suggest that these were at one time strung together. It has been pointed out, too, that in and after 1423 bills were no longer always enrolled in French but that some of them were in English. What has not been described, however, are the inscriptions which appear on commons bills in and after 1423 and the relations existing between the bills themselves and the statutes which were framed upon them.

---

[1] See above, pp. 229-233.

Above the text and usually to the left of each of the three surviving bills of 1423 is written the words, "Soit baille as seigneurs." The same is true of the surviving bills of 1425. The hand in which these inscriptions is written is a careless cursive, apparently, in the bills of 1425, not always the same; and it is always different from the various hands which characterize the bills themselves.[2] In the parliament of 1429 and in the immediately succeeding parliaments the inscription "Soit baille as seigneurs" seems to be always in the same hand[3]; and this circumstance suggests that the commons had come to empower some official, perhaps the speaker or a clerk, to indicate their approval of a bill by dispatching it to the lords. That the bills, themselves, were written in different hands implies, too, that they were introduced by different persons or groups and on approval were sent on without further copying. In these respects, therefore, commons bills were already by 1429 like those of the second half of the century.

In another respect, however, they were unlike the later ones. On the dorse of the latter was always written the response of king and lords. On the back of none of the commons bills of 1423 or 1425 does such a response appear,[4] and for the most part this is true of the parliaments of the next ten years. Of the thirteen commons bills presented in 1429 not one was endorsed with a response. The absence of endorsed response is scarcely what we should expect at the time. The new individual commons bills were in many respects like contemporary private bills. Indeed, it is likely that the substitution of them for the comprehensive commons bill was suggested by the flexibility in procedure enjoyed by private bills.[5] But private bills had from an early time been endorsed with the king's response.

[2] Of the bills of 1425, some were written in a heavy cursive (A. P. 1192, 1194, 1198), some in a neat, formal hand (ibid., 1193, 1196, 1195), some in an open half-formal one (ibid., 1197).

[3] C., P. & C. P. 19/6-25; A. P. 7383, 1226, 1204, 5387.

[4] Several are rebacked, but this is done in so careful a manner that inscriptions would have been left uncovered, did they exist.

[5] See below, p. 374.

A clue, but not a very convincing one, as to why the usage was not at once transferred to commons bills may lie in a type of response which at just this time we find endorsed on private bills themselves. In the parliament of 1423 a petition was addressed by the earl of Huntingdon to the commons, who in turn presented it to king and lords with a request for its adoption. It asked that provision be made for the earl's release from captivity in France, and this was granted in a response of some length touching upon the exchange of prisoners. On the dorse of the original bill this response does not appear but instead " Respons[a] patet in rotulo." [6] Whether the " rolulus " was the roll of parliament or was a membrane containing the royal responses to all private and public bills presented in parliament is not clear. Since we have no evidence for the existence of a roll containing replies to both private and public bills, it is more likely that the " rotulus " was the roll of parliament. If so, we must picture the clerk as faced with the prospect of copying the response twice, once on the dorse of the bill and once on the parliament roll. Perhaps in an endeavour to simplify his labours he decided that the record of the roll was sufficient and referred to it anyone who might seek the response where it was normally to be found — on the dorse of the bill. The same brief cross reference, " Responsa patet in rotulo," appears on the dorse of certain private bills of 1423 and 1427.[7]

The pertinence for commons bills of these illustrations lies in the fact that in the mind of the clerk of parliament the dorse of a bill was not indisputably the place where a response must appear. The valid record might be inscribed elsewhere and the inscription of it on the dorse of the bill might be sec-

[6] A. P. 4229; R. P., IV, 247.

[7] C., P. & C. P. 15/5, 15/9 (both of 1423), 17/8 and A. P. 4211 (a. 1423), 1220, 1224 (both of 1427); R. P., IV, 199, 212, 322, 200, 321, 325. All of these responses are long except that to A. P. 4211. Yet this exception shows that avoidance of labour was not the clerk's only reason for neglecting to inscribe the response on the dorse of a private bill.

ondary. If this conjecture is correct, it may explain why the responses to individual commons bills did not at once appear on them in and immediately after 1423.

In due course, however, responses came to be noted on commons bills. What appears to be the first instance of the practice was in 1427.[8] From the parliament of this year only two original commons bills are preserved, the two which are enrolled last on the parliament roll.[9] On the dorse of the first of them, which is a request that staple commodities may be shipped freely from Melcombe to Calais, is the incription " Le Roi le voet." The bill, however, has some characteristics of a group bill adopted by the commons at the end of the session. Its interest was local, it was not introduced by " Item priount les Communes " as were most of its predecessors on the parliament roll, and it was followed by a bill confessedly introduced on the last day of parliament. The inscription may, therefore, be of the sort which was characteristic of private or group bills of the period. On the dorse of the bill which was enrolled after it, a genuine commons bill, nothing was written.

More curious if not more convincing as the earliest surviving response inscribed on a commons bill is one of 1429. In this instance the bill was a normal commons one, was dis-

---

[8] On the dorse of a commons bill of 1426 there is an inscription, but it merely notes the content of the bill, not the response made to it. The petition asked that claims for the remission of customs on wool lost at sea be brought before the treasurer and barons of the exchequer rather than before the council, but the response maintained the council's jurisdiction. The inscription on the dorse of the bill, itself injured, runs, " Pur les merchauntz englois quo [gone] lour prouves de [gone] devaunt le Tresorer . . . chief Baron ou autre Barone du escheker " (A. P. 1203; *R. P.*, IV, 303). On the dorse of a bill of 1425 there is a still more abbreviated and injured note. The bill asked that purchasers of lands held of the king should acquire by virtue of the fine paid for alienation the same estate relative to the king as they had acquired relative to the heirs of the seller. While the response of the parliament roll is a refusal, the inscription on the bill runs " . . . pur alienacion de terres tenuz . . . du Roy . . . " (C., P. & C. P. 16/10; *R. P.*, IV, 294).

[9] A. P. 1225, 1306; *R. P.*, IV, 333-334.

patched to the lords with the usual inscription, was enrolled in a series of similar bills in accordance with the numeral noted upon it, and, incorporating the response to it, finally became a statute.[10]   After an explanation of how malicious indictments were made against men in counties in which they did not reside and of how the accused, failing through ignorance to appear, were outlawed and their property confiscated, it asked, with long specification of conditions, that in such indictments a second writ of *capias* be issued in the county where the accused was supposed to be resident and that, if he could not then be found, the justice should make proclamation in county court touching his appearance.   The response to this petition, as enrolled, granted it with the reservation that a statute of the last parliament remain in force, with a change in the date for the return of the second writ, with a regulation that the proclamation be made in two county courts and with a restriction that the statute to be enacted remain valid until the king should declare his will otherwise in parliament.   This response does not appear on the dorse of the original bill; but a considerable part of it is written on the face of the bill below the text.   The phraseology of this inscription, which, as far as it goes, is practically that of the enrolled response, is as follows: " Soit fait come il desire, lestatut fait en le darrein parlement des processes affairs en tielx cas devaunt le Roi en son Bank esteant en sa force et qe la proclamacion qest desire festre fait en plain countes soit fait en deux countees devant le retourn d'icelle [" delcapais " has been elided].   Et durera ceste estatut tanqil plerra au Roi a declarir autrement sa volunte en ceo cas en parlement." [11]

[10] C., P. & C. P., 19/15; *R. P.,* IV, 353; *Stats.,* II, 246.   The faint numeral upon it is XVIII, and its number on the roll is XIX.

[11] The enrolled text has " il est desire," " Et qant al Proclamation a faire soit il fait en deux Countees " and " autrement declarer."   It adds a sentence which does not appear on the bill and which runs: "Et qant al space del secunde Capias soit l'espace de troit sepmains de la date du Br[ief] ou les Countees se teignent de moys en moys.   Et ou les Countees sount tenuz de sys sepmains en sys sepmains soit l'espace de Quatre moys."

What distinguishes the enrolled response from this inscription on the face of the bill is the added item in the former changing the date suggested in the petition for the return of the second writ. The inscription omits this item altogether. What is equally strange is that the statute which usually incorporates all the additions or changes of the enrolled response fails to incorporate this one. It does incorporate the other three changes, which are also those of the inscription. The latter, therefore, had for the drafters of the statute greater validity than the enrolled response. Perhaps the best explanation of this curious dissimilarity of inscription, enrolled response and statute, is that the inscription was not the original response but an adaptation of it written later on the bill, perhaps by the drafters of the statute. If this is true, we have still to seek a convincing instance of a response inscribed on a commons bill.

The next surviving bill which is enrolled as a commons petition and in its original form has the response written upon it is number XIII of the commons petitions of 1431. It is a group bill addressed by the burgesses of Dorchester to the commons asking the intervention of that body with the king for the maintenance of their privilege of weighing all commodities sold by weight within twelve leagues of the borough despite a statute of the preceding parliament which required towns to secure a balance accordant with the standards of the exchequer. The enrolled response, while maintaining the standards of the exchequer, secured to the burgesses their privilege. As printed, it comprises some ten lines, but on the bill it appears below the text in two long lines written in a fine irregular hand.[12] Although it offers an early instance of a response inscribed on a so-called commons bill, it is not quite normal in that the bill was really a group bill approved by the commons and in that the response was written on the face rather than on the dorse of the original. In the next parliament in 1432 a private bill of the duke of York addressed

[12] A. P. 1242; *R. P.*, IV, 380.

to the king and approved by the commons but naturally not enrolled with the commons petitions, had its response also written on its face.[13]   At the moment, therefore, it was not entirely irregular for the response to a group or a private bill to appear on its face rather than on its dorse.

Although sixteen of the commons bills which survive from the parliament of 1433 have no responses written upon them, three others have. One, which requested that alien merchants be obliged to pay in cash or merchandise for their purchases was refused; and the words of the refusal, " Le Roy s'advisera," were written in a fine careless hand on the face of the bill above the text and to the left. A second bill asked that men imprisoned for non-payment of recognisances of debt but released to bring suit to justify themselves should at the time of their release furnish sureties to pay if judgment was not found in their favor. The enrolled response explained that, since the king had an interest in such sureties, they should henceforth be named for himself as well as for the interested party. The original bill is much injured, the right third of it being torn off. But below the text of the petition and to the right is the beginning of a line which records the opening words of the response, " Pur ceo [gone] Tielx seurtees a luy mesmes par le. . . ." A third bill asked that anyone who chanced to capture smuggled goods at sea should share them with the king and that all smuggling from creeks be felony. The first request was refused, the second granted in a brief response. Again the original bill is injured. But all of the response except three missing words appears written below the text in a clumsy cursive.[14] In these bills of 1433 we have at length three indubitable instances of responses to petitions written on the face of the bill. The awkward, casual and irregular manner in which this was done and the absence of any

[13] A. P. 1260; *R. P.,* IV, 397.
[14] C., P. & C. P. 21/8, 12, 19; *R. P.,* IV, 450, 452, 454. The inscription on the third bill runs: " Qant al serche affaire sur le meer le Roy sadvisera; qant al peine de felonie desuis ex[presse, soit fait] come il est desire par la Petition."

similar inscription on most of the bills of the same parliament show clearly that the practice was still a new one.

It was still in an incipient stage at the time of the next parliament held in 1435. Of the twelve " communes petitiones " then presented seven survive in their original form, and on two of them a response is written. One of these responses is simply " le Roy le voet," and like two of the responses of 1433 it is written on the face of the bill below the text. The other petition began " Item priount les Communes " and asked that abbots and priors should not be appointed collectors of clerical tithes in dioceses where they had small possessions but only in those in which their principal house was situated. In this case the response was written on the dorse of the bill and runs as follows: " The Kyng will, for as moche as the deputyng of the collectours . . . belongeth to the saide Archebishoppes and Bisshoppes, that the matier contyned in this saide petition be committid to theym to putte such remedie thereynne as may be thought best after their wysdoms and discrecions." On the parliament roll, however, there is nothing of this, the response being abbreviated to " Le Roi s'advisera." [15] Since the bill itself was in essence, though not in form, a group petition, one explanation of the discrepancy between the two responses might be that the response was inscribed upon it as if it had been a group petition, but was abbreviated by the clerk when he came to enroll the bill. Such procedure would, however, be most unusual, for the clerk seldom, if ever, changed a response. A better explanation would be that the enrolled response was the one made first, and was later expanded to the form in which it appears on the bill. Some such procedure seems to have given rise to the discrepancy already noticed between the enrolled response and the inscribed response of the bill of 1429. That the former sometimes antedated the latter has been further suggested by inscribed responses on private bills which refer the petitioner to the enrolled responses in the words " Responsa patet in

[15] C., P. & C. P. 22/5, 22/9; *R. P.*, IV, 490, 493.

rotulo." It is clear that not yet in 1435 had it become usual to inscribe a response on the dorse of a commons bill.

Pronounced steps in this direction were taken in the parliament of 1437. Of the eight "communes petitiones" which survive in their original form from that year five show responses written on the dorse.[16] Although no inscription appears on two others, each has been partly rebacked and inscriptions which may have been there are possibly obscured. The eighth is an official bill to which no response was made.[17] Of the five responses written on the dorse, only one was of any length. This was the reply to a bill framed in the interests of the staplers, if not indeed written by them. Since it was addressed to the king and makes no mention of the commons, we should think it a group bill advanced by the staplers themselves, were it not included in the commons petitions.[18] Of the four short responses one was a refusal; and the other three, which gave brief assent either "until the next parliament" or "as long as it shall like the King," are followed each by an unusual monogram. It is pretty clearly a sign manual and was possibly that of the king himself.[19] If so, the responses which were nearly if not quite the first ones to be written on the back rather than on the face of undoubted commons bills were initialed by the young king, who was at the moment assuming the duties of state.

The triumph of the new usage came with the parliament of 1439. As it happens, all of the twenty-nine so-called "communes petitions" of this parliament except two are preserved in their original form. On the dorse of each of the twenty-

---

[16] The five are C., P. & C. P. 22/10, 11, 13; A. P. 7768, 5481; *R. P.,* IV, 500-510, nos. 2, 3, 16, 17, 18.

[17] A. P. 1306, 1308; C., P. & C. P. 22/12; *R. P.,* IV, 506, 509, 504, nos. 14, 19, 11.

[18] A. P. 5481. The original is curious in that two paragraphs have been elided and the usual superscription, "Soit baille as seigneurs," is wanting. Inasmuch as the two paragraphs do not appear in the enrollment, their elision constituted a revision of the bill. Whether this revision was connected with the omission of the superscription is not clear.

[19] C., P. & C. P. 22/11, 10, 13; A. P. 7768. See above, pp. 167-68.

seven is inscribed the response which follows it on the parliament roll.[20] There is no trace of the king's sign manual after any of them, but the inscription is in the formal chancery hand which was to be usual henceforth. Although most of the responses were short, indicating briefly assent or dissent, a half dozen of them were of some length. Hence, quite apart from the length of the response, the custom of inscribing it on the back of a commons bill had become established.

For the most part it was observed in later parliaments. Wherever no response can be discovered on the backs of bills after 1439, this may sometimes be due to rebacking. Of the surviving bills of 1441 seven are endorsed with the response, three show no endorsement but have been rebacked, and one notes that the response appears on the roll and on a separate membrane.[21] Nearly all of the surviving commons bills of 1443 have been rebacked wholly or in part, and on none of them is an endorsement visible.[22] If there actually was a failure to inscribe responses on the bills in this year, we must infer that the usage was still flexible. In the surviving four bills of the parliament of February, 1449, it is again clearly in evidence, all of the bills bearing responses.[23]

Although the custom of treating commons bills like private or group bills by endorsing them with the royal response had become established by 1439, we are as yet without explanation of how responses were recorded between 1423, when the comprehensive commons bill was abandoned, and 1439. They may, of course, have been drawn up together on a separate membrane, as they presumably had been before 1423. They would then have been read on the last day of parliament, and soon transcribed to the parliament roll. It has been pointed

---

[20] C., P. & C. P. 23/11-20, 24/1-12; A. P. 1324-1328; R. P., V, 23-33. For nos. 18 and 29 no originals survive. The former was a group bill addressed to the commons and refused by the king; the latter was an official bill.

[21] C., P. & C. P. 25/1-2, 4-13. For the last see below, p. 301. 25/6 is injured and it is doubtful whether a response is written on the dorse.

[22] Ibid., 26/2-9, 50/1, 68/16; A. P. 1337, 9901, 9467.

[23] C., P. & C. P. 27/11-14.

out that in 1423 responses to private bills were sometimes to be read on a "rolulus," probably the parliament roll, rather than on the dorse of the bills; and this suggested that the parliament roll may soon have become the authoritative record for responses to commons bills as well as for some made to private bills. There was better reason for inscribing on the parliament roll the responses to commons bills than for inscribing there the responses to private bills. All private bills were not enrolled, and it was usually necessary that the responses to them appear on the bills themselves. Since practically all commons bills were enrolled, the enrolled responses constituted as complete a record as if they had been inscribed on the bills themselves.

Were the responses, however, first drawn up on a single membrane, or was there a separate response for each bill? Certain surviving evidence tends to show that, if a response was long, it was drawn up separately. In 1429 a group petition was addressed to the commons asking that the earlier statute giving justices power to correct slight clerical errors in the record of proceedings held before them be re-enacted. The commons presented the bill as one of their own. The response, in assenting to the petition, rephrased it somewhat and excepted records written in Wales. In this form the response became a statute. Differing from all responses hitherto examined, it first appears inscribed separately on a strip of parchment; and the strip, as stitching and perforations show, was attached to the petition which it answered.[24] The instance is somewhat unusual in that the petition was a group one adopted by the commons and in that the response was a restatement of it appropriate to be a statute. Possibly for these reasons combined it was written on a separate membrane. By itself the instance would scarcely be evidence of a usage, but as it happens it does not stand alone.

In 1433 the commons presented a bill, which after reciting the penalty imposed by a statute of 1404 for assault on

[24] A. P. 1204; C., P. & C. P. 19/20; *R. P.,* IV, 356; *Stats.,* II, 252.

knights of the shire attending parliament, asked that this statute be expanded in certain specified respects. The response,
assenting in general, made four further minor specifications.
It included lords as well as knights and burgesses, attendance
at "Counseil du Roi" as well as at "Parlement," ordered
that proclamation be made on three several days, and made
more definite the date set for the misdoer's appearance in
court. A statute combined the essential facts of the petition
and the response. As it happens both bill and response are
preserved as separate membranes, the latter, however, so
injured that only the left half of it survives. The fragment
nonetheless is sufficient to show that the response was written
in English, in precisely the phrases which appear on the parliament roll in French. From this instance it would seem
that by 1433 a response might be made separately and in English to a petition presented in French, the response itself to
be in turn enrolled in French.[25]

In 1439, as we have seen, the rule had become established
that responses were to be inscribed on the dorse of the bill.
Nevertheless one commons bill of the year shows not only the
response inscribed there but the same response written on a
separate membrane attached to the bill. This attached response has further characteristics of interest. The bill, which
as usual bears the inscription "Soit baille as seigneurs," asked
that citizens and burgesses be not appointed collectors of
fifteenths and tenths in a county outside of their city or borough unless they had lands and tenements there to the value
of 100 s. The attached response grants this and introduces
explanatory matter about the usual method of naming collectors. It is in English whereas the petition is in French. The
response inscribed on the back of the bill accords with the
record of the roll of parliament. But the response written on
the attached membrane shows three interlinings and six era-

---

[25] C., P. & C. P. 21/13, 14; *R. P.*, IV, 453; *Stats.*, II, 286. It is possible,
of course, that the response preserved is a copy of the response enrolled in
French. But there would have been little reason for making such a copy.

sures with corrections. Below is written " a ycest cedule les co[mmun]es sount assentuz." What we have is clearly the response of king and lords written on a separate membrane, corrected and emended either by them or when returned to the commons and formally assented to by the latter body. That the response on the attached membrane antedated the response on the dorse of the bill is evident from the emendations embodied in the latter. A final change occurred in the drafting of the statute. This combined the preamble of the petition which was written in French with the response which was written in English, and to avoid an awkward combination the statute translated the response into French, attaining in this way linguistic unity.[26] In 1439, therefore, the response to a commons bill might take the form of an amendment written on a separate membrane which might in turn receive the commons approval and then be copied on the dorse of the bill before being edited as part of a statute.

From 1441 comes a further illustration of a response first written on a separate membrane and there amended. A commons bill asked that the privileges of the Hansards, except the men of Cologne, be suspended in view of the ill-treatment of English merchants in the towns of Prussia and of the Hanse. A long reply explained that the king had sent ambassadors to demand just treatment before Martinmas, failing which he would take the action requested. On the dorse of the petition is written, " Responsa patet in rotulo et in quadam cedula h[ic annexata]." Both references are correct. The parliament roll records the response in final form, and on a membrane, which perforations for stitching show was once attached to the bill, is written the same response save that here three long additional lines have been crossed out. Clearly this detached response, itself amended by deletion, was the first reply of king and lords or, in other words, the amendment to the commons bill. It bears no mark of the commons' acceptance.[27]

[26] C., P. & C. P. 23/14; *R. P.,* V, 25; *Stats.,* II, 305.
[27] C., P. & C. P. 25/12, 13; *R. P.,* V, 64.

Touching the form first assumed by the response to commons bills between 1423 and 1439 we may, therefore, draw certain tentative conclusions. Not until the latter date was the response normally and usually inserted on the dorse of the bill. If it was occasionally so inscribed before that date, the bills on which it appeared were likely to be group bills adopted by the commons; and the usage in the case of private bills was not new. The response in and before 1439 was also sometimes written on a separate membrane attached to the bill. In these instances it was usually rather long and was sometimes corrected. It might be in English and on enrollment be translated into French. Probably along with the two new methods of treating the response, the old usage of grouping responses on a single membrane from which they were read on the last day of parliament persisted; such is more likely to have been the case with simple approvals or disapprovals or approvals with slight changes. In whichever way the responses of 1423-1437 first appeared, they were later enrolled on the parliament roll and there became an authoritative record. To this record a note on the back of a bill might itself refer. After 1439 a new usage prevailed. Nearly always responses appeared on the back of bills as well as on the parliament roll. If an endorsement occasionally, as in 1441, referred to the parliament roll or to a separate "cedule," this was exceptional. The transitional period was past and endorsed bills had assumed what was to be their final form.

During the same transitional period another usage appeared relative to commons bills which, however, was not so uniformly followed after 1439 as was the practice of endorsement. On sixteen of the twenty-seven commons bills preserved from the parliament of 1439 there are written in a fine hand above the bill and to the left the abbreviated words le[git]ur et r[espondetur]. They appear on bills refused as well as on those approved. Of the eleven bills which were enrolled last on the parliament roll and bear numerals indicating this order of enrollment the abbreviations are wanting. These bills, like their predecessors, were sometimes approved, sometimes rejected.[28]   On no surviving commons bills of the next parliament do the abbreviations appear and on the bills of later parliaments their appearance is sporadic.   We must conclude, therefore, that the relatively numerous inscriptions of 1439 were incidental.   Perhaps at a certain stage in the proceedings of a session and for reasons of his own the clerk of parliament or some other clerk jotted down the abbreviations. They were not new in 1439, although the instances surviving before that date are not numerous.   On one commons bill of 1426, on one of 1429, and on one of 1437, they appear in the upper left corner.[29]   On at least five of the bills of 1433 they are to be noted in the same place.[30]   On two private bills of the first parliament of the reign is written *legitur,* and on others from the reign of Henry V is written the same word or an equivalent phrase.[31]   These instances substantiate the conjecture that a clerk sometimes for his own convenience made an annotation to show that the bill had been acted upon.   The annotations as a whole suggest that action followed upon a single reading and that the second reading of the end of the century was not yet developed.

Of the characteristics of commons bills which emerged in the reign of Henry VI the most significant, therefore, were the drafting of each bill as a unit rather than as one of several articles, the inscription which dispatched it to the lords, the further inscription of the response on the dorse, and the occasional note that the bill had been received and read.   We may now return to the inquiry which has been pursued relative to the four preceding reigns, the inquiry whether commons bills formed the basis of most legislation which appeared on

[28] C., P. & C. P. 23/11-20, 24/1-4; A. P. 1324, 1325. One bill bearing the abbreviations is in the midst of the eleven which are without them.

[29] A. P. 1203, 7768; C., P. & C. P. 19/8.

[30] Ibid., 21/7, 4, 12, 20; A. P. 1281.

[31] A. P. 1170, 1186. On a private bill of 1423 is written in the upper left corner " non legitur . . . " followed by two or three illegible words (ibid., 4211). See below, p. 375.

the statute roll. It will be recalled that this had come to be the case in the first two Lancastrian reigns. The method already adopted will again be useful, the ascertaining whether official bills rivaled commons bills as the precursors of statutes and whether commons bills were extensively amended before they became statutes. We shall for the time disregard commons bills which were rejected.

During the years 1422-1451 eighteen parliaments met and in them were presented " communes petitions " to the number of 307. In response to these so-called commons bills 185 statutes were enacted. Our first inquiry must be whether there had by this time crept in among the 307 any official or lords bills in the manner which later prevailed. Whenever before 1423 an official or lords bill became the basis of a statute, it appeared on the parliament roll before the caption " communes petitions " and the caption introduced only genuine commons bills. After 1453, as we have seen, this was no longer the case.

As soon as commons bills were presented separately, as they were in and after 1423, it would at least be possible to introduce among them when they were enrolled an occasional official bill. It would, of course, be incorrect to do so. But the clerk may have excused himself for the inaccuracy by the reflection that, even if the commons had not proposed the bill, they had assented to it. From his point of view bills were, it is likely, significant principally as the basis of statutes. Doubtless, if official bills had been numerous in any parliament, as they became under Henry VII, they might have been enrolled as such; but, if there was usually none of them or at best only a few of them, the employment of a separate caption might not readily have occurred to the clerk. Before 1423 there had been no caption for the occasional official bills which became statutes. However the clerk may have excused himself, he actually did begin to enroll official or lords bills under the caption " communes petitiones." The first instances occur in 1425 and 1429. Since the originals of these bills survive only from 1429, it will be well to describe first the instances of that year.

In the busy parliament of 1429 twenty-seven statutes were drafted on the basis of thirty-nine so-called commons petitions and one preceding group petition which the commons sponsored.[32] On examination it appears that at least one and probably four of the twenty-seven were actually or in essence official or lords bills. The clearest instance is the petition numbered 22, which gave rise to the statute numbered 13. The statute differs from the petition in omitting considerable introductory matter and in transforming an appeal into an imperative. It agrees with it in repeating almost verbatim provisions for the legal protection, especially in pleas of novel disseisin, of men who would go with the king on his journey to France. That the statute reproduced the essential part of the petition was natural since the response to the latter was "Le Roi le voet." The petition itself differed from the usual form of a commons bill in that it was introduced by no "priont les Communes" but substituted as petitioning clause, "priont les Seigneurs, Chivalers et Esquires qi passeront ovesque notre dit Seigneur le Roi en son dit viage qe please a notre dit tres soveraigne Seigneur de l'advys des Seigneurs Espirituelx et Temporelx et auxi des Communes de ceste present Parlement . . . d'ordiner. . . ." Clearly this was primarily a group petition; but nearly all group petitions which in these years evolved into statutes were first presented to the commons, were dispatched by them to the lords with the inscription "Soit baille as seigneurs" and then awaited the endorsement of king and lords. In this instance, however, the procedure was reversed. The original of the bill bears no inscription dispatching it to the lords but bears instead below the text the inscription, "A cest bille les Communes sont assentuz."[33] Such approval is what we should expect from the

---

[32] *R. P.,* IV, 345, 347-362; *Stats.,* II, 238-262. Statute 29 has no prototype on the parliament roll and there is no statute 28.

[33] C., P. & C. P. 19/18; *R. P.,* IV, 355.

words of the petition itself which asks that it be granted with the assent of the commons. Since this appeal of the petition is answered by the inscription on the original, no doubt remains that the bill was a group bill first sponsored by the lords or by the government. Such sponsoring of a group bill was, of course, nothing unusual; but that a bill so presented and approved should have been enrolled among the " communes petitions " was a matter of considerable moment.

Another " communes petition " of 1429 resulting in an almost identical statute was also probably of official origin, although the original does not survive to make the proof complete. Opening without the usual appeal from the commons it ran, " Item . . . ordine soit par auctorite d'icest Parlement " that the mayor of the staple in office at the moment continue so to act for some two years longer. The response was " Le Roy le voet." The failure of the commons to appear as petitioners and the substitution of " authority of parliament " for " authority of the lords " suggests that the bill did not originate with the commons.[34]

Similarly without the confirmation of the original bills are three so-called commons petitions of 1425 which without much question originated with the government or the lords. One asked for the continuance of a statute of 1421 empowering justices to correct errors which clerks might make in recording proceedings; another requested that writs or suits affecting men created knights during the current parliament should not

---

[34] *R. P.*, IV, 361; *Stats.*, II, 257. The last statute of 1429 to be enrolled on the statute roll was also of official origin but has no antecedent on the parliament roll. It reconciled an earlier ordinance and an earlier statute relative to the qualifications of jurors in inquests involving alien merchants. It made no mention whatever of the commons and its enacting clause was, " le Roi . . . de ladys et assent des seigneurs espirituelx et temporelx esteantz en c'est present parliament ad declaree " that the statute be not prejudicial to the ordinance. What we have is the instance, unusual in this century, of a royal ordinance enrolled on the statute roll along with statutes, all of which except itself were of commons origin or had received the commons' assent. It was probably set down after the others for the sake of convenient record (*ibid.*, p. 261).

therefor be impaired; and a third asked that protection granted by an ordinance of 1421 to men serving the king abroad be continued as a statute for three years.[35] To the last two the king gave unconditional assent, to the first assent with a brief amendment. What is common to the three is the request that they be granted with the assent of the commons. The first appeal runs: "Please au Roi . . . par assent de les Seigneurs Espiritualx et Temporelx et des Communes de cest Parlement . . . d'ordiner . . ."; the second, "Please a . . . le Roy de ordiner par auctorite de cest present Parlement par avis de toutz les Seigneurs . . . et les Commynes du dit Parlement . . ."; the third, "Please a Roi . . . et a les Seigneurs Espirituelx et Temporelx de cest present Parlement . . . par assent des Communes en cest present Parlement d'ordiner. . . ." Obviously these appeals did not originate with the commons themselves but either with the lords or the government, presumably with the latter. Their petitioning phrases are those characteristic of official bills both of an earlier and of a later time.[36] The testimony of the phraseology is sufficient to assure us from the enrolled record alone that the bills were official ones and that, did we have the originals, each would be inscribed, "A cest bille les communes sont assentuz." Supported by the original bill of 1429, official and thus inscribed, we may conclude that by 1425 and 1429 the custom of enrolling official bills under the caption "communes petitions" had arisen. It was a natural and an almost immediate outcome of presenting commons bills separately. The clerk of parliament, no longer constrained by the single commons bill of several articles, became careless of the integrity of the traditional caption.

Two bills of 1429 enrolled as commons petitions differed from those just described in having characteristics of both commons bills and official bills. One related to the amendment of judicial records, imposing penalties for the misuse of such

---

[35] *R. P.,* IV, 307; *Stats.,* II, 230-231.
[36] Cf. above, pp. 249-50, 252, 56-57.

records; the other corrected abuses in the taking of inquests by escheators and in the too speedy leasing of escheated lands. Like commons bills both were introduced by "Item priont les Communes"; but in both instances the appeal was that the king act, not with the assent of the lords, as was usual, but "par auctorite de cest present Parlement." The variation might pass unnoticed were it not for the testimony of the original bills, which fortunately survive. After the text of each bill is written the inscription always reserved for official bills, "a cest bille les communes sount assentuz."[37] In view of the inscriptions there can be little doubt that the bills were official ones approved by the commons and that the appropriate phrase in the appeal is the one which substituted for the approval of the lords the approval of parliament. The introductory "priont les communes" must have been an attempt to put the bills in the mouth of the commons, perhaps that the two might the more fittingly be grouped with bills which were really commons bills.

A commons bill, inscribed somewhat like these two but in another respect different from them, has come down from the parliament of 1432. Beginning "Please unto the Kynge . . . and to all the Lordes Espirituell and Temporell of this present parlement," it asked that with the assent of the lords a statute providing money for the repair of the harbour of Calais but repealed by a later statute be "of newe reformed." As enrolled, the petition has all the features of a commons bill; and its character as such seems further guaranteed by the inscription on the original, "soit baille as seigneurs." But on the original there is also written below the text, "les Communes a cest bille sount assentuz."[38] This is a strange confusion of two inscriptions which do not elsewhere appear

---

[37] C., P. & C. P. 19/16, 17, 21; *R. P.*, IV, 354, 357; *Stats.*, II, 248, 252. To the first of these bills the commons' assent was given with a proviso, which is one of the earliest commons amendments (see above p. 194). The inscription of the commons' assent follows the proviso but relates to both bill and proviso.

[38] A. P. 9865; *R. P.*, IV, 405.

together and which should be mutually exclusive. If we affiliate the bill with the two just described as official in origin but
put in the mouth of the commons to look like a bill of their
own, we must add that the commons adopted it more completely
than they adopted the other two by not only permitting the
use of their introductory phrase but also writing upon it the
words which dispatched it to the lords. The three bills in their
confusion of types, should probably be looked upon as phe-
nomena of a period of transition such as these years actually
were.

Although it may be true that two official bills in 1429 and
one in 1432 disguised themselves as commons bills in order
that they might the more readily be enrolled as commons petitions, the usage was not persisted in. Henceforth, when official
bills were so enrolled, there was no attempt other than the
enrollment to conceal their character. The next official bills
of the reign which became statutes were two enrolled last
among the commons petitions of 1439. The first of them
asked that captains be fined for detaining their soldiers'
wages; the second that deserting soldiers be punished as felons. Instead of the usual introductory " Priont les communes "
each bill begins " Forasmuch as . . ." and, after reciting the
pertinent circumstances, proceeds " therefore that it like the
King . . . to ordeyne [remedy]." Both were inscribed, " Le
Roy le voet." The original of the first survives but not the
original of the second. On the surviving original is written
" a cest bille les Communes sount assentuz," a confirmation
of the official character of the bill such as without doubt also
appeared on the lost original of the second.[39]

Only one other official or lords bill became a statute before
1453. This one belongs to 1451 and was enrolled as a commons petition, following two genuine commons bills and followed by a group bill and a private bill. Although no original
of it survives, the introductory sentence " Be it ordeyned and

---

[39] C., P. & C. P. 24/12; *R. P.,* V, 32; *Stats.,* II, 314-315. The endorsement of the first was omitted in the enrollment.

established" reveals its character. It extended the provisions of a statute of Henry V defining procedure against truce breakers on the high seas. The response, besides giving the king's assent, added the date from which it should become operative.[40]

This description of certain official bills of the reign of Henry VI before 1453 has revealed not only that official bills were sometimes enrolled as commons petitions but also that this occurred infrequently. If the three curious instances of 1429 and 1432 are classed as official bills the total is only eleven. In contrast were 162 statutes which arose from genuine commons petitions.[41] The figures are illuminating as to the character of the legislation of the thirty years. We have seen how in the times of Henry IV and Henry V official bills practically disappeared as the source of legislation. Nor did such become very numerous, as we have also seen, before 1484.[42] In a general way, therefore, it is correct to say that the statutes of the first half of the fifteenth century were framed almost entirely upon commons bills, those of the third quarter of the century somewhat less so, and those of the last quarter markedly upon official or lords bills. The significance of this generalization in the history of the commons is patent; for it implies that the period when legislation arose almost entirely from commons bills was a period of considerable commons' influence upon public affairs so far as this could express itself in legislation. Before emphasizing this influence, however, it is necessary to inquire whether the commons bills which gave rise to legislation were in any considerable degree amended in the process.

Of the 162 statutes which were framed from commons bills

---

[40] *R. P.*, V, 224; *Stats.*, II, 358.

[41] Of the twelve other statutes of the years 1422-1451, one arose from a bill of the clergy, nine from private or group petitions enrolled before the "communes petitions" and two have no counterpart on the rolls of parliament (*Stats.*, II, 238, 214-215 (nos. 4-6), 217-219 (nos. 2-6), 269, 213 (no. 1), 216 (no. 29); *R. P.*, IV, 347, 177-178, 249-252, 375).

[42] Cf. above, pp. 137-38.

during the years 1422-1451 one-half underwent no change
save the substitution of an imperative for an appeal and save
the occasional omission of introductory and explanatory matter. In every parliament except the first bills were presented
to which the king gave unqualified assent and often the majority were thus approved. Half of the statutes of these years,
however, arose from bills the royal response to which embodied
some change or amendment. Since the scope of these amendments measures the degree to which commons' proposals failed
of precise enactment, it is desirable to scan them somewhat
closely. They fall into five general groups. One group specifically reserved the king's prerogative; one defined more
closely some clause of the bill, perhaps relating it to earlier
statutes; one made some change in the penalties imposed or in
the disposition of them; a fourth limited the duration of the
statute which it authorized; and a fifth altered in some respect
the administrative machinery of the bill.

Reservation of the king's prerogative was the purport of the
amendments to only four bills. The king granted a petition
that the ordinance of the staple regarding bullion be continued
for three years, reserving his right to modify it with the advice
of his council. He promised to introduce no *Vidimus* clause
in a safe conduct unless a " great cause " should lead him to
do so. He agreed that cheese and butter need not go to Calais
but reserved the right to restrain the traffic in these commodities. Lastly, he assented to the request that hostlers and
brewers should not have letters patent to take horses for the
king and queen, yet reserved his " prerogative and pre-emi-
nence." [43]

Definition of some clause of a bill or the relating of it to
other statutes was more usual. Some thirteen instances occur.
Often the amendment was so obvious that it might well have
been in the original bill. Liberties of church, lords and boroughs were confirmed so far as they were " bien usez et nient
repellez ne par le Commune Leye repellablez." Where a bill

[43] *R. P.,* IV, 454, 500; V, 24, 202.

provided that any offender who shipped wool elsewhere than
to Calais be punished, the amendment added that, if he should
himself confess at the exchequer, he should be convicted by
his own confession. Where a petition asked that aliens be
not suffered to receive gold for their merchandise, an amendment rephrased this to the effect that they should not bind
anyone to make payment in gold and should not refuse payment in silver. Permission that the borough of Dorchester
have its privileged weights and measures was phrased more
concisely than in the petitioners' bill. A commission to survey the river Lee was authorized provided someone could be
found willing to do so without disturbing the right of anyone.
The merchandise of friendly aliens taken in enemies' ships
might be retained by the captors but only so far as this was not
contrary to existent treaties. A request that anyone harassed
by a writ of subpoena in an action determinable at common
law might recover damages was granted with the addition that
the writ should not issue until surety was found to satisfy the
accused if the action should fail. A requirement that security
be given that shipments cleared for Calais proceed thither was
authorized subject to the liberties of the Italians. The activities of alien merchants were regulated but without prejudice
to any alliance or truce. Denizens were to pay alien rates
when they shipped wool or tin elsewhere than to Calais, excepting those who already had licences. Woolen yarn might
not be exported as thrums, but with the reservation of advan-
tages secured to the king by an earlier statute. Newly created
wardens might inspect worsteds in Norfolk, but they might
make no new ordinance without submitting it to king and council. Welsh outlaws might be taken in Herefordshire but also
the statute of Westminster I touching like matters should be
put into execution.[44] Thus the characteristics of these thirteen amendments were, not that they modified in any appreciable degree the respective bills to which they were appended,
but that they noted limitations or additions which naturally

[44] R. P., IV, 253, 358, 360, 380, 381, 492, 501, 508; V, 24, 54, 104, 105, 106.

arose out of existent statutes, treaties or concessions, or out of accepted procedure.

The amendments made to eight other commons bills of 1422-1451 changed the penalties imposed or the disposal of them. To a penalization of cordwainers for practicing the trade of tanners and for tanning badly was added a penalty for tanners whose tanned hides might prove defective. When the king assented to the issue of commissions to survey impediments in the Thames, the penalty of 100 marks proposed for persistent offenders was changed to such action as the justices of the bench might see fit to take. A penalty for imprisonment, fine and forfeiture of "trible dammages" proposed for deceiving men who might bring money to the mint to be coined was changed to the forfeiture of double damages; and this penalty was extended, as it was not in the petition, to the requirement that the king's assayer and the controller of the mint take no fees. When certain abbots and priors of Yorkshire and Lancashire requested that they be represented in court by attorneys, as had been granted by an earlier statute, seneschals and bailiffs to forfeit £12 if they should refuse to receive the attorneys, the king replied with a renewal of the statute but a disregard of the penalty. To a bill providing punishment for purveyors who did not observe the statutes, the response added that the statute of 36 Edward III affecting also purveyors of persons other than the king should likewise be observed. On the other hand, in response to a petition that the gauging penny be not paid until the gauger of wine had done his work and that a statute of 1439 stipulating the forfeiture of wine sold before gauging be repealed, the first request but not the second met with approval.[45] Finally, an amendment to a bill touching false measures reserved a part of the penalty for the informer; and an amendment to another bill requiring sureties for the bailing out of imprisoned debtors added that, since the king had income from such sureties, security be given to him

[45] *Ibid.*, IV, 253, 255, 257, 381; V, 55, 116.

as well as to the creditor.[46]   Although in these eight instances
the changes of penalty constituted amendments more considerable than those which arose from changes in definition, the
departure from the intent of the petitioners was not great and
did not noticeably alter the resultant statutes.

Much more serious were the amendments which limited the
duration of statutes, and they also were more numerous.   In
the parliaments of 1422-1451 amendments which did this and
no more numbered twenty-nine, while seven amendments limited the duration of statutes and contained other provisions
as well.   Sometimes the duration accorded was for a period of
years — three, five, seven or ten.[47]   Sometimes it was only
until the next parliament; or until the next parliament and
longer if the statute in question did not then seem inexpedient
to king and lords.[48]   Sometimes it was at the will of the king.[49]
In one instance it was made dependent upon peace or war on
the northern border and in another was to apply to outlawries
of the future but not to those of an interim period.[50]

To limit the duration of a statute until the next parliament
or to a period of years was undoubtedly to impose upon it a
serious restriction.   It was akin to outright rejection.   Yet
rejection was, as the commons had recognized in 1414, always
within the competence of the king.   At that time they had
asked that no statute be enacted from a petition without their
assent "nother by addicions nother by diminucions by no
maner of terme ne termes the whiche that sholde chaunge the
sentence and the entente axked. . . ."[51]   We might, of course,
interpret the word "terme" as meaning a term of years and

---

[46] *Ibid.*, IV, 256, 452.

[47] *Ibid.*, IV, 333, 381, 450; V, 53, 61, 150, 200, 202.   As part of the amendment, *ibid.*, p. 105.

[48] *Ibid.*, IV, 255, 258, 260, 330, 404, 500; V, 28, 29, 30, 55, 64, 151, 152,
155.   As part of the amendment, IV, 255, 256.

[49] *Ibid.*, IV, 352, 377, 507.   As part of the amendment, *ibid.*, pp. 328, 353,
381, 492.

[50] *Ibid.*, IV, 490, 407.

[51] *Ibid.*, IV, 22.   See above, pp. 261-62.

thus applicable to precisely the type of amendment which we are considering. But the reiteration of " terme " in the plural and the explanation that the "entente" must not be changed seem rather to imply that evasive provisos instead of terms of years were in the petitioners' minds. We have seen that in the following parliaments of Henry V the commons' consent was at times got to a change in the clauses of a bill but apparently not got to a limitation of its duration.[52] Whether this same disregard of their assent to a limitation of duration prevailed from 1422 to 1451 cannot, in the absence of the original responses, be determined. On the whole it seems that this sort of amendment was the one which the commons at the time admitted to be independent of their approval, a half-step toward complete rejection, which they would have been unable to protest.

The type of amendment to which in 1414 the commons seem particularly to have claimed the right to assent was the kind which we have now to examine. It may be called an administrative amendment, being concerned primarily with a change in some administrative feature of a bill. In one guise or another it was appended to bills twenty-seven times between 1422 and 1451, nearly as often as the amendment limiting the duration of a statute. Its importance varied with the magnitude of the change introduced. Speaking generally, the change was slight, but in some four instances it did considerably alter the character of a bill. In view of the bearing of this type of amendment upon the commons' control of legislation during the reign of Henry VI, it may be permissible to enumerate briefly these amendments. For the most part a chronological order will be followed except that the four more sweeping ones will be left to the last.

At the beginning of the reign there was granted a request that Irishmen, except graduates of the schools, beneficed clerks and a few others, might be expelled from the realm. In pursuance of this end an amendment was added that all Irish

---

[52] See above, pp. 281-85.

scholars of the king's obedience, other than graduates who were allowed to remain, find security for good behaviour and that they and other Irishmen entering the realm show to the chancellor letters under the seal of the lieutenant or justice of Ireland testifying that they were of the king's obedience. A bill of the following parliament proposed further that in the case of these Irishmen the surety for good behaviour be given in the presence of a justice of the peace or of the mayor of a town. An amendment now added the chancellors of Oxford or Cambridge as officials competent to receive the security of scholars resident in either town. In the same parliament of 1423 a request that wardens of the brauderers of London be empowered to search for and seize unlawful embroidery at certain fairs was evasively answered by the amendment that unlawful embroidery should be forfeit. In this case an administrative proviso was omitted. Another bill of 1423 required that goldsmiths mark their silver and punished offences of the master of the mint at common law. Amendments added that the marks must be known to the wardens of the goldsmiths and that the master of the mint be held according to the terms of his indenture. In 1425 a petition asked that men who summoned or attended masons' assemblies be declared felons; but an amendment reduced the penalty for attendance to imprisonment and failed to give justices of the peace the jurisdiction asked for. Equally restrictive was an amendment to a bill which asked that butter and cheese be no longer staple merchandise necessarily sent to Calais. The amendment authorized shipment elsewhere but only in virtue of licences issued by the chancellor. Where a petition of 1427 asked for a period of three months before the return of a writ of *capias,* the reply reduced the time to six weeks or longer at the discretion of the justices. Again in the following parliament an amendment reduced the period of time at the end of which a second writ of *capias,* the subject of a new bill, was returnable. In 1427, a reduction of seven days to six and of ten to eight relative to time of announcement took place in virtue of an amendment to a bill which defined the conditions under which special assizes should be granted and held, a penalty being added for failure to observe these conditions.[53]

In the parliament of 1429 a long bill touching forcible entries was amended by exempting from its provisions tenants who had been in possession for three years or more. Another bill touching riots was amended by the requirement that before a writ of *capias* could issue two justices of the peace must testify that the occurrence of the riot was a matter of common fame. Another bill, permitting justices to rectify clerical errors in the returns of sheriffs and other officials, was by amendment made not applicable to Wales. To the bills of the parliaments of the three following years four administrative amendments were made, some of them rather blunting the edge of the remedies asked. A bill which asked that disturbers of traffic on the river Severn be speedily tried before justices of the peace was granted in substance, but the complainant was referred to the common law without specific mention of justices of the peace or of the writs to be used. Instead of the letters of marque, asked for against subjects of the king of Denmark from whom no satisfaction could be got for injuries done, the king's reply promised suitable remedy to be devised by the council. A bill limiting the prices of the wares of wax chandlers was accepted but was made inapplicable to whatever might be purchased for the funerals of nobles. In contrast with these restrictions, punishment for assault on knights of the shire and burgesses coming to parliament was by amendment extended to lords spiritual and temporal and to any coming to the king's council, while the time at which assailants should appear before the king's bench was noted.[54]

The years 1439-1444 produced six administrative amendments. To a bill that all justices of the peace have an income of £20 the king's reply added that if no one so qualified was available in the county the chancellor might appoint other

[53] *R. P.*, IV, 190, 254, 255, 256, 292, 293, 327, 353, 328.
[54] *Ibid.*, pp. 353, 356, 379, 402, 453.

suitable men. To a request for the reaffirmation of all ordinances enacted in 1421 to endure until the next parliament but
expired because of the death of Henry V and especially for
the reaffirmation of the ordinance against false indictments,
the king's reply approved the re-enactment of the ordinance
most desired but not of the others. To a commons petition
for the reform of the ordinance of partition (which required
the recoinage at Calais of a part of merchants' proceeds from
the sale of wool) the king replied that the staplers should
themselves reform it but that if they did not do so shortly the
petition would stand approved. To a request for the continuance of a statute of 1427 which created commissions of sewers
and for new provisions touching residence and wages the reply
granted the continuance for fifteen years but disregarded the
new provisions. To a bill regulating servants' wages and contracts there was general assent except to the clause which required any servant making a new contract to make it before
the constables of the town where he was in service and to another clause which penalized the givers of excess wages. To
a bill stipulating how knights of the shire and burgesses should
be elected the only amendment was that the knights must be
men of birth and not yeomen. Following these six amended
bills of the second half of the reign was one other of 1449.
When the commons petitioned that priests charged with rape
or with taking excessive salary be pardoned in return for a
subsidy payable by the priests, the king replied that the grant
of such a subsidy lay with convocation but that if it was
voted in convocation he would on his part grant the pardon.[55]

A characteristic of the twenty-three administrative amendments so far noted is that the changes which they made in the
provisions of the bills to which they were respectively appended were relatively slight. This is less true of four other
amendments of the same sort. In 1422 a commons petition
asked protection against the king's purveyors by requiring a
bailiff or constable of a village or hamlet in which anyone

[55] *Ibid.,* V, 28, 64, 109, 112, 115, 152.

might be aggrieved by the purveyor to prepare a "bille" noting the injury done and to deliver it to a justice of the peace, who in turn should hear the complaint at his next session. The response neglected this procedure, which was undoubtedly the principal interest of the petitioners, and contented itself with reaffirming all statutes against purveyors, which it enjoined sheriffs to proclaim four times yearly. Scarcely less serious was the omission of certain procedure asked for in a group bill of 1433 presented by the commons. The bill, reciting how faint and false pleas introduced to delay grand juries in the consideration of cases before them were not penalized, asked both for a procedure which would avoid such delay and for damages payable to the plaintiffs whose suits were delayed. The response granted the damages but ignored the procedure. Two other amendments dealt with export licences. In 1425 the commons requested that Kentishmen might ship corn, beasts and other victuals to Picardy as freely as they once had done without the licences of late required. The answer reaffirmed a statute of 1394, which permitted free exportation of corn subject to the council's control, but refused any relaxation of regulations touching other merchandise. Finally, a group petition of 1435, voicing the oft-repeated request of the commons that no licences be granted to export wool elsewhere than to Calais, was answered not only with a reservation of the benefits of licences already issued and of the liberties of the Italians and the burgesses of Berwick but also with a reservation of the king's authority to modify on the advice of his council the statute now to be granted.[56] Clearly this proviso left the door open for the issue of such licences as the king might please to grant.

The evasion, in the replies to these four petitions, of precisely what the commons asked is patent. It may be noted, however, that two of the bills were professedly group bills adopted by the commons, while the one regarding Kentish exports was virtually such. Only the bill about purveyance was

[56] *Ibid.*, IV, 190, 448, 307, 490.

a rebuff to the commons at large. But full assent to bills which closely touched the royal household was in general difficult to secure. Viewed as a whole the twenty-seven administrative amendments to commons bills from 1422 to 1451 did not seriously modify the substance of the petitions to which they were appended. When they were incorporated in the resultant statutes, as they always were, the statutes so closely enacted the petitions that the outcome may correctly be termed popular legislation. If these twenty-seven statutes were on the whole popular, the twenty-nine others which incorporated amendments limiting their duration were equally so. They also constituted popular legislation but of a sort which the king might in the future allow to lapse. Of the twenty-five other bills which in these years were amended we have seen that the amendments were largely formal in character. Reservation of the royal prerogative, reference to existing treaties, definition of inadequate clauses, might properly be added as amendments to bills the phraseology of which had not been made sufficiently precise. Over against these eighty-one amended bills stood as many more which were accepted by king and lords without amendment; and it is on the whole surprising that half of the commons bills of these years needed no amending whatever. Such extensive freedom from amendment and the insignificance of nearly all amendments which were added, along with the almost entire absence of official or lords bills, mark the period 1422-1451 as one of dominantly popular legislation.

This characterization would be further justified if we could be assured that the commons assented to the amendments made to their petitions from 1422 to 1451. We have seen that in 1414 they had asked that no additions or diminutions be made to their bills and had been promised that henceforth nothing would be enacted contrary to their asking whereby they should be bound without their assent, saving to the king his prerogative to grant and deny what he wished. We have seen, too, that the roll of the following parliament testified that the commons' assent was then got to amendments added to the commons petitions but that during the remaining years of Henry V we have no such assurance. Since amendments of these later years changed the bills little, it may have been assumed that slight changes did not involve the principle of binding the commons without their assent.[57]

This assumption would not be inapplicable to the legislation of 1422-1451. Our examination has shown that amendments to commons bills altered them little; and because the amendments were inconsequential, it was possible to argue that no departure had been made from the spirit of the various bills. With the appearance of separate commons bills in 1423 we might perhaps be led to hope that evidence would be forthcoming to show how the commons treated the royal response. Unfortunately, as we have seen, responses came to be endorsed on commons bills only slowly and gradually. Most responses earlier than 1439 have disappeared other than those enrolled on the parliament roll. In one of the responses of 1439, however, there is testimony relative to the commons' treatment of an amendment made to one of their bills. It has been described above to illustrate the appearance of a response written on a separate but attached membrane. Where the bill asked that citizens and burgesses be not appointed collectors of tenths and fifteenths outside of their city or borough unless they held lands and tenements outside, the amendment added details about the method of naming collectors. As written on the attached membrane it shows three interlinings and six erasures with corrections, all neatly done, and below it is written "a ycest cedule les communes sount assentuz."[58] This is clear enough testimony that in 1439 the commons were doing what the parliament roll tells us they were doing in 1415 — assenting to amendments made to their bills. Indeed, they may have revised this particular amendment touching the collection of subsidies; for the interlinings and erasures must have

[57] See above, pp. 261-63, 281-85.
[58] C., P. & C. P. 23/14. See above, p. 301.

been those of either the lords or the commons. If they were the work of the commons the inscribing of the commons' assent may have been preparatory to returning to the lords an amendment which had originated with the latter and was now being re-amended. Or, of course, the interlinings and erasures may testify merely to vacillations in the first drafting of the amendment.

In the same parliament another commons petition asking that no one be appointed justice of the peace in any county unless he had lands and tenements to the annual value of £20 was amended to the effect that if there were not in the county enough such men, the chancellor might appoint other suitable men. The response appears both on the dorse of the bill and on an appended membrane. But on the latter there is no record of the commons' assent.[59] Thus the positive testimony of one amendment of this parliament is more or less counterbalanced by the negative testimony of another. It might seem that the commons' assent was recorded only when changes were made in the amendment — made perhaps by the commons themselves.

Between 1439 and 1451 two other amendments to commons bills are preserved, one of which may bear record of the commons' approval, while the other certainly does. The first amends a bill of 1442 asking retaliatory measures against Hansards, inasmuch as English merchants were being ill-treated in Prussia and the Hanse towns. A long response promised this in case an embassy shortly to be sent to the offending authorities should secure no remedy before Martinmas. On the back of the bill is written: "Responsa patet in rotulo et in quadam cedula h[ic annexata]." The schedule survives and four small perforations show that it was once attached to the bill.[60] Unfortunately the right half of it is gone, the half on which an inscribed commons' assent would have been written. On the left half is visible, however, not only the text as it was enrolled

[59] Ibid., 24/2; R. P., V, 28.
[60] C., P. & C. P. 25/12, 13; R. P., V, 65.

but also three lines which have been elided. The elision may, of course, have been made by whoever drafted the amendment; but it may also have been the work of the commons, changing an amendment while perhaps affixing to it the signature (now destroyed) of their approval.

In the parliament of 1444 the commons asked for the punishment of one John Bolton, who had murdered and robbed a woman for resisting his attempt to rape her but who, before his crime was known, had received a charter of pardon in return for becoming an informer against others. Voidance of similar charters issued to any other man similarly guilty was also requested. For some unexplained reason no response to this bill is enrolled on the parliament roll, although a space is left for one. But a response is preserved on a membrane formerly attached to the bill. The king consigned Bolton to perpetual imprisonment but refused the general request. Below is written, " a cest cedule les Communes sount assentuz." [61]

This is the second unmistakable instance from the years 1422-1451 of the commons assenting to an amendment added to one of their bills. If the schedule of 1442 were not injured we might have another instance. Slender as the evidence is, it does, nevertheless, suggest that amendments to commons bills were submitted to the originators of the bills, especially when they were of some length and were written on separate membranes or schedules. Regarding briefer amendments, especially such as limited the duration of the proposed statute, we are left in some doubt. The uncertainty arises in part from our further uncertainty about how the responses were recorded. Only in and after 1439, or at best in 1437, was a response normally inscribed on the dorse of a bill. Even then such endorsement may not always have been the first record of the response. Since, however, it is difficult to suppose that some amended bills were sent back to the commons while others were not, it is best to infer that by 1439 the commons

---

[61] C., P. & C. P., 26/5, 6; *R. P.,* V, 111. The petition and the space for the response appear on membrane 4 of the parliament roll (C. 65/97).

were usually asked to give their approval to any amendment to one of their bills. If this inference is correct, the commons' control over legislation in the first three decades of the reign of Henry VI was nearly complete. Nearly all legislation originated as commons bills, these bills were amended either not at all or only in a minor way, and such amendments as were added received sometimes and perhaps always the commons' assent.

It only remains to glance at commons bills which were entirely rejected. The commons themselves did not question the king's right to reject their bills, presumably with the advice of the lords; for such rejection did not give rise to legislation without their assent. Nevertheless a persistent tendency to reject commons bills would scarcely be characteristic of an era of popular legislation. Hence, although an extended consideration of rejected commons bills between 1422 and 1451 cannot here be undertaken, some estimate of the number and importance of them is desirable. A brief consideration of those of the first ten parliaments of the reign of Henry VI will at least give some clue as to how far the attitude of the government or of the lords was non-acquiescent.

As it happens, the commons bills presented in the parliaments of the first decade of the reign and the statutes arising from them corresponded closely in number with the bills and statutes of the two following decades. The bills numbered 151 and the statutes 90.[62] Not all of the 61 bills which gave rise to no statutes were, however, rejected. Ten of them were approved but were of a kind not particularly appropriate for proclamation as statutes. One, for instance, in the first parliament of the reign asked for the confirmation of offices granted by Henry IV and Henry V. Others requested respectively the giving of surety by certain misdoers in Herefordshire, the appointment of a commission of sewers, the issue of licences for alienation by the chancellor without suit to the

---

[62] In comparison with 154 bills and 95 statutes from the two following decades.

council (hitherto requisite), the entrusting of the conservation of the Thames and Medway to the mayor and guardian of
London rather than to county officials, the reference of the
unanswered petitions of parliament to the council and the
justices, the enforcement of a statute which limited the jurisdiction of the constable and the marshal of England to
appeals arising outside the realm, the authorization of the purchase of lands in Cambridgeshire from which income could
be got to pay a part of the wages of the county's representatives in parliament, the inspection of Gascon wines, and the
repeal of a subsidy granted in the preceding parliament.[63]   To
the difficult question of why such approved bills did not become statutes we shall have to return; but for the moment it
will suffice to note that the appearance of a bill on the parliament roll and its non-appearance on the statute roll did not
necessarily imply that it had been rejected.

Certain other commons bills which did not give rise to statutes were not altogether rejected but were answered with a
remedy other than that proposed by the petitioners.   Several
of the remaining 51 bills from the first decade of Henry VI
were of this sort.   To a request for the repeal of a statute of
9 Henry V, which allowed sheriffs and escheators to hold office
during four years and for the relief of certain sheriffs from a
part of their farm the response was that the statute would be
retained for the time being but would be reformed and that allowance would be made on sheriffs' farms from year to year as
had already been promised.   Two bills touching the church
were referred to existing law, spiritual and temporal, and to
the archbishops.   One of them asked for a commission to report on neglected services in chapels attached to parish
churches, the other urged penalties for the non-residence of
parsons and vicars.   When the latter was again presented at
the next parliament with more precise provisions it was again
referred to existing law with the assurance that the lords spir-

[63] *R. P.*, IV, 191, 254, 258, 329, 330, 334, 349, 382, 405, 409.

itual had promised execution.[64]   Just as petitioners were
referred to ecclesiastical authorities, so they were at times referred to the council.   Such was the reply to a petition for the
abolition of head-pence in Northumberland, to another for
the issue of letters of marque against offending subjects of the
duke of Burgundy, to another which complained of the quar-
tering of soldiers upon divers villages, especially in Kent, and
to a fourth which asked that justices of the two benches and
barons of the exchequer survey grants of felons' goods for
which allowance had not been made in accounts of sheriffs and
bailiffs.   In the last case authorization was given to bring the
matter before the next parliament if it should prove too difficult for the council to deal with.[65]

Sometimes a response was acquiescent but explained that
other action had been or would be taken.   Complaints against
the results of fixing the Danish staple at Northbarne were
answered with the explanation that the king had sent to Denmark ambassadors whose return should be awaited.   A request
that justices of the peace try for treason Welshmen who were
exacting a "raithe (oath of 300 men) from inhabitants of the
Welsh border received the king's assurance that he wished to
provide against such violence and had bidden the lords marchers act.[66]   Sometimes, finally, the response might evade the
petition by promising that the matter complained of would be
duly rectified.   In 1425 a petition that the subsidy payable on
wool lost at sea should be remitted by the exchequer was
answered by the provision that the council rather than the
exchequer should examine the claim.   But when a bill of the
following parliament protested that this would involve a
"poursuite infinite," the response to this promised that the
council would act with speed.   Again, when a petition asked
that one William Larke, servant of a member of parliament,
be freed from prison during the session and added a general

[64] Ibid., pp. 191, 290, 305.
[65] Ibid., pp. 291, 350.
[66] Ibid., pp. 378, 329.

request that all lords, commons and their servants coming to or being in parliament be not arrested except for treason, felony or violation of the peace, the response assented to the privilege for Larke but refused the added request.[67]

Illustrative of petitions in which the emphasis in the reply was put on the reaffirmation of earlier statutes rather than on the additions proposed are three bills of 1432. One requested the observance of a statute of 1404 which required alien merchants to reside with English hosts and to sell their merchandise within a certain period of time. When it added penalties for neglecting hosts and extended the time allowed for the sale of merchandise, the king replied that he wished to see the existing statutes and thereupon would execute them to the advantage of himself and of the realm. Another bill asked that a man's failure to be present at the sheriff's tourn in Cornwall be not amerced severely but " after the quantite of his trespas," as the Great Charter and other statutes provided and as men of the hundred might determine. The reply was, " Let the common law be kept." A third bill urged that cloth once sealed by the ulnager be not henceforth subject to seizure as unsealed. In reply the observance of existent statutes was enjoined.[68]

Although the disregard in the first two of these replies of the concrete remedies proposed was not very serious, similar disregard elsewhere might prove to be so; and in the grudging responses made to five commons bills of the decade a rejection of important measures may be seen. In 1422 the commons asked that a writ of subpoena might not issue until the complainant had drawn up a bill specifying his grievances and until two justices of either bench had declared that these were not remediable at common law. Failure in the suit would bring with it a penalty of £20. The king's reply ordered the enforcement of a statute of 1394, which in all these matters confined itself to authorizing the chancellor to award dam-

[67] *Ibid.*, pp. 289, 303, 357.
[68] *Ibid.*, pp. 402-404.

ages to an innocent defendant.   As to writs of subpoena under
the privy seal the issue between the commons and the government was thus sharply drawn.[69]   In the same parliament a
further attempt to limit the use of writs of privy seal was
equally unsuccessful.   The commons petitioned on behalf of
the staplers that the privileges of the latter be ratified, that
no writ of privy seal interrupt pleas begun in the court of the
mayor and constables and judged in accordance with the law
merchant, so far as this was in accord with the common law
of the land, and, finally, that the mayor and constables execute
judgments within the bounds of the staple.   When in 1427 a
similar bill was introduced with the revision that if the
mayor and constables failed to do justice according to the
law merchant they might be summoned before the chancellor
or the council, it met with the same reception.   Existent privileges were approved, the remainder of the petition was refused.   Thus the growing authority of chancery and of the
council was maintained in the face of the commons' protest.
Insurance against what seemed arbitrary judicial action was
once more requested in a petition presented in 1425 and again
in 1426.   Complaining of accusations made irresponsibly by
persons in sanctuary, it asked that an accuser find surety to
prove his charge, unless he was at the time himself in prison.
Since the responses to both bills merely referred the petitioners
to the common law, the finding of security was virtually ignored and the situation left at it had been.[70]

Quite as serious as the indifference to new judicial regulations asked for in connection with existing privileges or statutes
was the government's aloofness toward a proposed measure
for checking livery and maintenance.   A bill of 1427, pointing out that existing statutes against the giving of liveries
could not be enforced because of the " graund mayntenaunce "
of the offenders, proposed that justices of assize and justices
of the peace have power to issue writs of attachment and

---

[69] *Ibid.*, pp. 189; *Stats.*, II, 88.
[70] *R. P.*, IV, 191, 328, 291, 305.

distress or of *capias* and *exigent,* the latter as in cases of armed breaking of the peace, and, if the accused appeared, to examine him and require him to pay as if he had been duly convicted by inquest. These proposals, looking toward the restraint of maintenance, were waived aside with the admonition that statutes already made be put in execution.[71]

Along beside these bills, the essence of which was evaded by a response which merely enjoined the enforcement of existing statutes, stood others which were openly rejected. To them the response was the stereotyped " Le Roi s'advisera." Among the 151 commons bills of the first decade of Henry VI some thirty-one were answered in this way, one-half of the number which did not become statutes.[72] But just as some of the bills virtually rejected through disregard of new means of enforcement were important and others were not, so there was considerable difference in the significance of bills undisguisedly rejected.

Many of them dealt with matters of special or local interest. One, a group petition, asked that tallies or debentures issued by the treasurer or receiver of the chambers of Henry IV and Henry V be paid at the exchequer. Another, twice presented, would have given justices of the peace power to convict any who might obstruct the free passage of the Severn. One proposed that men of Kent be reimbursed for whatever soldiers or captains might take from them by deductions from the wages of the latter. One asked that denizens might bring suit for trespass against Hansards in London and that special panels of jurors might pronounce the verdicts. Another would have made perpetual a statute of 1431 enacted for three years to prevent extortion of sheriffs in Herefordshire. One would have amended another statute of 1431 which empowered attorneys to represent certain non-resident abbots and priors of Lancashire and Yorkshire by penalizing

[71] *Ibid.,* p. 329.
[72] See above, p. 324. Two of the thirty-one were bills presented a second time. Another was granted in the following parliament.

seneschals who might refuse to accept the attorneys in good faith.   Three rejected bills reflected the interests of wool traders.   One protested against charges that wool brought to Calais weighed more than the cocket indicated and explained that increased weight might arise from the wool getting wet at sea.   Another urged the restraint of licences which permitted Irish hides to be shipped to Flanders.   A third demanded that lambs' wool and shorlyngs should pay, as had been usual until of late, only poundage and not the wool-custom and subsidy.   Finally, it occasionally happened that a bill, though of wider scope, was still of restricted interest. Such was one asking that a statute of 1413, which enjoined the writing in a writ of the full name of a man accused in order that an innocent person might not be mistaken for him, should be effective before 1413 as well as after that date.[73]

While it is true that many of the commons bills rejected were of local or special interest, it is also true that some of them were of considerable significance.   We have already seen that four or five important bills of the first decade of Henry VI were virtually rejected by ignoring their essential provisions.   It remains to note a dozen others of importance which were flatly rejected.   Three dealt with security of title.   In 1423 the commons in a group bill asked that, in pleas of novel disseisin, inquest might be taken to determine whether the defendant was delaying the action by falsely alleging that the reversion or remainder lay with the king, and asked further that the disseisor might not after the death of Henry V make feoffment with such reversion.   Since the allegation complained of involved procedure by petition to the king and since pleas of novel disseisin were numerous, the bill looked to the remedy of what was possibly a serious abuse.   In the next parliament a petition that purchasers of tenements held in tail or fee simple of the king might have toward the king the same estate in such tenements as they would have toward the heirs of the alienator was rejected, although the request seems reasonable.

---

[73] *Ibid.*, pp. 292, 332 and 351, 403, 406, 407, 290, 332, 352, 377.

A third bill asked that in suits charging that lands were held by forged documents one-half of the jurors should be chosen from the county in which the lands lay, the other half from the county of the accuser, since the latter was acquiring unfair advantage when all jurors were from the county in which he brought suit and in which the lands did not lie. This, too, seems a reasonable request.[74]

Six bills dealt with the administration of justice, four of them involving the competence of various courts. One, twice presented, asked that rovers of the sea, or pirates, be looked upon as felons and be tried as such by justices of the peace; another petitioned that amercements for trespass and other offences be not made in the sheriff's tourn and to his advantage but in sessions of the justice of the peace and by two, three or four substantial men of the hundred; a third requested that no one be subjected to examination in parliament or in any other court or council on any matter touching his free tenement or inheritance, since this was contrary to common law; a fourth, twice presented, would have limited the jurisdiction of the courts of the duchy of Lancaster, as had been done temporarily in 1421, by providing that outlawries pronounced in them should not be effective in other parts of the realm. Two other bills sought to protect defendants. One asked that men accused on appeals of mayhem might have their attorneys; and the other, asserting that jurors made false oaths in inquests, asked that the plaintiff might recover on a writ of attaint from them as well as from the defendant and further that every juror on a jury of attaint should have an annual income of 100 s. from free tenements.[75] Some of these bills may have been rejected because they would unwisely have limited the competence of courts; but there seems apparent in all of them a reforming spirit which deserved consideration.

Three rejected bills had been drawn up in the interest of members of parliament. One, lamenting the failure of sub-

[74] *Ibid.*, pp. 253, 294, 378.
[75] *Ibid.*, pp. 350 and 376, 401, 403, 331 and 407, 401, 408.

stantial burgesses to come longer to parliament, urged that the customary wage of two shillings the day be henceforth paid the representatives of cities and boroughs; another asked that all towns and villages which did not themselves send members to parliament contribute to the expenses of knights of the shire; and a third, in order to establish parliamentary privilege, formulated elaborate provisions for the serving of a writ of trespass and for subsequent legal proceedings if any knight of the shire, citizen or burgess should be molested in coming to parliament.[76] It was natural for the commons to present such bills as these and it is not altogether clear why they should have been rejected.

Two rejected petitions of some importance, finally, concerned themselves with the conduct of the church and one with the privileges of alien merchants. Of the former, one, protesting against the neglect of divine services, urged that if a vicarate was left inofficiate for six months by any religious who held such church to his own use, the church and its appurtenances should be disappropriate and disamortized; and the other, reviving an old complaint, asked that presentment of aliens to benefices, forbidden by statutes of Richard II and Henry IV which had been observed by the king's ancestors, should be void whether made with or without the king's licence. Touching alien merchants, a bill urged the enforcement of a statute of 1404, which enjoined such merchants to go to host, to sell their merchandise within three months, to expend their money on English merchandise and not to sell to other aliens, while, as means of enforcement, it added stringent penalties to be imposed for three years.[77] Ecclesiastical and mercantile petitions of this sort were normal and not unnatural commons' requests.

It now seems possible to draw some conclusions about the rejected bills of the first decade of the reign of Henry VI. Of the 151 bills presented 61 did not become statutes but not

[76] *Ibid.*, pp. 350, 352, 404.
[77] *Ibid.*, pp. 404, 304, 328.

all of the latter were rejected. Ten of them were approved as acts of parliament but as unworthy of the statute roll. Several others were not rejected but were answered by assigning a remedy other than that asked for, or by explaining that other action had been taken. Eight others evaded requests by referring the petitioners to earlier statutes and in five of these instances the evasion was serious. Thirty-one bills, or about one-fifth the number presented, were flatly rejected. Of these many dealt with matters of special or local interest but about a dozen were bills of importance, half of them relating to the administration of justice. If to this dozen of frankly rejected bills we add the five important ones which were answered evasively, it appears that about one-tenth of the commons bills presented in the first ten parliaments of Henry VI were significant ones which did not meet with the approval of lords and king. As many more of minor importance also met with disapproval. In contrast were the other four-fifths of the commons' requests which were either entirely or largely granted. The two following decades of the reign probably witnessed much of the same ratio of approvals to rejections. If so, we may conclude that the veto of commons bills, which the commons themselves had in 1414 recognized as entirely within the king's prerogative, was not widely exercised.

The questions which we asked relatively to the first three decades of the reign of Henry VI may now be answered. These were, it will be remembered, to what extent did commons and official bills then assume the form which characterized them in the second half of the century, and on the other hand, were Lancastrian precedents followed as to the preponderance of commons bills over official bills and as to the slight degree to which commons bills were amended by king and lords? The three decades witnessed noteworthy changes in procedure. At the very beginning of the reign the comprehensive commons petition gave place to separate commons bills. Upon each of these there appeared from the outset the superscription indicative of the commons' approval, " soit baille as seigneurs." A little later, but apparently during the decade of the thirties, there arose the custom of inscribing on the dorse of each bill the king's response, the established usage for private bills. At times we find on the face of a commons bill an abbreviated note to the effect that it had been read and answered in the lords; but the occurrence of this abbreviation is casual, varying from parliament to parliament. The substitution of separate commons bills for the comprehensive commons petition made possible the intrusion among them of an occasional official bill when the clerk drew up the parliament roll. This illogical practice began in 1425 and instances of it occur in the parliaments which follow. Such of these official bills as survive bear the appropriate inscription recording the commons' assent. All these features of procedure we have met with in our study of the bills of 1453-1465. We are now able to add that they date from the earlier years of the reign of Henry VI.

On turning from the form to the number and content of commons bills, we find during the first three decades of the reign a continuation of the situation which disclosed itself under Henry IV and Henry V. Nearly all bills which became statutes were of commons origin. Of the 185 statutes of the period, 162 arose from commons bills and not more than eleven from official bills, the remainder being largely from private or clerical bills. Nor were the commons bills seriously amended in becoming statutes. One-half of them were accepted as presented, and of the amendments added to others not more than a half-dozen thwarted greatly the wishes of the commons. Moreover, we get some evidence that during the three decades certain amendments were submitted to the commons for their approval. That all amendments should be, in so far as they changed the intent of any bills, had been requested and granted in 1415; and perhaps the promise was largely observed. In any event, the trivial character of most amendments, even if some were not ratified by the authors of the bills, did not detract greatly from the commons' contribution to the legislation of the period. As to commons bills frankly rejected, they, too, were relatively infrequent and were not in many cases of great moment. Thus, the three decades, in testifying to the commons' influence over parliamentary legislation, continued the traditions of the two preceding reigns, while, in adopting several innovations in procedure, they gave to both commons and official bills many of the characteristics which these displayed in the next half century.

CHAPTER X

PRIVATE BILLS AND GROUP BILLS IN THE COMMONS

WE have seen that in the reigns of Edward I and Edward
II nearly all petitions presented in parliament were either private or group bills and that there were a great many of them.
Not until the reign of Edward III did commons bills assume
importance. We have seen, too, that in the second half of
the fifteenth century a few private bills were likely to be enrolled on the parliament roll preceding the " communes petitions." At this time they were either addressed to king and
lords and after acceptance sent to the commons, who inscribed
upon them their assent, or they were addressed to the commons and, on dispatch by them to the lords with an inscription which was a mark of approval, were accepted by lords and
king. In the fourteenth century the private bills of individuals were treated in none of these ways. Seldom and only for
special reasons were they enrolled on the parliament roll.
Almost never were those addressed to the king and lords submitted to the commons for approval. And not until the end
of the century were any of them addressed to the commons.[1]

Frequently they were addressed to the king and his council,
the latter word, as used in these petitions, meaning the council in parliament.[2] But the council in parliament was the body

[1] Of the 111 unenrolled private bills printed in the *Rotuli* for the reign
of Richard II, 29 were addressed to the king alone, 3 to the lords alone,
30 to the king and lords, and 42 to the king and his council. Of the
remainder, four were addressed to king, lords and commons, one to lords
and commons and two to the commons alone. In earlier reigns no mention was made of the commons in the address.

[2] In 1379, for instance, the archbishop of York addressed a bill " A . . . le
Roi et son bon Conseil " but the appeal expanded this to " plese a notre
Seigneur et son sage Conseil en cest present Parlement " (A. P. 914; *R. P.*,
III, 69).

of the lords spiritual and temporal. In two petitions of 1383-4 the address and appeal were to "le Roy et son sage Counseill en cest present Parlement," but the response was "le Roy voet par assent des Seigneurs en Parlement . . ." In another bill of 1379 the address was to king and council but the reply ran, "Il plest au Roy depuis qe les Seigneurs de Parlement l'ont ordeyne."[3] Equivalents of this sort frequently occur and the term council was as yet not regardful of the commons. The century of the three Edwards remains one during which the commons were practically non-existent for anyone who wished to offer a petition in parliament. They stood in the same position as did the petitioner himself. They, too, asked favours of the king and lords and were not themselves a source of authority or influence.

Group bills, although to contemporaries they were private bills, fared differently from the private bills of individuals. Not so much in the fifteenth century, to be sure, when like the latter they were addressed either to the king and the lords or to the commons, were passed on to the other house for approval and appeared not infrequently on the parliament roll; but rather in the fourteenth century when, unlike private bills of individuals, they were often adopted by the commons and were presented to the king and the lords as articles of the comprehensive commons petition. This practice continued in the fifteenth century and was even extended; but by that time both group bills and private bills had come to secure the commons' approval in another way. Our problem, therefore, is to ascertain when the private bills of individuals came to be addressed to the commons as well as to the king and the lords, and when those which continued to be addressed in the latter way were submitted to the commons for approval. We shall have to note how group bills were treated. And we shall particularly have to attend to the way in which both private bills and group bills were enrolled.

Since the great mass of the private bills of individuals in

[3] *Ibid.,* pp. 181, 182, 68.

the fourteenth century had nothing to do with the commons as
a body, little need be said about the procedure which was
adopted to expedite them.   Maitland has discussed it admir-
ably for the beginning of the century and Messrs. Richardson
and Sayles have continued the discussion, extending it to
1377.[4] The latter writers explain quite correctly that commons bills were presented to the lords and the king in one way,
but private bills and most group bills in another way. Whereas
the former were delivered to the clerk of parliament, the latter
were delivered to the so-called receivers of petitions, who in
turn passed them on to " triours " or auditors of petitions. The
distinction appears most clearly in the parliament roll of 1346
where at the beginning we read: " Et puis fu comandez qe
chescun qe se sentist grevez et vourroit mettre Petition en cel
Parlement le mettroit avant [a fixed day] . . . Et furent
assigner certeins Clercs de resceivre les Petitions et Prelatz,
Barons, et justices d'oier meismes les Petitions. . . ."   These
private petitions were grouped as those of England and Ireland on the one hand and as those of Gascony, Wales, Scotland and the " Isles " on the other.   One chancery clerk was
assigned to receive each group, and as auditors for the English
and Irish petitions were named a bishop, an abbot, a baron,
and four justices, the auditors for the other group being fewer.
Farther on in the roll, just preceding the comprehensive commons petition, we read relative to the latter: " Et puis fu
demandez des ditz Chivalers, Citeyns et Burgeys qe, s'ils vou-
sissent mettre nulle Petition en dit Parlement qe purroit tour-
ner a commune profit et en ese de eux, q'ils la liveroient au
Clerk du Parlement; laquele Petition ils liverent le Vendredy
proschein . . . laquele Petition fu maignee devant les Grantz
du Conseil le Samady, Dymenge et Lundy proschein suantz;
et meisme le jour de Lundy fu responduz a la dite Petition.
Desqueux Petitions et Respons la copie est souzescrite. . . ."[5]

<hr/>

[4] Maitland, *Memoranda,* pp. lv-lxxiii; H. G. Richardson and G. Sayles,
The King's Ministers in Parliament, in *Eng. Hist. Rev.,* vols. xlvi, xlvii.
    [5] *R. P.,* II, 157, 160.

Although the contrast between private bills given to the receivers and commons bills given to the clerk of parliament is not elsewhere so clearly drawn,[6] there is every reason to think that the procedure was maintained throughout the fourteenth and fifteenth centuries. Receivers and triours antedated 1346, and later in the century their numbers were increased. In particular the auditors came to include a greater number of lords and a relatively smaller number of justices.[7] Already in 1341, the chancellor and the treasurer might be associated with the auditors "quant miester serra"; and in 1352 to these optional members were added the seneschal, the chamberlain, the sergeants-le-Roi, and, if a bill touched the king's chamber, Sir Thomas de Brembre or Sir Henry de Graystock.[8] In later parliaments the household officials were seldom mentioned, but, whenever there was need, the chancellor, the treasurer and the king's sergeants were to sit with the auditors. Among the latter there were always named one of the justices and usually two.[9] The committee two centuries after its inception was a dignified and representative one. By 1509 it had come to include four members of the commons.[10]

The functions of the triours of petitions in the parliaments of Edward III are described by the verbs "oier et trier"; but in the parliament of 1379-80 the phraseology is happily expanded. We are told that, "si aucune persone del Roialme . . . se vorra pleindre a . . . Roi en cest son Parlement de greef ou tort a luy fait dont remede n'ad este encores purveuz ne ne poet estre sanz Parlement, . . . le Roi . . . ad fait assigner . . . certains Prelatz, Seigneurs et Justices pur oier, discuter et terminer mesme les Billes ou Petitions quelconques. . . ."[11] What may be called a committee of lords and justices, afforced by the principal officers of state was here given authority to

[6] Cf. *ibid.*, pp. 201, 304(8), 374(87).
[7] Richardson and Sayles, *op. cit.*
[8] *R. P.*, II, 126, 236.
[9] *Ibid.*, IV, 198, 261, 295, 316 *et passim*.
[10] See above, p. 29.
[11] *Ibid.*, III, 71. Cf. above, p. 206.

terminate grievances for which no remedy could be found outside parliament. Already in 1354 the grievances were defined as those "qe ne purroient estre esploite hors du Parlement[12]; and in 1347 we hear of a case which had been before the council and chancery but which, it now seemed to the council, should come before "le Conseil en Parlement."[13] Maitland, who discussed at some length the functions of the triours, concluded that their business clearly was to dispatch petitions to the person or court appropriate to consider them and possibly to hear testimony in support of them.[14]

There is evidence to support both of his conclusions. Already in 1305 the auditors were to answer all Gascon petitions which could be answered without the king.[15] In 1362 complaint arose that petitions which touched the king were dispatched by the auditors *Coram Rege* and that in consequence no redress was got. A commons petition now asked and secured that such bills "soient veues devant les ditz Seigneurs [i.e. the auditors] et par avis de Chancellor, Tresorer et autres du Conseil le Roi responduz et endocez en manere come droit et reson demandent. . . ."[16] The success of the petition shows that the auditors, afforced by the more important ministers, were sometimes expected to draft an answer rather than refer the case elsewhere. Which of these two courses they took in any particular instance must have depended largely upon the nature of the case itself. We find endorsements which declare "Quia istud negotium videtur arduum, terminetur coram magno Consilio"; and this is frequently reduced to the simple, "Coram Rege et Magno Consilio."[17] On grounds of propriety bills were sent also to the common law courts, to the exchequer, to chancery or even to franchise courts.[18] Prob-

[12] *Ibid.*, II, 254.
[13] *Ibid.*, p. 197.
[14] *Memoranda*, pp. lxi, lxviii-lxxii.
[15] *Ibid.*, p. 4.
[16] *R. P.*, II, 272.
[17] *Ibid.*, pp. 391, 178, 180, 185, 189.
[18] *Ibid.*, pp. 378-419 *passim*. Evidence of how the action of the auditors

ably most petitions were thus referred to various courts or to the great council rather than answered definitely by the auditors, at least before the time of Richard II.

In the fifteenth century private bills often came before the lords for answer if we may judge from the phrase which frequently on the parliament roll followed the text of those enrolled: "La quell Supplication devant le Roi et les Seigneurs leeu en le dit Parlement fuit respondu a la mesme en manere come ensuit." [19] It is thus clear that the lords often sanctioned the answers given to private bills. Whether as a body they framed these answers is another matter. When answers were simple they could easily have done so. But when, as often happened, answers were long and technical, it is not improbable that a smaller body than the lords drafted them. If this happened, no more appropriate body could have been found than the auditors. In any event they were required to familiarize themselves with the subject matter of all private bills; and they comprised not only men of great political authority but men learned in the law, who would have been competent to draft any answer decided upon. It is possible, therefore, that the auditors sometimes continued to do what

---

was followed by action of the great council, i.e. the lords, is furnished by the endorsements on an unprinted petition of *c.* 1322 in which Nicholas de Stapelton asked the king to postpone an annual " fyn " and to restore his lands which the Scots had wasted. On the back of the bill at the bottom is written " Coram Rege," undoubtedy the minute of the auditors. Above, however, is the response, " Il semble a conseil s'il plest au Roi qe la chose est afaire." In this instance the auditors sent the petition to the council which answered it subject to the approval of the king. The fortunes of another bill were similar save that this one had to go before the king. Soon after 1321 the men of Aukland asked that in payment of money due the king they might have allowance on a wardrobe bill which they held. On the dorse and below is written " Coram Rege "; above " videtur consilio quod est faciendum si placeat Regi, set tamen coram Rege." (A. P. 13548, 13516). The wardrobe bill dated from the time when Roger de Northburgh was treasurer of the wardrobe, 1316-1321 (*C. C. R., 1313-1318*, p. 333; *1318-1323*, p. 478).

[19] *R. P.,* IV, 130-2, 139, 173, 178, 188.

they had probably sometimes done at first—draft the final responses to private bills.

The private bills of individuals whether approved or rejected were in the fourteenth century almost never enrolled on the parliament roll. Until the time of Edward III special rolls recording them were kept by the receivers but were then discontinued.[20] On the parliament roll of 1368 and on those of Richard II we do find private bills addressed to the king but on closer inspection these prove to be petitions preliminary to instituting suits in parliament. In most instances some account of the judicial proceedings follows.[21] Only two or three private bills seem to have been enrolled not as an integral part of judicial proceedings but as a matter of record. In 1383 Robert de Plesyngton, chief baron of the exchequer, asked the king for confirmation of a pardon already granted him. The bill, read in parliament before Richard in the presence of many lords and other " Sages du Conseil," was granted by the king, who carefully reserved his " Regalie." It was enrolled curiously and alone at the end of the commons petitions. Again in 1390 the king's uncles, the dukes of York and Gloucester, asked that there be assigned each of them £100 annually in lands and rents. The bill was enrolled, as similar private bills of the fifteenth century came to be, before the commons petitions.[22] The importance of the two bills may explain the deviation from the usage of the century. It was not until the reign of Henry IV that it became at all usual to enroll private bills on the parliament roll.[23] By this time, as we shall see, they were coming within the survey and competence of the commons.

Group bills as contrasted with the private bills of individuals often came in the fourteenth century to have a close

[20] Richardson and Sayles, *Bull. Inst. Hist. Research*, IX, 3.

[21] *R. P.*, II, 297; III, 7-9, 39-41, 78-79, 105, 109, 170, 186, 258-261, 286, 289, 302-303, 310-315. There are a few enrollments of this sort in the early years of Henry IV (*ibid.*, pp. 430, 488-490, 530).

[22] *Ibid.*, pp. 164, 278.

[23] *Ibid.*, pp. 461, 464, 492, 532-538, 550-552, 610.

association with the commons and were frequently enrolled on the parliament roll; for some of them were adopted by the commons and were thus ensured of enrollment among the commons petitions. We have seen that certain articles of the earliest comprehensive commons petitions were appeals for groups within the realm.[24] There could, of course, scarcely be a sharp differentiation between a petition for the commonalty and one for a section of the commonalty. A bill from a county or a group of counties or from the borders, or from several ports or even from one town was, in a way, a commons bill. As such, bills of this sort were enrolled in greater or smaller numbers throughout the two centuries. While petitions from what may be called topographical sections of the community were by far the most numerous, especially at first, others might originate with economic or social groups. In 1365 the commons presented among the articles of their comprehensive petition one from " les Seigneurs de Niefs " and in 1368 one from " la Commune qe vivent par geynerie de lour Terres ou Marchandie et qe n'ont Seigneuries ne Villeins pur eux servir."[25] But in general it was left for the commons of the fifteenth century to adopt bills of such groups. The number of group bills sponsored by the commons varied in different parliaments. In the first ten parliaments of Richard II, for instance, they sponsored in each of four parliaments four or five of them but in each of six parliaments only one, two or three of them. Of the 61 articles presented by the commons in 1377 nine were group petitions and in 1376, of the 150 articles, some twenty-seven were such. The phraseology of group bills which were adopted by the commons underwent a slight change. Until 1383 they began with a direct appeal, e.g., " Item prient les Communes de les Countees de Somerset et Wilteshire . . ."; but in that year we find an indirect appeal, " Item prient les Communes pur les povres

---

[24] See above, pp. 213-14, 216, 240-42.
[25] *R. P.*, II, 287, 296.

Burgeises et Gentz de votre Ville de Scardeburgh. . . ."[26]
Henceforth the latter form grew in favour.

While the commons were altogether ready to adopt the petitions of counties, towns or economic groups, they were very chary about adopting the petitions of individuals.[26a] It was assumed that these should be presented by the petitioner himself to the receivers of petitions. How much any departure from this usage was deprecated in the fourteenth century is shown by "une Ordenance faite en mesme le Parlement [of 1372] en manere q' ensuyt: Purce qe Gentz de Ley qe pursuent diverses busoignes en les Courts le Roi pur singulers persones ove queux ils sont procurent et font mettre plusours Petitions en Parlementz en noun des Communes qe rien lour touche mes soulement les singulers persones ove queux ils sont demorez, [it was agreed in parliament that such men of law should not in the future be returned as knights of the shire]."[27] Since the ordinance did not arise from a commons petition, the disapproval expressed by it was primarily official. Since, too, the offenders were "Gentz de Ley," the condemned practice testifies to the respect shown by the lawyers to the influence of the commons. If they were prohibited from having their clients' bills presented in the name of the commons, i.e., sponsored perhaps much as group bills were, it was not unlikely that they would seek a new method of procedure which would secure for private bills the support desired.

There is not much evidence from the reigns of Edward III and Richard II that the commons actually were presenting the private bills of individuals in their own name.[28] Among the 150 articles of the enormous commons petition which was presented in the Good Parliament of 1376, although one-

---

[26] *Ibid.*, II, 312; III, 162.
[26a] See above, p. 243.
[27] *Ibid.*, II, 310.
[28] It is possible, of course, that the offense of the men of law in 1372 was the attempted formulation of articles of the comprehensive commons bill which would be primarily of advantage to their clients rather than to the nation at large and yet give no verbal indication of this.

sixth of the number were group petitions, only two were strictly private bills. In one the prince of Wales asked for the restoration of certain franchises in Cornwall and Devon; in the other Sir John Hawkwood and Sir John Clifford asked that the king grant to each of them a charter of pardon. Both bills were incorporated as they had been written, the second beginning, "A tres-excellent et tres-redoute notre Seigneur le Roy." [29] Not until eleven years later were other private bills similarly presented. In 1388 among the enrolled commons petitions was one beginning "Item les Communes prierent a Roi" and asking that the bishop of Ely, the chancellor, who had been translated to the ruinous see of York, should be given assistance. The king, answering by the mouth of his seneschal, said that he would act so that "sibien le dit Evesque comes les ditz suppliants soy tendront pur contentz." Immediately following is another bill beginning in the same way and asking the king to increase the estate, both in honour and in property, of his brother, John. In 1390 among the commons bills was one beginning "Item supplient les Communes pur Johan Norhampton" and asking that sentence of treason procured by his enemies against him as a result of his upright behaviour when mayor of London be annulled. In 1391 the commons presented among the articles of their bill two which were in behalf of individuals. In the first they asked pardon for John More who had been associated with John Norhampton and condemned in the same way; in the second they begged that John de Roches, once keeper of the castle of Brest, be recompensed for a bastion which he had built there. [30] All of these five bills of Richard's reign were of some importance. The chancellor, the king's brother and the mayor of London were personages who must have commanded influence in the commons, and the payment for a bastion was properly an item in the budget for war. The same importance, however, did not attach to a petition of Robert atte Mulle and his wife enrolled

[29] *Ibid.*, II, 371, 372.
[30] *Ibid.*, III, 250, 282, 293.

among the commons petitions of 1393. In it they asked that
they be pardoned the payment of £600 adjudged against them
as discoverers of treasure trove in Guilford. The response
in this instance was the disapproving one, "Suent a Roi pur
ce qe ceste Petition n'est pas Petition del Parlement."[31] No
other private bills of Richard's reign apart from group bills,
were enrolled as commons petitions and the shortness of the
list justifies the conclusion that the commons at the time very
seldom adopted the bills of individuals as their own.

Two other bits of evidence suggesting that in Richard's
reign the commons sponsored private bills should, however, be
examined. In the parliament of 1397-1398 they asked that a
committee of lords and commons be authorized to deal authoritatively with unanswered petitions; for, they explained, "ils
aient devers eux diverses Petitions si bien pur especials persones come autres nient luez ne responduz. . . ." To what
did they refer as petitions "pur especials persones"? We can
in a measure discover this since the committee actually sat
and answered petitions which the parliament roll professes to
record. As recorded, the petitions answered were two commons bills and two group bills, one of the latter presented
respectively by "les Marchantz de votre Roialme denizeins
et aliens" and the other presumably by the craft of tanners,
who complained that an earlier statute which was to their
advantage had not been observed.[32] The bills "pur especials
persones" were, therefore, so far as they were recorded, group
bills; and such had long been received by the commons. We
have, as it happens, another group of bills similarly referred
to a committee at about the same time and similarly described.
This group was not enrolled but survives largely in manuscript
and was somewhat carelessly printed by the editors of the
Rotuli after the parliament roll of 1 Henry IV. The bills
seem rather to date from the first parliament of 1397.[33] On

---

[31] *Ibid.*, p. 307.
[32] *Ibid.*, III, 368-372.
[33] *Ibid.*, pp. 447-448. They cannot belong to 1 Henry IV since one of

the back of the first of them is a memorandum which runs as
follows: "Fait a remembrer qe celles des [dix] peticions qe
sont annexez ensemble feurent envoier au Roy par les Communes en parlement ent priant au Roy de sa grace qil plerroit
tendrement prendre a coer la matiere compris en ycelles et
faire graciouse remedie en celle partie. Sur quoi le Roy
endendus mesme les peticions les livera en parlement par ses
mains propres et mesmes les peticions de sa grace par assent
du parlement ad commis a certeins seigneurs, cest assavoir, Lar-
cevesq de Cantirbirs, le Duc de Lancastre, levesq de Wyn-
cestre, levesq de Sarum, le conte de R[utland], le Conte
Mareschall ovek les officers le Roy pur trier, regarder et ex-
aminer les ditz peticions a la quinzeime de Pasque proschein
. . . ."[34] Of the ten petitions, eight, now widely scattered, survive.[35] According to the memorandum the ten were given by

the petitions was an appeal from the commons of Westmorland to be relieved of one-fourth part of a half-fifteenth granted "en votre Parliament
. . . l'an de votre regne *quinzisme*," a relaxation already granted by the
bishop of Salisbury "nadgairs vostre Tresorer." The bishop was still
treasurer of Richard II on 21 February, 1395, but was no longer so on
the following 2 September (*C. P. R., 1391-6*, pp. 555, 620). The petition,
therefore, belongs to one of the last two parliaments of Richard's reign.
Since another committee heard the similarly unanswered petitions of the
later parliament, as has been explained above, the committee here described must have been named in the first, i. e. in the Hilary parliament
of 1397. The provision that the bills should be examined at the "quinzeime de Pasque" is well satisfied by that parliament. Finally, another
petition of the group, not printed in the *Rotuli*, was from John Holland,
earl of Huntingdon. In the second parliament of 1397 John Holland was
created Duke of Exeter (*R. P.*, III, 355). From all these considerations it
is safe to date the petitions 1397.

[34] The words printed in the *Rotuli*, "Responsio ad decem praecedentes
Petitiones" are not found on the original manuscript. Indeed, what follows is not a response but an explanation. The words, "les livera . . . mesme
les peticions," an important phrase, were omitted by the editors. They
could have found at least another of the ten in good condition, although
they say that the three which they did not print were almost completely
destroyed.

[35] Seven are printed in the *Rotuli*: A. P. 5867, 5616, 6033, 7353, 1071, 1070,
1069. An eighth, unprinted, is A. P. 5726. On the back of each is a
Roman numeral indicating the order in which they were first grouped.

the commons to the king, who with the assent of the lords referred them to a committee. Were any of the petitions thus first sponsored by the commons private bills? Of the eight which survive, one was a commons bill and one was a private bill addressed to the commons, a bill from the same Robert atte Mulle whose bill of 1393 has been noted above. Both were naturally in the commons' hands. Of the remaining six, five were group bills expressing the wishes respectively of the burgesses of Ipswich and of Great Yarmouth, the citizens of Lincoln, the commons of Westmorland and the merchants and seamen of the realm. The sixth was the request of the wardens of the Scottish marches for assistance against the Scots, who were threatening the king's castles and lieges. All of the six, as bills affecting groups of the population were, therefore, appropriately presented by the commons. Thus we are assured that at the end of the fourteenth century the commons were seldom sponsoring private petitions but were confining their activities to presenting their own petitions or the petitions of various groups. The latter, to be sure, in contrast with commons bills were often called by contemporaries private bills, but the terminology should not mislead us as to the facts.

What had become clear was that the petitions of individuals could not well be incorporated in the comprehensive commons petition. To do so would be to distort the meaning of the latter and to distend its bulk beyond what would be seemly. But was there no other method by which the support of the commons could be got for private bills? Such support had seemed so desirable to the men of law in 1372 that some of them had abused their position as members of the commons to secure it. Could not the commons be got to give their approval as a body to a private bill brought before them and then send it to lords and king with a request that it be granted? If they were to be induced to do so, bills ought to be addressed

The order of the printed petitions is different, this being X, V, VI, IV, III, II, I. The unprinted petition was no. VII.

to them rather than to the king and the appeal should be that they intercede with the king. We are led then to inquire whether in the fourteenth century such address and such appeal are found and if so to what extent. It is a question which was asked at the beginning of this chapter before we glanced at the treatment usually accorded to private and group bills during the century.

If we take the address of a private bill as our best clue we shall find that toward the end of the fourteenth century a few addresses associated the commons with the king and lords and that a still smaller number mentioned the commons alone. In what is perhaps the earliest of these bills, the knights of the shire, although not the commons as a body, were included in the address. In asking redress for violent disseisin committed in 1362 and followed by false indictment, Robert Ridel and wife presented a bill "a notre seigneur le Roi, son tres-sages conseille et as chevaliers des Countees pur le communes Dengleterre." In the appeal they contracted this to "priont as seigneurs de parlement." Beside the lords were thus mentioned somewhat incidentally those members of the commons who seemed to the petitioners best to represent them in parliament. A group bill of about 1381 was addressed in a similar way "As tres graciouses seignours et chivalers de touz les countees dengleterre en cest present parlement ensemblez . . ." and continued "pleise a votres tres nobles seigneurs et tressages conseille dordeigner. . . ." It was an appeal of "les lieges communes de la Roialme" for protection against oppression by the great and their maintainers and is without endorsement.[36]

A few bills from the earlier years of Richard's reign associated the entire body of the commons with the king and lords in the address. Typical of them is a group petition which was presented soon after 1378 by holders of knights' fees in

---

[36] A. P. 6870, 5012. I am indebted for reference to these two petitions as well as for reference to A. P. 11182, 4569 and 4758, which are described below, to Dr. G. O. Sayles.

Kent. It urged that the wages of Kentish knights of the shire in parliament should be paid not by them alone but by tenants of all kinds in the county, since it was this larger body which was represented. Although the text is imperfect, the petitioners seem to say that, whereas the sheriff had been instructed to levy the wages in this way, he had failed to do so, alleging that the custom of the county made holders of knights' fees responsible. This seeming reference to earlier efforts on the part of the petitioners points to a bill of 1378 in which Kentish holders of knights' fees made what was probably their first appeal, asking re-adjustment of the burdensome wages. The response then was "Soit use come avant ces heures ad este" and the response to the later bill was substantially the same, "Ent soit fait come de encien temps y ad este uset." What differentiates the two bills, apart from the reference to the sheriff's action, are the addresses. Whereas the earlier bill was addressed, "a notre Seignour le Roy et as tres-sages Seigneurs Peres de Parlement," the second address ran, "A notre seigneur le Roy et as seigneurs et communes du parlement." There is no evidence, however, that the second bill was treated differently from the first, and the identity of the responses indicates that nothing was gained by including the commons in the address.[37]

A little later, in 1381, a private petition was presented which ran, "A notre tres redoute seigneur le Roi et as tres nobles seigneurs et bons Communes de cest present parlement monstre un poure homme William Skele del Counte de Kent" that he had been wrongfully dispossessed of land which he had purchased and that he had exhausted all his substance in attempting during three years to recover it in the courts of common law. Wherefore he appealed "a voz tres nobles Seigneuries" for remedy. It will be noticed that the commons did not figure in the appeal as they did in the address. Apart from this the interesting feature of the bill is that it survives

[37] A. P. 5921; *R. P.,* III, 53.

in two copies precisely alike and written in the same hand.[38] We might be tempted to surmise that one was intended for presentattion in the lords, the other for presentation in the commons. It happens, however, that copies very much alike survive also for two bills presented two years later, which did not, as Skele's did, mention the commons but restricted their address to king and council.[39] That the second of these should do so was natural since it was a petition of the clergy. The survival of two copies of a bill, therefore, even when addressed to king, lords and commons need not imply that the copies were to be used differently. They were probably made merely as a precaution. Neither of Skele's bills has on it any inscription to show that attention was given to it.

Three private bills of the last decade of the reign were like Skele's in addressing king, lords and commons and in disregarding the commons in the appeal. Only one copy of each survives. In the first John de Strathum and his wife complained of an attack of eighty men upon their house and property; in the second John d'Autry, Kt. and Alice, his wife, asked a hearing for the recovery of the manor of Sudbury, Norths., of which they had unsuccessfully tried to take possession; in the third John Harowe and his wife, Margaret, asked redress for violence done them when, fortified by an order of the council, they had attempted to enter upon certain tenements in Berkhamstead but had met with such resistance that Margaret persisting was thrown "en la channell." Although in each of the three addresses there was reference to the commons, the second appeal ran "a voz tres graciouses et tres excellente seigneuries," while the first and third continued simply "dont ils priont remedie."[40] Like them in mentioning the commons in the address only was the enrolled group petition of the mendicant orders in 1397. It began

[38] A. P., 958, 959; R. P., III, 130.
[39] A. P. 969 and 973, 975 and 976; R. P., III, 175-176 (nos. 3, 4).
[40] A. P. 6937 (c. 1391), 1056 (a. 1394), 5730 (c. 1394). Only the second is printed (R. P., III, 326).

" . . . Regi, Prelatis et Dominis et etiam Communibus Parliamenti presentis . . ." but did not again refer to the commons.[41]

Different were two bills of 1388 which referred to the commons in the appeal as well as in the address. The first was
a request of the mariners of England for higher wages, the
second a request of the masters of ships for compensation
when their ships were in the king's service. The former, beginning "A . . . le Roy et as autres nobles et Communes du
Parliament," continued, after explaining the inadequacy of
the existent wages, " Pleise a vos tres nobles Seigneurs et Communes du Parlement ordeigner . . ." and the second did practically the same. But there is no evidence that the commons
played any part in the expedition of the bills. To the first
the response was "Le Roi par l'advis de son Grant Conseil
ent ferra qe luy semblable qe soit a faire"; and to the second
"Le Roi en era bone voluntee de reguerdoner touz ceulx qi
l'ont deserviz."[42] Like these two bills in showing regard for
the commons in appeal as well as in address were two others
which, however, confined their address to lords and commons,
neglecting the king. In 1380 Elizabeth, wife of the late Gil-
bert of Elsfield, Kt., petitioned " As tresreverentz et tressages
seigneurs et comunes de la parlement" for restitution of the
manor of Drayton, Berks., which through lease had come into
the hands of Alice Perrers and thence into the king's hands
through forfeiture. The appeal like the address was "as
ditz seignours et comunes." No particular influence of the
commons, however, is reflected in the response which ordered
the petition sent to chancery, where the king's sergeants at
law and others should be summoned and the evidence in the
case be heard.[43] The second petition, similar in address and
appeal, gave to the appeal, however, something of the form
which it was to assume in the future. In 1389 Michael de la

[41] *Ibid.*, p. 341.
[42] A. P. 1007, 1008; *R. P.*, III, 253.
[43] A. P. 11182.

Pole and his wife, Katherine, explained "as honorables Seigneurs et les bones Comunes en cest present Parlement" that the settlement upon them of certain manors had not been sufficient to provide the annual £100 granted them in the last parliament. "Sur quoi," they continued, "please a vous honorables Seigneurs et les bones Comunes susditz de prier notre dit Seigneur le Roy" to instruct his officers to settle upon them other lands. The response was that the king wished the petitioners to have lands worth £100. The disregard of the king in the address is explained by the request that lords and commons should beg him to act.[44] The bill in its appeal differs from the future fifteenth-century type only in asking both lords and commons to intercede with the king instead of asking the commons alone to do so.

Regarding all these bills in which the commons were somewhat casually included in the address or even in the address and the appeal, we should like to know whether that body was asked to give its assent. In later days such assent was indicated in one way or another on the bill and the clerk of parliament on enrolling the bill made mention of it. But nothing of the kind was written on any of the original bills just described or was mentioned in the enrolled record of the bill of the mendicant orders. Indeed, regarding no private bill of Richard's reign do the *Rotuli* note the commons' approval. Touching two enrolled restorations of land in 1351 and 1353, both attendant upon reversal of sentence of banishment, the commons' assent was, to be sure, recorded, and this although the petitioners had not included the commons in their address.[45] Probably this assent was noted in the record to make the restoration as binding as possible. Up to 1400 there is little further indication that, whether the commons were or were not associated with king and lords in the address of a private bill, they were asked to assent to the bill.

Only some four private bills of Richard's reign addressed

---

[44] A. P. 1026; *R. P.,* III, 274.

[45] *Ibid.,* II, 243, 267.

to the commons alone and disregarding king and lords are discoverable. Perhaps the earliest of them was that of Thomas Felton, at the time a captive in France. He asked for assistance to pay his ransom which was soon due; otherwise he must languish in prison. Since Felton died before September, 1381, and had probably been released from captivity before December, 1380, when he again entered the king's service, the petition cannot be later than 1380. It is addressed " A tres honourez et sages chevaliers des comtes et les citoyens et bourgeois esteans pour les communez a cest present parlement." After recounting his misfortunes at length, Felton " suplie . . . que . . . Il vous plaise . . . avoir pite . . . En supliant . . . a notre dit seigneur et son treshonure conseil que ledit Thomas soit aide. . . ." This appeal was in advance of that of de la Pole, as well as of an earlier date, in requesting the commons alone to intercede with king and council. Together with the address it exemplifies the essential features of fifteenth-century bills presented to the commons; for these were that the commons should be addressed, not in association with the king and lords, but alone, and that they should be asked to intercede with the king or with the king and council in behalf of the petitioner. The petition, apart from initiating a new procedure, is further interesting as being one of two offered by Felton at about the same time. The other was addressed " a notre tressouverain seigneur le Roy et son treshoneure conseil " and related more briefly the circumstances of his captivity and his need of ransom. It was written on paper whereas the petition to the commons is on parchment. Were it not for the difference in the addresses, we might think that the shorter bill was a draft for the longer one. Although both are somewhat injured, neither seems to be endorsed with an answer and we are left in doubt as to the fortunes of the two.[46]

A second bill was addressed to the commons in 1389, some ten years after Felton had appealed to them. It was the re-

[46] A. P. 5514, 5513. Cf. *C. P. R.*, *1377-81*, pp. 600, 604; *1381-1385*, p. 45.

quest of the friends of Thomas Rushok, once bishop of Chichester but then exiled to Ireland, that sustenance be provided
for him. The address was "As tres sages comunes de cest
present parlement" and the appeal ran, "Pour quoy supplient ses ditz amys qe vous plese de faire requeste a notre
Seigneur le Roy et as Seigneurs du Parlement. . . ."[47] In
both phrases the characteristics of Felton's bill were repeated.
Two later bills, which should probably be dated 1397 and
1394 respectively, seem to be the only ones which maintained
the innovation in Richard's reign. The second of them, moreover, was also less definite in the phrasing of the appeal. The
first was the bill of Robert atte Mulle, for whom the commons
had petitioned in 1393 and who now explained that, of the
£600 demanded from him as the finder of treasure trove at
Guilford, he had paid 500 marks and could pay no more.
Addressing the "honourables et sages Communes d'iceste
present Parlement," he continued, "plese a voz tres sages
discreciouns avoir compassion . . . et sur ceo mettre voz
graciouses aides a dit suppliaunt . . . qe notre dit Seigneur le
Roi de sa grace especial . . . estre gracious a dit Suppliaunt. . . ."[48] The appeal differed from those of Felton and
the friends of the bishop only in its verbosity. A fourth bill
addressed to the commons in 1394, while less specific in its
appeal, introduced, however, a new item of interest. In it
John Banberye of Bristol explained that a great ship of his
laden with wine and merchandise from Gascony had struck
a sandbank in the Severn and thereupon had been pillaged
and broken up by Welshmen who had come in 300 or 400
boats. His request for redress survives in two copies, one
addressed "a tresredoute et tresexcellent seigneur le roi et as
ses tressages seigneurs de cest present parlement," the other
"a tressages Comunes en cest present parlement." Since the
second bears the endorsed response, it must have been the

---

[47] A. P. 1025; *R. P.*, III, 274.

[48] A. P. 1071; *R. P.*, III, 448. For the dating of this bill see above, p. 346,
n. 33.

copy upon which action was taken. Although its appeal asks only for remedy instead of asking the commons to intercede with the king, an inscription which it bears explains how the commons actually proceeded. Above the text to the left is written "Soit parle as seigneurs" a variant of the fifteenth-century inscription which was to have so significant and long-continued a history.[49] Its appearance here on Banberye's bill seems to be its first, and in consequence is most note-worthy.[50] It completes the characteristics which were to distinguish many private bills of the fifteenth century. All of these have now been discerned in the fourteenth century — the address to the commons alone, the appeal that the commons intercede with the king in behalf of the suppliant and the dispatch of the bill to the lords, the last a mark of the commons' approval. We may now turn to the fifteenth century.

The private bills of the reign of Henry IV adopted and developed the innovations of the two preceding decades. While most of them were still addressed to the king or to the lords or to both or to the king and council, an increasing number were addressed to the commons and to the commons alone. In only two or three instances were the commons associated with king and lords in the address as they had inconsequen-

---

[49] A. P. 4758, 4569. The bill is not printed in the *Rotuli*.

[50] It might seem that it was soon to have several successors; for above seven of the ten petitions of 1397 already described (*supra,* pp. 324-325), as sent by the commons to the king and by him referred to a committee to answer, is written, "As seigneurs" and above an eighth, "As seigneurs de ordein[er] remedie." It happens that the last, although printed at the end of the group, actually was first when the petitions were filed. On the dorse of it is both the numeral I and the memorandum describing the series. Each of the seven inscriptions, therefore, was a shortened form of the longer one. At first glance we might assume that "As seigneurs" implied the dispatch of the petitions by the commons to the lords, as Banbery's bill had been dispatched. But the longer inscription, appropriate to the special treatment which the petitions received when they were referred to a committee of lords, explains the inscriptions as a whole. They originated not with the commons dispatching the bills to the lords but with the king referring them to a committee. They were not, therefore, successors to the inscription on Banbery's bill.

tially been in a few bills of Richard's reign. It was still possible in 1402 for Isabelle, wife of the late William le Scroop, to address king, lords and commons and for John Attewode and wife to appeal to lords and commons; [51] but this type of address scarcely recurs. On the other hand there survive nearly a dozen petitions of the reign addressed to the commons. Most of them date from 1401-1404, but this is because we have few private bills of any sort from the middle and later years of the reign. In all of them the appeal was, as it had been in three petitions of Richard's reign, that the commons would intercede with the king in behalf of the petitioner. This convention thus seems definitely established at the beginning of the fifteenth century.

Except in the case of four of these bills we have also the commons' superscription to explain how that body reacted toward them. The four bills without superscription date from 1402 and the absence of any record of how they were received by the commons is not strange in view of the fact that we have only one indication of such action before this time.[52] Indeed it is rather surprising that the others, which for the most part are as early, should testify to the commons' approval of them.

[51] A. P. 1076, 1083; R. P., III, 483, 513.

[52] The four bills received consideration much as if they had been presented to king and lords, as the endorsements testify. In one John Hall and his wife asked for the restoration of a manor and hundred of which they had been disseised. The endorsement referred the case to the council for examination. In another Sir William Bonvyle and his wife similarly asked redress for disseisin and were told to sue at the common law. In the third the Master of the Order of Burton St. Lazar asked for recovery of the guardianship of the hospital of St. Giles outside London for which the order was bound to pay forty marks yearly at the exchequer but which was at the time withheld from them. The endorsement ordered the petition sent to chancery where the chancellor with the advice of the justices would do justice. The fourth also was referred to the chancellor. It was the appeal of men to whom certain abbeys had sold "annuities" that the abbeys should not be protected in exacting excessive sums and in escaping suits at common law. (A. P. 1080, 1097, 9870, 1095; R. P., III, 512, 520.) The third is not printed; the first, second and fourth were addressed "A tres sages Comunes de cest present Parlement," the third "A tressages Chivalers, Citezonis, Burgeis et communes du parlement."

How varied were the superscriptions in which as yet this approval was expressed is shown by the treatment of three of these others, which, as it happened, were members of a series of a half-dozen group bills. The six, all presumably of 1401 and all presented by townsmen asking relief from financial burdens, were at one time filed together. One of them, that of the burgesses of Grimsby, did not mention the commons in address or appeal and apparently did not receive their superscription. The bill of the burgesses of Ipswich and that of the tenants of Dunwich, Suffolk, were addressed to the king alone but must have passed through the commons' hands since both were inscribed "Soit prie a Roy." The bills of the burgesses of Truro and Lyme were both addressed to the commons, asked their intercession with the king and were inscribed respectively "Suez a Roy" and "Sue a Roy." The sixth bill, that of the mayor, bailiffs, and commonalty of Cambridge was addressed to the commons, begged them to intercede with the king and was inscribed "Soit baille as seigneurs pur parler a Roi." That the variety of the inscriptions meant little is shown by the circumstance that the bills from Truro, Lyme, Ipswich and Cambridge, each bearing a different commons inscription, were all endorsed with the same answer, "Suent au Roy et il ent ferra come meult lui semblera en le cas." [53]

The inscription on the Cambridge bill is most illuminating, since it was less abbreviated than the others. It expanded what became the usual later commons' superscription, "Soit baille as seigneurs," by explaining that a bill was to be sent to the lords that the lords might speak to the king about it. An inscription appearing on three other bills of Henry's reign, all

---

[53] A. P. 1085, 1086, 5609, 1120, 6030, 5169; R. P., III, 514-515. The printed text omits the inscriptions. On the Grymsby bill there seems to have been an inscription which has been erased. That the bills were once filed together is shown by five similarly placed perforations in the left margin of each. The date is inferred from the fact that the Truro bill seems to be earlier by nine years than another bill presented by the same burgesses in 1410 (A. P., 1120; R. P., III, 638; C. P. R., 1401-5, p. 3; C. P. R., 1408-13, p. 215)

of them private bills, says the same thing in a slightly different way — "Soit parle a Roi par les seigneurs." Two of these bills were enrolled on the parliament roll of 1402 with the note that each was "une Petition baillez en Parlement par les Communes d'Engleterre." Each began "A les tres honorables et tres sages Communes de cest present Parlement" and each charged Sir Philip Courteney with forcible entry and violence, in one case to the injury of Sir Thomas Pomeroy, in the other to that of the abbot of Newnham. The enrolled record makes no mention of the superscriptions which the original bills reveal.[54] We find the same words on a third bill of about the same year, neither enrolled nor printed. It presented together the separate appeals of three men of London each asking restoration of a messuage in the city. Each was addressed, "As honorablez et sages comunes de cest present parlement" and above the three was written, "Soit parle a Roi par les seigneurs."[55]

The full superscription of these three bills and of the bill of the men of Cambridge was elsewhere abbreviated, much as it was on the bills of the other townsmen. In a petition of 1402 which the commons themselves presented "en relevacion de voz Countez de Northumberland, Cumberland and Novell Castell sur Tyne," a sponsored group bill, it became "soit parle [a] Roy."[56] To an abbreviated form there might, however, be added a new word appropriately introducing the imperative (or subjunctive). On a bill addressed to the commons by Rustyn Villenove and others in 1404 the approving inscription ran, "Conc[essum est] soit parle as seigneurs."[57] Presumably the word here added is to be understood as in general introducing the superscription, whatever form the remainder of it might take. It reappears in French in an

[54] A. P. 1078, 6261; *R. P.,* III, 488, 489.

[55] Below the text has also been written " parler " and above it " respond'." On the dorse appears the king's response ordering the dispatch of the petitions to chancery, where the chancellor would do justice (A. P., 7367).

[56] A. P. 1090; *R. P.,* III, 518.

[57] A. P. 1110; *R. P.,* III, 565.

unusually expanded commons' approval written above a bill of 1402 in which John Whaplode appealed to the commons to beg the king to authorize the issue of writs which would enable him to recover a messuage in London. This time they wrote "Est grante et debailler la bill a Roy et as seigneurs de parlement." [58]   There was little advantage in using this longer form.

Varied as were the superscriptions on the bills which were addressed to the commons under Henry IV, the bills which bore them were not actually very numerous. Several of them were group bills, a type which for a long time had been sponsored by the commons and in Richard's reign had sometimes been addressed to them. Yet to find the superscription even on group bills was novel. Of the private bills of individuals addressed to the commons not more than a half-dozen survive which were thus inscribed. A bill of 1410 may be added to the list, although for an obvious reason it was addressed to the king instead of to the commons. It was the appeal of John Drayton, one of the knights of the shire from Gloucestershire, asking redress for assault made upon him when he was coming to parliament. As involving parliamentary privilege, it was assured of the support of the commons and stood in no need of being addressed to them. In evidence of such support the commons wrote upon it "soit prie a Roi et as seigneurs." [59]

We may extend somewhat our knowledge of the attitude of the commons toward private bills under Henry IV by the consideration of those which were enrolled but for which, of course, no superscription was noted. We shall see that the commons' approval was given in three if not in four different ways. It was given, as it had been under Richard II, by the commons presenting the wishes of an individual in a bill of their own; it was given, if the bill was addressed to the commons, by their presumably writing on it an approving superscription, as has just been described; it was given, even if the

[58] A. P. 5822.
[59] A. P. 5291.

bill had been addressed to the king, in some obscure manner which the roll describes as " at the request of the commons "; it was given, finally, in most instances when the bill was addressed to king, if indeed, it was given at all, not at the request of the commons but with their assent. These methods may be briefly noted as they are reflected in enrolled bills and in such originals of these as survive.

In seven instances the commons presented the wishes of an individual in bills of their own. Four of them, all from the first parliament of the reign, were like the half-dozen similar bills of the preceding reigns in being incorporated as articles of a comprehensive commons petition. The first of the four ran, " Item priont les Communes pur . . . Thomas Ercevesque de Cantirbirs " that, since he had lost heavily while Roger de Walden displaced him in the see, he might have execution on Roger's goods and that his tenants might be freed from obligations which they had undertaken toward Roger. The three following articles asked similar favours. In one it was the restoration to the earl of Arundel of the title and estates of which his father had been deprived by Richard II; in another it was the replacement at the treasury of the lost fines and records of these estates; in a third it was the restoration of the title and estates of the earl of Warwick.[60] All were political bills, making amends for injuries inflicted by act of parliament under Richard II. With the close of the century, however, the introduction of an appeal for an individual among the articles of the comprehensive commons petition passed for the most part out of fashion. Henceforth, when the commons wished to make such an appeal, they made it, except in one parliament of Henry V, by presenting a separate bill which was enrolled before their comprehensive petition.

An early instance of this adaptation, although not strictly in the form of a bill, was the commons' appeal in 1401 that the king restore to William Bagot his lands and possessions; [61]

[60] *R. P.,* III, 434-436.
[61] *Ibid.,* p. 458.

and fully formulated as commons bills were two appeals of
1407 and 1411. In the former year, the parliament roll, before it reached the comprehensive commons petition, recorded,
" une Petition feust baille en Parlement par les Communes pur
Mestre Thomas Sye, de quele Petition le tenure s'enseute:
A . . . notre Seigneur le Roy supplient voz povres Communes
[that the guardianship of the priory of Hinkley be regranted
to Sye's advantage]." The response duly noted that the petition was granted with the assent of the lords and at the prayer
of the commons. Slightly less specific was the petition of 1411
which asked that John Lumley recover the property of his
father and brother forfeited through treason. The parliament
roll begins as before, " une Petition feust baille en Parlement
par les Communes d'Engleterre pur Monseigneur Johan Lumley . . . : Pleaise au Roy . . . par advis de toutz les
Seigneurs . . . graunter a votre liege Johan de Lumley, Chiv-
aler. . . ." Although the commons do not in the petition
declare themselves the petitioners, this may properly be inferred, and the response notes that the bill was granted " a la
request des Communes en Parlement." [62]

Along with this testimony to the first method of getting the
commons' approval for the wishes of an individual, the parliament roll yields a little further information about the second
method, in accordance with which the commons wrote an approving superscription upon bills addressed to them. Two
such bills, those of Sir Thomas Pomeroy and the Abbot of
Newnham, which survive in their original as well as in their
enrolled form, have been described. Four others, of which
no originals survive, were undoubtedly like these in being
dispatched to the lords with the commons' superscription.
One was presented in 1401, two in 1410 and one in 1411.
All were read in the lords and were passed — in two instances,
it was said, at the request of the commons.[63]

[62] *Ibid.*, pp. 610, 655.
[63] *R. P.*, III, 460, 632, 633, 657. In the first the duchess of Ireland begged
the commons to request the King to protect her dower; in the second

More perplexing are three other bills which, the parliament roll relates, were granted at the request or at the special request of the commons, although it appears that each of them was addressed to the king rather than to that body. The earliest, dating probably from 1404, survives also in its original form. It is the appeal of Bartholomew Verdon, Kt. and three companions, all of Ireland, for restitution of their lands, which had been forfeited through condemnation for felony resultant upon indictment by Irish enemies but now annulled by the king's pardon. The original bears no commons' superscription and, were it not for the endorsed response that the king granted the request with the assent of the lords and " a les especialx prier et request de les Comunes en plein Parlement," we should not know that the commons had anything to do with it.[64] The two other bills, which like Verdon's were addressed to the king but yet are said to have been granted at the request of the commons, bear date of 1411. In one William Laysyngby asked for the restoration of property which he had forfeited through attainder and in the other John Colvyle asked that the church of Newton be appropriate and without endowed vicar. Whether the commons wrote their superscription on the two we cannot tell in the absence of the originals. Both, however, had a characteristic which Verdon's bill did not have. Although they were not addressed to the commons yet each in the appeal asked the king to grant the request with the advice and assent of the lords and com-

Walter Hungerford asked that the sheriff of Wiltshire impanel only jurors of substance to hear his plea that he had not, as guardian, wasted the priory of Farley; in the third William Doyly and his wife sought the recovery of the manor of Hynton, Norths; and in the fourth the abbott and convent of Furness asked that they might name attorneys to appear for them in suits in which they could not make answer in person.

[64] A. P., 1415; R. P., III, 484, 537, 552. The original is printed as of 1402. The bill was twice enrolled, once in 1404 and again in the second parliament of the year, but the answer the second time was more acquiescent than the first. There is another original bill, not enrolled or printed, which is like this one except that it was presented by Verdon's three associates. (A. P. 5618).

mons.[65]   It was not, however, quite the same thing for a bill to ask the assent of the commons as for it to be granted at their request.   Without satisfactory explanation, therefore, we must for the time leave these three puzzling bills [66] to note the last and weakest type of commons' support, their assent to a bill addressed to the king.

That the assent of the commons was not asked for bills of Richard's reign which were not addressed to them has been pointed out.   Under Henry IV, however, such assent was at length sought.   The first occasion seems to have been in 1401 in the case of a bill presented by the archbishop of Canterbury.   The parliament roll both records this and describes the manner of its acceptance.   " Item, une Petition feust baillez en Parlement touchant l'Ordre de Cisteux, laquele par comandement du Roy feust envoiez as Communes pur ent estre advisez et dire leur advis.   De quele Petition les paroles s'ensuent. . . ."   The request was that a bull recently purchased from Rome by the Order excepting it from the payment of tithes should be void.   In response the king with the assent of " les Seigneurs en Parlement " declared that the bull should not be put in execution and that he would ask the pope to annul it.   Earlier on the roll we read of what had happened in the commons.   They themselves reported " Coment leur feust baillez une Petition par l'Ercevesque de Canterbirs touchant l'Ordre de Cisteux pur estre enfourmez de mesme la Petition et ent dire leur advis; Et coment mesme l'Ercevesque leur dist, coment le Roy et les Seigneurs feurent accordez sur le respons d'icelle. A quel respons les ditz Communes s'agrerent bien et rebaillerent la dite Petition en Parlement." [67]   The circumstance that the archbishop himself took the bill from one house to the other shows that the machinery for automatically passing bills on had not yet been perfected.   Probably in this instance the seriousness of defying a papal bull

[65] *R. P.,* III, 655, 657.
[66] See below, p. 369.
[67] *R. P.,* III, 464, 457.

stimulated both king and archbishop to get the support of the commons. While, therefore, the procedure indicates that the approval of the commons to an important private bill had become something worth having, it shows equally that ordinary private bills addressed to the king were not yet usually brought before them.

The next private bills addressed to the king which are said to have had the commons' assent date from 1404. They were the requests of the countess of Huntingdon and the lady Dispenser respectively for the recovery of dower. Later in the year the earl of Somerset's bill, requesting that he inherit his son's annuity of 1000 marks, asked for and secured the commons' approval. In 1410 the petition of Richard Hastyngs that he inherit the forfeited lands of his brother received the assent of the commons as well as that of the lords.[68] The formal character of these four bills, which, of those addressed to the king, were the only enrolled ones of the reign of Henry IV, except the archbishop's bill, to be approved by the commons, suggest that the commons' assent was as yet got rather to strengthen titles than as a matter of course.

The four methods which the parliament rolls show were used to get the commons' support for private bills under Henry IV are also discernible in the reign of Henry V. Since from this reign few private bills survive in manuscript other than those printed in the *Rotuli* "ex originalibus," we shall have to draw conclusions largely from these and from the bills enrolled. By referring to the originals of the printed unenrolled bills we shall be able, however, to repair certain omissions of the editors. Where in some instances they neglected the superscription, we can supply it.[69]

Under Henry V the number of private and group bills which in one way or another received the commons' support was

---

[68] *Ibid.*, pp. 533, 550, 633.

[69] They failed to print the superscriptions which are found on A. P. 1125, 1132, 1148, 1147, 1146, 1168, 1174, 1176; *R. P.*, IV, 27 (no. 2), 32 (no. 12), 87 (nos. 1, 2, 3), 159 (no. 5) 163, 164 (no. 2).

relatively much greater than ever before. Although private and group bills of various reigns printed from the originals in the *Rotuli* are far from being all that survive, they are at least representative and may serve to indicate in a quantitative way the growth of the new procedure. Of the 104 printed from the reign of Richard II only two were addressed to the commons; of the 53 printed from the reign of Henry IV eight were so addressed; but of the 51 printed from the reign of Henry V, thirty were addressed to the commons and to them alone.[70] The enrolled private and group bills of the three reigns tell the same tale. In Richard's reign no such bill was addressed merely to the commons and none is said to have been granted at their request. In the next reign, of the 43 such bills enrolled, six were addressed to the commons and three others were said to have been granted at their request. Finally, under Henry V, of the 52 enrolled private and group bills, twenty-six were addressed to the commons and fifteen others were said to have been granted at their request. It is clear that the new method of presenting private bills had become popular.

When under Henry IV the commons wished to sponsor the plea of an individual, one of their ways of doing so was, as we have seen, to present it as a bill of their own. Apart from the presenting of four such bills as articles of the comprehensive petition of 1399 they did this by offering separate bills which were enrolled before the " communes petitions." Under Henry V they repeated this procedure but with a greater number of bills sponsored in the second way. It was in the parliament of 1415 that they included among the articles of their comprehensive petition three which were pretty clearly requests for individuals.[71] But elsewhere, when in a half-dozen instances they wished to present such requests as their own, they did so in separate bills which in due course were enrolled

---

[70] Two others under Henry IV and seven others under Henry V mentioned the commons along with the lords in the address.

[71] *R. P.*, IV, 83, 85.

before the "communes petitions."[72] Of the half-dozen, two were group bills such as the commons often adopted and two were bills put in the mouth of the commons by the bishop of Winchester. Behind a fifth there had clearly been a private bill addressed to the commons which, when presented to the king, received a new introduction. In it the commons asked remedy for Alexander Meryng, who was the victim of an error which a clerk had made in recording an assize of novel disseisin. The appeal retained the phrase utilized by private bills addressed to the commons, "Please a voz tres sages discretions . . . du prier a . . . le Roy et a toutz les Seigneurs . . . "; but the address had become that of the commons to the king, "Item priount les Communes." Obviously the use of the two clauses in the same petition was illogical. To avoid such contradiction and to escape the alternative of changing the words of the appeal, this method of giving the commons' sanction to a private bill was henceforth little used. It was simpler, though of course less impressive, to write on a private bill a sentence embodying the commons' support.

This second method was primarily and appropriately applicable to a bill addressed to the commons with a request that they intercede with the king. If they decided to intercede, they wrote on the bill a superscription which dispatched it to the lords. As was noted above, some twenty-six such private and group bills were enrolled on the rolls of the various parliaments of Henry V before the "communes petitions"; and unenrolled bills printed in the *Rotuli* add thirty others. En-

---

[72] In one the commons asked that the king pardon John Baskervyle and restore to him his forfeited lands; in another that a clerical error be corrected; in a third that the wardens of the girdlers of London be authorized to inspect the work of anyone exercising the craft within a league of the city; in a fourth that two drapers, a "woder" and a dyer be named to govern the dyers of Coventry and to restrain them from making high charges for their services and from manufacturing cloths; in a fifth and a sixth that letters patent be ratified authorizing the repayment to the bishop of Winchester of £14,000 which he had lent to the king (*R. P.*, IV, 72, 73, 75, 111, 132).

rolled or unenrolled they outnumbered private and group bills
addressed in any other way. The type had been evolved
under Richard II and had been occasionally employed under
Henry IV. The superscriptions of such bills in the reign of
Henry IV have been described and have shown considerable
variety. Superscriptions appear on practically all of those
which are preserved from the reign of Henry V and are likewise of interest; [73] for the diversity of the earlier reign was
being replaced by a growing uniformity. At first it seemed
that the accepted superscription was going to be " Soit prie
au Roy," one of the forms appearing under Henry IV, or the
variant, " Soit baille au Roy." Most of the original bills of
the early years of the reign bear one or the other of these
phrases.[74] But in the last parliament of the reign in 1421
they were superseded by " Soit baille as seigneurs." [75] The
transition is indicated by a superscription of 1414, " soit baille
a Roy et as Seigneurs du Parlement," and by one of 1415,
" soit prie au Roy et as Seigneurs." [76] In the latter year four
other superscriptions abbreviated these phrases to " A Roi et
as Seigneurs." [77] The tendency, therefore, was to neglect to
mention the king and to indicate only the first step in the
approach to him. While, as a superscription of 1402 had explained, a bill was sent to the lords in order that they might
intercede with the king and while for some time under
Henry V the emphasis was on interceding with the king, the
final assumption came to be that the sending of a bill to the
lords implied the sending of it to the king. In this way there
was established in the last years of Henry V a convention
which was to persist for centuries. A bill first proposed in

[73] The only originals which seem to show no superscription are A. P.
1123, 1158; *R. P.*, IV, 27 (no. 1), 131 (par. 14).

[74] A. P. 1125, 885, 1124, 1130-1133, 1135-1137, 1139, 6091, 1140, 5161,
6090, 1151-1153, 1155; *R. P.*, IV, 27, 28, 30, 32, 36-38, 40, 55, 88-90, 92.

[75] A. P. 1157, 1167, 1160, 6459, 1161, 1168-1170, 6236, 6097, 1173, 1174,
1176; *R. P.*, IV, 130, 132, 141, 143, 159-160, 162-164.

[76] A. P. 1141, 1149; *R. P.*, IV, 56, 89.

[77] A. P. 1146-1148, 1150; *R. P.*, IV, 87, 89.

the commons and approved by that body was dispatched with the superscription, " Soit baille as seigneurs." [78]

Among the private bills of the reign of Henry IV we met with three which were addressed not to the commons but to the king, and yet the parliament roll noted that they were approved at the request of the commons. Whether any commons' inscription contributed to this was not, in the absence of two of the originals, altogether clear. From the time of Henry V we have some nine bills addressed in the same way and enrolled with the same comment.[79] But the survival of the commons' superscription on two of them dating from 1421 removes doubt as to the method employed. On the two we read, as we do on bills addressed to the commons, the phrase " Soit baille as seigneurs." [80] Clearly, therefore, a private bill addressed to the king might be sponsored by the commons

[78] In 1421 the commons wrote an unusual inscription on a group bill addressed to them by the abbots and priors of the realm asking that the bishops be forbidden to name abbots and priors to be collectors of clerical tenths in archdeaconries and counties in which they were not resident. The words were " soit baille a mons[eigneur] lercevesque de Cantirb[irs]." (A. P. 1159; R. P., IV, 131). This was, of course, a reference of the petition to convocation.

[79] Of the nine bills four asked for ratification of letters patent already granted by the king and it is likely that they were introduced in the commons in order to strengthen the authority of these documents. The same may have been true of the bill which asked for the restoration of the title and lands of Thomas Montague, earl of Salisbury. So, too, this explanation would apply to an appeal of the bishop, dean and chapter of Lincoln that an existent statute and existent letters patent limiting the jurisdiction of officials of the city be clarified. Two other bills were appeals of Welshmen for the removal of disabilities resting upon them because of their nationality, and were naturally enough sponsored by the commons. One of these seems to have intended to address the commons; for, while the address was " A . . . le Roy et tres reverentz Seigneurs de cest present Parlement," the appeal was " plese a Vous tres honurez Seigneurs . . . de supplier a . . . le Roy." In the same way a bill of Thomas Chaucer, looking toward the strengthening of his title to lands granted him by various princes, implies in its address that it was to be presented by the commons. It began, " Please a Roy . . . grauntier par assent des Seigneurs Espirituelx et Temporelx et a la request des Communes." (R. P., IV, 40-43, 72, 141, 74, 6, 130, 39).

[80] A. P. 1157, 1160; R. P., IV, 130, 141.

before it reached the lords and the king; and when this happened they wrote on it the superscription which they used in dispatching bills addressed to themselves.

A final form of commons' approval for a private bill under Henry IV was that in which a bill addressed to the king was enrolled with the explanation that it had the assent of lords and commons. We saw how the archbishop of Canterbury got such assent for his bill in 1401 and we read of four other bills which were so approved. But while only five out of thirty-three enrolled bills of the reign addressed to the king were said to have secured the commons' approval, under Henry V, of ten such enrolled bills, six are said to have had it, two others asked for it, one of these together with another bill secured the "assent of parliament" and the tenth asked for this.[81] Thus the securing of the commons' assent to private bills introduced in the lords was fast becoming an established custom.

How now was this assent expressed? Unfortunately no original survives for any of these ten enrolled bills of Henry V. And of unenrolled bills addressed to the king in this reign there seems to be only one bearing the inscription of which we are in quest. In the *Rotuli* there is printed as of the year 1415 a group bill requesting the king to declare whether the freedom from escheat, which he had sold on 12 November, 1415 for £1000 to tenants of lands in Wales (that in this matter Welsh law might be followed), extended also to his tenants of the duchy of Lancaster in Wales, now that the duchy had been severed from the crown. Above the text is written "Les Co[mun]es ount donez lour assent." Although the petition probably belongs to some year of the reign later than 1415 and although the inscription differs slightly from the one later adopted, the inscription itself seems to be the earliest surviving written expression of the assent which the commons were be-

---

[81] *Ibid.*, III, 533 (pars. 46, 47), 550, 633; IV, 44-45, 100, 138, 140, 36, 37, 74, 130.

ginning to give to private bills sent them from the lords.[82]

The reign of Henry V thus seems to give evidence of an innovation, while adopting and extending the usages of its two predecessors. The earlier usages were, of course, more in evidence. Private bills were adopted by the commons as their own, once as articles of a comprehensive commons petition and a half dozen times as separate commons bills; they were more often, and in what was becoming an approved manner, addressed to the commons and on acceptance forwarded to the lords with the superscription, "Soit baille as seigneurs"; they were, finally, if still addressed to the king, sometimes adopted by the commons who wrote upon them this same superscription or, if they had already been approved by king and lords, were, although rarely, inscribed with a phrase recording the commons' assent.

It only remains to inquire whether these same methods of expediting private bills continued in use under Henry VI. We may be content with a glance at the records of the seven parliaments which were held during the first decade of the reign. On the parliament rolls of these years, although we find no private requests adopted by the commons and enrolled under the caption "communes petitions," we do find seven commons bills incorporating such requests and enrolled separately before the caption. Two others are printed which were not enrolled.[83] Thus the first and most convincing method of getting commons' support for private bills was still resorted to. Much more favoured was the second method, the addressing of private bills to the commons and the dispatch of them, when approved, with the superscription which had now become usual, "Soit baille as seigneurs." The editors of the *Rotuli*

---

[82] A. P. 7489; *R. P.*, IV, 91. The petition can scarcely date from 1415, since it explains that uncertainty has arisen about the interpretation of letters patent patent of November of that year (cf. *C. P. R., 1413-1416*, p. 380); but it belongs to the reign of Henry V, since it describes the letters patent as granted by the king who is addressed.

[83] *Ibid.*, IV, 250, 322 (pars. 18, 19), 325, 392 (pars. 16, 18), 394, 314, 315; A. P. 1222, 1224, 1255; C., P. & C. P. 17/8, 20/9, 10, 17/4, 5.

print several of these in their original form[84]; and the parliament roll records several, always entered, so far as they were not group bills, before the caption "communes petitions." In the case of the latter, which, of course, were enrolled without note of any superscription, we are often able to supply from the originals the omitted phrase. It is always "soit baille as seigneurs."[85]

Private petitions addressed not to the commons but to the king were presented in each parliament in considerable numbers. Of the originals printed in the rolls several probably did not come up for consideration since they received no response; and others were answered without the assent of the commons, a survival of fourteenth-century usage.[86] When, however, we turn to the enrolled petitions addressed to the king, we find that with very few exceptions they are said to have been approved either at the commons' request or with their assent.[87] Even in one instance where the assent is not noted, the original records it.[88] Of the three or four which were accepted *at the request* of the commons, two originals survive and show that the commons' request was expressed as it had been under Henry V by the words "soit baille as seigneurs."[89] And now, when for the first time we have a few originals of enrolled bills addressed to the king which he approved with the commons' assent instead of at their request, these originals show that until 1431 the assent was expressed also by, "soit

---

[84] *Ibid.*, pp. 193, 194, 313, 384-387, 414-418.

[85] *Ibid.*, pp. 212, 247, 249, 285, 287, 321, 324, 372-375, 393-399; C., P. & C. P. 15/9, A. P. 4229, 1189, 9914, 4235, 1191, 1220, 1223, 1237, 1239, 1240, 5186, 1256, 1259, 1263-4, 9900.

[86] Among the latter were A. P. 1180, 1182, 1184-1186, 1214-1216, 1246; *R. P.*, IV, 192, 194-196, 314, 385.

[87] Exceptions are A. P. 1178, 1200, 1201; *R. P.*, IV, 179, 280, 300, 303.

[88] A. P. 1219 A; *R. P.*, IV, 319. It is the petition of Thomas, lord Roos, to have livery of his brother's lands, and the superscription is " soit baille as seigneurs."

[89] C., P. & C. P. 49/2, A. P. 1257 A & B; *R. P.*, IV, 283, 395. But another petition, said to have been presented at the request of the commons bears no inscription (A. P. 1202; *R. P.*, IV, 302).

baille as seigneurs." [90]   In that year and in the next, however, two such bills show a different inscription.   On one is written above the text "les Co[mun]es sount a cest bille assentuz," and on the other below the text "les Co[mun]es a cest bille ount donne lour assent."   On a similar bill of 1432 not en- rolled there is also written below the text "A cest Bille les Co[mun]es ount donne lour assent." [91]   It thus becomes clear that not until the end of the first decade of the reign of Henry VI did the commons' approval of private bills addressed to the king definitely assume the form which it had assumed at least once under Henry V and was to retain in the future. For some years it was more often expressed in the inappro- priate phrase which had been devised somewhat earlier to indicate the commons' approval of private bills addressed to them.   By 1431, however, the new type of commons' in- scription had, as an earlier chapter has shown us, already been used to indicate approval of an official public bill sent to the commons and eventually enrolled with the "communes petitions." [92]   The use of it in this connection perhaps empha- sized its appropriateness for private bills in preference to an inscription devised for another purpose.

This conjecture leads to another.   In an earlier chapter we have also seen that in 1423 the comprehensive commons peti- tion gave place to individual commons bills.   Before that time there was no need for the commons to write an inscription on their comprehensive bill, inasmuch as the introductory words presented it to the king; and the occasions on which they pre- sented separate commons bills, usually in behalf of individuals, were rare.   As it happens, no originals of the latter survive but it is likely that they were inscribed in token of approval, in the same manner as were private bills addressed to the commons.   At any rate there was ready to hand in 1423 an

[90] C., P. & C. P., 49/1, A. P. 1199, 1219 A, 1236, 1238, 7165; *R. P.,* IV, 284, 301, 319, 371-373.

[91] A. P. 1235, 1260, 1268; *R. P.,* IV, 370, 397 (par. 25), 415 (no. 5).

[92] See above, p. 305.

inscription which had been evolved in the preceding twenty-five years. Since it was this which was at once adopted by the new separate commons bills, there can be little doubt that it was borrowed from private bills or at most from the occasional commons bills which presented private or group requests. Henceforth commons bills as well as private bills sponsored by the commons were inscribed in token of approval " Soit baille as seigneurs."

Whether the commons' experience in forwarding private bills to the lords with a note of their approval suggested to them the abandonment of the comprehensive commons petition cannot be demonstrated but is not unlikely. Two decades of such experience must have shown them the antiquated character of the accepted method of presenting commons' requests. More time for preparing a commons bill and more time for debating it in the lords would be allowed if such bills were sent up as soon as formulated instead of waiting until all could be grouped together as articles of one large petition. For flexibility of procedure such a new method would mean much. And it must have come to seem illogical that private bills could be individually and readily sent from commons to lords, while more important common bills could not be. If these conjectures are correct, the development of procedure regarding private bills had a two-fold effect upon procedure regarding commons bills. It contributed to the abandonment of the comprehensive commons petition and it supplied a superscription which could be written on the new separate commons bills.

One other point of procedure deserves notice in connection with early private bills sent from the commons to the lords. It is the reading of a bill in parliament; or rather, since we have no early information about the reading of bills in the commons, the reading of a bill in the lords. Something has already been said about such reading in the second half of the fifteenth century[93]; but it was not then a new custom. That

[93] See above, pp. 164-66.

bills were formally read in the lords is noted on the parliament roll from the early years of Richard II.[94] The statement nearly always refers to private bills which instituted a suit in parliament, practically the only sort of private bill which was enrolled during the reign. On none of the originals of such of these bills as survive, however, nor on any other original bill of the reign is there note that it was read. Under Henry IV the roll continues to record the reading of bills, including now private bills of a less judicial character.[95] Again, no original of the enrolled bills records a reading; but an unenrolled and undated commons bill, which may come from this reign, bears the inscription *leg[it]ur coram d[omi]nis.* It may, however, belong to the early years of Henry V.[96]

Not until the early parliaments of Henry V do we get several bills upon which it is noted that they were read in the lords. Below the text of each of four private bills of 1414, three of them addressed to the commons, there is written *leg[it]ur;* and above the text of each of five from a later parliament of the year, all of them addressed to the commons, is inscribed *leg[it]ur coram d[omi]nis.* Upon several of these there had already been written *Soit baille au Roy* or *Soit prie au Roi.*[97] Later private bills sent by the commons to the

[94] *R. P.,* III, 8, 40, 79 *et passim.*

[95] *Ibid.,* pp. 429, 430, 488-492, 532-538 *et passim.*

[96] The bill, which is written on a membrane about 15 inches wide by 4 inches long, consists of two articles, one asking that no Welsh rebel be allowed to be sheriff or escheator, the other that no Englishman be indicted in the courts by any rebel for thirty years to come. The articles do not appear in this form in any comprehensive commons petition of the time nor are they otherwise enrolled. An article of the comprehensive petition of 1402, however, forbids a Welshman to hold the office of sheriff or escheator in Wales as well as many other offices there (*ibid.,* p. 509). The undated bill may be a little earlier than this, since it is simpler; but it may also be later, since the response to it enjoins that the statutes and good customs already made for those parts be kept and executed. The type of commons' superscription, which it also bears, "soit prie . . . [illegible]," scarcely admits of its being later than the early years of Henry V (C., P. & C. P. 13/18).

[97] A. P. 1122-1124, 1132, 1136, 1137, 1139, 1140, 1142; *R. P.,* 17, 27 (no. 2), 28 (no. 4), 32 (no. 12), 38, 40a, 55 (nos. 1, 3), 56 (no. 4).

lords, however, do not often bear a note to the effect that they were read in the lords; and it seems to have been a matter of chance whether the reading was or was not noted on the bill. As for commons bills, when at length they emancipated themselves in 1423 from the comprehensive commons petition, they, too, occasionally bore note that they had been read. The inscription, however, now became *le[git]ur et r[espondetur]*, a record of reading and answer. In such form we find it on two commons bills of 1426-1429 and on four private bills of the same years.[98] The infrequency of these instances, however, strengthens the inference that the inscribing on a bill a note that it had been read in the lords was for a long time a matter of chance.[99] It mattered less that this should be done than that there should be inscribed on bills of all sorts the commons' approval.

We may at this point bring to a close our survey of early private bills. Whatever may have been the influence, in certain points of procedure, of such bills upon commons bills in and soon after 1423, there can be little doubt that the new practice of submitting practically all private bills to the commons for approval greatly enhanced the influence and prestige of that body. Private bills in the early years of Henry VI had come to be treated very differently from private bills at the end of the reign of Edward III. In 1377 they were still, as they had been for three-quarters of a century, submitted to receivers and auditors of petitions, then came before the lords, so far as they came before parliament at all, and were in no way referred to the commons. Fifty years later they had become private bills in the modern sense of the term. They were introduced at the will of the petitioner in either house; and there is evidence of a preference for introducing them in the commons. When so introduced they were, if approved, dispatched to the lords with a superscription which had already

---

[98] C., P. & C. P. 19/8, A. P. 1203, 6024, 1219 A., 1232, 1233; R. P., IV, 348 (no. 4), 303 (no. 1), 313 (no. 9), 319, 364 (no. 4), 365 (no. 6)

[99] See above, pp. 302-303.

become stereotyped.[100]   If introduced in the lords, they were
now usually sent down to the commons to acquire there an
inscription betokening approval.[101]   This, too, was quickly to
become stereotyped.   Hence the form assumed by private bills
and the method of dealing with them which in an earlier
chapter we discovered were charactristic of the middle of the
fifteenth century had been fully developed some two decades
earlier.   Like important features in the development of commons bills they were the achievements of the early years of the
house of Lancaster.

Henceforth the treatment of private bills underwent little
change throughout the fifteenth century.   During the reign of
Henry VI petitioners continued to prefer to address their petitions to the commons, if we may judge from those that were
enrolled.   Under Henry VII, however, when, as we have seen,
the triumph of official bills over commons bills was complete,
private bills reflected a new attitude on the part of their
authors.   Of those enrolled, the greater number was addressed
to the king, in this reverting to earlier usage.   The change is
illustrated by a comparison of the enrolled private bills of the
parliament of 1439 with those of the parliament of 1487.   In
the former such bills enrolled before the "communes petitions" and addressed to the commons or introduced in their
name were ten and those addressed to the king were six; in the
latter these numbers had become three and six respectively.
The usage which had risen to popularity under Henry V had
now suffered a certain eclipse.   Not that the change greatly
mattered so far as securing the commons' assent to private
bills was concerned; for under Henry VII private bills, how-

---

[100] It may have been at this stage that bills introduced in the commons
came before the triours of petitions, these men being a committee of the
lords (see above, p. 338).   By 1509, however, when the triours had come
to include certain members of the commons (above, p. 22), private bills
may have come before the triours before being presented in either house.

[101] As has been pointed out, this gave the commons a certain share in
the administering of justice in parliament, a responsibility which they had
disavowed in 1399 (see above, p. 79, n. 15).

ever addressed, were submitted to the commons. This had been the permanent result of the new procedure. But just as the earlier tendency reflected and contributed to the increasing influence of the commons, so the later tendency reflected a decline in their contribution to legislation. Although commons bills had risen to favour some decades earlier than had private bills addressed to the commons, the decline of the two sorts was synchronous.

CHAPTER XI

STATUTES AND THE STATUTE ROLLS

IN the preceding chapters it has been implied that parliamentary legislation in its final state usually assumed the form of statutes. Much attention has been given to the process by which this came about. Most of the statutory legislation of the fourteenth and fifteenth centuries, we have seen, arose from petitions presented in parliament by the commons. Since a petition required an answer from lords and king, the final parliamentary pronouncement upon it was the combination of petition and answer. In making the combination the answer was at first added to or inserted in the petition or amalgamated with it, but later was in part appended to it in the form of an amendment. In combining the text of petition and answer, the changes made were sometimes slight, consisting of the substitution of an imperative for an appeal or of minor verbal alterations. But, sometimes, especially in the fourteenth century, the answer so modified the petition that the new enactment was couched largely in its phraseology. In the preceding chapters the new enactment has been called a statute without much regard to whether contemporaries would always have given it this name. It is now time to ask whether they would, and to consider a little more closely the final record which was made of parliamentary legislation. Has it, therefore, been entirely correct to prefer the term statute in a study of fourteenth- and fifteenth-century parliaments? To whom was the task of combining petition and response entrusted? What was the origin and character of the so-called "statute roll," in which we find the legislation in its edited and final shape? And, finally, why were some approved bills edited as statutes while others were not? Although answers to these questions do not immediately concern the commons influence on legislation, they suitably conclude the story of how during two centuries such influence became effective in the life of the nation.

The term most widely applied to an amalgamated petition and response in the first half of the fifteenth century was ordinance. It already had a rival in the briefer term "act," while an earlier rival, the term "statute," was falling into disuse. The verbs properly corresponding with these words were ordain, enact and establish, but they were not very precisely used. Ordain was the favourite verb; and statutes or acts as well as ordinances were often ordained. In 1327 the commons begged the king and his council "ordener . . . par Estutut" and in 1351 statutes were said to be ordained by the king.[1] In petitions of all sorts the usual request in the fourteenth and fifteenth centuries was that the king ordain or that the commons beg him to ordain. In the numerous bills of the parliaments of 1442 and 1444 "ordain" and "ordinance" were the words almost always employed to describe the king's action and its outcome.[2] The so-called statute roll adopted the usage of the parliament roll. Although its caption for the legislative measures of a parliament was "ordinances et estatutz," the term which it usually applied in the fifteenth century to each particular one was ordinance. Even if there were no statutes there were ordinances. So generic was the term that others than the king might ordain.

When, however, in the fourteenth century it was desired to give to a bill approved in parliament the most dignified name possible, the word chosen to describe it was statute. This designation towered above its contemporary, ordinance, and for some time had no acquaintance with its successor, act. It gave in turn its name to the final record of the most important measures adopted in a parliament, the statute roll. Its force was greater than that of an ordinance. In 1377 the lords of

---

[1] *R. P.,* II, 5, 238 (no. 3).
[2] "Establish" and "grant" were occasionally joined with "ordain."

parliament who in 1376 had been present at the making of an ordinance against Alice Perrers " recordont qe lours entencion fuist qe mesme l'Ordinance serroit Estutute et porteroit force du Statut "; and in the same parliament the commons asked that any of their petitions approved by Edward III in 1376 by the usual " Le Roi le voet " be " afferme pur Estatut " and also that others which had been answered only by ordinances and not by statutes ("ne fuist qe Ordenance et nemie Estatut ") should be shown them in order that any which was reasonable should also be declared a statute — " soit ordene pur Estatut." [3] Thus toward the end of the fourteenth century an ordinance could be exalted into a statute.

What then at the time were the characteristics of statutes which differentiated them from ordinances? Some hint about their essential nature is found in such remarks as, " les Leys, si bien la Commune Ley come les Estatuz " are not kept; " les Leis eues et usees en temps passez . . . ne se purront changer saunz ent faire novel Estatut "; and the commons pray " qe par Estatut cest Ley soit amendez." [4] A statute, therefore, was something which extended the common law and had the same validity as the common law.

On various occasions the distinction between statute and ordinance was elaborated by emphasizing the quality of permanence which inhered in the former. In 1340 certain requests of the commons were heard by a committee of prelates, lords, knights and burgesses. The points and articles which were " perpetuel " the committee " firent mettre en Estatut " but the points and articles which were not perpetual and were " einz pur un temp " the king had sealed as letters patent. The statute, the king bade, should be engrossed and sealed and firmly kept throughout the realm.[5] The same distinction between statutes and letters patent was drawn in 1344.[6] Again

[3] *Ibid.*, III, 14, 17.
[4] *Ibid.*, II, 238, 203, 202.
[5] *Ibid.*, p. 113.
[6] *Ibid.*, p. 133 (par. 61).

at the close of the parliament of 1363, in which was made, along with various ordinances, a long one touching apparel, the king pointed out to lords and commons that the things granted in this parliament were novel and asked " s'ils voleient avoir les chose issint acordez mys par voie de Ordenance ou de Statuyt.   Qe disoient qe bon est mettre les choses par voie d'Ordinance et nemi par Estatut aufin qe si rien soit de amender puisse estre amende a preschein Parlement et issint est fait." [7]   A few years before in the parliament of 1354 the commons had prayed that the ordinances of the staple and all other ordinances " faites au darrein Conseil tenuz a Westminstre . . . soient affermez en cest Parlement et tenuz pur Estatut a durer pur touz jours." [8]   Finally, in the parliament of 1373, when the clergy disregarded an ordinance recently made on the ground that it could not impair their ancient privilege " et ne fust mye afferme pur Estatut," the commons petitioned that it please the king " d'afermer la dit Ordinance pur Estatut a durer pur temps a vener." [9]   A statute was thus something enduring, unchangeable and as valid as the common law, whereas an ordinance might be transient and subject to change.   To change an ordinance into a statute was to give it permanence and greater validity.[10]

If, however, a statute, despite its intended permanence, was found to be in conflict with the law of the land or the prerogative of the king, it might be held void or might be repealed.   In the parliament of 1343 it " acordez est et assentuz qe l'Estatut [of 1341] soit de tut repellez et anientez et perde

[7] *Ibid.*, p. 280.   Despite this, the last of the ordinances, one which attempted to strengthen an earlier ordinance, ended, " Par quoi est ordeine et par Estatut establi en cest present Parlement [a new penalty]."

[8] *Ibid.*, p. 257.   In the chief justice's opening speech almost the same words occur (p. 253).

[9] *Ibid.*, p. 319 (par. 21).

[10] This feeling about the permanence of a statute was revealed in 1379. The commons asked that all bills, both private and common, be answered before they departed from any parliament " et sur ce due Estatut soit fait en ce present Parlement et enseale a demurrer en tout temps a vener . . . " (*ibid.*, III, 611).

noun d'Estatut come cel q'est prejudiciel et contraire a Leys et Usages du Roialme et as Droitz et Prerogatives notre Seigneur le Roi"; nevertheless the articles of it which were accordant with law and reason might, with the advice of the justices and other "Sages" be made anew into a statute to be kept for all time.[11]   The assenting answer to a commons petition of 1368 declared that, "si nul Estatut soit fait a contrarie [to the Great Charter and the Charter of the Forest and all statutes earlier than 1368], soit tenu pur nul."[11a]   In Richard's parliament of 1397, the clergy and the lords, replying to the Lords Appellant, "assenterent expressement qe le dit Parlement [of 1388] et toutz les Estatutz, Juggementz, Ordenances et toutz autres choses ent faits . . . soient cassez et adnullez . . . ," the appellants having declared them "encontre la Volunte et Liberte du Roy et le Droit de sa Corone."[12]   Henry IV, in turn, in his first parliament adopted the same attitude toward the parliament of 1397. Asked by lords and commons for his opinion, he said that it seemed to him "qe le dit Parlement . . . ensemblement ove toutz les Juggementz, Establissementz, Estatuz et Ordinances faites et renduz en ycell . . . sont revocables" and that he wished them repealed and annulled. At this lords and commons were rejoiced and humbly thanked him.[13]   In one of the charges formulated against Richard it was incidentally stated as an accepted principle that statutes were binding only so long as they were not repealed by another parliament.[14]   A still more

---

[11] *Ibid.*, II, 139. Stubbs notes that the annulment of the measures of the Good Parliament by John of Gaunt was analogous, but that these measures had not taken the form of a statute (*Const. Hist.*, II, 611).

[11a] *R. P.*, II, 295; *Stats.*, I, 388. The statute based on the answer to the petition mentions only the Great Charter and the Charter of the Forest omitting — without warrant — the mention of "touz autres Estatutz." Professor McIlwain fails to note the omission in his discussion of the "Fundamental Law" (*High Court of Parliament*, p. 59).

[12] *R. P.*, III, 357.

[13] *Ibid.*, p. 426.

[14] "Item, postquam in Parliamento suo certa Statuta erant edita, que semper ligarent donec auctoritate alicuius alterius Parliamenti fuerint

indifferent attitude toward the permanence of statutes was shown by the commons in this same parliament when, touching the statute of provisors, they assented that the king might "mesme l'Estatut casser, repeller, irriter et de tout adnuller selonc sa haut discretion" and according to what he thought most expedient and necessary for the honour and profit of his royal estate, of his realm and of his people.[15] No further justification for the repeal of a statute was longer needed than expediency.

This playing fast and loose with statutes was bound to come despite fourteenth-century ideas about their permanence; for it could not have been easy for a parliament to tell whether one of its measures might not in the future be with advantage repealed. The putting of the question in the parliament of 1363 whether the requests granted should become ordinances or statutes shows that there was nothing inherent in them which logically made them one or the other. It was even then a matter of expediency, a question whether at the next parliament it might be well to revise them. In the course of the fifteenth century men ceased to attempt to maintain the distinction. Ordinaces and statutes came to be terms used synonymously, and for this reason the distinctions elaborated by Hallam and Stubbs became inapplicable.[16]

specialiter revocata . . . " (ibid., p. 419). Richard had violated unrepealed statutes.

[15] Ibid., p. 426.

[16] Hallam noted the permanence of statutes and their relation to the common law, contrasting them with ordinances made by the king with the advice of his council, promulgated in letters patent or charters and subject to recall (H. Hallam, View of the State of Europe during the Middle Ages, 11th ed. (London, 1855), III, 49, 50). Stubbs went further and emphasized the distinction between statutes and ordinances as that between measures which were respectively legislative and executive in character (op. cit., II, 616-618). Doubtless the distinction did to some degree exist; but the term ordinance was not long reserved for measures taken by the king and council. It was soon extended to those taken by the king and parliament. Even in 1353, in a great council at which the commons were present, certain proposed ordinances of the staple were sub-

In the parliament of 1399 it was "ordeignez et establiz" by king, lords and commons that liveries of certain kinds might not be given and "cestes Ordinance et Estatut" was to become effective at a certain date.[17] Being uncertain which term was applicable, the drafters of the regulation applied to it both of them. More curious still was the usage of 1401. In the parliament of that year the commons asked that an "Ordinance" of 1388 be not enforced. In the reply this is called an "Estatut" and it is ordered that an "Ordinance" of 1399, which already potentially conceded the favour, "soit fait Estatut et proclamation ent faite en chescun Countee." The resultant statute called the condemned regulation of 1388 both statute and ordinance.[18] Thus in almost the same breath statute and ordinance are used indifferently and yet it is ordered that an ordinance of one year become a statute two years later.

A reason, however, is suggested for an order of this sort, one which introduces a new characteristic of a statute. Since it was desirable that the regulation of 1399 be proclaimed in the counties, as it apparently had not been when it was an ordinance, the ordinance should be made a statute.[19] In general, of course, ordinances were proclaimed in the counties, as the statute roll of the parliaments of Richard II so often shows them to have been. But many ordinances were probably also not proclaimed, as this one of 1399 seems not to have been. Statutes, on the other hand, were still looked upon as closely

mitted to lords and commons for debate and approval. Only afterward were the ordinances made (*R. P.,* II, 246).

[17] *Ibid.,* III, 428.

[18] *Ibid.,* p. 478; *Stats.,* II, 130.

[19] The commons petition which gave rise to the ordinance of 1399 asked for a restoration of the legislation of the parliament of 1388 and also that any part of this which seemed unprofitable might later be so designated by the commons in their petitions. The commons petition of 1401 came within the scope of the second part of the request. Meanwhile an ordinance, presumably not proclaimed in the counties, had merely restored the legislation of 1388, apparently making no mention of possible exceptions as it should have done (*R. P.,* III, 425; *Stats.,* II, 112).

enough related to the law of the land to require proclamation in the counties.

As for their permanence, although statutes might still be thought a little more enduring than ordinances, it was not long before a statute could be ordained for a short period of time. In 1406 the commons requested and secured that a bill against the Lollards be enacted " et tenuz pur Estatuit tanq'al proschein Parlement." [20] In 1425 a petition was introduced in parliament touching an ordinance made in the last parliament of Henry V in 1421. This ordinance related to the judicial rights of men serving with the king in France and was to be effective until the first parliament after the king's return. Under the circumstances, as the petition notes, the ordinance became ineffective with the death of the king. Now in 1425 it was ordained with the assent of the commons that the earlier ordinance " esoise come Estatut et ley effectuel et availlable " for all men serving in France, this " a durer de la darrein jour de cest present Parlement tanque al fyn de trois ans." [21] It was sharp logic which called this three-year prolongation a statute but the earlier similar one an ordinance. In point of fact there was no longer any attempt to make the distinction and in the reign of Henry VI statutes were sometimes ordained for terms of years just as ordinances often were. All that remained characteristic of a statute was that it must be proclaimed; and to this characteristic we shall have occasion to return. [22]

As it happened, the term statute came to be less and less used in the fifteenth century. In the voluminous records of the parliaments of 1442 and 1444 it was seldom applied to the legislation of the moment, although many petitions were approved, became ordinances and appeared on the statute roll. There is no reason why much of legislation might not have been called statutes and, indeed, the introductory phrases of the statute roll still stated that the king had made, ordained

[20] *R. P.,* III, 583. See above, p. 195.
[21] *R. P.,* IV, 308; *Stats.,* II, 232.
[22] See below, pp. 390-94.

and established certain statutes and ordinances.[23]   The word persisted longer in this stereotyped phrase than elsewhere; but even at the end of the reign of Henry VI it sometimes occurred in the body of legislation.   Perhaps the accepted usage of the statute roll tended to keep it alive.

While in the early years of the fifteenth century the term statute was coming to be distinguished less and less from the more generic ordinance, there appeared beside the latter a rival, in no wise distinguishable from it in meaning.   This was the term "act," that which the king with the advice and assent of the lords and commons enacted.   Appearing rarely in the fourteenth century, it did not then have its later connotation. When in 1380 the lords and commons reported before the king that a case referred to them by the justices was treasonable, the following paragraph began "ceste darrein acte issint faite. . . ."[24]   An act was not yet the enacted approval of a petition or even the approved enactment of the royal will. It became the latter at least in 1421 when the royal bestowal of the manor of Isleworth upon the newly-founded nunnery of Sion was described as "un certein acte . . . fait et accordez en ceste present Parlement" by the king with the assent of lords and commons.[25]   In 1423 *actus* had come to be used as a generic term for all the enactments of a parliament; for we are told that the clerk of parliament read before the council the "actus habiti et facti" in the last parliament.[26]

At length in 1439 a group petition, one asking for the incorporation of the town of Plymouth, ended with a reservation to the king of all rights "que in presenti Actu prefatis

[23] E.g., *Stats.*, II, 295, 301.

[24] *R. P.*, III, 75.

[25] *Ibid.*, IV, 140.   There is no evidence that the king acted in response to a petition.

[26] *Proceedings*, III, 22.   In somewhat this sense the term is used in the parliament roll of the year.   To a request in a commons petition which ran, "Et qe cest notre commune request et Petition soient enactez en le rolle du Parlement duraunt ycell," the reply was, "Et quant a l'Acte et l'enrollement du dit Petition, soit fait come il est desire par icell."   Here "Acte" meant "enactment" (*R. P.*, IV, 254).

Maiori et Communitati aut predictis Personis in eodem Actu nominatis . . . non conceduntur"; and the favourable reply of the king refers to "this present Act and Ordinance."[27]   The same parliament established the usage by applying the term act to an approved commons petition.   This, which provided that alien merchants have hosts, ended with the provision " qe cest Act et Ordenaunce comence" at Easter to endure for seven years and that before Easter certain commissions be made rehearsing "tout mesme le Act et Ordenaunce."[28]   After this the term "act" is used interchangeably with ordinance. Approved bills, whether private, group, official or commons, became indifferently ordinances or acts.   In the middle of the fifteenth century, the grant of a subsidy by the commons was also called an "act."[29]

The combining of petition and answer into a statute, ordinance or act was little else than a process of editing.   It was not a very difficult task, since the editor or editors had no authority to change the subject matter before them but only the opportunity to combine, rephrase, re-arrange and at times elide.[30]   It was scarcely beyond the competence of the clerks

[27] R. P., V, 21-22.

[28] Ibid., p. 25.

[29] See above, p. 45.

[30] How much they might still be required to do as late as 1449 is illustrated by the editing of a commons bill of that year which asked that fairs and markets be not held on the sabbath or on feast days. In so doing, the bill explained at length the evils arising from the existent practice, the people "nothyng, alas, havyng in mynde the horrible fowlyng of here Soule in gylefull bying and sellyng, moche liyng and fals forsweryng with drounkenshipp and debatyng, and specially in withdrawyng hemself and all her meyny holich fro divine service. . . ." These evils the ordinance translated into Latin neglecting certain details about unfed and overworked beasts of burden; but the next items the ordinance omitted entirely.   These related how men now "provoke our meke Saviour and his holy Seints . . . , directly doyng not onlich ayenst ye commaundement of all holy Chirch but also ayenst our Lordis irrevocable wordis in the Gospell of Matheu: Si vis ad vitam ingredi serva mandata etc., not dredyng ye sharpe sentens of David . . . nether aferd of the message sent . . . to Kyng Harry ye II at Cardyf . . . [as] write in ye Cronicle of Policronicon the VII boke, ye XXII Capitle. . . ." Certain alluring rewards promised

of chancery. Since, as we shall see, it was they who engrossed the statutes for publication, it might seem that they also might have edited them from material supplied by the clerk of parliament. A passage, however, in the council records of 1423 suggests that the editing was left to the more competent hands of the justices. It runs, " Eodem die lecti fuerunt per clericum parliamenti coram dominis [de consilio] actus habiti et facti in ultimo parliamento, qui ibidem habuit in mandatis de ostendendo dictos actus justiciis Regis utriusque banci ad effectum quod illi actus qui erunt statuti regni per ipsos videantur et redigantur in mundum et postea quod ostendantur dominis et proclamentur et quod aliorum actuum tangencium gubernacionem dominorum de consilio et regni dimittantur copie cum clerico consilii Regis et quod simul omnes reducti in scriptum irrotulentur in Cancellaria ut moris est." [31] The clerk of parliament was thus directed by the council to show the acts of parliament, i.e., its approved bills, to the justices of both benches that those acts which were to be statutes might be seen by them and put into clear language before being proclaimed. It was the justices who edited the enactments of parliament preparatory to their proclamation.

When at length a statute, ordinance, or act had been created by editing a bill and the response to it, what was to be its future? One distinction in store for it we have long taken for granted. It was to be enrolled on a "statute roll." The name statute roll applies most appropriately to the record of the approved and edited statutes and ordinances of the fourteenth century; for, at the time, statutes were looked upon as having greater permanence and hence greater dignity than ordinances and any enrollment of both of them would naturally, if brevity was desired, be called a statute roll. When ordi-

the king in the body of the petition were also not unnaturally omitted in the ordinance. By this omission of edifying but unenforcable matter the petition is cut to one-half its length . . . from 90 to 47 lines (*R. P.*, V, 152). But the instance is unusual and few fifteenth-century petitions stood in need of much elision or change.

[31] *Proceedings*, III, 22.

nances and acts largely replaced statutes, the traditional designation survived and the statute roll became a record primarily of certain ordinances or acts. We must now inquire
what features of these, as well as of all statutes, distinguished
them from other ordinances and acts enrolled on the parliament roll but not on the statute roll. Just as the study of
petitions led us in chapter V to an analysis of the parliament
roll, so an inquiry about statutes, ordinances and acts leads us
to an examination of what is usually called the statute roll.

There is, of course, no "statute roll." There are, up to
1468, eight rolls, each calling itself a *rotulus* of the statutes of
one or more reigns or of the part of a reign. Another roll
or other rolls, now lost, seem to have continued the record
to 1489 but after that time statutes were recorded elsewhere.[32]
The editors of the *Statutes of the Realm* had great respect
for these rolls, always using them as their preferred text and
supplementing them from what they thought inferior sources.
On the whole they were probably justified in this attitude and
their transcription seems correct. But it is one thing to accept
an enrollment as the best final record of the matter enrolled
and another thing to accept it as the first authoritative statement of this matter. Relative to the statutes of the fourteenth
and fifteenth centuries it is desirable to inquire what lay behind the statute rolls, supplying to the enroller the matter
which was to be enrolled.

A preliminary and simple answer to this question is to be
had from a glance at the enrolled statutes of the reign of
Richard II. The editors of the *Statutes* print them from the
single roll of twenty-four membranes catalogued in the Public
Record Office as Statute Roll 3.[33] In this, statutes of Richard's various parliaments are grouped under such marginal
captions as "De Statuto apud Gloucestre nuper edito, irrotu-
lato anno secundo"; and there is a general caption on the

---

[32] *Stats.*, I, pp. xxxiii-xxxv.

[33] C 74/3; *Stats.*, II, 1-110. Another roll (C 74/4) contains a duplicate of
the statutes of 1397-1398.

dorse of the first membrane calling the collection "Rotulus diversorum statutorum tempore Regis Ricardi Secundi."[34] It is apparent from the changing penmanship that the entries relative to successive parliaments were made by different hands and presumably at different times. The proceedings of a parliament would naturally have been enrolled soon after its conclusion. The first, or "great" roll of statutes, recording those of the reigns of Edward I, Edward II, and Edward III, shows the same diversity of hands after 1295. Statutes before that date were written in one hand. From this it would seem that in 1295 statutes already existent were enrolled and that to the record thus begun the statutes of successive parliaments were added soon after they were drafted. Statute Rolls 1 and 3, therefore, have the value of nearly contemporary records for the period 1295-1397.

The form assumed by the enrolled statutes of the early years of Richard II is somewhat surprising.[35] Those of each parliament are not baldly recorded but are embedded in the midst of letters close addressed to the sheriff. The formula runs: "Richard . . . a notre Viscont de Midd', saluz. Sachez q[e] . . . a notre parlement tenuz a Westminstre . . . [nous] avons fait ordeigner et establer certeins estatutz . . . [which follow]. Et pur ce vous mandons qe toutes les dites estatutz facez crier et publier et fermement tener. . . . Donne par testmoignance de notre grande seal a Westminstre [1 February, 1 Richard II]." And it is further noted, "Consimiles lettere diriguntur singulis Vicecomitibus per Angliam sub eadem data."[36] The statutes of all of Richard's ten parliaments held before 1384 assume this form except a short statute of 1379, which may well have been appended to the more extensive statute dispatched to the sheriffs in that year.[37]

---

[34] There is a similar general caption on Statute Roll I for the statutes of the three preceding reigns.

[35] The marginal caption describes the legislation of each parliament as a *statutum*, except in 1393 when the plural *statuta* was used. (*Stats.*, II, 87).

[36] *Ibid.*, pp. 1-5. The Latin sentence is often in a different hand.

[37] *Ibid.*, pp. 8, 12.

In 1384 the form changed somewhat. The statute was no longer embedded in the writ but preceded it. The statement that similar writs were sent to other sheriffs was added as usual. Although the writ follows the statutes on the enrolled record, it is likely that it was attached to the large membrane or membranes on which the statutes were written to be sent to the sheriff. Such a change of form made it possible for statutes and writ to get separated and we shall expect to find sheets of statutes to which no writ is longer appended. On the statute roll of Richard II the new form is more usual after 1384, the statutes of the six parliaments of the years 1388 (September)-1394 being recorded in this way.[38] The statutes of 1386 and one fragment from 1389 were still embedded in the writs.[39] There is no writ, either enveloping or appended, for statutes of the four parliaments of 1385, February, 1388, January, 1397 and September, 1397.[40] In 1388, however, a concluding note runs, "Et memorandum quod proclamatio istius statuti facta fuit in singulis Comitatibus Anglie."[41] If we may assume that in the case of these four parliaments the writs had not yet been attached to the originals from which the statutes were enrolled, or had perhaps got detached, or had seemed to the enroller so usual as to be unworthy of record, we may hazard the generalization that the statutes of each of the parliaments of Richard II were, in their original form, either embedded in writs to the sheriffs or had such writs attached to them.

Although an examination of the enrolled record makes such an inference almost unavoidable, it is reassuring to recover some of the originals so inferred. For the parliaments of 1377, 1391 and 1392, the statutes survive written in each case in a formal hand on a large sheet of parchment some two feet

[38] *Ibid.*, pp. 55-92.
[39] *Ibid.*, pp. 39, 74.
[40] *Ibid.*, pp. 38, 43, 92, 94.
[41] *Ibid.*, p. 55.

wide.[42]   In 1377 the document is a letter close directed to the
sheriff of Middlesex, embodying the new statutes of the year.
Since the enrolled record also addresses the sheriff of Middlesex, this document or one like it must have been before the
clerk who made the enrollment.   In 1391 and 1392 the recital of the statutes stands alone.   It is likely that a writ was
once attached to each sheet but has vanished.   Although the
documents are injured, they justify the inference that the
statute roll of Richard II was derived from originals of this
sort.   The comparison of an item in one of the three with its
enrolled form strengthens the inference.   The scribe who enrolled the statutes of 1391 overlooked a passage and had to
write it between the lines.   The writer of the large sheet made
no such blunder.[43]

The practice of enrolling statutes from original sheets directed to the sheriffs was not peculiar to Richard's reign nor
was it new at its beginning.[44]   Although the juxtaposition of
statute and writ in the enrolled record perhaps appears more
frequently then than either before or after, it was usual
enough in the three preceding reigns.   The first recorded instances of it date from 1299.   The statute roll shows that
two statutes of that year were embedded in the writs by which
they were sent to the sheriffs.   And in regions where there
were no sheriffs other officials received copies — the warden
of Berwick, of the Cinque Ports and of Guernsey and Jersey,
the justices of Chester, of Ireland, of North Wales and of
West Wales.   Copies were sent also to the treasurer and
barons of the exchequer.[45]   A month earlier another statute
had been similarly embedded in a writ sent to the sheriff of

---

[42] E 175, 3/1, 7, 8.   The lower margin of each of the three sheets, where
the great seal would have been attached, has been so cut away that no
trace of the attachment survives.

[43] Cf. C 74/3, m. 7, par. 6 with E 175, 3/7.

[44] In 1327 a commons petition asked that all preceding petitions, so far
as granted, be sealed with the great seal " et livere as Chivalers des
Cuntes severalment pur chescum Cunte au Viscunte. . . ."   (R. P., II, 10).

[45] C 74/1 membs. 37-36; Stats., I, 131-134.

Lancaster. Although we are not told that like writs were sent to other sheriffs, they undoubtedly were. Regarding this statute the roll notes that a part was sent to the treasurer and barons of the exchequer and to the justices of the common pleas and of the king's bench.[46] In 1306, when a statute was sent to the sheriffs, it was also sent in its entirety to the justices. The latter were told to proclaim it "publicly" in the bench. "Istud statutum missum fuit Justiciis de Banco et in singulis Comitatibus per Angliam. Et mandatum est prefatis Justiciis quod statutum illud in dicto Banco publice faciant proclamari et quantum ad ipsos pertinet firmiter observari. Eodem modo mandatum est singulis vicecomitibus per Angliam."[47] In 1318 the writ to the justices of the king's bench was itself enrolled with the information, "Quedam statuta per nos in presenti parliamento apud Eboracum convocato . . . edita vobis mittimus. . . ."[48]

Whether the dispatch of copies of the statutes of a parliament to the justices continued after the time of Edward II cannot be discovered from the enrolled statutes. No mention is made of such dispatch, although, as we have seen, the sending of statutes to the sheriffs in the reign of Richard II is on the statute roll thrust into greater prominence than is any other use made of these documents.[48a] Only at a much later time and in a casual way do we learn that the statutes of 25-33 Henry VI were sent to the royal courts.[49] Under the circumstances it is hardly safe to infer that the practice was usual. As for the exchequer, it was customary in the fifteenth century to send to it one or more statutes of a parliament if the enforcement of these concerned the exchequer. But it was per-

[46] *Ibid.*, pp. 126-130.
[47] *Ibid.*, p. 147.
[48] *Ibid.*, pp. 177-9.
[48a] Dr. Sayles tells me that under Edward III as well as under his predecessors statutes were often enrolled in the records of the two benches and of the court of the exchequer. Such enrollment implies that copies of the statutes had been sent to these courts.
[49] See below, p. 399.

haps not customary to send a sheet containing all the statutes of a parliament. In 1433 a copy of the ordinances and statutes of 1414 was sent with an accompanying writ to the exchequer; but the need of such action nineteen years after the date of the statutes possibly implies that a copy had not been dispatched at once.[50]

The statutes of the parliaments of Henry IV and Henry V apparently assumed much the same form as did those of the later years of Richard II. Large parchment membranes upon which they were formally inscribed seem to have been sent to the sheriffs with writs attached. The older practice of embedding the statute in the writ survived in 1407 and in 1417 and 1419; but the statutes of these years, especially of the last two, were brief.[51] Large membranes upon which were written the statutes of the parliaments of 1401, 1402, 1404 and 1414 survive.[52] For the statutes of each of the first two and of the fourth, two sheets were necessary but for those of the third one sufficed. No writ is attached to the statutes of the last three of these parliaments and the one now attached to the statutes of the first — certainly not to a sheriff — probably does not belong with it.[53] On the upper left hand corner of the membrane of 1414, however, are four perforations through which a writ may well have been sewed on. In two respects these sheets are more revealing than are those of the parliaments of Richard II. At the bottom of each of them are slits through which there once passed a parchment ribbon attaching what a later exemplar shows to have been the great seal.[54]

[50] E 175, 3/18. The membrane is narrower than the contemporary sheets on which statutes were written for the sheriffs and there are no slits for the affixing of the great seal. The exchequer may, of course, have had an earlier copy which had been lost.

[51] *Stats.*, II, 159, 200, 201.

[52] E 175, 3/11, 3/14, 3/17, roll 29. For the parliament of 1414 only one of two sheets survives and this is somewhat narrower than the sheets which record the statutes of the three parliaments of Henry IV.

[53] It is almost illegible. There is reference to Thomas Holand of Kent and apparently to others. T. Holand was never sheriff of Kent.

[54] See below, p. 398.

And in particular on the dorse of a sheet of each of the first three parliaments has been written " Ingrossatur in libro de Statutis." [55]

What now was this "book of statutes" into which the statutes of the parliaments of Henry IV were copied from the large sheets? Was it really a book or was it a roll like the great roll of the statutes of the Edwards or the smaller roll of the statutes of Richard II? There is a roll of twenty membranes of the statutes of Henry IV and Henry V which continues the tradition of the other two and which was used by the editors of the *Statutes* as a basis for their text. [56] It is very well written and in hands which reflect entries made after successive parliaments. The roll has no comprehensive caption as the earlier rolls had, but there is a marginal caption for each parliament e.g. "Statuta de anno quarto." No writs to sheriffs are transcribed except in the three instances in which the statute is embedded in the writ. It would be reasonable to conclude that we have here the "liber de statutis," were it not for the difficulty of assuming that contemporaries did not distinguish between a roll and a book.

That the *liber* referred to was very likely a book which could be opened becomes clear from a chronicler's account of the proceedings of the Good Parliament of 1376. When Sir Peter de la Mare, as spokesman of the commons, wished to show the lords that the transfer of the staple from Calais to the home ports was in violation of an existent statute, he " avoit une liver des estatutes prest sur lui et overa le liver et luyst lestatute. . . ." [56a] Since it is not likely that this book was the great roll, it seems that in 1376 a book of statutes was available for reference in the commons. Whether it was a copy which belonged to them or was one borrowed from the lords or from the courts, or whether it was one made for pri-

---

[55] The dorse of the sheet of 1414 is so black with dirt that no trace of this phrase is visible, even if it was once written there.

[56] C 74/5; *Stats.*, II, 111-212.

[56a] *An Anominalle Chronicle, 1333 to 1381*, ed. Galbraith, p. 86.

vate use must, in the present state of our knowledge, be left in doubt. But the *liber de statutis* of 1401-1404, which must likewise for the time remain veiled in obscurity, was without doubt an authoritative record.

The statutes of the reign of Henry VI are far more imperfectly enrolled than are those of preceding reigns. There is no comprehensive statute roll for the reign but only fragmentary rolls which record the statutes of its earlier and its later years. One roll contains the statutes of 1-8 Henry VI (1422-1429), another those of 25-39 Henry VI (1447-1460), a third is a duplicate of the second.[57] The rolls themselves differ from earlier ones in being written each in one hand, not as before in different hands which reflect the enrollment after each parliament. We have, therefore, reached a stage in the development, or rather in the deterioration, of the statute roll in which it becomes a tardily-made copy of the statutes of several parliaments written some time after the latest of them. It would not be surprising to find enrollment of this sort altogether neglected; and as a matter of fact the numerous statutes of the seven parliaments of 9-23 Henry VI (1430-1444) seem not to have been enrolled at all. No statute roll of them survives; and the editors of the statutes in printing them were obliged to depart from their custom of printing enrolled statutes and to rely upon other sources which they thought of inferior value.[58]

These other sources are large parchment sheets upon one or two of which are usually written the statutes of a single parliament. Already such sheets recording statutes of three parliaments of Richard II and of four parliaments of Henry IV and Henry V have been described. None survive for the first eight years of Henry VI but after that no parliament before 1453 is without at least one such record. There is one for each of the parliaments of 10, 11, 14 and 23 Henry VI, one for the four parliaments of 25-29 Henry VI, three for the

[57] C 74/6, 7; E 175, roll 35.
[58] *Stats.*, I, pp. xxxiii, xxxvi; II, 263, n.

parliament of 9 Henry VI and eight for each of three parliaments, viz. those of 15, 18 and 20 Henry VI.[59] Usually a single sheet sufficed for the record of the statutes of a parliament but two sheets were required for the statutes of 23 Henry VI and 25-29 Henry VI.

The sheets, like those of the earlier reigns, are each some two feet wide and are written in a formal hand. Where the bottom margin of each is turned over the double thickness is pierced in the center by two slits. The purpose of these is revealed by the sheets which record the statutes of 25-29 Henry VI. Through the two is passed a parchment ribbon to which is affixed the great seal. There can be little doubt that the other sheets either had a great seal appended or were to have had. It is clear, therefore, that all the sheets emanated from chancery.

There is further evidence about their origin. A name is sometimes written at the bottom of one of them in the scribe's own hand. On the eight copies of the statutes of each of the parliaments of 15, 18 and 20 Henry VI seven names appear, viz., Preston, Wedon, Selby, Colyns, Asshecombe, Shelford and Westhorp. The first three appear on other sheets as well, while the sheet recording the statutes of 1432 adds the name of Faukes. Certain of these names can be identified as those of clerks of chancery and all were probably of this affiliation.[60] Their signatures together with traces of the affixing of the great seal make it apparent that the sheets of statutes were chancery transcripts.

The sheets are probably chance survivals of several drawn up after each parliament. Primarily, such were probably engrossed to send to the sheriffs; for, although it is not certain

---

[59] E 175, file 11, nos. 3-8; file 4, nos. 4, 6, 11, 13; C., P. & C. P. 25/14, 25/15.

[60] Chancery writs of 1441-1445 directed to the treasurer and barons of the exchequer and to the keeper of the hanaper ordering the payment of various sums were drawn up by Selby and Faukes (E 101, 216/11). On one occasion Selby received attorneys who came to chancery (*C. P. R., 1436-41*, p. 101).

that under Henry VI new statutes were still sent to the sheriffs to proclaim, it is likely that they were. In 1423 we have testimony that they were proclaimed in some way. The council minute quoted above directs that acts of parliament which were to be statutes should, after being edited by the justices, be shown to the lords "et proclamentur." No writ to a sheriff, however, seems to be associated with any of the surviving sheets. Moreover, from each of the parliaments of 15, 18 and 20 Henry VI eight sheets are preserved. These can scarcely have been sent to sheriffs and later have drifted back to chancery. Probably copies were made for other persons in authority as well as for the sheriffs. In the time of Edward II, as we have seen, copies of the statutes were sent to the justices, who were directed not merely to enforce them but to proclaim them. After this we do not hear that statutes were thus sent until in the reign of Henry VI there is testimony, susceptible perhaps of the interpretation that they were. On the dorse of a commons petition of 1449, itself seemingly once the outermost of a bundle of commons petitions of the five parliaments of 1449-1454, there is written in a contemporary hand, "Communes petitiones quinque parliamentorum unde statute sunt edite et de tribus parliamentorum in Regias curias misse et deliberate."[61] It is possible that the inscription was intended to describe the procedure of 1423, the sending of commons petitions to the justices to be edited; but it actually states that statutes already edited were sent to the courts. Whatever interpretation is put upon it, there must always have been need that the justices have official copies of new statutes, at least to consult and enforce, if not to proclaim. The eight surviving copies of the statutes of each of three parliaments of Henry VI may originally have been prepared for some group of justices who either did not use them or later returned them to chancery. But the significant thing about these and other transcripts of the statutes of a parliament is that in all probability they antedated the statute roll.

[61] C., P. & C. P. 27/11 "de tribus parliamentorum" is written above.

The latter was evolved by transferring to it the statutes which the sheets made known to the nation and the courts. It then became the finished, final and available record of parliamentary legislation.

The last question which must be asked about the statutes of the fourteenth and fifteenth centuries, is why some of the approved bills recorded on the parliament roll did not become statutes while others did. One phrase in the council minute of 1423 suggests an answer. The minute, while directing that the acts of the recent parliament after being edited by the justices should be shown to the lords and be proclaimed, also directs that copies of other acts, which presumably were not submitted to the justices for editing, should be given to the clerk of the council. This second group of acts were those " touching governance to be exercised by the lords of the council and of the realm." They were pretty clearly administrative measures which affected the conduct of the government in its central departments, not the conduct of the king's subjects at large. When in 1449 the commons petitioned for and secured the adoption of an act of resumption, this measure, to which schedules of exemptions were finally appended, was not appropriate for publication throughout the realm.[62] Yet it was vastly more important for the welfare of the realm than was the ordinance that priests should be relieved of certain indictments, an ordinance proclaimed in the preceding spring and entered on the statute roll.[63] The editing and proclaiming of an approved bill in the manner traditional to statutes did not, therefore, depend upon its importance or significance. It depended upon whether the subject matter was of general concern for the population at large or at least for one class or group of men. Regulations touching the staple, for example, or touching Welshmen in Herefordshire were appropriate for editing and proclamation, brief though their announced duration might be. Certain measures looking to the reform of the

---

[62] R. P., V, 183-199.
[63] Ibid., p. 152; Stats., II, 352.

king's household, though of much greater moment, were not. The latter were to be carried out by the personnel of the household and by the exchequer.

To decide whether an approved bill was of general import or was properly to be referred to the administrative departments of the government cannot have been very difficult. The decision may have been made in parliament before the close of the session and corresponding instructions may have been given to the clerk. Such is the strict implication of the instructions of 1423 which direct that some of the acts of the last parliament be sent to the justices "quod illi actus qui erunt statuti regni per ipsos videantur." It is possible, however, that the clause should not be too strictly interpreted and that the justices themselves may have had a voice in the decision; for the inspection which they were to give to the acts (implied in *videantur*) may have included a consideration of whether these were suited to be statutes or not. No one would have been better qualified to decide this than they.[64] If some acts put before them were unsuited to be statutes, there was no need of editing these since enrollment on the parliament roll would suffice.

The question whether an approved bill of parliament should or should not be enrolled on the statute roll leads us naturally to inquire into the relationship of this roll to the parliament roll. Was the former merely selective, taking certain approved bills from the parliament roll, which by implication was the first of the two to be drawn up? It would be natural to think so. But the council minute of 1423 has just told us that statutes were edited from approved petitions in their original form and that the customary enrollment in chancery followed. Probably it was desirable that statutes be proclaimed promptly, whereas the enrollment of parliamentary activities might be a

---

[64] That a decision was carefully made by someone is implied by the inscriptions which appear on certain bills of 1449. Above the text in the right-hand corner of each bill is written "statutum" (C., P. & C. P. 27/11-14, 16). But such annotation was not usual.

more deliberate proceeding. That there was this sequence in procedure would become likely should we find statutes edited from approved bills which were never enrolled on the parliament roll. Such, as it happens, we do find. In 1449 a commons petition, asking that alien merchants who imported wheat, corn, or other merchandise be obliged to expend the money received on English commodities, was granted, though only to endure until the next parliament. Inasmuch as the regulation was to be proclaimed in all parts of the realm where foreign merchants trafficked, it naturally became a statute and is on the statute roll.[65] But it was not enrolled on the parliament roll. Since it differed in no way from many approved bills which were enrolled, the only explanation of the omission is that the clerk of parliament was negligent. Elsewhere the enrolled record of this parliament seems incomplete, there being no account of its termination. But the instance fortifies the conjecture that the sheets of statutes, if not the statute roll, were sometimes drawn up before the proceedings of parliament were enrolled.[66]

While it is probable that the editors of statutes did not rely upon the parliament roll, it seems equally probable that the compiler of the latter came to be influenced by a knowledge that certain approved petitions had become or were to become statutes. We have adopted this hypothesis to explain a phenomenon which, when we first noticed it in the middle of the fifteenth century, was puzzling and misleading. It was the enrollment of a certain number of official bills under the caption "communes petitions." Later we discovered that such enrollment was not characteristic of the fourteenth century but made its appearance very soon after 1423. The further knowledge that before this year commons petitions had been presented as a single bill made clear that any enrollment of

---

[65] R. P., V, 155; Stats., II, 349-350.

[66] There is, however, an instance of the commons asking that a petition be "enactez en le rolle du Parlement duraunt ycell," apparently during the session (see above, p. 387, n. 26).

official bills in the midst of them would not then have been likely. After 1423, however, when commons bills were presented separately, it would have been easy to enroll a few official bills among them, if there had been adequate reason for doing so. A very good reason, it may have seemed to the clerk, was that a few official bills were to be affiliated with commons bills in becoming statutes. Later when the number of these grew, the custom had become established. In this way it was that the late fifteenth-century parliament roll came to present the illogical grouping of many official bills as "communes petitions."

For the preparation, proclamation and recording of statutes in the fourteenth and fifteenth centuries, therefore, it seems that the procedure was somewhat as follows. The clerk of parliament gave certain of the approved bills of a parliament, which the parliament itself perhaps had already decided should be statutes, to the justices for editing. When edited, this group of statutes was engrossed by chancery clerks on large sheets of parchment, enough copies being made to send to the sheriffs and probably to the courts. From these sheets the text of the statutes was copied on at least one authoritative roll. This was called the statute roll, since, when it took form in the thirteenth and fourteenth centuries, statutes were the most noteworthy enactments of parliament, having, it was held, a permanence and authority greater than ordinances had. Later it was recognized that a statute might be of limited duration and the term was gradually displaced by the more flexible terms ordinance and act. But the roll was still called the statute roll. The sheets of statutes and the statute rolls were of importance as conveying the will of parliament to the nation and to the courts. They seem even to have influenced the writer of the parliament roll; for he came to include under his caption "communes petitions" bills which were not such, presumably on the ground that these like many of the "communes petitions" were to become statutes. Thus in immediate and in later influence the sheets of statutes and the statute roll outshone the parliament roll.   But the parliament roll, none the less, remains the more full and more vital record of parliamentary activity.

CONCLUSION

In this volume an attempt has been made to examine certain parliamentary documents of the fourteenth and fifteenth centuries in a new way. The novelty lies in interpreting enrolled records with which we have long been familiar, in the light of the antecedent material from which they were compiled. The enrolled records are primarily the parliament rolls and the statute rolls; the antecedent material comprises bills of various sorts and sheets of statutes. There was reason for thinking that a new interpretation of the rolls would throw light on the details of parliamentary procedure and perhaps on the forces behind parliamentary legislation. To acquire some familiarity with the former the procedure of the early seventeenth century and of the early sixteenth century was first briefly examined. In particular the earliest journal of the lords was enlisted to serve as an introduction to the parliament roll. What now have we ascertained?

Our first discovery has been that in the middle of the fifteenth century certain types of bills carefully described by a speaker of the commons in the seventeenth century had already become sharply differentiated from one another. Apart from rare bills of general pardon and rather numerous subsidy indentures, the principal types which then came before parliament were private bills and two sorts of public bills. The latter were those which originated with the commons and those which originated with the lords or with the king and his council. The first of them we have called commons bills; the second, since it is difficult to distinguish the hand of the lords from that of the government, official bills. During the fifteenth century, although a considerable number of private bills were considered in parliament and some of those approved were enrolled as a matter of record, the activities of that body related largely to the acceptance or rejection of public bills. Some business, to be sure, other than the granting of subsidies and the passing of bills, was at the time transacted in parliament, notably business of a judicial character. But, in general, parliamentary interest was concentrated on the consideration of commons bills and official bills. It was markedly so in the journal of 1509 and the less explicit parliament rolls of earlier years indicate that it was so in the fifteenth century.

Such being the case, it becomes highly desirable to distinguish commons bills from official bills; for, though private bills might in the middle of the fifteenth century be introduced more or less indifferently in the lords or commons, it was not so with the two sorts of public bills. The origin of a public bill in one house or the other presumably indicated whether the forces behind it were, on the one hand, popular, or, on the other, aristocratic or official. To discover to what extent the legislation of any parliament originated with the commons, it is necessary to ascertain the number and importance of the commons bills introduced in it as contrasted with the number and importance of official bills similarly submitted and the degree to which each sort was accepted, amended or rejected. Commons bills can easily be distinguished from official bills, we have discovered, if the bills survive in their original form; nor is it difficult, if the originals survive, to perceive the origin of amendments.

No conclusion about the dominance of commons bills or of official bills in any parliament can, however, be drawn merely from a consideration of surviving original bills; for these are at times so few that they furnish no ground for general conclusions. They can, however, be utilized to disclose how they and others like them were enrolled on the parliament roll, a selective enrollment of what happened in any parliament. Parliament rolls for all or nearly all parliaments after the middle of the fourteenth century survive and each contains what seems to be a complete record of all public bills

approved as well as of some which were rejected, not neglecting the amendments to the former. If, from a consideration
of all such bills, assurance can be got as to which originated
with the commons and which with the king and lords, it ought
to be possible to interpret in the light of its origin the legislation of the fourteenth and fifteenth centuries. To this end we
have made at the outset a comparison of several public bills
as well as of several private bills of the years 1453-1465 with
the forms which they assumed when enrolled; and the comparison has given us a key with which to interpret the parliament
rolls.

It quickly appeared that an interpretation was needed; for
the parliament rolls of the middle and late fifteenth century
prove to be misleading. Their deception lies in their enrolling as " communes petitions " some bills which were not commons bills but were official bills. Fortunately, however, the
comparison also shows that both commons bills and official
bills can, even if no originals of them exist, be recognized on
the roll from certain phrases employed in the bills themselves.
By giving close attention to these we can reclassify all the
bills of the parliament rolls, distinguishing them as originating
with the commons or with the king and lords. In another respect, too, the parliament roll needs interpretation, viz., in its
entry of amendments. The earliest modifications of commons
bills were the answers which were made to them by king and
lords; but from the middle of the fifteenth century the
answers began to assume the modern form of amendments.
The parliament roll in its enrollment of these became less informing than it had been when it recorded answers, not always
now revealing with whom an amendment originated. Again it
is necessary to refer to the original amendments for assurance
on this point and for a clue wherewith to interpret the rolls.

The ultimate success of a public bill was usually demonstrated by its becoming in its amended form a statute, an
ordinance or an act. The first term was in favor in the fourteenth century, the last in the fifteenth, the second in both

centuries. Although there was in the fourteenth century an effort to define a statute as legislation which extended the common law and was to endure forever, the attempt was abandoned by the beginning of the fifteenth century. So far as statutes, ordinances and acts of the fifteenth century can be distinguished from approved bills which did not become such, the distinction lies in their being usually applicable to a considerable number of persons or even to all persons within the realm. For this reason they were proclaimed, presumably by the sheriffs, and finally interpreted by the courts. Sometimes, although not very often, approved commons bills did not become statutes, not being widely applicable. Official bills, especially when they were enrolled as " communes petitions," sometimes became statutes; and we have conjectured that the reason for their being so enrolled in the fifteenth century was that they might be proclaimed as such.

At the end of a parliament the approved bills which it seemed appropriate to embody in statutes were edited. Usually the editing was the simple process of combining whatever response or amendment had been made with the provisions of the original bill. The latter might, of course, be greatly changed thereby. Sometimes the phraseology of combined bill and response was improved by elision or rephrasing. Who did this editing is not too clear but the editors were probably the justices. As soon as the statutes of a parliament had thus been formulated, they seem to have been engrossed by chancery clerks on large sheets of parchment, to each of which was appended the great seal. Not only were such sheets prepared for proclamation but copies were made from them of the statutes which they recorded accompanied sometimes by the writs by which statutes were dispatched. These copies on long membranes sewed together, sometimes for one reign or a part of one, sometimes for two or more reigns, constituted, when they were rolled up, a statute roll. Thus the statute rolls, like the parliament rolls, were enrolled records. While they were not as close to the source of legislation as were

the latter, they do supply a convenient record of the edited
bills of successive parliaments which it was thought desirable
to have proclaimed. Although many approved bills do not
appear on them, nearly all approved commons bills do, as
well as many official bills of general purport. Since these
two groups embodied in a general way the legislation of the
two centuries, the ascertaining of the commons influence on
this legislation narrows to an investigation of how many and
how important statutes arose from commons bills in contrast
with those which arose from official bills, due allowance being
made for the extent to which each sort was amended.

Such being our method, what has it profited us? The examination of certain parliament rolls of the middle of the
fifteenth century in disclosing that the caption " communes
petitions " had at the time no consistent meaning suggested
that in earlier years it may have had. We turned, therefore,
to a study of the earliest commons petitions of which we have
record. Petitions from the commons as a body, we discovered,
were almost never presented in the parliaments of Edward I.
As soon as they came to be, but still rarely, in the reign of
Edward II, they tended to assume a peculiar form. While
occasionally they were like private petitions in making a single
request, they usually grouped together a series of requests
making them articles of one petition. This embodiment of
the commons' grievances in any parliament we have called
the comprehensive commons petition. The parliament roll in
enrolling it applied to it the caption " communes petitions,"
the one which in the middle of the fifteenth century we found
misleading. In its origin and for the first century of its history, the caption described accurately what came after it.
The one deviation of any of the articles from commons petitions lay in the occasional admission among them of private
petitions relating to groups, a type of bill which the commons
from the outset sometimes adopted as their own. The composite document, written on one sheet of parchment, was
presented to lords and king and was on the last day of par-

liament answered article by article. The answers at first were written on the back of the petition, afterward probably on a separate membrane. When articles and answers were enrolled, each article was followed by its appropriate answer.

For a century after its inception the comprehensive commons petition pretty clearly did not change its character, although few originals survive to assure us of this. In enrolled form, its introduction, its phrasing of bills and the tongue employed (practically always French) point in this direction. Not only do few originals of comprehensive commons petitions survive but few bills or drafts of bills which much have preceded the drawing up of the document are to be found. Sometimes certain private bills are referred for answer to an article of the current commons petition and sometimes a group bill survives which, we can see, was incorporated. We may have one or two original drafts of bills. This obscurity about the preparation of the comprehensive commons bill persists up to 1423. In that year such a bill was no longer presented to lords and king but, instead, the several bills from which one would have been composed. As enrolled, these show diversity in address and language. Originals of them at once appear and from subsequent parliaments are numerous. Henceforth all bills comprised under the caption " communes petitions " were in their original form separate bills. The change at once permitted the insertion of official bills among the commons bills when the clerk enrolled both sorts; and he promptly availed himself of the opportunity. He reasoned, apparently, that, since nearly all statutes were framed from the " communes petitions " any official bill which was to be a statute could well be enrolled under this caption.

What led to the abandonment of the antiquated comprehensive petition we can only conjecture. It may have been the influence of a new type of private bill which had been coming into fashion for some twenty years. Instead of the usual private bill addressed to king or to king and lords and presented to the receivers and triours of petitions, we find from the close of the fourteenth century an increasing number of private bills addressed to the commons asking them to intercede with the king in behalf of the petitioner. In itself this was an important innovation inasmuch as it attributed new importance to the influence of the commons. And the opportunity thus given to a private petitioner of introducing his bill in either house brought with it a flexibility which may have suggested to the commons that it would be well to present their own requests in a better way. If each commons bill could be presented separately, opportunity for debate in either house, somewhat apart from other bills, would be given, and this ought to guarantee more mature deliberation.

The new type of private bill introduced, too, a phrase into parliamentary procedure which the new commons bills at once adopted. Above the text of a private bill which the commons saw fit to approve they wrote, "Soit baille as seigneurs," in order that the lords might in turn use their influence with the king in behalf of the petitioner. Since in the same way the lords' support of a commons bill was necessary, the new phrase was after 1423 inscribed also on commons bills. Not only was a new inscription evolved for dispatching both private and commons bills to lords and king but a corresponding one was devised for recording on private bills and on official bills, which it was now becoming the custom to submit to the commons, the approval of this body. The second phrase was, fittingly, "A ceste bille les communes sount assentuz." Like its counterpart it perhaps appeared first on private bills.

The newly individualized commons bills may soon after this have borrowed another usage from private bills. On the dorse of the latter it had been customary from the days of Edward I to write the king's response. Upon the commons bills of 1423 and the years immediately following no response is written. The responses may still have been given together on the last day of parliament. But in the course of the third decade of the century the usage of private bills seems to have been adopted. On many, although for a time not on all commons bills, the response was written on the dorse.

The first third of the fifteenth century thus witnessed important innovations in the treatment of private bills, commons bills and official bills, all of them to persist for centuries. In so far as later procedure involved the presentation of bills of any of these types in one house or the other, the inscribing on them of some phrase indicating the commons approval and the recording on the dorse of each the final answer made by king and lords, it had been evolved by the early years of Henry VI. Another characteristic of later procedure did not appear until the reign of Edward IV; for it was then that amendments to commons bills, which had hitherto been expressed in the answers to each, began to be cast in the form of provisos written often on separate membranes and appended each to the bill to which it related. This fostered, so far as official bills and private bills were concerned, a further innovation in procedure but one less significant than it is usually thought to have been. Official bills, which assumed new importance in the second half of the fifteenth century, had long been cast in the phraseology which, barring rare changes in the commons, they retained if they became statutes. Since the practice was so well established, it was a verbal rather than an actual change when in the reign of Edward IV we find such a bill described on the parliament roll as "billa formam actus in se continens." Considerable importance has been attached to the phrase because of an interpretation which Stubbs put upon it. Without due regard to the connotation in which it occurred, he surmised that it ushered in a change in procedure. Procedure by petition, he suggested, was giving place to procedure by bill, an evolution which enhanced the authority of the commons by guaranteeing that the words of their bills would not henceforth be changed without their assent. As a matter of fact the phrase was not applied to commons bills; and the commons had as early as 1414 got from the king a ratification of what they then described as accepted custom, the submission to their approval of any change made by king and lords in their bills. It is true that the new Edwardian custom of phrasing as provisos the reservations which the king's answer sometimes imposed on commons bills contributed to the propriety with which a bill could be described as containing in itself the form of an act. But it is doubtful whether this custom was in the minds of the authors of the phrase, who probably used it merely to describe the finished form assumed by an official bill. That the phrase was later extended to describe private bills does not strengthen Stubbs' hypothesis.

If our new method of interpreting the parliament roll in the light of the bills from which it was compiled has revealed to us innovations in procedure, can we also draw conclusions of wider scope concerning the significance of commons bills, now that we know somewhat more accurately their characteristics? How did they, during the two centuries under survey, compare in number and importance with official bills, so far as either sort became statutes? In other words, what was the influence of the commons on legislation in comparison with that of king and lords?

Under Edward I all legislation which appears on the statute roll arose from the action of the king, at most with the assent of the lords and only once or twice with the assent of the commons. Under Edward II the new comprehensive commons petition gave rise, on two of the three instances when we catch glimpses of it, to brief statutes. It was a momentous innovation and was fully exemplified in the first parliament of Edward III in 1327. Owing largely to the disappearance of many parliament rolls during the next quarter of a century and perhaps to the failure of the commons to gain as much favour for their comprehensive bill as they had in the critical parliament of 1327, we can discover little about the embodiment of commons petitions in statutes until after 1352. But from that year the traditions of 1327 were resumed for two decades. The series of comprehensive commons bills is impressive and the derivation of statutes from their articles is flattering. In the last decade of the reign, however, adverse influences checked the movement toward popular legislation and these continued effective in the opening years of Richard II. Twice during this reign the attainment of the commons' desires through statutes derived from their petitions was again realized. In 1382-1383 and in 1388-1394 more statutes were enacted in this way than from official bills. But in the intervening interval as well as at the end of the reign, the two periods of Richard's tyranny, more statutes arose from official bills than from commons bills. Nor is there evidence that any of the official bills of Richard's reign were submitted to the commons for approval. That the demonstrable influence of commons petitions upon statutory legislation fluctuated widely under Richard is in accord with what we know from other sources about the changing political currents of the reign.

With the revolution of 1399 the advance of commons legislation, three or four times checked in the preceding century, was immediate and impressive. Almost without interruption during a half century statutes were to a very large degree derived from commons bills. It made no difference whether these, as before 1423, took the form of the articles of a comprehensive petition or, as they did after 1423, the form of separate bills. The only difference dating from this year was that henceforth official bills occasionally crept in among the enrolled commons bills and like them were enacted as statutes. The total number of such official bills was small, throughout the half-century not more than one-twentieth as many as the commons bills which became statutes. They came, further, to be submitted to the commons for approval and to be inscribed with the words indicative of this, "A ceste bille les communes sont assentuz." We find them so inscribed in 1429 and there were probably earlier instances. Both in their infrequency and in their dependence upon the commons' assent official statutes thus recognized the growing influence of the commons in legislation.

Not only did commons bills come to preponderate over official bills but their content was not greatly modified by the answers made to them by king and lords and, of course, incorporated in the statutes to which they gave rise. We have examined at length the answers to commons bills of the first half of the fifteenth century. Half of them were simple approvals, which resulted in transforming the appeal of the bill into the imperative of the statute. Of the other half, many limited themselves to making changes in phraseology or in minor administrative details or in the penalties imposed, some guarded the king's prerogative, several limited the duration of the statute to be enacted, but only a very few disregarded to any degree the commons' requests. Moreover, the commons seem to have brought it about that these answers to their bills, which were virtually amendments, should be to a considerable degree submitted to their approval. In 1414 they put forward the claim that, although the king's prerogative authorized him to reject any of their bills, it had already become established that he could not change the purport of them "nother by addicions nother by diminucions by no maner of terme ne termes the which that sholde chaunge the sentence and the entente axked." [1] The royal approval given to this claim found fulfilment at once relative to amendments made in the succeeding parliament; and the inscription of the commons' approval found on the originals of certain amendments of the time of Henry VI and of later reigns indicate that to a considerable degree the commons continued to make good their claim. This success, along with the parallel one of getting official bills submitted to them, was their final triumph in securing control over the legislation of the first half of the fifteenth century. Tendencies in this direction, which had shown themselves during the middle years of Edward III and

[1] *R. P.*, IV, 22.

on two occasions under Richard II, were at length fully realized.

After 1450, however, the commons' influence upon legislation began to wane. At first this manifested itself in the rejection of several important bills which they presented in 1453 and 1455. Under Edward IV it was disclosed by the paucity of legislation in general, except in 1465, and by the dominance of class interests in many of the statutes which were still based on commons bills. Under Richard III and particularly under Henry VII a change occurred, rivaling in importance the one which ushered in the century. Just as after 1399 most legislation came to be derived from commons petitions and these little amended, so in and after 1484 most statutes arose from official bills. Not that commons bills disappeared or were entirely disregarded. A considerable number of them was still sent up by the commons to lords and king, but the content of these was seldom significant. In contrast, the far-sighted, well-devised and influential statutes of the reign of Henry VII arose from official bills. That official bills were at the time enrolled as "communes petitions" is misleading; the usage had originated soon after 1423 and such bills then influenced legislation little. When at length they again played the part in the formulation of legislation that they had under Edward I and at certain periods in the fourteenth century, it did not seem worth while to change the structure of the parliament roll. One service of original bills to our investigation has lain in revealing the antiquated formalism of this roll and thereby disclosing the true authors of the legislation of the time of Richard III and Henry VII.

The conclusions just summarized are in no way revolutionary. Long ago Stubbs described the Lancastrian reigns as a period of popular influence on the affairs of state, in so far as the commons themselves were a popular body. The reign of Henry VII has, on the other hand, been recognized as a period of growing absolutism in so far as this implied government by king and council. The Yorkist reigns might well be transitional. It is true that the inferences of Professors McIlwain and Pollard as to the continued importance of parliament as a "High Court" from the time of Edward I to the time of the Tudors may need modification. Professor Lapsley's caution that "emphasis on the judicial aspect of the medieval parliament should not be allowed to obscure what might be called the political side of that growth" is altogether pertinent.[2] By the fifteenth century the interest of parliament had come to center in legislation; and a certain irony inheres in the fact that the rolls first refer to parliament as a high court at about the moment when its judicial functions were being superseded by its legislative functions.[3] In this volume we cannot raise the question of the degree to which at one period or another the commons represented the popular will. In the middle years of Henry VI an effort was made by the commons themselves to define the qualifications of electors of knights of the shire and of burgesses. The qualifications were such as presumably to confer the suffrage upon property holders of moderate means. How far conditions of election gave effect to these intentions must also here be left unascertained. But if we may assume that the commons really were throughout much of the fifteenth century and perhaps throughout much of the fourteenth a body representative of the middle classes of the nation, we may say that legislation at times during the last fifty years of the fourteenth century and throughout all of the fifty years following was popular in character. After 1450 it gradually ceased to be so and in the last fifteen years of the century had come to be in origin dis-

[2] Preface to Pasquet, *An Essay on the Origins of the House of Commons,* p. xi.

[3] In 1399, the Chief Justice of the "Commune Bank" in pronouncing sentence against condemned lords spoke of "this hegh Court of the Parlement"; and in 1384 the Chancellor in defending himself against a charge brought against him had referred to "Parlement q'est la pluis haute Courte del Roialme." The term occurs rarely on the parliament rolls of the first half of the fifteenth century but frequently after 1450 (*R. P.,* III, 451, 169; V, 102, 240, 244, 246, 285, 495, 632).

tinctly not so. The fortunes of popular statutory legislation thus rose on an ascending curve only to decline to a level not much higher than that from which they started.

INDEX

INDEX

Act, 387-88, *see Formam actus* ...
Address of bills, 49, 52, 56, 62-65, 305, 349-57, 360-65, 369, 372.
Administrative amendments, 315-20.
Administrative bills, 96-97, 105-106, 400-401.
Alien merchants, bills touching, 124, 139, 142-43, 147, 268, 312, 327, 332.
Amendment of bills, 4, 9, 11-12, 41-42; by king and lords, 22-24, 168-89, 199, 261-85, 310-20, 334; by the commons, 24-26, 189-200.
Apparel, bills touching, 110, 136, 154.
Appeal in bills, 49, 52, 56-57, 62-65, 349-57, 360-64.
Assent to bills, by the king, 10, 27, 29, 42-43, 50-51, 55-56, 58, 166-67; by the lords, 10-11, 166-67, 341; by the commons, 10, 12, 50, 53, 55-56, 59, 161, n. 50, 305-309, 353, 364-66, 370, 372-73, 411; by the commons to amendments to their bills, 4, 25, 174-77, 261-63, 301, 320-23.
Attainder, bills of, 23, 57, 80, 88-89, 102-103, 107, 113, 115, 179, 192.
Attorney, the king's, 5, 18-19, 22, 42.
Auditors of petitions, 29, 74, 338-41, 377, n. 100.

Bacon, 141-42.
Bills in parliament, identical with petitions, 46-47; types of, 5-7, 39-69; *see* address, amendment, appeal, assent, debate, dispatch, endorsement, engrossing, reading, rejection, response, presentation, provisos, administrative bills, commons bills, group bills, lords bills, official bills, private bills,

public bills, subsidy bills.
" Bones gentz," 207, n. 9, 211-12, 219.
Burgundy, bills relating to, 112, 127, 171, 184, 326.

Calais, bills touching, 66-67, 84-86, 110-12, 120-21, 129, 153, 158, 254, 311, 318-19.
Calendar of parliament, 72-74, 84.
Caption " communes petitions," 30-31, 87 ff.
Carlisle, statute of, 210.
" Cedule," 40, 179, 191, 193-94, 301, 323.
Chancery, 220, 398.
Clergy, bills touching the, 124-25, 143, 149-50, 217, 239, 265, 273-74, 296, 325, 332.
Clerk of the crown, 13, 27.
Clerk of parliament, 7-14, 22, 27, 28, 338.
" Comen House," 184.
Committees in parliament, 4, 9, 20, 164.
Commons bills or petitions, xv, 30-32, 48, 62-64, 85 ff., 181-82, 230-87, 304-10, 361, 405-407, 413-16; origin of, 201-203, 338.
" Communaute," 202, 204, 207, n. 9, 209-10, 238, 249.
" Commune " or " communes," 205-206, 207, n. 9, 213, 216-17, 219, 221, 225, 234, 238, 277, n. 173a.
Comprehensive commons petitions, 203 ff., 286, 348, 409-11; under Edward II, 207-14; under Edward III, 215-27; under Richard II, 227-28; persistence of, 229-34; formulation of, 235-47.
Conference between houses, 4, 25, 279.